Online Investing

10th Edition

by Matt Krantz

for
dummies®
A Wiley Brand

Online Investing For Dummies®, 10th Edition

Published by: **John Wiley & Sons, Inc.,** 111 River Street, Hoboken, NJ 07030-5774, www.wiley.com

Copyright © 2019 by John Wiley & Sons, Inc., Hoboken, New Jersey

Published simultaneously in Canada

No part of this publication may be reproduced, stored in a retrieval system or transmitted in any form or by any means, electronic, mechanical, photocopying, recording, scanning or otherwise, except as permitted under Sections 107 or 108 of the 1976 United States Copyright Act, without the prior written permission of the Publisher. Requests to the Publisher for permission should be addressed to the Permissions Department, John Wiley & Sons, Inc., 111 River Street, Hoboken, NJ 07030, (201) 748-6011, fax (201) 748-6008, or online at http://www.wiley.com/go/permissions.

Trademarks: Wiley, For Dummies, the Dummies Man logo, Dummies.com, Making Everything Easier, and related trade dress are trademarks or registered trademarks of John Wiley & Sons, Inc. and may not be used without written permission. All other trademarks are the property of their respective owners. John Wiley & Sons, Inc. is not associated with any product or vendor mentioned in this book.

For general information on our other products and services, please contact our Customer Care Department within the U.S. at 877-762-2974, outside the U.S. at 317-572-3993, or fax 317-572-4002. For technical support, please visit https://hub.wiley.com/community/support/dummies.

Wiley publishes in a variety of print and electronic formats and by print-on-demand. Some material included with standard print versions of this book may not be included in e-books or in print-on-demand. If this book refers to media such as a CD or DVD that is not included in the version you purchased, you may download this material at http://booksupport.wiley.com. For more information about Wiley products, visit www.wiley.com.

Library of Congress Control Number: 2019945516

ISBN 978-1-119-60148-7 (pbk); ISBN 978-1-119-60149-4 (ebk); ISBN 978-1-119-60150-0 (ebk)

10 9 8 7 6 5 4 3 2 1

Contents at a Glance

Table of Contents

Introduction

You might be wondering why you need a book like this one to help you invest online. After all, if you're looking for information about investing online, you can certainly type *investing online* in a search engine and get thousands of search results.

But that's the problem. You'll get thousands of search results. Some of the sites you'll find by using a search engine might have secret agendas and push financial products hazardous to your goals. Yet other sites offered up by a search engine might be filled with bad information, causing you to unknowingly make poor investment decisions. Worse yet, you might stumble on fraudulent websites determined to steal your identity or money. Sure, you might find some good websites through a web search, but how can you tell the good from the bad when you get hundreds, if not thousands, of results?

Along came *Online Investing For Dummies*, 10th Edition. This book is here to act as a down-to-earth guide for getting started with online investing. I steer you clear of unnecessary investing gobbledygook, and I point you to resources that you can trust. I've already done all the mucking through the thousands of investing websites to find good ones — you shouldn't have to do so as well!

About this Book

Online Investing For Dummies, 10th Edition has been updated and refreshed to be your intelligent guide through this often-confusing and constantly changing world of investing online. As the author, I can share the tricks, tips, and secrets I've learned from a career writing about online investing for readers just like you. This book can save you the trouble of fumbling through the Internet looking for the best online resources.

In this edition, you'll find online sites that may be even more relevant to you now if you missed out on the powerful bull market that kicked off in 2009. After watching stocks more than quadruple their value between March 2009 and March 2019, you're probably more aware than ever of the potential gains of investing. Sadly, some investors allowed their fear to convince them to bail out of stocks at just the wrong time. Many investors panicked and pulled the ripcord in March 2009, scared to death by the vicious financial crisis that raged in 2008 and 2009. Stocks lost more than half their value between October 2007 and March 2009, prompting some investors to write off investing as being too risky or just a bad idea.

And that's why this book is so important. If you don't have a strategy, the emotions of fear and greed take over and short-circuit your reasoning. Investing based on emotion is typically a good way to lose money and miss opportunities. The Internet can help you keep emotions out of investing and make you a smart and skilled investor. This book shows you how to use the information you find online to become a more informed investor who is better able to stomach the market's ups and downs.

Foolish Assumptions

No matter your skill or experience level with investing, you can get something out of *Online Investing For Dummies*. I assume that some readers haven't invested in anything other than baseball cards or Pez dispensers and have no clue where to even start. If that describes you, the first part of the book is custom-made for you, taking extra care to step through all the key points in as much plain English as possible. (When I have no choice but to use investing jargon, I tell you what it means.) But I also assume that more advanced investors might pick up this book, too, looking to discover a few things. The book takes on more advanced topics as you progress through it and carefully selects online resources that can add new tools to your investing toolbox.

Icons Used in This Book

REMEMBER

These icons highlight info that you should etch on the top of your brain and never forget, even when you're getting caught up in the excitement of investing online.

TIP

Read these sections to quickly pick up insider secrets that can boost your success when investing online.

Some of the things covered in the book get a bit hairy and complicated. This icon flags such sections for two reasons. First, you may decide to avoid the headache and skip over them — the info isn't vital. Second, the icon is a heads-up that the paragraph is probably loaded with investment jargon. Don't be embarrassed if you need to read the section a second or third time. Hey, you didn't want this book to be too easy, did you?

Avoid the landmines scattered throughout Wall Street that can decimate your good intentions at building wealth with these sections.

Beyond the Book

In addition to the content in this book, you'll find some extra content available at the www.dummies.com website:

>> **The cheat sheet for this book is at** www.dummies.com/cheatsheet/ onlineinvesting. The cheat sheet covers how to get started with online investing and how to protect your identity and online money, and provides some helpful tips for investing and a useful investor's glossary.

>> **This book includes two bonus chapters, which you can find at** www. dummies.com/bonus/onlineinvesting. These bonus chapters cover how to broaden your horizons with international stocks, and how to take your knowledge further with technical analysis and initial public offerings.

>> **Updates to this book, if any, will be at** www.dummies.com/extras/ onlineinvesting.

Where to Go from Here

If you're a new investor or just getting started investing online, you might consider starting from the beginning. That way, you'll be ready for some of the more advanced topics I introduce later in the book. If you've already been investing online, have a strategy you think is working for you, and are pleased with your online broker, you might skip to Part 2. And if you're dying to know about a specific topic, there's nothing wrong with looking up terms in the index and flipping to the appropriate pages.

1

Getting Started Investing Online

IN THIS PART . . .

Discover everything you need to know to get yourself and your computer or other device ready to pick, buy, and sell investments online.

Learn all the key terms you need to know to set up investment accounts, pick a broker, and get started.

Understand the main ways to invest online, and quickly gain the wisdom of more experienced investors.

Find the answers to two of the most commonly asked questions investors ask me: "How do I get started investing online?" and "How much money do I need to invest online?"

IN THIS CHAPTER

» Analyzing your budget and determining how much you can invest

» Taking the basic steps to get started

» Understanding what returns and risks you can expect from investing

» Getting to know your personal taste for risk

» Understanding your approach to investing: Passive versus active

» Finding resources online that can help you stick with a strategy

Chapter **1**

Getting Yourself Ready for Online Investing

Before doing something risky, you probably think good and hard about what you stand to gain and what you might lose. Surprisingly, many online investors, especially those just starting out, lose that innate sense of risk and reward. They chase after the biggest possible returns without considering the sleepless nights they'll suffer through as those investments swing up and down. Some start buying investments they've heard that others made money on without thinking about whether those investments are appropriate for them. Worst of all, some fall prey to fraudsters who promise huge returns in get-rich-quick schemes.

So, I've decided to start from the top and make sure that the basics are covered. In this chapter, you discover what you can expect to gain from investing online — and at what risk — so that you can decide whether this is for you. You also find out how to analyze your monthly budget so that you have cash to invest in the first place. Lastly, you find out what kind of investor you are by using online tools that measure your taste for risk. After you've become familiar with your inner investor, you can start thinking about forming an online investment plan that won't give you an ulcer.

It's only natural if you're feeling skittish when it comes to investing, especially if you're just starting out. After all, it's been a brutal couple of decades even for veteran investors. First came the dot-com crash in 2000, then the vicious credit crunch in 2008 that threatened to drop-kick the economy, and then a nasty bear market in 2008. The stock market then proceeded to soar starting in March 2009, roughly quadrupling in value through mid-2019. But even that rally wasn't pain-less, because the stock market short-circuited in May 2010, due in part to com-puterized trading, causing its value to plunge and largely rally back in just 20 minutes. Don't forget the 2015 Greek debt crisis and fears of a major economic slowdown in China that rattled investors. Confused yet? Get this. Even good news can hurt the market. Stocks dropped roughly 20 percent in late 2018. Why? The economy was doing so well that investors worried that the nation's central bank, the Federal Reserve, would slow it down.

Some think all this chaos is just too much to bear and choose to avoid stocks altogether. That decision is a mistake, though. Prudent investing can be a great way for you to reach your financial goals. You just need an approach that will maxi-mize your returns while cutting your risks. And that's where this book comes in.

Why Investing Online Is Worth Your While

Investing used to be easy. Your friend would recommend a broker. You'd give your money to the broker and hope for the best. But today, thanks to the explosion of web-based investment information and low-cost online trading, you get to work a lot harder by taking charge of your investments. Lucky you! So, is the additional work worth it? In my opinion, taking the time to figure out how to invest online *is* worthwhile because

- >> **Investing online saves you money.** Online trading is much less expensive than dealing with a broker. You'll save tons on commissions and fees. (Say, why not invest that money you saved?)

- >> **Investing online gives you more control.** Instead of entrusting someone else to reach your financial goals, you'll be personally involved. It's up to you to find out about all the investments at your disposal, but you'll also be free to make decisions.

- >> **Investing online eliminates conflicts of interest.** By figuring out how to invest and doing it yourself, you won't have to worry about being given advice that might be in your advisors' best interest and not yours.

REMEMBER

You may still decide to hire a financial advisor. For some people, the extra guidance or piece of mind you get from a person whose job it is to watch your portfolio makes a ton of sense. Even so, it's a good idea to know how investing and markets work so you can understand what your advisor is doing with you money. Advisors, too, appreciate it when clients comprehend the plan. It's like when you travel to different parts of Europe — the locals like to see you at least try to speak their language.

Getting Started

I can't tell you how many investors just starting out write me and ask the same question. Maybe it's the same question that's running through your head right now: "I want to invest, but where do I start?"

Getting started in investing seems so overwhelming that some people get confused and wind up giving up and doing nothing. Others get taken in by promises of gigantic returns and enroll in seminars, subscribe to stock-picking newsletters with dubious track records, or invest in speculative investments hoping to make money overnight, only to be disappointed. Others assume that all they need to do is open a brokerage account and start madly buying stocks. But as you'll notice if you look at the Table of Contents or flip ahead in this book, I don't talk about choosing a broker and opening an account until Chapter 4. You have many tasks to do before then.

However, don't let that fact intimidate you. Check out my easy-to-follow list of things you need to do to get started. Follow these directions, and you'll be ready to open an online brokerage account and start trading:

1. **Decide how much you can save and invest.**

   You can't invest if you don't have any money, and you won't have any money if you don't save. No matter how much you earn, you need to set aside some cash to start investing. (Think saving is impossible? I show you digital tools later in this chapter that can help you build up savings that you can invest.)

2. **Master the terms.**

   The world of investing has its own language. I help you to understand investing-ese now so that you don't get confused in the middle of a trade when you're asked to make a decision about something you've never heard of. (Chapter 2 has more on the language of online investing.)

3. **Familiarize yourself with the risks and returns of investing.**

   You wouldn't jump out of an airplane without knowing the risks, right? Don't jump into investing without knowing what to expect, either. Luckily, online resources I show you later in this chapter and in Chapter 8 can help you get a feel for how markets have performed over the past 100 years. By understanding how stocks, bonds, and other investments have done, you'll know what a reasonable return is and set your goals appropriately.

REMEMBER

I can't stress enough how important this step is. Investors who know how investments typically behave don't panic — they keep their cool even during times of volatility. Panic is your worst enemy because it has a way of talking you into doing things you'll regret later.

4. **Get a feel for how much risk you can take.**

   People have different goals for their money. You might already have a home and a car, in which case you're probably most interested in saving for retirement or building an estate for your heirs. Or perhaps you're starting a family and hope to buy a house within a year. These two scenarios call for different tastes for risks and *time horizons* — how long you'd be comfortable investing money before you need it. You need to know what your taste for risk is before you can invest. I show you how to measure your *risk tolerance* later in this chapter.

5. **Understand the difference between being an active and a passive investor.**

   Some investors want to outsmart the market by owning stocks at just the right times or by choosing the "best" stocks. Others think doing that is impossible and don't want the hassle of trying. At the end of this chapter, you find out how to distinguish between these two types of investors, active and passive, so that you're in a better position to choose which one you are or want to be.

6. **Find out how to turn your computer, tablet, or smartphone into a trading station.**

   If you have a computer, tablet or smartphone and a connection to the Internet, you have all you need to turn it into a source of constant market information. You just need to know where to look, which you find out in Chapter 2.

7. **Take a dry run.**

   Don't laugh. Many professional money managers have told me they got their start by pretending to pick stocks and tracking how they would have performed. It's a great way to see whether your strategy might work, before potentially losing your shirt. You can even do this online, which I cover in Chapter 2.

8. **Choose the type of account you'll use.**

   You can hold your investments inside all sorts of accounts, which have different advantages and disadvantages. I cover them a little in this chapter and go into more detail in Chapter 3.

9. **Set up an online brokerage account.**

   At last, the moment you've been waiting for: opening an online account. After you've tackled the preceding steps, you're ready to get going. This important step is covered in Chapter 4.

10. **Understand the different ways to place trades and enter orders.**

    In Chapter 5, I explain the many different ways to buy and sell stocks, each with very different results. (You also need to understand the tax ramifications of selling stocks, which I cover in Chapter 3.)

11. **Boost your knowledge.**

    After you have the basics down, you're ready to tackle the later parts of the book, where I cover advanced investing topics. These topics involve choosing an asset allocation (covered in Chapter 9), researching stocks to buy and knowing when to sell (covered in Chapter 13), and evaluating more exotic investments (the stuff you find in the bonus chapters at www.dummies.com/bonus/onlineinvesting).

THE DANGER OF DOING NOTHING

After reading through the 11 steps for getting started, you might be wondering whether you've taken on more than you bargained for. Stick with it. The worst thing you can do now is put this book down, tell yourself you'll worry about investing later, and do nothing.

Doing nothing is extremely costly because you lose money if you don't invest. Seriously. Even if you stuffed your cash under a mattress and didn't spend a dime, each year that money becomes worth, on average, 3 percent less due to inflation. Suppose you won $1 million in the lottery and stuffed it in a hole in your backyard with the plan of taking it out in 30 years to pay for your retirement. In 30 years, all 1 million greenbacks would still be there, but they'd buy only $400,000 worth of goods.

Even if you put your extra cash in a savings account, you're not doing much better. Because savings accounts usually give you access to your money anytime, they pay low levels of interest, usually around 1 or 2 percent. Even high-yield savings accounts and certificates of deposit (CDs) typically pay only slightly higher interest than the level of inflation or usually below, meaning that you're barely keeping up — or falling behind. If you want your money to grow, you need to move money you don't need for a while out of savings and into investments, which have the potential to generate much higher returns.

Note: The Federal Reserve Bank of Minneapolis offers a free calculator that tells you how much something you bought in the past would cost today (www.minneapolisfed.org). The calculator is located on the right side of the website (you'll probably need to scroll down a bit to see it).

Measuring How Much You Can Afford to Invest

Online investing can help you accomplish some great things. It can help you pay for a child's college tuition, buy the house you've been eyeing, retire in style, or travel to the moon. Okay, maybe not the last one. But you get the idea. Investing helps your money grow faster than inflation. And by investing online, you can profit even more by reducing the commissions and fees you must pay to different advisors and brokers.

REMEMBER

One thing online investing cannot do is make something out of nothing. To make money investing online, you have to save money first. Don't get frustrated, though, because you don't need as much to get started as you might fear. If you have a job or source of income, building up ample seed money isn't too hard.

Turning yourself into a big saver

If you want to be an investor, you must find ways to spend less money now so that you can save the excess. That means you must retrain yourself from being a consumer to being an investor. Many beginning investors have trouble getting past this point because being a consumer is so easy. Consumers buy things that they can use and enjoy now, but almost all those objects lose value over time. Cars, electronic gadgets, and clothing are all examples of things consumers "invest" their money in. You don't even have to have money to spend — plenty of credit card companies will gladly loan it to you. Consumers fall into this spending pattern vortex and end up living paycheck to paycheck with nothing left to invest.

Investors, on the other hand, find ways to put off current consumption. Instead of spending money, they invest it into building businesses or goods and services that can earn money, rather than deplete it. The three main types of investments are stocks, bonds, and real estate; I cover others in later chapters.

Here are a few things you can do now to help you change from being a consumer to an investor:

>> **Start with what you can manage by putting aside a little each month.**

>> **Keep increasing what you put aside.** If you do it gradually, you won't feel the sting of a suddenly pinched pocket.

>> **Hunt for deals and use coupons and discounts.** Put aside the saved money.

>> **Buy only what you need.** Don't be fooled into buying things you don't need because they're on sale.

SCOURING THE WEB FOR SAVINGS HELP

Even fastidious savers have unavoidable basic expenses. Investors, though, find ways to be smart about even these routine costs. These sites can help you boost your savings:

- **360 Degrees of Financial Literacy** (www.360financialliteracy.org) urges you to stop wasting money and offers tips to help you get out of debt by cutting excess spending. The site can calculate how to get out of debt and even how much you can save by packing a lunch instead of buying one. It's run by the American Institute of CPAs, so you know some serious brainpower is behind the calculations.

- **Get Rich Slowly** (www.getrichslowly.org) provides tips, calculators, and online tools to help you save more so that you can invest more. The site's front page has daily entries of note to savers and investors. The site is a blog, or web log, which features posts offering suggestions on how to better manage your money.

- **The Penny Hoarder** (www.thepennyhoarder.com) turns saving money into a life-style. The site explains how to find lucrative side hustles, such as tutoring or editing resumes, save money on purchases, and get a better job. This site provides a daily stream of posts with tips and suggestions for consumers.

Using desktop personal finance software

The word *budget* is a real turnoff. It conjures up images of sitting at the kitchen table with stacks of crumpled-up receipts, trying to figure out where all your money went. As an investor who prefers to do things online, this image probably isn't too appealing.

It's worth your while to find other ways to see how much money is coming in and how much is going out. You can get help in many ways, including personal finance desktop software, apps, and websites.

Traditionally, the best way to track your spending and investments was *personal finance software*. Even today, in a world of websites and apps for smartphones and tablets, personal finance software is one of the most powerful tools for investors who want to know where every penny is going.

The rise in personal finance websites has narrowed the choice of personal finance software to essentially one. Quicken remains the top choice for people looking for the most powerful software to help them measure how much money they can afford to invest — and maintain privacy of their data. Quicken can help you determine how much money you spend, where it goes, and how much excess you accumulate each month that you can channel into investing. You can view the results in charts, such as the one shown in Figure 1-1.

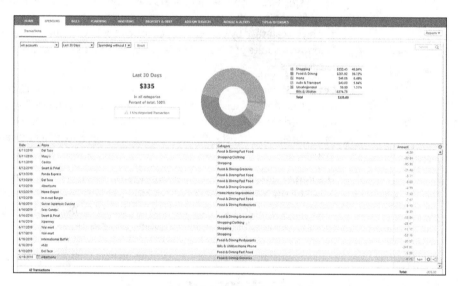

FIGURE 1-1:
Quicken allows you to slice and dice your budget and find out where your money is going.

Quicken can also create a budget for you, essentially at the click of a button. The software alerts you if you're spending more on a certain category than you budgeted for. The biggest gripe against the software is that you have to get your transactions into it first. You can type them in, which is kind of a hassle, or you can download them from your credit card company, bank, or brokerage. Like most software these days, Quicken requires you to subscribe. It costs $60 for a two-year subscription to the Deluxe edition. Note that Quicken's online features, including stock-quote downloads, stop working unless you renew your subscription.

Quicken does more than help you set and stick to a budget. It helps you with more advanced topics, such as managing your portfolio and taxes — stuff I cover later in this book.

Quicken might be the big kid on the block, but it isn't completely alone. Be sure to check out these other options (some of which are free!):

>> **Moneydance** (www.moneydance.com) comes in versions for Windows, Macintosh, and Linux. If you're already using Money or Quicken, no worries — Moneydance can translate your files. It's comparably priced at $50 and offers a trial that lets you use the software until you hit 100 transactions. There's also a version for a smartphone running iOS or Android.

>> **Money Manager Ex** (www.codelathe.com/mmex) tries to make the power of software like Money and Quicken free. It's *open-source* personal finance software, programmed by hobbyists and offered to the public as a service. If you like it, you can donate to the programmers who have created it. Money Manager Ex is also available for Android smartphones — showing how the line between personal finance software and personal finance mobile apps is blurring.

>> **GnuCash** (www.gnucash.org) has one big thing going for it: It's free. The software is updated and maintained by a host of freelance programmers, much like Money Manager Ex. Be warned, though, that GnuCash lacks the polish of some of the other personal finance software and is harder to navigate. Some versions of the software are considered unstable even by the programmers who coded them — at least until all the bugs are fixed.

>> **Buddi** (http://buddi.digitalcave.ca/index.jsp) is another free option. But unlike the other personal finance software, Buddi is designed to track budgets and spending, not investment portfolios.

TIP

Some investors prefer creating a spreadsheet to track all their finances. Microsoft provides several helpful budgeting spreadsheets, which you can find by entering the word **budget** in the search field of the Office Templates & Themes home page (http://templates.office.com).

Perusing personal finance websites

Before you can put personal finance software to work, you often need to download and install it on your computer. You then need to spend some time figuring out how to use it. If that's exactly the kind of thing that scared you away from making a budget in the first place, you might want to consider *personal finance websites.* The main benefits of personal finance websites are that they let you see your information from any PC connected to the Internet, and you generally don't have to install software to make them work. Most personal finance websites have created mobile app versions, too, which will be discussed in the following section. But first, here are a few personal finance websites to check out:

- >> **Mint.com** (www.mint.com) built a loyal following with its simplicity. Mint was so successful, in fact, that Intuit bought the company in 2009, shut down its own Quicken Online site, and turned Mint into its online personal finance site. Mint pulls in all your bank and brokerage accounts and imports all your financial information. For users just looking to get up and running fast, Mint is tough to beat. It's also free. However, Mint lacks many of the powerful investment-tracking features in Quicken, including the capability to precisely track how much you paid for certain investments — your *cost basis* — which is important, as you discover later. And you'll need to be comfortable handing over all your account numbers and passwords to a third party. A version of Mint for mobile devices is also worth paying attention to.

- >> **Personal Capital** (www.personalcapital.com) was built by some of the same people who created Quicken. The site is best known for its powerful investment portfolio tools, which I discuss further in Chapter 8. But Personal Capital also allows consumers to download their banking transactions and spot trends in their spending. Personal Capital provides a *dashboard* that shows you where all your money is coming from and going to, and a cash manager to help you keep a handle on your expenses. What's the catch? If you use Personal Capital, you will be contacted by a financial advisor who will talk to you about signing up as a client.

- >> **YNAB** (www.youneedabudget.com) is built to make budgeting look good. With a slick website and matching app, YNAB pulls in all your spending in one place and helps you wipe out debt. You can check your progress toward saving for financial goals and join online workshops with budget counselors. The service is free for the first 34 days and then costs $6.99 a month.

WARNING

Putting all your financial data online with a third party is simple and convenient, but it can be a bad idea for some investors. First, there are security concerns with entrusting all your financial data to strangers over the Internet. Every year, hundreds of companies' sites are breached and their data compromised. Even giant companies such as retailer Target, credit-rating service Equifax, and hotel chain Marriott lost customer data in breaches. But beyond that, if a website calls it quits one day, you might lose access to the historical financial and investing records you kept on the site. For example, Wesabe had been a leading online financial tracking site until it pulled the plug in July 2010. The investment-tracking site Cake Financial was bought by E*TRADE in January 2010 and, without warning, shut down — leaving investors without access to their financial information. Geezeo had been a leading online financial tracker website until the company shut down its public website in 2010 and moved to sell its products to banks instead. These examples are a big reason why personal financial software, such as Quicken, can still be preferable because your data is stored on your computer's hard drive, where you can always access it (unless it fatally crashes, and you failed to maintain a current backup copy, of course).

If you're not ready to trust your financial data to a website, you can still benefit from the wisdom of the web. *Personal finance information sites* don't track your transactions, but they're still able to give you the big picture. The following sites are worth checking out:

>> **The Financial Planning Association's Life Goals** (www.plannersearch.org/financial-planning) lets you click financial goals, such as Saving for Retirement, and get advice.

>> **SmartAboutMoney.org** (www.smartaboutmoney.org) provides various tips on how to save more and boost your financial strength.

>> **The Financial Literacy and Education Commission** (www.mymoney.gov) is a government-run site that steps you through everything from saving more to avoiding frauds. It's also a good directory of useful information available from other government agencies.

Capitalizing from personal finance apps

The rise of smartphones and tablets has given investors a new way to track their money. A large and growing group of investors see desktop personal finance software as being too clunky or complicated for them. Meanwhile, the poor performance of many websites on smartphone web browsers has led many investors to get into the habit of downloading personal finance apps to their devices to help them manage their lives. Most of the key players in personal finance apps are also leaders with personal finance websites. But because mobile apps are so important, they now deserve special treatment. The key rivals follow:

>> **Mint.com** (www.mint.com): Given the popularity of Mint online, it's only natural it's a leader in the app world, too. Mint makes sense for many consumers because it's free and familiar; backed by a large company with the resources to update it; and available on many mobile devices including those running Apple's iOS and Google's Android operating system. The app does everything you'd expect, such as downloading balances. It also works nicely with the web — allowing you to safeguard your data if you lose a mobile device.

>> **Mvelopes** (www.mvelopes.com) can be your spending cop, telling you when you're spending too much. Mvelopes is a spending tracker that tries to be the digital version of envelope-based budgeting. Rather than stuffing cash in envelopes set aside for certain expenses, Mvelopes lets you decide before you

get a paycheck how much you're willing to spend in certain categories (such as dining out) and plan your spending for the month. As the month progresses, you download all your spending from banks and credit card companies and subtract each transaction from the envelopes you set aside. That way, if you're spending too much on restaurants, for instance, you know to cut back or to skimp in other areas. It's $4 a month to sign up for the basic service, which is limited to budgeting. The Complete version allows you to get a monthly call from a financial coach to see how your plan is going. The Complete version is not a cheap tool, though, setting you back $59 a month. With the Plus version, which costs $19 a month, your financial coach calls you quarterly. Mvelopes is available for iOS and Android.

>> **MoneyPoint** (www.microsoft.com/en-US/store/apps/MoneyPoint/9WZDNCRFJCCD) is an innovative take on mobile apps that attempts to blend the power of Quicken with the convenience of an app. Unlike Mint and other apps that rely on your entering banking information and downloading the data, MoneyPoint allows you to enter the data yourself, and your data is saved on your computer. It's available on any devices running Windows 10, and it's free.

>> **Personal Capital** (www.personalcapital.com) brings its personal finance chops to the mobile app game. The app gives investors high-level and convenient access to their accounts, as well as the ability to track spending and monitor investments. The tools are free to use. Available for iOS and Android.

>> **MoneyStrands** (www.moneystrands.com) tries to make saving your money hip, if that's possible. The site is full of colorful diagrams, making it appear fun to use, which might make it seem less intimidating to some people. The site not only helps you track how you're doing financially but also compares you with others and provides savings tips. MoneyStrands is available for free on iOS and Android.

>> **Digit** (www.digit.co) aims to take the sting out of saving money. The app for iOS and Android monitors your spending and automatically calculates how much you can afford to save. The app then moves money you don't need into a separate savings account. If you have a hole in your pocket, this might be the kick in the pants you need. But if you're the frugal kind, you might try one of the other apps because Digit charges a monthly fee of $2.99. Paying money to save money seems a bit strange.

Saving with web-based savings calculators

If personal finance software, apps or sites seem too much like a chore or too Big Brotherish, you might consider these free web-based tools that measure how much you could save, in theory, based on a few parameters that you enter:

- **MSN Money's Savings Calculator** (`www.msn.com/en-us/money/tools/savingscalculator`) allows you to enter six assumptions to find out how much you'd have to save to meet a specific goal. You enter your initial deposit, annual savings amount, increase in contributions, number of years to save, what return you expect to get on your savings, and your tax bracket. The calculator does the rest of the work.

- **Bankrate.com's Savings Calculator** (`www.bankrate.com/calculators/savings/saving-goals-calculator.aspx`) asks you what you're saving for, be it college or buying a car. It then breaks down your financial objective and tells you how much you need to save monthly to meet said objective.

- **Financial Industry Regulatory Authority's (FINRA's) Savings Calculator** (`https://tools.finra.org/savings_calculator/`) lets you enter different combinations of variables, such as how much you've put away already and how much additional money you intend to save. It then gives you a realistic estimate of how much you can expect to add to your savings account.

Relying on the residual method

Are you the kind of person who has no idea how much money you have until you take out a wad of twenties from the ATM and check the balance on the receipt? If so, you're probably not the budgeting type, and the previous options are too strict. For you, the best option might be to open a savings account with your bank or open a high-yield savings account and transfer in money you know you won't need. Watch the savings account over the months and find out how much it grows. That can give you a good idea of how much you could save without even feeling it. You can find out where you can get a high rate of interest on your savings from Bankrate.com (`www.bankrate.com/banking/savings/rates/`). The site lists rates on savings accounts based on how much money you've saved.

Using web-based goal-savings calculators

All the previous methods help you determine how much you can save. But the following sites help you determine how much you *should* save to reach important goals, specifically, the ultimate goal of retirement:

- **Vanguard's Retirement Calculator** (`https://personal.vanguard.com/us/insights/retirement/saving/set-retirement-goals`) prompts you to enter how much you make and how long you have until retirement to help you figure out how much you need to save. Vanguard offers similar tools to help you decide how much you need to save for other goals, such as paying for a child's college tuition.

» **T. Rowe Price's Retirement Income Calculator** (www3.troweprice.com/ric/ric/public/ric.do) uses advanced computerized modeling to show you how much you need to save no matter what the stock market does. It runs your variables through a Monte Carlo simulation, which simulates what happens to your savings no matter what and gives you the odds that you'll have enough money.

» **Nationwide's On Your Side Interactive Retirement Planner** (https://isc.nwservicecenter.com/iApp/isc/rpt/launchRetirementTool.action) asks you some questions and then rates your ability to retire when and how you plan to. It also suggests tips on improving your odds of saving as much as you hope.

» **Index Funds Advisors Retirement Analyzer** (www.ifa.com/montecarlo/home) uses a sophisticated analysis to give you a range of possible outcomes in your retirement savings. Most retirement analyzers require you to make guesses at things such as the return you might get. The IFA Retirement Analyzer uses history to give you a good idea of what your best-case and worst-case scenarios might be.

BEING PREPARED FOR EMERGENCIES

When creating your budget and moving money from savings to an investment account, be sure to keep an emergency fund on hand. This money is readily available in case of a personal financial crunch, stored in an account you can access immediately, such as a bank savings account. A decent guideline is to always have enough cash handy for at least six months of living expenses. Knowing how much you spend monthly or annually, or your *run rate*, is a good idea. Your run rate is a key input in many financial decisions, including determining how much you need to save to retire. Several of the apps, software and websites in this chapter will calculate your run rate.

You can always measure your run rate manually. Add up how much you spend each month on necessities, such as housing (rent or mortgage and property taxes), food, utilities, insurance (home, car, and health), and transportation. Multiply by six to get a general idea of how much you should have for emergencies. During the 2008 financial crisis, some experts increased their recommendation for an emergency fund to 9 to 12 months of cash on hand. That's not a bad idea even now that the crisis is a distant memory.

Deciding How You Plan to Save

After you've determined how much you need to save and how much you can save, it's time to put your plan into action. The way you do this really depends on how good you are at handling your money and saving. The different methods are as follows:

>> **Automatic withdrawals:** Ever hear the cliché "pay yourself first"? It's a trite saying that actually makes sense. The idea is that before you go shopping for that big-screen TV or start feeling rich after payday, you should set money aside for savings. Some people have the discipline to do this themselves, but many do not. For the latter group of people, the best option is to set up *automatic withdrawals,* which is a way of giving a brokerage firm or bank permission to automatically extract money once a month. When the money is out of your hands, you won't be tempted to spend it.

>> **Retirement plans:** If your goal is investing for retirement, you want to find out what retirement savings plans are available to you. If you're an employee, you might have access to a 401(k) plan. Or if you're self-employed, you might consider various individual retirement accounts (IRAs). When you're starting to invest, taking advantage of available retirement plans is usually your best bet. I cover this in more detail in Chapter 3.

>> **On your own:** If you have money left over after paying all your bills, don't let it sit in a savings account. Leaving cash in a low-interest-bearing account is like giving a bank a cheap loan. Put your money to work for you. Brokers make it easy for you to get money to them via electronic transfers.

To Be a Successful Investor, Start Now!

The greatest force all investors have is time. Don't waste it. The sooner you start to save and invest, the more likely you will be successful. To explain, take the example of five people, each of whom wants to have $1 million in the bank by the time he or she retires at age 65. The first investor starts when she is 20, followed by a 30-year-old, 40-year-old, 50-year-old, and 60-year-old. Assuming that each investor starts with nothing and averages 10 percent returns each year (more on this later), Table 1-1 describes how much each must save per month to reach his or her goals.

See, youth has its advantages. A 20-year-old who saves less than $100 a month will end up with the same amount of money as a 60-year-old who squirrels away $12,914 a month or $154,968 a year! That's largely due to the fact that money that's invested early has more time to brew. And over time, the money snowballs and *compounds,* which is a concept I cover later in this chapter.

TABLE 1-1   How Much Each Must Save to Get $1 Million, Part I

An Investor Who Is	Must Invest This Much Each Month to Have $1 Million at Age 65
20 years old	$95.40
30 years old	$263.40
40 years old	$753.67
50 years old	$2,412.72
60 years old	$12,913.71

Note: Assumed 10% annual rate of return

Learning the Lingo

Just about any profession, hobby, or pursuit has its own lingo. Car fanatics, chess players, and computer hobbyists have terms of art that they seem to learn through osmosis. Online investing is no different. You might have heard but not completely understood many terms, such as *stocks* and *bonds.* As you read through this book and browse the websites I mention, you'll probably periodically stumble on unfamiliar words.

Don't expect a standard dictionary to help much. Investing terms can be so specialized and precise that your dusty ol' Webster's dictionary might not be a big help. Fortunately, a number of excellent online investing glossaries explain in detail what investing terms mean. Here are few for you to check out:

>> **Investopedia** (www.investopedia.com) has one of the most comprehensive databases of investing terms, with more than 5,000 entries. The site not only covers the basics but also explains advanced terms in great detail. It's also fully searchable so that you don't waste time getting the answer.

>> **Harvey's Hypertextual Finance Glossary** (people.duke.edu/~charvey/ Classes/wpg/glossary.htm) is all about quick answers. The database, written by Campbell Harvey, a professor of finance at Duke University, explains most basic investment terms in one or two sentences.

>> **InvestorWords** (www.investorwords.com) has a fully searchable database of investment terms, but it also makes the dictionary a bit more interesting with unique features such as a term of the day and a summary of terms that have recently rewritten definitions.

>> **The U.S. Securities and Exchange Commission's Glossary** (www.investor. gov/additional-resources/general-resources/glossary) is operated

by the government agency primarily responsible for overseeing most investing activity. The title doesn't disappoint. You'll find quick descriptions of all the basics and also some more advanced industry topics.

Setting Your Expectations

Have you ever talked to a professional investor or financial advisor? One of the first things you'll hear is how much experience he or she has. I can't tell you how many times I've been told, "I've been on Wall Street for 30 years. I've seen it all."

Some of that is certainly old-fashioned bragging. But these claims are common because in investing, experience does count. It's easy to say you could endure a bear market until you're watching, white-knuckled and sweating bullets, as your nest egg shrivels from $100,000 to $80,000 or $50,000. Experience brings perspective, which is very important.

But if you're new to investing, don't despair. Online tools can help you develop the brain of a grizzled Wall Street sage. And don't forget that I'm here to set you straight as well. In fact, I'm set to start talking about how much you can expect to make from investing. And you'll be hearing a great deal about a little something called the rate of return.

Keeping up with the rate of return

Don't let the term *rate of return* scare you. It's the most basic concept in investing, and you can master it. Just remember that it's the amount, measured as a percent, that your investment increases in value in a certain period of time. If you have a savings account, you understand the concept already. If you put $100 in a bank account paying 2.5 percent interest, you know that by the end of the year, you will have received $2.50 in interest. You earned a 2.5 percent annual rate of return. Rates of return are useful in investing because they work as a report card to tell investors how well an investment is doing, no matter how much money is invested.

You can calculate rates of return yourself with the following:

>> **A formula:** Subtract an asset's previous value from its current value, divide the difference by the asset's previous value, and multiply by 100. If a stock rises from $15 to $32 a share, you would calculate the rate of return by first subtracting 15 from 32 to get 17. Next, divide 17 by 15 and multiply by 100. The rate of return is 113.3 percent.

- » **Financial calculator:** You can use the Hewlett-Packard 12c calculator, which financial types always carry. Find out how to crunch a rate of return with an easy-to-follow tutorial at http://h20331.www2.hp.com/Hpsub/downloads/HP12Cpercents.pdf. (Look for Example 5.)

- » **Financial website:** Many handy sites can calculate rates of return for you, including CalcXML (www.calcxml.com/calculators/rate-of-return-calculator) and Bankrate (www.bankrate.com/calculators/retirement/roi-calculator.aspx).

WARNING

When you calculate the rate of return for a portfolio you've added money to or taken money from, you must take an extra step. I explain the process in Chapter 8.

The power of compounding

Famous physicist Albert Einstein once called *compounding* the most powerful force in the universe. Compounding is when money you invest earns a return and then that return also earns a return. (Dizzy yet?) When you leave money invested for a long time, the power of compounding kicks in.

Imagine that you've deposited $100 in an account that pays 2.5 percent in interest a year. In the first year, you'd earn $2.50 in interest, which brings your balance to $102.50. But in the second year, you'd earn interest of $2.56. Why? Because you've also earned 2.5 percent on the $2.50 in interest you earned. The longer you're invested, the more time your money has to compound.

TIP

You can enter your own information and see how powerful a force compounding is at this site: www.dinkytown.net/java/CompoundSavings.html.

Compounding works on your side to fight against inflation. Calculator Pro has a web-based calculator (www.calculatorpro.com/calculator/real-rate-of-return-calculator) that tells you whether your rate of return is keeping you ahead of inflation. The calculator also tells you what your real rate of return is — in other words, how much of your return isn't being eaten away by inflation.

Determining How Much You Can Expect to Profit

Why bother investing online? To make money, of course. But how much do you want to make? Understanding what you can expect to earn is where you need to start. Whenever you hear about an investment and what kinds of returns it promises, you should be able to mentally compare it with the kinds of returns you can expect from stocks, bonds, and other investments. That way, you know whether the returns you're being promised are too good to be true.

How do you do this? By relying on the hard work of academics who have done some heavy lifting. Academics and market research firms have ranked investments by how well they've done over the years. And I'm not just talking a few years, but decades — in many cases, going back to the 1920s and earlier. The amount of work that's gone into measuring historical rates of returns is staggering, but if you're using online resources, you're just a click away from finding out how most types of assets have done.

What you expect to earn is a number that can affect most of your investment decisions, usually dramatically. The following table is a revised version of Table 1-1 — the one that showed how five different people could expect to save $1 million. Table 1-2 looks at how much they must save to make their goal changes based on how much they think they will earn from their investments.

TABLE 1-2 **How Much Each Must Save to Get $1 Million, Part II**

An Investor Who Is	Must Invest This Much Each Month if She Earns 5%	Must Invest This Much Each Month if She Earns 10%	Must Invest This Much Each Month if She Earns 15%
20 years old	$493.48	$95.40	$15.28
30 years old	$880.21	$263.40	$68.13
40 years old	$1,679	$753.67	$308.31
50 years old	$3,741	$2,412.72	$1,495.87
60 years old	$14,704.57	$12,913.71	$11,289.93

The 20-year-old must save nearly $500 a month extra if she thinks she will earn only 5 percent a year from her investments instead of 15 percent. But even scarier, if she saves $15.28 thinking she'll earn 15 percent a year, but earns only 5 percent, she'll have just $30,963 instead of the $1 million she was counting on.

Studying the past

When people ask you how stocks are doing, they often want to know how much they went up or down that day. Financial TV stations and websites reinforce this preoccupation with the here-and-now by scrolling second-by-second moves in stock prices across the bottom of the screen.

But, second-by-second moves in stocks don't tell you much. If a stock goes down a bit and a company didn't report the news, did anything change during that second? Watching short-term movements of stock prices doesn't mean much in the overall scheme of things.

To understand how investments behave, it's more helpful to analyze their movements over as many years as you can. That way, recessions are blended with boom times to get you to a real, smooth average. Doing this requires the painstaking method of processing dozens of annual returns of stocks and analyzing the data. Luckily, some academics and industry pioneers have done much of the work for you, and you can access their findings if you know where to look. And I just happen to know a few places where you can start your search:

>> **Bogle Financial Market Research** (www.vanguard.com/bogle_site/ bogle_home.html) is the website maintained by the founder of Vanguard, John C. Bogle. Bogle revolutionized the investment industry by creating the world's largest index mutual fund, the Vanguard 500, which is designed to replicate the performance of the Standard & Poor's 500 stock market index. *Stock market indexes*, such as the Standard & Poor's 500 index and Dow Jones Industrial Average, are benchmarks that let you track how the market is doing.

   Bogle passed away in 2019, but his site is still invaluable because he explained that the market, on average, returns about 10 percent a year. That benchmark will be important later as you evaluate different stocks. Indexes are covered in more detail in Chapter 8.

>> **Annual Returns on Stock, T. Bonds and T. Bills: 1928 – Current** (pages. stern.nyu.edu/~adamodar/New_Home_Page/datafile/histretSP.html) doesn't have the catchiest title, but it's great information for investors. The site, maintained by New York University Professor Aswath Damodaran, lets you see how stocks and bonds have done every year since 1928. This is one site you'll want to bookmark.

>> **FTSE Russell's US Index Performance Calculator** (www.ftserussell.com/ index-series/index-tools/russell-index-performance-calculator) lets you look up how all types of stocks, ranging from small to large, in addition to bonds, have done over the years. You'll find a handy Index Returns Calculator that lets you see how different types of stocks have done at different points in history. FTSE Russell provides a variety of *market indexes*, or measuring sticks for the various markets.

>> **Kenneth R. French's website** at http://mba.tuck.dartmouth.edu/pages/ faculty/ken.french/data_library.html#HistBenchmarks. This site is complicated but worth the effort. French, a professor at Dartmouth, along with University of Chicago's Eugene Fama (faculty.chicagobooth.edu/ eugene.fama), revolutionized investing with an analysis that found that

essentially three things move stocks: what the general market is doing, how big the company is, and how pricey the shares are. Both profs keep statistics on their sites on how stocks move.

>> **Index Funds Advisors** (www.ifa.com) compiles much of the research done by Fama and French and helps explain it in plain language. You can download a colorful book from the site, *Index Funds: The 12-Step Recovery Program for Active Investors,* by Mark T. Hebner (IFA). The book explains how different types of stocks perform in the long term and shows how much you can expect to gain. It also shows long-term returns of bonds. You can also calculate the information yourself using the IFA Index Calculator (www.ifa.com/calculator/?i= port100_ifa&g=100000&s=1/1/2000&e=7/31/2015&gy=true&aorw=false& perc=true). Figure 1-2 shows you what kind of data this calculator can churn out.

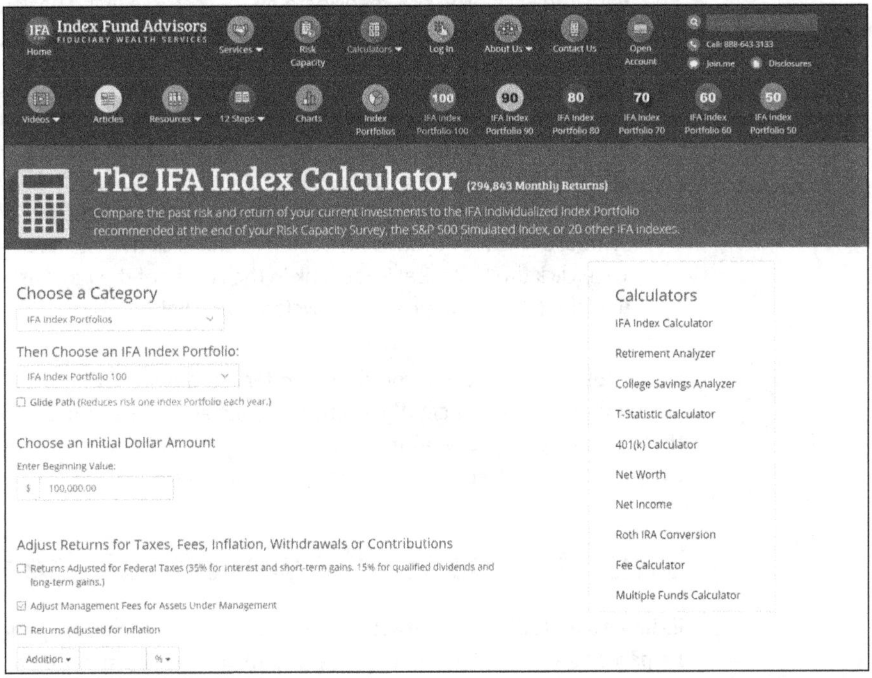

FIGURE 1-2: IFA.com's Index Calculator allows you to get detailed information on how different types of investments have performed over the years.

>> **Robert Shiller's website** (www.econ.yale.edu/~shiller) contains exhaustive data on how markets have done over the long term. You can view the data and make your own conclusions. Shiller is a well-known economics professor at Yale University.

- **S&P Indices** (us.spindices.com/indices/equity/sp-500) contains a full record of the returns from the Standard & Poor's 500 index going back for decades. This is invaluable data because you can understand how markets tend to move, instead of worrying about things that have never happened. Click the down arrow to the right of the Additional Info button. Scroll down and click the S&P Market Attributes Web File link, which then prompts you to open an Excel file. Click the Prices-Annual tab and scroll down the spreadsheet's annual returns. That information can give you an idea of how volatile stocks can be and also what returns are possible if you stay invested.

- **FreeStockCharts.com** (www.freestockcharts.com/legacy) allows you to download the stock trading history of most investments. After the site loads, just start typing the name or symbol of the investment you're interested in. A box will pop up with the names of stocks that match what you entered. Click the name of the company you're interested in. If you click the Export Chart icon (two small cylinders) along the top of the chart, you can download data into Excel. The site keeps data on most stocks going back to 1985. The site works with only the Internet Explorer web browser and requires the Silverlight plug-in.

- **Yahoo! Finance** (http://finance.yahoo.com) is a well-known source for historical stock data, and for good reason. You can download historical prices on many stocks going back to their first days of trading. And downloads are free. In the Search for News, Symbols or Companies field, just enter the symbol of the stock you're interested in and click the magnifying glass button. Then click the Historical Prices link in the center of the page. If you want to download the data, click the Download Data link.

TIP

Don't get too hung up if you don't understand everything on these sites. Several are sophisticated, especially French's. Just scan through the annual returns so that you can get a general feel for how markets behave over time. The idea here is for you to gain perspective, not cram for an econ PhD.

What the past tells you about the future

Exhaustive studies of markets have shown that stocks, in general, return about 10 percent a year. Through the years, 10 percent returns have been the benchmark for long-term performance, making them a good measuring stick for you and something to help you keep your bearings. But long-term studies of securities also show that, to get higher returns, you usually must also accept more risk. Table 1-3 shows how investors must often accept more risk to get a higher return.

TABLE 1-3   ## No Pain, No Gain

Investment	Average Annual Return	Relative Risk
Stocks	10.0% (based on S&P 500 since 1926)	Riskiest
Corporate bonds	6.0%	Moderately risky
Treasury bills (loans to the U.S. government that come due in a year or less)	3.4%	Least risky

Source: Morningstar through 2018

TIP

Don't make the mistake of thinking that investing in stocks guarantees you a 10 percent return every year, like a savings account. That's not the case. Stocks are risky and tend to move in erratic patterns, and they test your confidence with sudden drops. In fact, each year stocks typically posted a total return, including dividends, somewhere between a loss of 10 percent and a gain of 28.6 percent, according to the folks at the Index Funds Advisors website (www.ifa.com). And get this: Since 1926, the Standard & Poor's 500 index has returned between 10.0 percent and 10.9 percent only twice and 10 percent only once, in 1966. The market's brutal decline in 2008, which chewed up a third of stocks' value, is a good reminder of how violently stock prices can change in the short term. Don't let short-term swings in stocks derail your long-term plan, but *do* be aware that markets move in violent ways. That way, you won't be tempted to do something that you'll regret later. Volatility is the price you must pay to get returns.

Table 1-4 shows you just how crazy the market's movements can be in the short term, using the history of the popular Standard & Poor's 500 index since 1928.

TABLE 1-4   ## Wild Days for the S&P 500

Event	Amount
Number of days up	12,447 (average gain 0.74%)
Number of days down	11,017 (average loss 0.78%)
Best one-day percentage gain	March 15, 1933, up 16.6%
Worst one-day percentage loss	Oct. 19, 1987, down 20.5%
Best year	1933, up 46.6%
Worst year	1931, down 47.1%
Best month	April 1933, up 42.2%
Worst month	Sept. 1931, down 29.9%

Source: S&P Dow Jones Indices as of the end of 2018

Gut-Check Time: How Much Risk Can You Take?

It's time to get a grip — a grip on how much you can invest, that is. Most beginning investors are so interested in finding stocks that make them rich overnight that they lose sight of risk. But academic studies show that risk and return go hand in hand. That's why you need to know how much risk you can stomach before you start looking for investments and buying them online.

Several excellent online tools can help you get a handle on how much of a financial thrill seeker you are. Most are structured like interviews that ask you a number of questions and help you decide how much volatility you can comfortably stomach. These interviews are kind of like personality tests for your investment taste. I cover several in more detail in Chapter 9, where I discuss how to create an investing road map, called an *asset allocation*. For now, answering these questionnaires right away is worthwhile so that you can understand what kind of investor you are:

>> **Vanguard's Investor Questionnaire** (https://personal.vanguard.com/us/FundsInvQuestionnaire) asks ten salient questions to determine how much of a risk taker you are with your money. It determines your ideal asset allocation. Take note of the breakdown. The closer to 100 percent that Vanguard recommends you put in stocks, the more risk-tolerant you are, and the closer to 100 percent in bonds, the less risk-tolerant you are.

>> **Index Funds Advisors Risk Capacity Survey** (www.ifa.com/SurveyNET/index.aspx) offers a quick risk survey that can tell you what kind of investor you are after answering just five questions. You can also find a complete risk capacity survey that hits you with a few dozen questions. Whichever you choose, the survey can characterize what kind of investor you are and even display a painting that portrays your risk tolerance.

>> **Charles Schwab Investor Profile Questionnaire** (www.schwab.com/public/file/P-778947/InvestorProfileQuestionnaire.pdf) gets you to think about the factors that greatly determine how you should be investing, such as your investment time horizon and tolerance for risk. The Schwab questionnaire can be printed so you don't have to be in front of a computer to take it. At the bottom of the questionnaire is a chart that helps you see how aggressive or conservative you should be with your portfolio.

Passive or Active? Deciding What Kind of Investor You Plan to Be

Investing might not seem controversial, but it shouldn't surprise you that anytime you're talking about money, people have some strong opinions about the right way to do things. The first way investors categorize themselves is by whether they are passive or active. Because these two approaches are so different, the following sections help you think about what they are and which camp you see yourself in. Where you stand not only affects which broker is best for you, as discussed in Chapter 4, but also affects which chapters in this book appeal to you most.

How to know if you're a passive investor

Passive investors don't try to beat the stock market. They merely try to keep up with it by owning all the stocks in an index. An *index* is a basket of stocks or bonds that track a market by measuring movement by all the investments in it. For instance, the S&P 500 index tracks a selection of the largest and most valuable 500 U.S. stocks. Passive investors are happy matching the market's performance, knowing that they can try to boost their real returns with a few techniques I discuss in Chapter 9.

You know you're a passive investor if you

>> **Aren't interested in choosing individual stocks:** These investors buy large baskets of stocks that mirror the performance of popular stock indexes such

as the Dow Jones Industrial Average or the Standard & Poor's 500 index. Passive investors don't worry if a small upstart company they invested in will release its new product on time and whether it will be well received. They typically own small pieces of hundreds of stocks instead.

>> **Want to own mutual and exchange-traded funds:** Because passive investors aren't looking for the next Microsoft, Facebook, or Apple, they buy mutual and *exchange-traded funds* that buy hundreds of stocks. (I cover mutual and exchange-traded funds in more detail in Chapters 10 and 11, respectively.)

>> **Want to reduce taxes:** Passive investors tend to buy investments and forget about them until many years later when they need the money. This approach can be lucrative because by holding onto diversified investments for a long time and not selling them, passive investors can postpone when they have to pay capital gains taxes. (I cover capital gains taxes in more detail in Chapter 3.)

>> **Do not want to stress about stocks' daily, monthly, or even annual movements:** Passive investors tend to buy index or mutual funds and forget about them. They don't need to sit in front of financial TV shows, surf countless financial websites, read magazines, or worry about where stocks are moving. They're invested for the long term, and everything else is just noise to them.

Sites for passive investors to start with

One of the toughest things about being a passive investor is sitting still during a bull market when everyone else seems to be making more than you. Yes, you might be able to turn off the TV, but inevitably you'll bump into someone who brags about his or her giant gains and laughs at you for being satisfied with 10 percent average annual market returns.

When that happens, it's even more important to stick with your philosophy. Following the crowd at this moment undermines the value of your strategy. That's why even passive investors are well served going to websites where other passive investors congregate:

>> **Bogleheads** (www.bogleheads.org) is an electronic water cooler for fans of Vanguard index funds and passive investors to meet, encourage, and advise each other. They call themselves Bogleheads in honor of the founder of Vanguard, John Bogle.

>> **The Arithmetic of Active Management** (www.stanford.edu/~wfsharpe/art/active/active.htm) is a reprint of an article by an early proponent of passive investing, William Sharpe, who explains why active investing can never win.

>> **Vanguard** (www.vanguard.com) contains many helpful stories about the power of index investing and offers them for free, even if you don't have an account.

How to know whether you're an active investor

Active investors almost feel sorry for passive investors. Why would anyone be satisfied just matching the stock market and not even try to do better? Active investors feel that if you're smart enough and willing to spend time doing homework, you can exceed 10 percent annual returns. Likewise, active investors question the logic of holding stocks even as markets plunge. Active investors also find investing to be thrilling, almost like a hobby. Some active investors try to find undervalued stocks and hold them until they're discovered by other investors. Another class of active investors are short-term traders, who bounce in and out of stocks trying to get quick gains.

You're an active investor if you

>> **Think long-term averages of stocks are meaningless:** Active investors believe they can spot winning companies that no one knows about yet or are underappreciated, buy their shares at just the right time, and sell them for a profit.

>> **Are willing to spend large amounts of time searching for stocks:** These are the investors who sit in front of financial TV shows, analyze stocks that look undervalued, and do all sorts of prospecting trying to find gems.

>> **Believe they can hire mutual fund managers who can beat the market:** Some active investors think that certain talented mutual fund managers are out there and that if they just give their money to those managers, they'll win.

>> **Suspect certain types of stocks aren't priced correctly and many investors make bad decisions:** Active investors believe they can outsmart the masses and routinely capitalize on the mistakes of the great unwashed.

>> **Understand the risks:** Most active traders underperform index funds, some without even realizing it. Before deciding to be an active trader, be sure to test out your skills with online simulations, as I describe in Chapter 2, or make sure that you're measuring your performance correctly, as I describe in Chapter 8. If you're losing money picking stocks, stop doing it. Be sure to know how dangerous online investing can be when trying to be an active investor by reading a warning from the Securities and Exchange Commission here: http://sec.gov/investor/pubs/onlinetips.htm.

WARNING

Many investors try, but few are able to consistently beat the market. Consider Bill Miller, portfolio manager for the Legg Mason Capital Management Value Trust mutual fund. Miller had beaten the market for 15 years and turned into a poster child for active investors and proof that beating the market was possible if you were smart enough. But even Miller's streak came to an end in 2006. That's when his Legg Mason Value Trust fund didn't just trail the market, it lagged by a mile, returning just 5.9 percent while the market gained 15.8 percent. The fund lagged the market by 12.2 percent in 2007 and again in 2008 by 18.1 percent. While the fund beat the market in 2009, active investors had already lost their hero. Even now, more than a decade later, there's yet to be a mutual fund with an equivalent record.

Sites for the active investor to start with

Ever hear of someone trying to learn a foreign language by moving to the country and picking it up through immersion? The idea is that by just being around the language, and through the necessity of buying food or finding the restroom, the person eventually gets proficient.

If you're interested in active investing, you can do the same thing by hitting websites that are common hangouts for active investors, picking up how these types of investors find stocks that interest them and trade on them. These sites can show you the great pains active investors go through in their attempt to beat the market. A few to start looking at follow:

» **TheStreet.com** (www.thestreet.com) collects trading ideas and tips from writers mainly looking for quick-moving stocks and other investments.

» **Investor's Business Daily** (www.investors.com) provides tools and research for investors looking for promising stocks. The site highlights stocks that have moved up or down by a large amount, which usually catches the attention of traders.

» **Seeking Alpha** (http://seekingalpha.com) provides news and commentary for investors of all skill levels who are trying to beat the market.

IN THIS CHAPTER

» Turning your PC or mobile device into an online investing station

» Pinpointing online media that can make you a more informed investor

» Turning blogs and podcasts into research tools

» Scouring the Internet with search engines

» Securing your computer from online financial crooks

» Practicing your techniques with online tutorials and simulations

Chapter **2**

Getting Your Device Ready for Online Investing

A pps and online services have reinvented convenience. Admit it — you've probably shopped online from the couch in your PJs. But with the ease of online transactions comes the assumption that you will do more tasks yourself. You compare routes and times and prices before booking your own airline tickets, and you research and compare medical plans before enrolling in a health insurance plan. The process is convenient, but you also need to know what you're doing.

The story is the same with investing. If you want to reach your financial goals and retire comfortably, it's up to you to make it happen. The age of employers looking after their workers' futures with pensions is vanishing and being replaced with do-it-yourself retirement plans such as 401(k)s.

If you ask for help, you're almost always directed to search online or do your own research. That sounds reasonable, except that the Internet contains billions of web pages, and you can find dozens if not hundreds of sources for investing advice, much of which is conflicting or, worse, wrong. No wonder many investors throw their hands up in utter frustration.

That's where this chapter comes in. In Chapter 1, I fill you in on what it takes to prepare yourself to be an online investor. Here in Chapter 2, it's time to prepare your computer, smartphone, or tablet for online investing and make it a tool that quickly provides you with the answers you need. This chapter helps you tweak your device until it's like your personal investing workstation. By the time you're finished, your trading device will feel as comfortable to you as an old leather chair. And by using mostly free online resources, you'll save yourself some money in the process.

I escort you through the morass of financial websites and apps and show you which ones you need to know. You find out what types of investing information are available online and how to access what you need from your computer or other device. You also find out how to use online simulation sites that let you take a dry run investing with fake money to make sure that you know what you're doing before using real cash.

Turning Your Device into a Trading Station

When you think of a stock trading floor, you probably picture a room full of traders wearing brightly colored jackets, throwing papers around, and yelling out market orders. Some of that drama still exists on the New York Stock Exchange floor, but it's largely a throwback from the old days.

Today, trading floors I've walked through look more like insurance offices. They have rows of desks with computers not unlike the ones you see, well, in insurance offices. Professional traders do have an advantage: Many have high-end trading systems and software that cost thousands of dollars a month. That might be beyond your price range, but you might be amazed at how much market information you can get, for free or for little money, if you know where to go.

REMEMBER

Mobile devices have become go-to devices for checking mail — and yes — playing Fortnite. When you're looking for a quick update on your portfolio or want to see how your stocks are doing, your smartphone is your trusty mobile companion. Because of the increased popularity of mobile devices, they are included in this section. But the emphasis, still, is on good ol' fashioned computers. Why? Online brokers tell me that most trading still happens on PCs. The bigger screen, dedicated keyboard, and better tools still make the PC the tool of choice when it comes to investing.

Using favorites to put data at your fingertips

The easiest way to turn your computer into a market-monitoring station is by bookmarking or creating favorites to key sites with data you need. *Favorites* (also sometimes called *bookmarks*) are links in your Internet browser that let you quickly reach a web page when you need it, without typing a long website address. Most Internet browsers have this capability, and they all work slightly differently. In the following steps, I show you how to create favorites by using Microsoft's Edge browser in Windows 10:

1. **Navigate to the website you're interested in saving.**

2. **Click the Favorites icon (star) in the upper-right corner of the screen, labeled in Figure 2-1.**

   A menu opens.

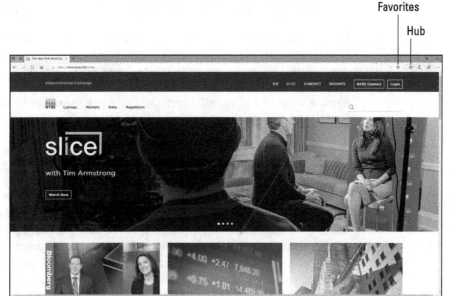

Favorites

Hub

FIGURE 2-1:
Setting financial websites as favorites is a matter of just clicking a few buttons.

3. Make sure the Favorites tab is selected, and **give the favorite a name.**

   Choose a name that will quickly identify the site for you.

4. **In the Save In space, choose the Favorite folder into which you want to put the favorite.**

   If you want to put this favorite in a separate folder, you can create a folder by clicking the Create New Folder option. If you're not sure, just use the default Favorite folder.

5. **Click the Add button.**

When you want to access that address again, click the Hub icon (labeled in Figure 2-1) and scroll down until you see the title of the page you're interested in. Again, make sure the Favorites tab is selected.

TIP

Don't worry — your favorites are still available when you're away from your office and PC. There's an app for that! You can download and install a free version of Edge for your smartphone, too, if you're using iOS or Android. Just download the Edge browser from your phone's app store, start the mobile browser, and log in using your Microsoft account (the same username and password you use on your computer). All the favorites and folders you created on your computer will be pulled over and accessible if you tap the Hub icon.

Putting key mobile apps a touch away

Investors are increasingly looking to their smartphones and tablets as a way to keep up with the markets, especially when they're away from the office. The computer is still the ideal place to do most of your work — given the spacious size of the screen, increased processing power, and greater storage. But some investors like the simplicity of a mobile device or use it to keep an eye on their money at all times.

Both of the major mobile platforms (Apple's iOS and Google's Android) provide an app store. That's where you go to download the apps you'll want to track your money.

To make it easier to find the apps you're looking for on your phone, consider creating an app folder called Investing or Money and putting all your finance-related apps there. You'll save yourself lots of wasted time scrolling through menus. If you're using a phone running Android or iOS, you create a folder by dragging one app's icon on top of another icon of a related app. A folder will be created automatically.

Compiling a list of must watch sites

So you know how to create favorites and organize your mobile apps. But what sites are worth creating as favorites? My suggestion is to take a page from the professionals and try to replicate the data they're most interested in. Most professional trading workstations are set up so that they can take on five distinct tasks:

>> Track the market's every move

>> Monitor news that has the potential to affect stock prices

>> Check in on Wall Street chatter

>> Access company financial statements and regulatory filings

>> Execute trades

TECHNICAL STUFF

The world between PCs and mobile devices continues to blur. Microsoft's Surface Pro is basically a tablet that's also a computer. And Windows 10 is designed to give you the power of a desktop computer but with the ease and apps that smartphone users have become used to. Apple followed with the iPad Pro — which still runs a mobile operating system — but touts a larger screen and the capability to connect and use a keyboard. Expect the distinction between computer and mobile devices to dissolve over time.

Tracking the Market's Every Move

You're probably hoping to study the market and find ways to score big and fast. Hey, everyone wants to get rich quick. Just remember that making money by darting in and out of stocks is extremely tough to do, and most investors, online or not, will be better off forming and sticking with a long-term investment strategy. The difference between long-term investing and short-term trading is discussed in Chapter 1, where I also give you the tools necessary to figure out which approach is best for you.

No matter what kind of investor you plan to be, watching real-time stock movements is fascinating. Seeing rapid price moves with stock prices dancing around and flashing on the computer screen is a guilty pleasure and a source of entertainment (or profit) for some investors.

TIP

You can find a great deal of overlap among online investing resources. Many of the following sites and apps do more than what I highlight here. Explore the different sites and see whether certain ones suit you best.

You can get stock quotes and see the value of popular market indexes such as the Dow Jones Industrial Average, Standard & Poor's 500 index, and NASDAQ composite index in many places. Therefore, a website must excel to earn a position as one of your favorites. In Chapter 6, I list multiple sites best suited for tracking specific parts of the market. The next section in this chapter has a quick list that can help you get started creating general-purpose online investing favorites or decide which apps are worthy of occupying space on your phone. The sites listed here make the cut because they not only provide stock quotes but also go a step further by being the best at a certain aspect of tracking the market.

REMEMBER

When you look up a stock quote on many sites or in an app, you'll usually see three quotes: the last sale, the bid, and the ask. The *last sale* is what you probably think of as the stock quote and is featured on most websites. That's the price at which a buyer and seller agreed to a transaction. The *bid* is the highest price other investors are willing to pay for the stock. The *ask* is the lowest price that investors who own the stock are willing to sell it for.

Getting price quotes on markets and stocks

Nearly any site or finance app can give you stock quotes for the day, including the financial news websites discussed later in this chapter. But a few sites deserve special mention because they make it easy to get stock quotes for days in the past and even download them to your computer for further analysis. And because they deserve special mention, they're getting it right here:

>> **MSN Money** (http://money.msn.com) is handy for looking up prices of stocks and market indexes because it's fast and gives you everything you need, ranging from the stock's closing price to the amount of trading activity to when dividends (cash payments) were paid to investors. One nifty trick of MSN Money is that it has companion apps for Windows 10, iOS, and Android that remembers which stocks you're most interested in. You can create this list by clicking the My Watchlist link on the website or on the Watchlist menu in the app.

>> **Yahoo! Finance** (http://finance.yahoo.com) lets you download historical data, a feature that's getting surprisingly scarce in non-professional tools. Enter a stock symbol and click the magnifying glass. Then, at the top of the page, click the Historical Data link. You'll see a page with a table of dates and the stock's prices on those dates. In the Time Period area near the top, you can choose a range of dates for which you'd like stock prices. On the right side is a link to Download Data. Yahoo! Finance also offers an app for several types of smartphones, making it a convenient choice.

KNOWING YOUR EXCHANGES

When you get a stock quote from most websites, you also see what exchange the stock trades on. This information is important. Most U.S. stocks typically trade on one of two major exchanges in the United States: the New York Stock Exchange (NYSE) and the NASDAQ.

You find foreign exchanges (which I cover in more detail in Bonus Chapter 1 on the web) and informal marketplaces such as the Pink Sheets, operated by OTC Markets Group, and the similarly named but separate OTC Bulletin Board. Many beginning online investors are attracted to the Pink Sheets and OTC Bulletin Board stocks due to their low share prices and high volatility, which is why they're called *penny stocks or microcap stocks.* Microcap, or micro-market capitalization, stocks a worth very little. But buying stocks on the Pink Sheets and Bulletin Board can be very risky. The Pink Sheets and Bulletin Board don't have the same oversight of their stocks as those listed on major market exchanges such as the NASDAQ. That makes them popular with fraudsters. You can read the Securities and Exchange Commission warnings to investors about these stocks at www.sec.gov/investor/pubs/microcapstock.htm.

>> **Google Finance** (www.google.com/finance) does a solid job of summarizing in one page many of the basics you need to know about a stock. You'll find not only the stock price but also a list of competitors, a summary of what Wall Street experts think about the stock, and basic financial information. Google Finance also offers free real-time stock prices.

>> **FreeStockCharts.com** (www.freestockcharts.com/legacy) gives you great flexibility in creating stock charts, allowing you to add different indicators that show you how a stock is doing. And unlike most other stock sites, FreeStockCharts lets you download the end-of-year values of investments. End-of-year data is helpful when you want to see how an investment has performed over the long haul.

Slicing and dicing the markets

Although quite a few market indexes exist — I discuss many of them in Chapter 8 — *all* online investors need to be familiar with some major market benchmarks. These benchmarks are so commonly discussed that they need to be part of your investor vocabulary. Table 2-1 presents them in all their market-dominating glory.

TABLE 2-1   ## Key Market Indexes

Index Name	What It Measures
Dow Jones Industrial Average	Thirty big, industrial companies. When investors hear about "the market," more often than not they think of the Dow.
Standard & Poor's 500 index	Large U.S. companies, including 500 of the nation's most well-known stocks. Moves similarly to the Dow, even though it includes more stocks.
NASDAQ composite index	Stocks that trade on the NASDAQ stock market. Tends to closely track technology stocks.
Wilshire 5000 Total Market Index	The entire U.S. stock market. Contains all significant stocks from the largest to the smallest.
Russell 2000 Index	Small-company U.S. stocks. Tends to be more volatile than indexes that track large companies — the S&P 500, for example.
MSCI ACWI (All Country World Index)	Stocks around the world. Includes shares of big companies in developed parts of the world and small companies in less-developed nations.

Nearly all financial websites let you track all the indexes listed in the table. Yahoo! Finance (`http://finance.yahoo.com`), though, makes it easy to monitor different slices of the markets, such as foreign stocks, specific industry sectors, and bonds. The Yahoo! Finance website offers several ways for you to dig beyond the market indexes, as the following list makes clear:

>> **A quick read on all U.S. market indexes:** To see how most of the key U.S. market indexes are doing, start at Yahoo! Finance's main page at `http://finance.yahoo.com`. Hover your cursor over the Markets option at the top of the page, and click the World Indices link that appears. The top of the next page displays key U.S. market indexes, such as S&P 500, Dow Jones, and NASDAQ.

>> **A rundown of the performance of foreign stocks:** Scroll down the list that appears under World Indices and you can monitor just about any foreign market you'd care to track. Bonus Chapter 1 on the web (`www.dummies.com/bonuschapters/onlineinvesting`) tells you more about investing in international stocks.

>> **A summary of the performance of industries:** The Yahoo! Finance page enables you to track the performance of different industries, if you know where to look. To find a list of industry group results, click the Industries link at the top of the Yahoo! Finance page or follow this link: `finance.yahoo.com/industries` — and set it as a favorite.

HOW THE DOW'S VALUE IS CALCULATED

Market measures, such as the Dow, are priced not by traders but by calculators. Mathematical formulas analyze the movements of the stocks in an index to arrive at the value of the index. To get the value of the Dow, for instance, the prices of the 30 stocks in the index are multiplied by a *divisor* and summed. The divisor is used to smooth interruptions caused when stocks are replaced in the index. For details on how the Dow is calculated, go to www.djaverages.com. You can read more about indexes in Chapter 8.

TIP

Don't confuse stocks with indexes. *Stocks* are shares in individual companies, such as Microsoft or Exxon Mobil. The prices of stocks reflect how much you would have to pay for a share of the stock. *Indexes* are mathematical formulas that tell you how much a collection of stocks has changed in value. For example, when the Dow Jones Industrial Average, which contains 30 stocks, hits 25,000, that doesn't mean you can buy it for $25,000. The 25,000 is just a number that represents relative value.

Your crystal ball: Predicting how the day will begin

Some investors like to get a jump-start on the trading day by watching the futures market. The *futures market* is an auction for future contracts, which are financial obligations that allow buyers and sellers to lock in prices for commodities and other assets in the future. The futures market allows investors to bet how much certain assets will be worth minutes, days, weeks, or years from today. Futures are commonly used with commodities, such as energy and food, as I describe in more detail in Chapter 6.

You can see what the futures market is saying about stocks, too. Bloomberg, a major financial news and data company, gives investors a sneak peek on how stocks could open the next trading day. On its Futures page (www.bloomberg.com/markets/stocks/futures), you can see how traders who apparently don't have anything better to do are betting after the stock market is closed and how major market indexes around the world will open. If you're the kind of person who doesn't like surprises, the Futures page is an easy way to see how investors are behaving even when the market centers are closed.

Getting company descriptions

Professional investors like to bone up on what a company does, who's in charge, and how profitable it is without poring through dozens of industry reports. You can get this type of quick snapshot information by reading online company descriptions. All the main investing sites I discuss have company description sections in. Here is one more site worth checking out, plus another way to use Yahoo! Finance:

>> **Reuters** (www.reuters.com/finance/markets) offers in-depth profiles on companies. Just click the magnifying glass, enter the name of the company, click the magnifying glass again, and then click the name of the company. The page that opens shows you all the vital information about the company, ranging from a company description to the names of members of its management team (if you click the People tab). To see a comprehensive rundown of the company's financial results, click the Financials tab.

>> **Yahoo! Finance** (http://finance.yahoo.com) offers a comprehensive summary of a company's vitals. From the site's main page, enter the stock's symbol in the search box located on the top of the screen and then click the magnifying glass. On the top of the next page, click the Profile link. On the screen that appears, you can also find particulars on the company's financial performance by click the Statistics and Financials links.

Keeping tabs on commodities

I have more on the exciting world of commodities — such as the oil, lumber, and coal that companies use to make their products — in Chapter 6. If you can't wait until then, check out the following websites:

>> **Bloomberg** (www.bloomberg.com/markets/commodities) has a professional-grade site that lets you watch movements in just about any commodity that you can imagine, including gold, silver, and platinum. Interested in live cattle? Yes, you can see the price. This data is necessary if you want to invest in commodities directly. And even if you don't buy or sell commodities, they're good to watch. For instance, if you own shares of Starbucks, wouldn't you want to know what the price of coffee is doing?

>> **CME Group** (www.cmegroup.com) lists prices on many major commodities, such as corn, soybeans, wheat, and ethanol. I describe this site (and other commodities-centric sites) in more detail in Chapter 6.

Tracking bonds and U.S. Treasurys

A *bond* is an IOU issued by a government, a company, or another borrower. An owner of a bond is entitled to receive the borrowed funds when they're paid back by a certain time in the future at a predetermined interest rate. Even if you have no interest in investing in bonds, you still should know what rates are doing. After all, if you could invest in *Treasury bonds* — bonds issued by the federal government that come due in 30 years — and get a 3 percent annual return guaranteed, wouldn't you be a bit less enthusiastic about a risky stock that you think will return only 4 percent? That extra return is not enough for the extra risk you're taking.

The U.S. government sells other Treasurys, including *Treasury bills* (T-bills), which generally come due in a year or less, and *Treasury notes* (T-notes), which come due longer than a year but no more than ten years. I provide details in Chapter 6 on how bond yields affect stock prices. For an introduction, check out the following sites:

>> **Bloomberg** (www.bloomberg.com/markets/rates-bonds) makes tracking bonds easy. At a glance, you can see the yields on just about any major bond or Treasury you can imagine.

REMEMBER

>> **The Federal Reserve Bank** (www.federalreserve.gov/monetarypolicy/openmarket.htm) is the online presence for the *Fed,* as it's affectionately called. The Fed is in charge of strongly influencing short-term interest rates, including the *federal funds rate,* which is typically the rate at which banks lend money stored at the Fed to other banks overnight. No, you can't borrow at that rate, but it's important to watch this interest rate because it affects long-term interest rates, which you *can* borrow at. You can see past federal funds rates at the Fed's site, as shown in Figure 2-2. Traders buy and sell long-term Treasurys and set interest rates based in large part on where short-term rates are or where they're expected to be.

TIP

Would you like to find out more about how the Fed affects the nation's money supply? The Federal Reserve Bank of Kansas City maintains a useful and simple site on the topic — designed for teens and college students, but useful for any investor — at www.federalreserveeducation.org/.

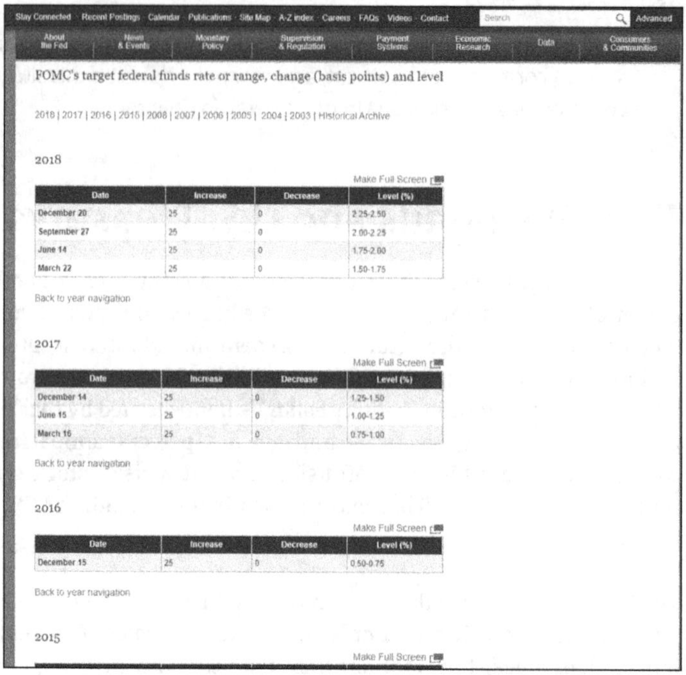

Date	Increase	Decrease	Level (%)
December 20	25	0	2.25-2.50
September 27	25	0	2.00-2.25
June 14	25	0	1.75-2.00
March 22	25	0	1.50-1.75

Date	Increase	Decrease	Level (%)
December 14	25	0	1.25-1.50
June 15	25	0	1.00-1.25
March 16	25	0	0.75-1.00

Date	Increase	Decrease	Level (%)
December 15	25	0	0.50-0.75

FIGURE 2-2: The Fed's website makes it easy to track important interest rates.

Monitoring Market-Moving News

Ever see a biotech stock skyrocket after the company announces a breakthrough treatment? Tech stocks routinely jump in price on the debut of popular new gadgets or software. That's the power of news — often called *market-moving news.* Markets are constantly taking in and digesting all sorts of developments and changes, both good and bad. To stay on top of these developments, you'll want to set as favorites a few leading financial news sites. The following sections explore the different kinds of financial news sites in greater detail.

Financial websites

Many of the financial sites mentioned previously in the chapter are also great places to get market-moving news. Yahoo! Finance and MSN Money pick up wire service stories on the markets and individual stocks, making them helpful resources. Bloomberg covers just about every type of traditional investment you can imagine, thanks to its network of reporters. Others include the following:

>> **Google News** (news.google.com) has a business section that pulls in important financial stories. Its best feature is the capability to search for news based on precise criteria, including keywords, the date the story appeared, or the geographic location of the news.

>> **Bing News** (www.bing.com/news) searches the Internet for business stories after you click the Business tab. Scroll down to the Interests section to set markets, personal finance, or individual stocks as interests, which means they will be covered more prominently online and also in the Bing mobile app (downloaded to your smartphone).

>> **Briefing.com** (www.briefing.com), shown in Figure 2-3, is a data service used by professional investors, who pay for its premium services. However, the site makes some of its content available for free. You can find running commentary on market-moving news and events. Briefing.com's stock market update is a great way to find out what's behind the market's day-to-day swings — and see how a random event can have a big effect on stocks.

FIGURE 2-3:
Briefing.com provides many free resources to online investors.

- >> **MarketWatch** (www.marketwatch.com) focuses on business stories that are so interesting that you can hardly resist clicking. The site attempts to separate itself from the competition by providing columns from various financial writers who opine about everything from companies' accounting practices to technology. You can instruct MarketWatch to email you articles of interest as well as note when a stock moves by a certain amount.

- >> **BigCharts.com** (www.bigcharts.com) is a service of MarketWatch that provides graphical information about the markets. The best aspect of the site is the set of BigReports lists that show you, at a glance, the biggest movers on Wall Street that day in terms of price or percentage price change.

- >> **Motley Fool** (www.fool.com) has a little something for everyone. You find content for the active trader, including stock tips galore, as well as tricks and techniques on how to deeply analyze companies' financial statements. Passive investors will appreciate the more general personal finance stories.

- >> **Reuters** (www.reuters.com) makes high-end systems used by many professional traders, but many of these tools are available to you as well. If you click the magnifying glass in the search box at the upper-right corner of the page, enter a company's name, and then click the company's name, you can see advanced statistics about the stock, including dividend yields and key ratios. (Don't worry. I cover these advanced topics in Chapters 14 and 15.)

TIP

Many financial websites and news stories use the terms *bullish* and *bearish*. When investors are *bullish*, they think the stock market is going to go up. And when investors are *bearish*, they think stocks will go down.

Traditional financial news sites

Many financial news providers that you might already be familiar with from websites, apps, newspapers, magazines, or TV also provide data that's useful to investors online, including the following:

- >> **Wall Street Journal Online** (www.wsj.com) is a source of breaking financial news. You might be familiar with the print edition of the *Wall Street Journal;* this is the online version. This site charges for much of its content.

- >> **Financial Times** (www.ft.com) is a London-based business publication, so it provides a unique spin on business events here. It's a good source of merger announcements.

- » **CNBC** (www.cnbc.com) routinely updates its website, and the financial TV channel's online presence has many of the same features as other financial news sites. What makes the site unique is that it lets you stream to your browser segments that aired on CNBC.

- » **CNN Money** (http://money.cnn.com) has a good mix of breaking financial news and general personal financial help. It contains specialized information on markets, technology, jobs, personal finance, and real estate.

- » **Investor's Business Daily** (www.investors.com) is largely geared to sophisticated investors; subscribers have access to all articles. You'll find articles for short-term active traders as well as for passive or mutual fund investors more focused on the longer term, as shown in Figure 2-4. The site also has tools to help you find stocks that are outperforming the rest of the stock market.

- » **Barron's** (www.barrons.com) is a weekly publication written mainly for advanced investors and is updated online during the day. Most of the features are available only to subscribers. Subscribers to the *Wall Street Journal*'s website get access to Barron's online site because both are owned by Dow Jones.

FIGURE 2-4: Investors.com's provides a detailed look at stocks.

DO YOU SPEAK TICKER SYMBOL?

Nearly every financial website is centered on the ticker symbol. These are the one-, two-, three-, or four-letter abbreviations used to symbolize stocks or investments. Originally, ticker symbols were used so that brokers could quickly read a *ticker tape,* a scrolling printout of stocks and prices. The symbol has taken on a new use in the online era, so much so that most sites enable you to search for a stock by its symbol.

Ticker symbols have become so popular that investors sometimes use them instead of a company's name. And sometimes companies have fun with their symbols to make them more memorable. In 2006, for instance, motorcycle maker Harley-Davidson changed its symbol from the boring HDI to the more exciting HOG, the nickname for its rumbling bikes. Other fun ticker symbols (and the company) include the following:

- BUD: Anheuser-Busch InBev
- CAKE: Cheesecake Factory
- EAT: Brinker (a restaurant company)
- FIZZ: National Beverage
- LUV: Southwest Airlines
- SAM: Boston Beer
- ZEUS: Olympic Steel (Get it? The Greek god)

Keep one other thing in mind regarding stock symbols. You used to be able to tell whether a stock traded on the NASDAQ or the New York Stock Exchange just by looking at the symbol. For many years, NASDAQ stocks traded with symbols with four letters, such as INTC for Intel and MSFT for Microsoft. But that changed in 2007 when NASDAQ began issuing symbols of one, two, and three letters to its member companies.

Checking In on Wall Street Chatter

Rumor and innuendo are key parts to traders' lives. Because stock prices are highly sensitive in the short run to what other traders and investors are saying about a stock, traders make it their business to follow any murmur. As an individual investor, you're at a disadvantage in this department because you don't have portfolio managers of giant mutual funds calling you and telling you what they're hearing. But you can use social networking and social investing, online tools that allow investors to swap information.

BEWARE OF RUMORS

Investors can't help themselves when it comes to rumors. And sometimes certain blogs and podcasts only feed your innate desire to get the inside scoop on an investment that's about to explode in value. Investment rumors are kind of like celebrity gossip: You're probably better off ignoring them, but sometimes it's impossible to resist. Just remember that making investment decisions based on rumors is usually a bad idea.

Even giant stocks can get swept up in rumors and result in pain for gullible investors. Here's an example: On May 17, 2012, Facebook, the world's largest social networking company, sold its stock to public investors for the first time for $38 a share. The website was (and is) so popular with consumers that the rumor mill went into overdrive. Many people with little to no experience with investing thought they had to jump into the initial public offering of Facebook since they thought it was bound to soar on its first day. But these rumors proved to be wrong. Shares of Facebook barely moved on their first day of trading, and by the end of May the stock lost 22 percent of its value from the offering price. Shares have performed very well since then, but investors who bought when the stock debuted had to endure a long period of pain.

Guess what? You might think investors would have learned their lesson from Facebook. But the same hype-fueled fever revved up again in May 2019. Unprofitable ride-sharing service Uber Technologies offered its shares at $45 each. Given how popular the service is, many expected fireworks. But the stock fizzled, falling nearly 8 percent on the first day. Even months later, shares of Uber traded below the $45 a share offer price.

Chat rooms were an early form of social investing, but the area has evolved to include online blogs and podcasts. Twitter has also become an important tool for investors. In addition, several online brokers' sites let users communicate with each other. I cover all these forms of communication in more detail in Chapter 7.

If you're a passive investor, you probably couldn't care less about rumors. Even so, you can take advantage of blogs and chat rooms that are dedicated to index investing.

Everyone is an expert: Checking in with blogs

Thanks to low-cost computers, mobile devices, and Internet connections, just about anyone with an opinion and a keyboard or smartphone can profess to the world his or her view of investments. Some of these opinions are worth listening to, but many are not.

One popular vehicle for sharing opinions is a *blog* (short for web log), which is a sort of an online journal. Blogs can vary greatly in quality. Some are the modern-day equivalent of a crazy person on the street corner yelling at anyone who walks by, whereas other blogs are thoughtful and well-informed. It's *buyer beware* with blogs — you have to decide whether the person is worth listening to. Ask yourself what the blogger's track record is and how the blogger makes money.

Finding blogs

With so many blogs out there, sometimes the toughest part can be finding the worthwhile ones. Here are several ways that you can locate them:

>> **General search engines:** All the leading search engines, including Google, Yahoo!, and Bing, let you search much of the blogging world. You're likely to find major general-interest finance blogs just by typing **investing blog**. You can also look for articles such as "The 7 best investing blogs" written by reputable publications like the ones described previously to get suggestions.

>> **Community sites:** Facebook (www.facebook.com) is best known as an online place for friends to keep tabs on each other and for families to share photos with each other. But some financial blogs are also lurking there. To find them, just log on to the site and search for the words *financial, money, investing,* and *stocks.* You can also find Facebook communities focused on investing for retirement or other goals.

>> **Mainstream media:** Almost all the news sites have some of their writers penning blogs as well. Many blogs are available from the mainstream media outlet's website.

Getting in tune with podcasts

Next time you see someone listening to a smartphone with Bluetooth buds jammed into his ears, don't assume he's rocking out. He might be researching stocks or learning about investing. A *podcast* is an audio broadcast that's transferred electronically over the Internet to your computer or smartphone — they're like radio shows for the Internet age. Some podcasts are created by major media, but others, like some blogs, are done by amateurs, so the same need for caution applies.

It's easy to find a radio or TV station: Just turn on the radio and start flipping. But finding podcasts takes a little more doing. It's not difficult, though, if you try these different methods:

>> **Podcast smartphone apps:** You'll probably be listening to podcasts on your smartphone in the car or on a train, so it makes sense to use your phone to find them, too. With Android, you can find podcasts in two ways. The easiest method is to launch the built-in Play Music app. Press the three lines in the upper-left corner, choose Podcasts, and search for podcasts. The other method is to download the Google Podcasts app, which gives you a little more control in finding a podcast you'll love. With iOS, fire up the Podcasts app, and search for and download podcasts from there. You can also use third-party podcast apps, such as Spotify (primarily a music streaming app) and Stitcher.

>> **Podcast search engines:** Search engines dedicated to podcasts, such as Podcasts.com (www.podcasts.com), provide a giant list of podcasts that meet your requirements. Stitcher Radio (www.stitcher.com) is another popular podcast search site. You can stream from these sites, too, but more likely you'll fire up a podcast app and listen from there.

>> **Desktop audio software:** Apple's iTunes software (www.apple.com/itunes) has a podcast search function as part of its iTunes Store. Click the Store link, click the Podcasts link, and then click Business. You can scroll through hundreds of available podcasts, including some from mainstream outlets such as *Bloomberg Businessweek,* CNBC, and National Public Radio. Not an iTunes kind of person? No problem. Spotify for the desktop, downloadable from the Windows 10 app store, also has a podcast feature. To get there, click Browse in the menu on the left side of the screen and then choose Podcasts from the option at the top. You can also stream podcasts to your computer using Stitcher.com if you click the Listen option.

Taming Twitter

Social media such as Facebook and Twitter are increasingly the go-to places to keep on top of real-time business news from major outlets. Here's the quick-and-dirty of what you need to get set up: Download Twitter from your device's app store. The app, which is available for computer and mobile devices, allows you to search for news outlets, bloggers, and other sources of market news and then follow them. After you follow these outlets, Twitter will present you with all the news being tweeted so you won't miss a thing. The app is free; you just need to sign up for Twitter. For more details on how to turn Facebook and Twitter into a treasure trove of investing information, see Chapter 7.

Keeping Tabs on the Regulators

Professional traders' computers also keep close tabs on regulatory filings from companies. Regulatory filings are often the best, if not the only, data that investors get directly from a company. If companies make any significant announcements, they're required to notify the appropriate government watchdogs, which in most cases is the Securities and Exchange Commission.

I cover these important documents and what they contain in more detail in Chapter 12, but for now, it's important for you to know how to monitor these documents and quickly find them online. You can get regulatory filings online through

>> **The company's website:** Most provide a section with their complete reports.

>> **Financial sites and portals:** Most of the sites I list previously in the chapter provide links to the documents.

>> **Aggregation sites:** These sites parse the filings from companies and make them easy to find and download for free. SEC Info (www.secinfo.com) sorts all the regulatory filings into easy-to-understand categories. Last10K.com (www.last10k.com) allows you to find quickly companies' financial reports.

>> **The Securities and Exchange Commission** (www.sec.gov)**:** For most investors, the free SEC site has as much info as any sane person would ever want, and it isn't too difficult to navigate to boot.

In fact, the Securities and Exchange Commission site is so easy to navigate that I'm going to show you how to do it right now. To find company regulatory filings, follow these steps:

1. **Point your web browser to** www.sec.gov**.**

    The SEC site makes an appearance.

2. **Click the Company Filings link in the upper-right corner.**

    The Search the EDGAR Company Filings page appears.

3. **Enter the company's name or ticker symbol in the appropriate box, and then click the Search button.**

    You see a giant list of company filings in the order in which they were filed, as shown in Figure 2-5.

The list is not entirely user-friendly because the filings are distinguished only by their *form*, which is regulatory code for the types of information the documents contain. Table 2-2 gives you the skinny on the most common form codes.

FIGURE 2-5:
The SEC website provides regulatory filings to investors at no cost.

TABLE 2-2   SEC Forms You Can Use

Form Code	What It Contains
8-K	A news flash from the company. 8-Ks can contain just about anything that's considered "material" or important to investors, ranging from the resignation of a top official to news of the win of a new customer.
10-Q	The company's quarterly report. This form displays all the information a company is required to provide to investors each quarter. Here you can find the key financial statements, such as the income statement and balance sheet, which are covered in more detail in Chapter 12.
10-K	The company's year-end report. This is one of the most important documents that a company creates. It provides a summary of everything that happened during the year, including comments from management and financial statements that have been checked, or *audited,* by the company's accounting firm.
DEF 14 and DEF 14A	The company's *proxy statement* — a document that describes company matters to be discussed and voted on by shareholders at the annual meeting. Contains all the important company information that's subject to shareholder approval and scrutiny. Most proxies contain everything that's up for a vote at the shareholder meeting, ranging from board members up for election, pay packages and other perks, and pending lawsuits. If you're going to read any document, make it this one.

REMEMBER

Companies don't make their regulatory filings easy to read. You have to be part lawyer, part investor, and part investment banker to read between the lines in these often-cryptic statements. *Investment Banking For Dummies* (Wiley), which I co-authored, goes into the nitty-gritty. I cover the basics in Chapter 12 of that book, where I teach you how to pick apart 10-Ks, 10-Qs, and DEF 14s.

Executing Trades

With all this talk about researching and analyzing, don't forget job number 1: buying or selling investments. You need to either log on to the website of your broker or download a smartphone app or special software from your broker that can handle the trades. I go over the dizzying number of choices you have for online brokers in Chapter 4.

Searching the Internet High and Low

At the risk of sounding obvious, search engines hold some gems of information for investors. Some of the most popular search engines include the following:

>> **Google** (www.google.com): Definitely the biggest and most popular web search engine, so much so that investors often say they'll *google* a stock. Because the site is so clean and Zen-like, it has the benefit of being easy to use. Type **stock:** and a ticker symbol, and you'll get basic price information. Click the Financial News, Comparisons and More link for more details.

>> **Bing** (www.bing.com): Microsoft's attempt to come up with a Google killer, Bing.com has a few handy features for online investors, including the capability to quickly pull up stock quotes and charts by entering **stock** and the company's name or ticker symbol. For example, to get a quick datasheet on General Electric, type **stock GE**. Clicking the information box takes you to MSN Money for more analysis.

>> **Wolfram Alpha** (www.wolframalpha.com): This lesser-known search engine has some valuable features. If you enter the ticker symbol of a stock, Wolfram Alpha generates an impressive page filled with all sorts of company information. Wolfram Alpha will calculate some advanced statistical information, for instance, that shows you how well the stock has done over different time periods.

>> **Yahoo!** (www.yahoo.com)**:** Yahoo! remains the go-to search place for many consumers. Yahoo! Finance has excellent resources for investors, as described previously in this chapter, so it's logical to try the site for searching, too.

Keeping the Bad Guys Out: Securing Your PC

If you're going to use your computer to process your investing and banking tasks, you'd better lock it down. Cyber-criminals are sophisticated and have targeted online investors in hopes of gaining control of a person's account and stealing money.

Please, don't let such concerns scare you off from investing online. After all, cars get broken into but you still drive. Just take the following precautions to make it harder for the bad guys to get into your PC:

>> **Turn on antivirus software.** A *virus*, which is sinister code designed to wreak havoc on your computer, can corrupt system files and make your computer unreliable or unusable. Antivirus software is the easy solution. It runs in the background, looks at any program that tries to run on your computer, and stops the program if it tries to do something improper.

TIP

You can go to great lengths to lock down your aging computer, but the best defense is upgraded equipment running a modern operating system. Windows Security, which is built into Windows 10, runs efficiently and is pretty much all you need. To make sure that it's turned on, choose Start ⇨ Settings ⇨ Update & Security ⇨ Windows Security. From here, make sure that Virus and Threat Protection is turned on. Also, check the Virus & Threat Protection Updates section for updates to install.

Many third-party antivirus software programs are available for purchase, but ignore all emails and ads pitching software to clean your computer or phone. You don't need them, and many will actually harm your device.

>> **Install antispyware software.** *Spyware* is software that attaches itself to your computer without your permission and runs behind the scenes. It's especially sinister because it might forward personal information to a third party, usually for marketing. Windows Security automatically scans your computer and makes sure that no spyware has hitched a ride. You can also find dedicated software programs designed to sniff out spyware. Malwarebytes (www.malwarebytes.org) works well (and has the greatest name).

>> **Use a firewall.** A *firewall* is an electronic barrier that (selectively) separates you from the Internet at large. A proper firewall is like a moat around a castle — only traffic that you lower the drawbridge for can get in. You can use the following types of firewalls:

- *Built-in:* If you have Microsoft's Windows 10, a firewall is turned on by default.

- *Router:* A *router* is a small box that sits between your computer and the wall jack that connects you to the Internet. Many routers work like a software firewall and can even make your computer invisible to other computers. Depending on your router, you might need to enable the firewall. Check the router's instructions to find out how.

>> **Protect your passwords.** Mobile devices are often locked down with fingerprint scans. But typed-in passwords are still surprisingly important online. Most online brokers require complex passwords, which include letters, numbers, and special characters. That requirement makes life harder for hackers but annoying for you because complex passwords are hard to remember.

TIP

You can keep track of all your passwords by using a digital vault such as LastPass (www.lastpass.com) or Dashlane (www.dashlane.com). These services encrypt all your passwords in one place, and allow you to access them by entering one master password.

>> **Be cautious when using Wi-Fi.** Jumping on a free Wi-Fi network to look up your investment portfolio might be tempting but dangerous. Hackers can take control of free Wi-Fi networks and commandeer your log-in credentials. It's always safer to skip the free Wi-Fi and use your smartphone's cellular connection instead. If you must use public Wi-Fi, make sure you also use a *virtual private network,* or *VPN.* The VPN puts your Internet traffic in a digital private lane that others can't look into. If your employer doesn't offer a VPN for you to use on your personal computer or device, subscribe to a VPN service. Search the Windows app store for VPNs. They aren't free — and it's best to stick with cellular anyway.

Mastering the Basics with Online Tutorials and Simulations

Online investing is like Vegas in that you get no do-overs. If you invest all your money in a speculative company that goes belly up, you lose your money. Period. Don't expect the government to bail you out, and don't think that you can sue the company to get your money back because it's most likely gone. If you're new to investing, you might want to try the tutorials and simulations I discuss in the following sections before using real money.

Online tutorials

Before you jump into any activity with risk, it's worthwhile to take a deep breath, relax, and make absolutely sure that you understand how the process works. Several excellent online tutorials can step you through the process to make sure that you know what to expect. If you're just starting out, run through one of the following:

» **Investing 101 at Investopedia (**www.investopedia.com/university/beginner**)** is a great primer. The site is shown in Figure 2-6.

» **The Investor's Clearinghouse (**www.investoreducation.org**)** has links to online resources on all sorts of investing topics, from ways to research investments to finding investing help. An affiliated site, Help For Investors.org (www.helpforinvestors.org), provides even more tips.

» **American Association of Individual Investors (**www.aaii.com**)** provides free resources to investors, including a virtual Investor Classroom that teaches the basics (www.aaii.com/classroom).

FIGURE 2-6:
Investopedia's
Investing 101
steps investors
through most of
the things they
need to know.

WARNING

Be careful about which online tutorials you read and pay attention to. Many so-called tutorials are thinly guised pitches for investment professionals trying to get you to hire them. Some also promote specialized trading techniques with the purpose of getting you to buy books and other materials.

Simulations

Online games, or *simulations*, let you buy and sell real stocks using funny money. Online simulations are a good idea for investors because they let you get a taste for investing before you commit to a strategy.

Following is a list of a few simulators you can try:

>> **How the Market Works** (www.howthemarketworks.com) sets you up with $100,000 in virtual cash so you can try your hand at investing. There are games and lessons for those who want to learn more about investing online.

>> **Wall Street Survivor** (www.wallstreetsurvivor.com), shown in Figure 2-7, enables you to buy and sell fake shares in real companies. You compete with others in the game, because it's more fun to be rich with fake money if you can brag about it. If you don't do well, watch the educational videos to improve your skill.

>> **MarketWatch Virtual Stock Exchange** (www.marketwatch.com/game) lets you try your hand at investing in a simulated environment. You can compete in existing games or recruit your own opponents.

>> **SmartStocks** (www.smartstocks.com) gets you started with a pretty generous portfolio stuffed with $1 million in virtual cash. You can use this cash to build a portfolio of investments to see how you perform, and compete against your friends.

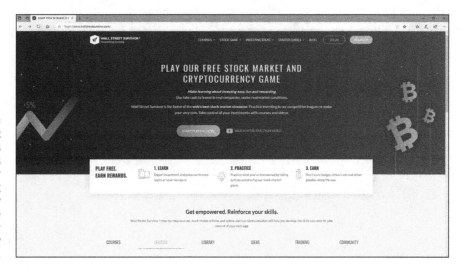

FIGURE 2-7:
Wall Street
Survivor's
simulator lets
you try your
hand at investing
online with play
money before
putting your
own money
on the line.

>> **Icarra** (www.icarra.com) is a powerful portfolio-tracking software program
that's so addictive, you might keep playing even after you set up an online
trading account and invest for real. After downloading the software, you enter
buys and sells. Icarra tracks the performance of your stocks and enables you
to view the portfolios of other members and share your own.

IN THIS CHAPTER

» Understanding how different brokerage accounts are taxed

» Distinguishing between taxable accounts and tax-deferred accounts

» Knowing the different ways brokers can assign ownership to accounts

» Seeing the advantages and disadvantages of 401(k)s and IRAs

» Finding out about ways to cut the tax bite when saving for college

Chapter **3**

Choosing the Best Account Type for You

Online investors tend to be do-it-yourself types, so it's unlikely that they'll have tax consultants on retainer just waiting to handle any tax issues they might have. No, many online investors are big on going it alone, which can be rewarding as long as such investors become tax savvy, especially when it comes to how taxes on the different accounts vary.

In this chapter, I explain how investments are taxed and discuss ways that picking the right kind of account can cut your tax bill. You'll want to understand the differences between the three main types of accounts — taxable, retirement, and education savings — before you sign up with an online broker. I also show how online tools can help you track and reduce your taxes. Finally, I step you through the different types of tax-advantaged accounts that can help you reach long-term goals, such as saving for your child's college education or for your retirement.

Knowing How Different Accounts Are Taxed

Brokerage accounts might all seem the same; after all, they're just holding tanks for investments. However, different types of brokerage accounts look different to Uncle Sam. Thanks to the unbelievable complexity of the tax code, you can use three main types of accounts to hold your investments: taxable, retirement, and education savings accounts.

Taxable accounts

Taxable accounts are the standard accounts that come to mind when you think about investing online. Taxable accounts are very accessible, meaning that you can easily take out the money without paying special penalties. But that flexibility comes at a cost: taxes. When stocks you own in taxable accounts go up, or *appreciate*, and you sell them, you owe capital gains taxes on your profit for that tax year. (*Capital gains* are gains you've made on the capital — cash — you've invested. Pretty simple, huh?) And if the stocks issue you cash payments, or *dividends*, you owe tax on those in the year they were paid, too. I discuss how capital gains and dividends are taxed in the section "Plain Vanilla: The Taxable Brokerage Account," later in this chapter.

Retirement accounts

Retirement is one of the largest and most intimidating things you must save for.

The bright side is that special *retirement accounts* make saving easier. Company pensions are vanishing, leaving retirement planning up to you. I explain the different types of retirement plans available to most people — and which ones could make the most sense for you — later in this chapter. The key retirement accounts to be aware of follow:

» **401(k)s** are typically retirement plans sponsored by a company. Oftentimes, the company matches the employee's contributions. 401(k) plans allow you to delay when you must pay taxes on your contributions and investment gains.

» **Traditional individual retirement accounts or arrangements (IRAs)** are available to people under the age of 70½ who have *earned income* and want to delay when taxes are due on retirement savings. Earned income is money you're paid from the fruits of your labor in the form of wages, salaries, tips or in many cases, earnings from self-employment. Your contributions might also be tax deductible if you're not covered by a company retirement plan or don't exceed income limits. You can look up the current limits on the Internal Revenue Service's website at www.irs.gov/publications/ p590a#idm140115509233456.

>> **Roth IRAs** are retirement savings accounts that let you put in money that's already been taxed so that it can grow and never be taxed again.

>> **Other popular retirement plans** include simplified employee pension (SEP) accounts, 403(b) plans for employees of tax-exempt entities, and Keogh plans, and each have different advantages and disadvantages. I cover IRA-like SEPs in more detail later in this chapter.

Check out the section "Retirement Accounts: Knowing Your 401(k)s from Your IRAs," later in this chapter, for more on your retirement plan options.

Education savings accounts

The cost of a college education keeps soaring. For the 2015 school year, the latest data available at press time, the tuition and fees for a four-year public college degree cost $39,400, on average, and private college costs were $134,600, according to Savingforcollege.com (www.savingforcollege.com/tutorial101/the_ real_cost_of_higher_education.php), citing data from The College Board. And it gets worse: Tuition prices go up faster each year, 5 percent on average, than prices on almost anything else you'd buy, including stamps, eggs, and milk. If you factor in the 5 percent annual rate at which tuition fees are increasing, in 18 years the tab will hit $94,800 for a public college and $323,900 for a private one. Online investors can get help from two types of *education savings accounts:*

>> **529 plans** are financially attractive state-sponsored education savings accounts. They can be used to shield money earmarked for college or, in some states, to prepay college tuition fees to lock in today's price. Tax reform in 2018 made 529 accounts even more useful. You can now use them to pay for primary and secondary education up to $10,000 a year.

>> **Coverdell education savings accounts** are more restrictive than some education savings accounts. How? The amount you can put into them annually is much lower than with a 529. Their primary draw was that you could use them to pay for primary and secondary education. But now that 529s can do this, following tax reforms in 2018, Coverdell accounts are less compelling.

I explain the different types of education savings accounts and discuss how you can use online resources to maximize your tax savings in the section "Going Back to School with Education Savings Accounts," later in this chapter.

Plain Vanilla: The Taxable Brokerage Account

If you want to talk intelligently about tax-advantaged accounts — accounts that are sheltered in some way for some period or other from the Internal Revenue Service — you would be well-served if you boned up on how regular taxable accounts are handled. It's hard to see why retirement accounts are such a boon for investors if you have no idea to what extent investments are usually taxed by Uncle Sam.

I give you online tools to help you crunch the numbers, but first, it's important to understand the basics of how the taxes work. Commit these basics to memory so that you can think about any tax consequences before you place a trade in a taxable account. Keep in mind that these are just the basics, and the rules can change slightly for people in different situations. If taxes are your primary concern with investing, consult with books on the topic or with a tax professional.

REMEMBER

You have a taxable event in a taxable brokerage account when one of two things occurs:

>> **Capital appreciation:** Imagine that you hit a veritable investing home run by buying a share of stock for $10 that soars to $100. When you sell the stock, that $90 per share gain is called *capital appreciation* or a *realized capital gain*. If you hold onto the stock and don't sell it, it's considered an *unrealized capital gain*. And with an unrealized capital gain, because you haven't cashed in the stock, you haven't profited in the eyes of the government and don't owe taxes. But the second you sell, everything changes. Your gain turns into a taxable one subject to rules I discuss shortly.

>> **Dividends:** You probably remember dividends from the Chance card in the *Monopoly* board game. *Dividends* are cash payments made by companies when they're making so much money they don't know what to do with it. The only thing they can think of is returning it to the shareholders. That way, shareholders can reinvest the cash rather than letting it pile up in the company's bank account.

I show you how to find out how much cash a company has on hand in Chapter 12, and in Chapter 13, I show you how to find stocks that pay fat dividends.

Capital appreciation is a fine thing to write about, and I do get to it eventually — right after the next section, to be precise — but dividends have that Somebody-Is-Sending-Me-Money-without-My-Really-Understanding-Why appeal, so I'm going to dive right in and talk about them first.

The importance of dividends

Dividends usually won't make you rich overnight, but don't think they're just for widows and orphans. Dividends accounted for more than a third of the Standard & Poor's 500 index's roughly 10 percent *total return* in its more than 50 years of existence. Total return measures your percentage gain on a stock resulting from both stock-price gains and dividends.

If you're not getting dividends, you could be missing out. Table 3-1 shows what stocks in the S&P 500 have returned each year since 2000 and the percentage that came from dividends. Note that dividends helped make up for losses in years when stocks declined in value. For instance, during the market bloodbath in 2008 when stocks lost 38.5 percent of their value, dividends were your only bright spot, albeit a small one. Dividends can play an even larger role in softening market declines. In 2018, for instance, the stock market declined by 6.2 percent. But investors' total loss was trimmed to 4.4 percent total return that year, thanks to the 1.9% dividend.

TABLE 3-1   ## The Importance of Dividends

Year	Price Change, %	Dividend, %	Total Return, %	% of Return from Dividends
2018	-6.2	1.9	-4.4	N/A
2017	19.4	2.4	21.8	11
2016	9.5	2.4	12.0	20
2015	-0.7	2.1	1.4	150
2014	11.4	2.3	13.7	16.8
2013	29.6	2.8	32.4	8.6
2012	13.4	2.6	16	16.2
2011	0.0	2.1	2.1	100
2010	12.8	2.3	15.1	15.1
2009	23.5	3.0	26.5	11.4
2008	–38.5	1.5	–37.0	N/A
2007	3.5	2.0	5.5	35.8
2006	13.6	2.2	15.8	13.8
2005	3.0	1.9	4.9	38.9

(continued)

TABLE 3-1 *(continued)*

Year	Price Change, %	Dividend, %	Total Return, %	% of Return from Dividends
2004	9.0	1.9	10.9	17.3
2003	26.4	2.3	28.7	8.0
2002	–23.4	1.3	–22.1	N/A
2001	–13.0	1.2	–11.9	N/A
2000	–10.1	1.0	–9.1	N/A

Source: S&P Dow Jones Indices

REMEMBER

Dividends are paid based on how many shares you own. If a company declares a $1 per share dividend and you own 100 shares, you will receive $100. To help compare the sizes of dividends, investors generally talk about the dividend yield. A *dividend yield* tells you how much return you're getting in the form of a dividend — in other words, how big the dividend is relative to what you've invested.

You can calculate a stock's dividend yield by dividing the annual dividend by the stock's price. But you can also get it from almost every financial website described in Chapter 2. Reuters, for example, has an extensive database of dividend information. To get a company's dividend yield using the Reuters website, follow these steps:

1. **Go to the Reuters stocks main page at** www.reuters.com/finance/markets.

2. **Click the Search icon (magnifying glass), in the upper right, and enter a ticker symbol or company name in the field. Click the name of the company when it appears**

3. **Select the Financials tab at the top of the screen.**

    In the new page that appears, scroll down to the Dividends section, shown in Figure 3-1 for General Electric. You can see what a company's dividend yield is now and what it was on average over the past five years. You can also see what kind of dividend yields other companies in the industry pay.

    Keep in mind that dividends vary greatly by industry. Companies in fast-growing industries such as biotechology tend to pay a small or no dividend so that they can reinvest profits to develop new products. Companies in more mature industries, such as industrial conglomerates, tend to pay out larger dividends to keep investors interested.

FIGURE 3-1: Reuters lets you find out how much of a dividend a stock pays and how it compares to its industry.

Table 3-2 shows what kinds of dividends are typical in various industries.

TABLE 3-2

Dividends That Industries Pay as of March 2019

Industry	Five-Year Average Dividend Yield, %
Pharmaceuticals	1.5
Conglomerates	2.2
Software	1.7
Real estate investment trusts	3.1
Multiline utilities (electric power and natural gas)	2.7

Source: www.reuters.com

TIP

Some online brokers and companies that sell their shares to investors directly allow you to use dividends paid by a stock to buy more shares of the stock. These programs are called *dividend reinvestment plans (DRIPs)*. If you're interested in these plans, keep them in mind when evaluating brokers, as I describe in Chapter 4.

How capital gains are taxed

When you sell a stock held in a taxable account that has appreciated in value, you usually owe taxes. Generally, such *capital gains taxes*, as they are referred to, are calculated based on how long you owned the stock — a period of time known as the *holding period.* There are two holding periods:

>> **Short-term:** The type of capital gain you have if you sell a stock after owning it for one year or less. You want to avoid these gains if you can because you're taxed at the ordinary income tax rate, which can be one of the highest tax percentages, as I explain shortly.

>> **Long-term:** The type of capital gain result you get if you sell a stock after holding it for more than one year. These gains qualify for a special discount on taxes, as I describe a little later.

WARNING

You must own a stock for *more than* one year for it to be considered a long-term capital gain. The holding period clock starts the day after you buy the stock and stops the day you sell it. Selling even one day too soon can be a costly mistake. If you buy a stock on March 5, 2019 and sell it on March 5, 2020 for a profit, that is considered a short-term capital gain.

The high tax price of being short-term

If you're interested in cutting your tax bill in a taxable account, you want to reduce, as much as possible, the number of stocks you sell for a profit that you've owned for only a year or less because the resulting gains will be taxed at your ordinary income tax levels. You can look up your ordinary income tax bracket at this Internal Revenue Service website: `www.irs.gov/pub/irs-pdf/i1040tt.pdf?portlet=3`. At press time, the IRS provided 2011 tax brackets. But just to give you an idea, Bankrate provides the tax brackets for 2019, as shown in Table 3-3.

TABLE 3-3   **Federal Tax Rates for 2019**

If You're Single and Earn between	If You're Married and File a Joint Return with Income between	Your Short-Term Capital Gains Are Taxed at
$0 and $9,700	$0 and $19,400	10%
$9,701 and $39,475	$19,401 and $78,950	12%
$39,476 and $84,200	$78,951 and $168,400	22%
$84,201 and $160,725	$168,401 and $321,450	24%
$160,725 and $204,100	$321,451 and $408,200	32%
$204,101 and $510,300	$408,201 and $612,350	35%
$510,301 or more	$612,351	37%

Source: Bankrate (`www.bankrate.com/finance/taxes/tax-brackets.aspx`)

Need an example? Remember the stock I mentioned previously that went from $10 to $100 a share (for a $90 per share gain)? Say that a single investor had $50,000 in taxable income that year and sold the stock after owning it for just three months. The investor's gain would fall from $90 to $70.20 after paying $19.80 in taxes.

How long-term capital gains are taxed

If you own stocks for more than a year, gains are taxed at what's known as the *maximum capital gain rate*. The rate you pay on long-term capital gains varies based on your normal tax bracket, but such rates are almost always much lower than your ordinary income tax rate, if not zero. Yes, that's right, between the 2009 and 2015 tax years at least, some investors' long-term capital gains were tax-free. Long-term capital gains rates, though, can change dramatically due to political pressure. Table 3-4 shows the maximum capital gain rates for 2019 for typical investments such as stocks and bonds.

TABLE 3-4

Maximum Capital Gain Rate for 2019

If Your Regular Tax Rate Is	Your Maximum Capital Gain Rate Is
37% or greater	20%
Between 12% and 37%	15%
12% or lower	0%

Source: Internal Revenue Service (www.irs.gov/publications/p17)

I'm trying to save you time (and money!) by providing you with all IRS tax brackets. But you can look them up yourself online at www.irs.gov/Forms-&-Pubs. And no, that 0 percent tax rate is not a typo. Keep reading and you'll find out more about how some capital gains, for now, are escaping taxation.

When you can win from your losses

If you're like most investors, you beat yourself up anytime you sell a stock for a loss. Nobody likes to lose money when the point of investing is to make it. But if there's a plus to suffering a loss, it comes at tax time. The IRS allows you to use capital losses to offset your capital gains and possibly your regular income. If your losses exceed your gains, you have a net capital loss to report on Schedule D, which can even cut your taxable income each year. This IRS rule presents several tax strategies that can cut your tax bill. The guidelines, when it comes to using losses to cut your capital gains taxes, include the following:

>> **Use losses to avoid short-term gains.** Make it your goal to never have a short-term capital gain. If you sell a winning stock you've owned for a year or less, go through your portfolio, find a loser, and sell it. (You can even use losses from stocks you've owned for more than a year to offset short-term capital gains.) If your long-term loss is greater than your short-term gain, the gain vanishes, and you have a *net long-term loss* instead. You can deduct up to $3,000 ($1,500 if you're married and file separately) from your regular taxable income. Not a bad deal.

For example, imagine that you scored a $1,000 profit from a high-flying stock you owned for a month. Normally, if you're in the 24 percent tax bracket, you'd have to pay $240 in taxes because it's a short-term gain. But you can pay no tax if you sell a stock at a loss of $1,000 by the end of the tax year. You get the entire $1,000 proceeds from the first sale free of tax, and you offload a bummer of a stock at the same time. Win-win!

>> **Dump your losers.** If you have losing stocks in your portfolio that you've lost hope in, sell them so that you at least get a tax break. Tax rules allow you to deduct up to $3,000 a year in capital losses from your regular income. It's a decent way to get out of stocks you're tired of and cut your tax bill.

>> **Don't forget tax-loss carryovers.** What if your net loss is greater than the annual limit of $3,000? Do you lose the deduction? Not at all; you just have to spread it out. You can carry over capital losses to your future tax returns until you use up the losses. The IRS (www.irs.gov/taxtopics/tc409.html) provides more information about how to carry over capital losses.

WARNING

Don't think you can sell a stock you're losing money on, take the loss for tax purposes, and just buy it back. The IRS's "wash sale" rule prohibits this. If you sell a stock or mutual fund for a loss, you're not allowed to deduct the loss if you bought back that investment or one that's "substantially identical" within 30 days before or 30 days after the sale. To avoid triggering the wash sale rule, you must wait 31 days after the sale to buy the investment back. Here are two sites that can help you understand the complexities of the wash sale rules:

>> **Fairmark** (www.fairmark.com/capgain/wash) provides a detailed description of wash sale rules and describes ways to avoid getting tripped up by this tax trap. (See Figure 3-2.)

>> **The Securities and Exchange Commission** (www.sec.gov/answers/wash.htm) also provides guidance on wash sales.

What to do with your worthless stock

Selling your losers is usually pretty straightforward: You swallow your pride, sell the stock, and take your tax loss. But sometimes the process is not that easy. Periodically, companies crash so badly that their stocks are *delisted* from the exchange, such as the New York Stock Exchange or NASDAQ, where they traded when you bought them. This happened to General Motors, before it sold stock to the public again as an initial public offering in 2010, fallen electronics seller Radio Shack in 2015, and Sears in 2018. They become what's called a *worthless security*.

You can still deduct the loss on a stock even if the shares aren't available for trading anymore. But the IRS is pretty clear about what you need to do. In most cases, even when a stock is delisted, it still trades on informal markets such as OTC Markets or Pink Sheets. It's best to sell the stock there so that you can recognize the loss and have a paper trail. It's often best to sell this way, even though some online brokers charge slightly higher commissions because proving something is worthless without being able to sell it can be difficult. If you can't sell the stock, you must prove it's worth less than a penny per share. Additional rules say that you can deduct your loss from a worthless stock only in the year it became worthless. If you didn't realize a stock wasn't worth anything until the year after it lost its value, you have to file an amended tax return for the year the stock became worthless.

PAY NO CAPITAL GAINS TAXES?

It almost seems too good to be true. Could it be the government cut the capital gains tax to 0 percent? The answer is yes and no. Congress in early 2008 approved a bill that cut long-term capital gains taxes for many taxpayers. The long-term capital gains rate for some investors fell to nothing from 5 percent. The lower rate affects only long-term capital gains because short-term gains are taxed at your ordinary income rate.

Before you start writing a thank-you letter to the IRS, though, you should know that there are some heavy restrictions. The 0 percent long-term tax rate applies only to people in the bottom two tax brackets, which means that in 2019 you'd have to have less than $39,475 in taxable income as a single person or less than $78,950 for a married couple filing jointly to qualify.

But for you taxpayers on the other end of the income spectrum, I have some bad news. Single taxpayers making more than $200,000 and couple filing jointly earning $250,000 or more are subject to an extra tax on investment gains and income. A net investment tax of 3.8% applies to investment income, including capital gains and dividends, for higher earners. This is just another reason to be aware of making moves that trigger tax events. Read more about this tax at www.irs.gov/newsroom/questions-and-answers-on-the-net-investment-income-tax.

Using technology to measure your capital gain

Taxes can have a dramatic effect on your online investing success, so you need to be aware of the rules. Most online brokerages won't stop you from placing a trade that could hurt you when tax time rolls around. It's up to you to manage your tax picture. And it's also up to you to track your capital gains.

You might think "Easier said than done," but keeping track of your capital gains isn't that complicated. Essentially, if you know the following about all your investment transactions, you have what you need to keep tabs on your capital gains:

>> **The date you bought the investment.**

>> **The amount you paid to buy it, which is known as your *cost basis*.** You can calculate the cost basis by multiplying the stock price you paid times the

number of shares you bought and then adding the commission you paid for the stock trade. All that added together is your cost basis.

For example, say you bought 100 shares of ABC Company for $50 and paid a $5 commission. Your basis is $5,005. You get that by multiplying the cost of the stock by the number of shares ($50 times 100 shares) and then adding the $5 commission.

>> **The date you sold the investment.**

>> **The amount you received for selling it, or your *proceeds*.** You can calculate the proceeds by multiplying the stock price you sold at by the number of shares you sold, minus the commission you had to pay.

Imagine now that you sold your 100 shares of ABC Company for $100 apiece and paid a $5 commission. The amount of your proceeds is $9,995. You get that by multiplying the price of the stock by the number of shares ($100 times 100 shares) and then subtracting the $5 commission.

At tax time, you must then report all your capital gains on Schedule D. For more help on this, check out what the IRS says about sales and trades of investments at www.irs.gov/publications/p550/ch04.html – d0e9488.

Because you're an online investor, you're probably loath to use a pencil and paper to keep track of all this information. Luckily, you have several alternatives:

>> **Online brokers' websites:** Most investors will get tax information from their broker's sites. Such sites often track when you bought investments, how much you paid, and when you sold them. Nearly all online brokerages have a place on their websites where you can see your realized and unrealized gains. And at the end of the year, online brokerages provide a document that shows all your trades and your bases in many cases. Here's why I say "in many cases": If you bought a stock in 2011 or later, it's your brokerage's responsibility to track your cost-basis information and report it to you at tax time. This is a big change for investors and eliminates the hassle of tracking the cost basis for any recently purchased stock. I offer more details on tracking sales later in the chapter. For now, know the change also means that your relationship with your brokerage is even more important, so you'll want to make sure you read Chapter 4, which helps you choose the best brokerage for you.

>> **Personal finance software:** Quicken (discussed at more length in Chapter 1) keeps track of everything you need to file Schedule D. It can also transfer all the data the government requires directly into tax-preparation software, such

as H&R Block's TaxCut or Intuit's TurboTax. Quicken can also print out a capital gains worksheet that you can give to your tax preparer.

>> **Portfolio-tracking sites:** Several of the web-based portfolio-monitoring sites discussed in Chapter 8 can help you track everything you need to calculate your taxes.

>> **Online capital gains calculators and sites:** These sits enable you to enter your stock buys and sells and help calculate your net capital gains or losses and carryovers. One example of an online capital gains calculator is the one at MoneyChimp at `www.moneychimp.com/features/capgain.htm`.

>> **Specialized online sites dedicated to optimizing your tax strategy:** This type of site might make sense if you have a particularly complicated situation. For instance, GainsKeeper (`www.gainskeeper.com/`) is a professional-level online service that helps you track your trades, tally your cost basis in stocks, and find ways to reduce your taxes. (Figure 3-3 shows the GainsKeeper site.) If you're an extremely active trader, the tax rules and keeping track of everything can get complicated, so software like this can be helpful. The system costs at least $70 a year. Before signing up, check with your broker — some offer discounted subscriptions. Or some brokers, including TD Ameritrade, offer free access to GainsKeeper.

FIGURE 3-3: GainsKeeper is a dedicated website that helps you find ways to optimize your tax strategy when it comes to investing.

Measuring your capital gains if you've lost your records

I know you meticulously track all your investments and trading records. But in the off case that you just can't find how much you paid for a stock bought before 2011, you can still figure out your basis by using the Internet, as long as you know when you bought it and it's still actively trading. 2011 is the key year — it is your responsibility to track your basis for stocks you bought before that year. You can use the historical charting, as I describe in Chapter 2, to look back in time and see where the stock was trading the day you bought it.

Here's how:

1. **Log on to Yahoo! Finance** (https://finance.yahoo.com).

2. **Enter the ticker symbol of the stock you're interested in and click the name of the company when it appears.**

   The page devoted to the stock you've chosen appears on-screen.

3. **Click the Historical Data option at the top of the page.**

4. **In the Time Period field, select the date you bought the stock, and then click Apply.**

5. **Calculate your cost basis:**

   a. *Under the Adj Close heading, find the price at which the stock traded on the day you bought it.*

   b. *Multiply that price by the number of shares you bought and add the commission you paid.*

6. **Calculate your proceeds:**

   a. *Find the price of the stock for the day you sold it (as shown in Figure 3-4).*

   b. *Multiply that price by the number of shares you sold and subtract the commission you paid.*

7. **Use the information and follow the previous instructions in the "Using technology to measure capital gains" section on how to calculate your capital gain or loss.**

TIP

If the company you invested in underwent some major changes before you sold the stock, the preceding method of calculating the cost basis does not work. For instance, the stock may no longer be trading, so no trading history will be available. You might also have obtained the stock indirectly and not bought it if the shares were distributed by a larger company as part of a restructuring.

FIGURE 3-4:
Yahoo! Finance allows you to look at what a stock's price was in the past to help you figure out your tax bill.

In these cases, you'll need a more heavy-duty technique. You could try to figure out the cost basis by digging through financial records most likely available at your library. If that sounds like too much work, an easier option is to use Intuit's TurboTax Premier software. Using technology from GainsKeeper, TurboTax Premier can do some major historical research online, even if the stock no longer trades or if the company underwent some major restructuring. The software isn't cheap — it'll set you back about $80 if you download the software to your computer — but it can also prepare all your tax forms for you.

TIP

For decades, it's been up to you, the investor, to keep track of your capital gains and losses. As a courtesy, some online brokers would keep track of your cost basis on any mutual funds or stocks you bought while you were their client. You couldn't always count on this service, though, because if you switched your account to another broker, poof, all your cost basis information was gone. This situation changed, though, starting in 2011. From 2011 on, brokers are required to keep track of the cost basis of any stocks you buy and provide necessary documentation to you at tax time. Brokers are also required to forward your cost basis information to your new broker if you move your account. The rules were put in place to help the government crack down on investors who didn't report all their gains, and no, we're not pointing any fingers here. But if there's a benefit, it's that the headache of cost basis is now your broker's headache. Even so, it's not a bad idea to know how to track your cost basis for tax planning during the year and also to make sure that your broker doesn't make a mistake.

How dividends are taxed

Thanks to the Jobs and Growth Tax Relief Reconciliation Act of 2003, dividends caught a big-time tax break that was later extended by the American Taxpayers Relief Act of 2012 and maintained after tax reform in 2018. Dividends that meet certain criteria are considered *qualified* and are taxed at the same favorable rate as long-term capital gains, as discussed in the preceding section. That was a huge break, because before that, dividends were taxed at the typically much higher short-term capital gains rate. But, to get the lower tax treatment, dividends must be

>> **Qualified:** Dividends from most companies that trade on U.S. exchanges are qualified. Important exceptions exist, though, including some dividends paid by *real-estate investment trusts,* or REITs, which typically own commercial real estate such as apartment buildings and strip malls. Also keep in mind that dividends paid by money market accounts and many bond funds don't qualify either because they're considered interest.

>> **Paid to a shareholder who holds the stock for the right amount of time:** To qualify for the lower rates, you must own the stock for a long enough time. The IRS says you must own the stock for more than 60 days during the 121-day period starting 60 days before the stock's ex-dividend date. The *ex-dividend date* is the day a new investor who bought the stock is no longer entitled to dividends declared by the company. For more information on this, Fidelity.com (`https://personal.fidelity.com/planning/tax/distributions/qdi.shtml.cvsr`) has a section that explains qualified dividends. The Securities and Exchange Commission (`https://www.sec.gov/answers/dividen.htm`) explains the ex-dividend date.

The big tax break that dividends have enjoyed since 2003 may not last forever. Some high earners have already lost it. A new 20 percent dividend tax rate was created for those of you lucky enough to be in the top tax bracket of 39.6 percent. The Patient Protection and Affordable Care Act also ushered in a new 3.8 percent net investment income tax that applies to dividends and capital gains for married taxpayers earning more than $250,000 and single taxpayers hauling more than $200,000. It's just a reminder that taxes aren't always low forever.

TIP

Investors who buy investments and hold them for a long time get a huge tax advantage over short-term traders. By holding stocks, you can put off the time when you have to pay tax on your gains. That allows your entire, untaxed ball of cash to snowball tax deferred. But even long-term investors have to pay taxes on dividends each year.

Retirement Accounts: Knowing Your 401(k)s from Your IRAs

If you made your way through the preceding section, you have a pretty good sense of just how complicated taxes can get when dealing with regular taxable brokerage accounts. The tax burden creates bookkeeping work for you when you buy or sell a stock (bad enough) and also eats into your profit (even worse). Being forced to pay taxes frequently means that the amount of capital you can invest gets whittled away, hurting your ultimate performance. With retirement accounts, you can delay the taxes you may have owed annually if the money was in a taxable account. That boosts the amount of money you can keep invested and allow to grow. Just remember that the downside to retirement accounts is that you might get socked with penalties if you take money out before you retire.

REMEMBER

In this section, I describe the main types of retirement accounts. The tax rules are complex and not as fascinating as the latest page-turner novel. If you just want the bottom line, many financial advisors recommend doing the following:

1. **Open a 401(k) account if your employer matches your contributions.**

   Put in at least enough money to get the match.

2. **If you have money left over and qualify, open a Roth IRA.**

   Most online brokers, as I discuss in Chapter 4, can open a Roth IRA for you.

If you'd rather use online tools to help you decide what to do, check out the following sites:

>> **Morningstar** (www.morningstar.com/invest-in-retirement.html) has a retirement calculator that helps you pick the right retirement accounts for you. This calculator is in addition to other resources dedicated to retirement issues. The site is free but requires you to register with a username and password first.

>> **Kiplinger.com** (www.kiplinger.com/retirement) has a retirement center where you can determine what accounts are best for you. If you're confused, some online brokers have financial advisors who can help you decide. For details, see Chapter 4.

>> **360 Degrees of Financial Literacy** (www.360financialliteracy.org/Topics/Retirement-Planning) is maintained by the American Institute of Certified Public Accountants. The site, shown in Figure 3-5, features advanced online tools that can help you make sure that you're saving enough for retirement and using the right types of accounts.

>> **Hugh's Mortgage and Financial Calculators** (www.hughcalc.org/retirement.php) provides a number of free online calculators that crunch complex financial problems. You'll find a complete section on retirement savings with several helpful tools.

>> **FIRECalc** (www.firecalc.com/) uses an advanced computerized model to help you determine how much you must save to retire. It bases its forecasts on historical data.

REMEMBER

The biggest downside to 401(k)s and most IRA accounts is that you get hit with a steep 10 percent penalty for taking money out before you turn 59½, unless you qualify for some exceptions. And you must start taking money out of a traditional IRA (not a Roth IRA) when you turn 70½ years old.

FIGURE 3-5:
360 Degrees of
Financial Literacy
is stuffed with
information to
make sure that
you plan your
retirement
correctly.

It's important that you understand all the catches, so I recommend doing a little 401(k)/IRA homework by checking out the following websites for complete descriptions of the different types of retirement plans:

>> **Vanguard** (https://investor.vanguard.com/ira/iras) contains an easy-to-follow chart that explains the advantages and disadvantages of traditional IRAs and Roth IRAs.

>> **Investopedia** (www.investopedia.com/terms/1/401kplan.asp) describes 401(k) plans in addition to a different type of 401(k) called the Roth 401(k).

REMEMBER

I want to be clear. Tax-deferred accounts such as 401(k)s aren't tax-free. Taxes are delayed, not avoided. When you use an account that lets you deduct contributions following the Pay Tax Later, Not Now principle — any 401(k) plan, for example — you'll still have to pay the ordinary income tax rate when you withdraw cash. Don't let this discourage you, though, because retirement accounts still provide tax savings to most investors.

401(k)s: A great place to get started

If your employer offers a 401(k) plan or the equivalent for public-service employees called the 403(b), don't pass it up. Thanks to the advantages that retirement accounts offer to employees and employers, 401(k)s have been extremely popular.

TIP

If your company offers a 401(k) and makes matching contributions, that's the first account you should open. Passing up on a company match is like turning away free money. Just be sure that you won't need this money until you retire.

Most 401(k) plans let you contribute up to $19,000 for 2019. If you're 50 years old or older, you can kick in an extra $6,000 as a catch-up contribution. The IRS (www. irs.gov/retirement-plans/plan-participant-employee/retirement-topics- 401k-and-profit-sharing-plan-contribution-limits) provides a table that shows the current 401(k) contribution limits and what they have been in the past.

Managing your 401(k) plan online

Just because your 401(k) is tucked away and invested for your retirement doesn't mean that you can't manage it online. You have several ways to tune and tweak your 401(k), including the following:

>> **The plan administrators' site:** Most 401(k) plans are easily accessible on a website. From there, you can set the variables that matter most. You can instruct the company that manages your employer's plan to withhold a set amount of money from your pay, decide which mutual funds you want to invest in, and shift money among mutual funds. You'll need to contact your company's human resources department to find out how to access the account.

>> **401(k) education sites:** Sites such as 5 Ways for a Secure Retirement (www.5waysin5days.com/) help you take a more active role in making sure that you'll have enough dough for your golden years. If you click the links to the five steps, you can see if you're on track.

>> **Regulators' sites:** These sites let you know your rights and the employer's obligations. Most retirement plans are overseen by the Department of Labor, which maintains extensive resources at www.dol.gov/dol/topic/retirement/ typesofplans.htm.

>> **BrightScope** (www.brightscope.com): Not all 401(k) plans are equal — and there's a way to see how yours compares. Your plan might be charging lofty fees or offering lousy investment choices. The BrightScope site helps you find out how your 401(k) plan stacks up against those at other companies. Choose the Research a 401(k) Plan option from the drop-down menu on the home page. Enter the name of the company offering the 401(k) plan and click it. The site shows you how your plan stacks up and how much longer you'll have to work to save as much as a worker at a company with a better 401(k) plan. If the plan is really bad, talk to your company's plan administrator and consider contributing only enough to get your company match.

TIP

Most employers require that you work for them for at least a year and that you be 21 or older before you can sign up for their 401(k) plans. But other than that, 401(k) plans vary among companies. Some 401(k) plans let you borrow money and pay interest to yourself. Some employers offer Roth 401(k) plans, which combine the benefits of 401(k)s with Roth IRAs, which you can read about in the next section.

Getting in tune with IRAs

Practically everyone can fund an IRA if he or she has the money. But IRAs are especially attractive if you don't have access to a 401(k) at work (perhaps because you're self-employed) or if the 401(k) at your company doesn't offer a match. IRAs, like 401(k)s, offer big benefits when you're saving for retirement.

Several types of IRA(s) exist, but you should really concern yourself with only the big three:

>> **Traditional IRAs** are available to anyone. They're a great place to save money for retirement because you can put away as much as $6,000 in 2019, and $1,000 more if you're over at least 50 years old.

Capital gains and dividends in a traditional IRA aren't taxed until you take out the money. And, you might be able to deduct your contributions if you're not covered by a company-sponsored retirement plan. If you or your spouse is covered by a company plan, the amount you can deduct is reduced based on how much you earn. The rules get complicated, but Fidelity has an excellent primer at www.fidelity.com/calculators-tools/all that explains how much you may contribute. Click the IRA Contribution Calculator link.

REMEMBER

Even if you can't deduct your contribution, a traditional IRA might still make sense for you. A nondeductible IRA can be a great place to stash investments that generate nonqualified dividends and interest, such as REITs and bonds.

>> **SEP IRAs** are designed for owners of small businesses, employees of small businesses, and people who work for themselves. They're easy to set up and allow employers — including self-employed people — to contribute up to 25 percent of compensation to a limit of $53,000 in 2015. Vanguard provides more information about these plans at https://personal.vanguard.com/us/whatweoffer/smallbusiness/sepira.

>> **Roth IRAs** can be one of the best things going. If you can open one, you should. With Roth IRAs, you pay now and play later. You can't deduct contributions when you make them, but you can take out the money in the future tax-free if you are at least 59½ years old and have owned the account for five years or longer. And unlike traditional IRAs, you're not required to take out the money at a certain age, allowing you to pass the giant, tax-free nest egg to your kids. Just imagine the power of compounding on an investment sitting untaxed for more than a lifetime. It doesn't get much better than that.

REMEMBER

Roth IRAs are generally best if you think your tax rate will be higher when you retire. It's impossible to know what Congress will do with tax rates in the future. That's why many financial advisors say it's better to go with a Roth, lock in the rates now, and protect yourself from the risk of higher tax rates later. But if you're certain you'll be in a lower tax bracket in the future, a Roth may not be for you.

SHOULD YOU TURN YOUR TRADITIONAL IRA INTO A ROTH?

Do you have a traditional IRA and wish you had a Roth? Taxpayers can choose to turn their traditional IRAs into a Roth. The tax rules surrounding such conversions are extremely complicated, so you'd better understand the ramifications before making the move. Several online resources can help, including the following:

- **General sources,** such as RothIRA.com (`www.rothira.com/roth-ira-conversion-rules`), provide guidelines about where a conversion would make sense.

- **Comparison websites** help you know what you stand to gain or lose from the transformation. The rules surrounding Roth and traditional IRAs are complex. If you're not sure about anything, check out Vanguard's comparison site at `https://personal.vanguard.com/us/whatweoffer/ira/whichira?Link=facet`.

- **Conversion calculators** take all your information, crunch the numbers, and tell you whether you can, or should, make the leap. Bankrate (`www.bankrate.com/calculators/retirement/convert-ira-roth-calculator.aspx`), DinkyTown (`www.dinkytown.net/java/RothTransfer.html`), and MoneyChimp (`www.moneychimp.com/articles/rothira/rothcalc.htm`) are a few. Most of the calculators, such as the Bankrate version shown in the figure, are easy to follow.

Setting up an IRA

After you've made your decision about what type of retirement account you're interested in — be it a traditional IRA, Roth IRA, or SEP IRA — you need to find a broker to set it up. Nearly all online brokers are equipped to set up all these accounts. But before signing up, make sure that the broker

>> **Does not charge extra fees or higher commissions:** In fact, online brokers might cut you special deals on your IRA accounts. This is something to look for when evaluating online brokers, as I describe in Chapter 4.

>> **Provides plenty of low-cost investments to choose from:** Most brokerages let you invest in both individual stocks and mutual funds with IRA accounts.

TIP

Okay, so you've decided on a plan for saving for retirement and you've picked the type of accounts best suited for that plan. But how much do you need to save? Most of the preceding sites help you answer that question. In addition, the following sites are even more focused on helping you measure how much you'll need to retire:

>> The Choose to Save site (www.choosetosave.org/ballpark) takes a simplified approach by giving you a Ballpark Estimate of how much you'll need.

>> Analyze Now! (www.analyzenow.com/) provides a Free Programs section stuffed with spreadsheets that can help you answer many of the questions you need to be asking yourself. In fact, the site even has an Investment Manager spreadsheet that can help you choose the right kind of accounts for planning your retirement. Analyze Now! is maintained by NewRetirement (www.newretirement.com/), which features an interactive retirement planner.

>> Index Funds Advisors' Retirement Analyzer (www.ifa.com/montecarlo/home) uses an advanced statistical analysis to examine the range of possible outcomes for your retirement savings. Using its statistical model, the IFA Retirement Analyzer tells you how much to contribute based on whether the market does well, poorly, or something in between.

>> CalcXML (www.calcxml.com/) features a calculator (www.calcxml.com/calculators/retirement-calculator) that tells you how much you need to save for retirement.

Going Back to School with Education Savings Accounts

Several special types of education savings accounts provide lucrative tax breaks, giving you a fighting chance to keep up with rising college costs. You need any help you can get because tuition costs rise at about twice the rate of most consumer goods.

The two main types of education savings accounts are the 529 plan and the Coverdell. Both 529s and Coverdell accounts work much like the Roth IRA, discussed in the preceding section, in that you put after-tax dollars into the accounts and watch them grow tax-free. You can take out the money, without paying any tax, as long as you use the cash to pay for qualified education expenses. The Internal Revenue

Service (www.irs.gov/publications/p970/ch08.html) describes qualified education expenses as "fees, books, supplies, and equipment that are required for the courses at the eligible educational institution." Reasonable room and board costs are also included for students who go to school at least half-time.

Three numbers you need to know: 529

TIP

When saving for college, it's tough to beat the 529. These are college savings plans typically run by states or educational institutions. The plans have several extremely positive attributes, such as

>> **Tax savings:** As the earlier example describes, the tax savings from 529 plans make them worthwhile. The tax savings can be even sweeter in some states that let you deduct your contributions to the state plan from your income.

>> **Control:** Even though your child is the beneficiary of the money, you remain the owner. That distinction is important because it means if Junior decides to run off and join the circus, he can't get the 529 money.

TIP

529 plans don't have to be used only for a kid. Open one for yourself if you're thinking about going back to school. And don't worry, your money won't be wasted if your child gets a scholarship. You can change the beneficiary to anyone else you want or even use the money to pay for more schooling for yourself. Normally, you may pay a 10% penalty on earnings in a 529 if you take the money out and don't use it for education costs. But there are exceptions — and your kid getting a scholarship is one of them. If that happens, you can withdraw up to the amount of the scholarship and not owe the 10% penalty. You will need to pay taxes on the earnings, but hey, at least you put them off.

>> **Availability and flexibility:** Unlike most other tax-advantaged accounts, which are mired with complex rules and restrictions, anyone can have a 529 account. The limit to how much you can contribute is generous, allowing you to contribute up to $14,000 a year in 2019 without triggering estate tax issues. You can also make a larger lump-sum contribution every five years. For information on the limits, the IRS has a helpful description (www.irs.gov/newsroom/529-plans-questions-and-answers) as does Dummies.com (www.dummies.com/how-to/content/529-college-savings-plan-contribution-limits.html).

>> **Lots of options:** Every state offers at least one 529 plan, and you can invest in any state's plan even if your child won't go to school in that state. So even if you invest in Utah's 529 plan, you can still use the money if your child wants to go to the University of California, Los Angeles. Go Bruins!

>> **Something for everyone:** Some states, but not all, offer two types of 529 plans: prepaid and savings. With *prepaid plans,* you transfer the investment risk to the state by agreeing to pay the current price of a college education and essentially locking in the price. Not all states offer prepaid plans. With *savings plans,* you

contribute any amount you want up to the allowed limits and try to increase it by choosing wise investments. If you save and invest wisely with a 529 savings plan, you could make enough to pay for your kid's college tuition and maybe part of a grandkid's, too. In fact, you can save for anyone's college using a 529, even for someone not related by blood.

Getting up to speed on 529 plans online

Some of the great things about 529 plans are that they're easy to sign up for, you can fund them without worrying about tax laws for the most part, and the investments are pretty much preselected. The biggest decision you must make is whether you'll opt for a plan offered by your state or go for one in another state.

TIP

Always evaluate and consider your own state's 529 plan before looking elsewhere. If your state lets you deduct contributions to its 529 plan, this might be a compelling feature you won't want to miss out on.

Here are the primary ways to research and find out about 529 plans:

>> **College savings information sites:** Savingforcollege.com (www.savingforcollege.com/) is a supersite when it comes to all things about college savings. You can find tutorials galore that show you how to pick a plan, decide which state's 529 plan is best for you, compare different 529 plans and fees, and even provide links to the plans so that you can sign up. Figure 3-6 shows you some of the information you can dig out from Savingforcollege.com. College Savings Plans Network (www.collegesavings.org/) helps you sort through the various options for saving for college.

FIGURE 3-6: Savingforcollege.com is the place to go for learning about 529 and other college savings plans.

>> **The states' 529 plan sites:** Each 529 plan runs its own website that gives you all the details about how much you can contribute, your investment options are, the fees, and other things you need to know. The best way to find links to states' plans is through the Savingforcollege.com site, although Table 3-5 contains links to some plans.

>> **Broker or mutual fund's sites:** Some states' 529 plans are administered by large brokerage or mutual fund companies. In those cases, you can find out more about the plans directly from the administration companies. Vanguard, for instance, handles the Iowa 529 plan in addition to the Vanguard 529 plan. You can find out about both plans, and 529 plans in general, at `https://personal.vanguard.com/us/whatweoffer/college`.

TABLE 3-5   **Website Addresses for Some States' 529 Plans**

State	Plan Name	Web Address
California	ScholarShare College Savings Plan	`www.scholarshare.com/`
Iowa	College Savings Iowa	`www.collegesavingsiowa.com`
New York	New York's 529 College Savings Program — Direct Plan	`www.nysaves.com/`
Ohio	Ohio CollegeAdvantage 529 Savings Plan	`www.collegeadvantage.com/`
Texas	Texas College Savings Plan	`www.texascollegesavings.com/`
Utah	Utah Educational Savings Plan	`www.uesp.org/`

Understanding 529 fees

As great as 529 plans are, you need to be familiar with their fees and charges. When evaluating plans, you want to see how the fee structures will affect your contributions and account balance to determine which are the best. The fees you need to know about include

>> **Enrollment fees** are up-front fees that some 529 plans charge to set up your account. Most 529s don't charge these, and you should try not to pay them if you can help it.

>> **Account maintenance fees** are charged on an ongoing basis to track and handle your account. These fees are a little more common than enrollment fees.

>> **Program maintenance fees** are charged by almost all 529 plans to cover the costs of running the 529. These fees generally run between 0.1 percent and 1.1 percent of assets.

>> **Fees charged by funds owned by the 529 plan** are also common. Say you invest in the Utah 529 plan, which invests in Vanguard funds. Those Vanguard funds themselves have fees that you must pay. These fees tend to be less than 1 percent of assets.

Industry regulator FINRA (`www.finra.org/investors/529-college-savings-plans`) maintains a website that can help you weigh all the different fees and choose the best plan for you.

TIP

You might worry that your child could have trouble getting financial aid if you stuff a ton of money into a 529 plan. Don't worry. It's not a big concern because the formula used for financial aid doesn't heavily factor in 529 plans. All that means, though, is that 529s do count a bit. If you want to keep the 529 completely out of the formula, you can legally name your child's grandparent as the owner of the account. Just make sure that you trust your parents to release the money to your child. That way, the 529 won't count against your child's financial aid application. Learn more about 529s and financial aid here: `www.savingforcollege.com/article/15-facts-about-financial-aid-eligibility`.

Living in the 529's shadow: The Coverdell

529s get most of the attention, and for good reason: They're a great tax shelter for money needed to pay for education. And following 2018, they got even better because up to $10,000 can be withdrawn to pay for primary and secondary school. That stole the Coverdell account's main party trick, because it used to be the way to shield some money used to pay for kindergarten, primary school, and secondary school, in addition to college. 529s are now your best bet because Coverdell accounts have several drawbacks, including the following:

>> Contributions are limited to $2,000 a year.

>> If you earn too much income, you won't be able to make the full contribution.

>> Contributions aren't allowed after the beneficiary turns 18 years old.

You can find out about Coverdell accounts, and whether they fit your needs better than a 529, at `www.savingforcollege.com/intro_to_esas`. You can also read about the tax ramifications of the account at a site maintained by the IRS (`www.irs.gov/taxtopics/tc310.html`).

IN THIS CHAPTER

» Understanding your choices of brokers

» Deciding what you need from a broker

» Knowing the differences between a self-service and full-service brokerage

» Making sure that your money is safe with your broker

» Scoping out how to access your account with your broker

» Setting up your account and getting started

Chapter **4**

Connecting with an Online Broker

I n this chapter, I dive into the offerings from all the major online brokerages to pinpoint which ones could fit your needs. Why can't I save you the trouble and just tell you which broker is the best? It's not that easy. Choosing "the best" brokerage is like choosing the most beautiful painting in an art museum. Everyone has an opinion based on what is most important to him or her. If you're most interested in dirt-cheap commissions and don't care much for service, you have one set of brokers to pick from. If you're looking for access to physical branches staffed with live people who can help you choose stocks or navigate the website, you have a different set of candidates. If you're all about the smartphone, you have other choices.

You might think you don't need this chapter because you like a certain broker's ads on TV or have a cousin who swears by his online broker. But don't underestimate the benefits that will accrue to you if you thoroughly research your broker options. Face it: Your broker is the gatekeeper to your money, and picking the right one will partly determine how successful you are as an investor.

Finding the Best Broker for You

People are constantly looking for the "best" of everything. Music buffs pore through online reviews and websites looking for the best earphones, commuters seek the best car, and new parents search for the best stroller. Similarly, investors are on a constant quest for the best online broker. But just as different headphones, cars, and strollers fit different people's needs, the same is true with brokerages. As I explain in the previous three chapters, investors have different goals, taste for risk, and resources. And that's why one person's broker can be perfect for him or her, but completely wrong for you.

REMEMBER

Not thoroughly researching your broker is a mistake. Your online broker is the most important member of your investing team, handling everything from tracking your portfolio to helping you buy and sell investments and tracking your taxable gains and losses. It's a relationship you need to be happy with to be a happy online investor. Above all, you want to make sure that your broker will be there for you if you run into any problems or have questions.

The nine main factors to consider

Brokers differ from one another in nine main ways. If you're aware of these things and understand what you're looking for, you can quickly eliminate brokers that don't fit your needs. The factors to consider are as follows:

>> **Commissions:** Perhaps the most important consideration for many investors when evaluating brokers is the price charged for executing trades, known as the *commission*. I discuss fees at length later in the chapter. There's good news here. Commissions charged by online brokers have been steadily falling since the 1990s, with most taking even lower dive during yet another price war that erupted in 2017. Also, most brokers now offer flat-rate commissions, meaning that all people pay the same commission no matter how many times they buy and sell or how many shares they trade. Some brokers have even started offering free commissions on certain trades. Roughly a third of self-directed investors said they're paying less than $5 a trade, according to a 2018 analysis by rating service J.D. Power.

>> **Availability of advice:** One way brokers separate themselves is whether or not they give you any help picking investments. On one end of the spectrum are the *full-service traditional brokers* that are all about giving you personalized attention. Not only can they pick stocks for you, but they'll also pour you coffee and serve you donuts when you visit them in their fancy offices. If you're not interested in paying for such perks, the *self-service brokers* are happy to oblige. Self-service brokers give you the tools you need, and then you're pretty much on your own. A few brokers fit somewhere between full service and self-service. J.D. Power found investor satisfaction was higher when brokers proactively reached out to offer help or guidance at least once a year.

>> **Access to an office:** Some brokers exist only online. It's up to you to have your own computer and Internet connection. But others have branch offices in certain cities and allow customers to stop in, do some trading, and sometimes take classes and fraternize with other investors or meet with advisors. You may not think that having access to a branch office will be important to you; after all, you're an online investor. But some find comfort in a bricks-and-mortar location.

>> **Other banking services:** A brokerage account doesn't have to be a financial island. Some brokerage firms let you move money from your trading account into other types of accounts, such as checking accounts. Some also provide ATM cards or credit cards.

>> **Speed of execution:** When you click the Buy or Sell button on the website, the trade isn't done. Your order snakes its way from your computer to other traders' computers on Wall Street, where it is filled. Some brokerages have spent a great deal of effort giving you the fastest path to other traders. That's generally beneficial because it means that you get a price that reflects the true value of the stock you're buying or selling. Depending on your strategy, you might not want your orders piling up in a bin, waiting to get filled. Speed of execution is tracked by broker-rating services, discussed later in this chapter, in the section "Finding Out What Reviewers Think."

>> **Customer service:** Do you have a question about your account or about making a trade? When you do, you'll need to reach the broker and ask it. The levels of service vary wildly. Some brokers have customer service reps available at your beck and call either in offices or on the phone. Others let you email a question and wait for an answer.

>> **Site reliability:** No one wants to be in the position of finding a promising investment only to discover that his or her online brokerage is down for repair. Some brokerages have focused on limiting system downtime, which might be important to you if you trade many times a day. Again, this is something brokerage-rating services measure.

>> **Access to advanced stock-buying tools:** Some brokerage sites are pretty bare-bones because they assume that the investors already have the software and tools they need. This is dramatically changing, however, as many third-party investing websites are vanishing, scaling back, or starting to charge for their services. Now, investors are increasingly looking to their brokerages to provide comprehensive tools that can track tax liabilities, help them go prospecting for stocks, or monitor market movements or breaking news.

>> **Ease of use:** Online brokers geared for people new to online investing or who plan to trade infrequently are minimalists and have as few buttons as possible. They're the Zen of trading. But those aimed for hyperactive traders who click Buy and Sell so many times they have calluses on their fingers tend to give investors dozens of options allowing them to do some advanced stuff. Some sites targeting advanced traders provide trading tools aimed at helping investors flip stocks or other options quickly and at set prices. But that might be overwhelming if you just want to buy 100 shares of General Electric stock every couple of months.

Gotchas to watch out for

WARNING

Brokerage firms often have confusing commission structures to fool you into thinking you'll pay less than you ultimately do. Make sure that you check to see whether the firm charges extra for certain types of orders, such as limit orders (I discuss limit orders in Chapter 5), large orders, or mutual funds. Some brokers zing you with fees or inflate commissions if you don't keep a balance of a certain size. Some brokers also charge you for switching to another broker. Always check before signing up for covert fees. The "Avoiding Hidden Fees" section, later in the chapter, can help you spot things to watch out for.

Separating the Types of Brokerages

Choosing a brokerage firm might seem intimidating, but it's no different than picking a restaurant. You can find fast-food restaurants, where you have to walk up to the counter, place your order, put on your own ketchup and mustard, and find a place to sit. Then there are full-service restaurants, where you're seated and pampered by dressed-up waiters who bring everything at your command and even clean the bread crumbs away when you're done.

The same goes for brokerages. Self-service brokers give you everything you need to get the job done and let you have at it. Because you're doing much of the work yourself, unless you ask for help, self-service brokers tend to have the lowest commissions. Following price wars, self-service brokers are commonly grouped into two baskets: deep discounters and discounters. Then you have the full-service traditional brokerages, which hold your hand through the whole process, down to suggesting investments, analyzing your portfolio, and offering estate-planning services. Remember that these are general brokerage categories, and sometimes the lines blur a bit because some self-service brokers let you buy advice from them if you ask.

TIP

If you can't find a page on the broker's site that lists all its fees, commissions, and other charges in less than three mouse clicks from the home page, look elsewhere. I've found that brokers that bury fees do so for a reason.

How do you decide what you need? Determine how often you intend to trade, what types of investments you plan to buy, and how long you'll hold them. It's difficult to know this in advance, but there are ways to figure it out. For instance, did you perform the trading simulations I mention in Chapter 2? If so, how often did you trade? Next, familiarize yourself with the four types of online brokers: deep discount, discount, premium discount, and full-service traditional. Read the following descriptions and see what you can expect to get at each level. Decide whether the extra whistles and bells are worth the extra cost. To make things easy, the key stats are summarized in charts after each section. I include the standard commissions to give you the most realistic scenario for each broker.

Here's another caveat. Some brokers will greatly reduce or eliminate their commissions if you buy certain investments. Consider Schwab. The company's standard online commission is $4.95. But if you buy one of the firm's exchange-traded funds, or ETFs, there's no commission. *ETFs* are baskets of investments that you can buy or sell just like a stock. ETFs are enormously popular and a great choices for investors. You owe it to yourself to learn more about these unique investments in Chapter 11.

REMEMBER

Double-check brokers' fees before signing up because they change frequently. Also remember that some brokers might charge lower commissions if you pay a monthly subscription fee, meet certain balance thresholds, or hold other types of accounts in addition to the brokerage account.

Paying the minimum with a deep discounter

The deep discounters are the Walmarts and Home Depots of the brokerage world. When you sign up for a deep discounter, you are on your own. But if you know what you're doing, that's a good thing because you don't have to worry about getting pestered by a salesperson trying to pitch stocks you have no interest in. And you'll get all the basics that you truly need, such as year–end tax statements, access to stock quotes and research, and the ability to buy and sell stocks and other investments. But the real beauty of these brokers is their sweet, low price: Because they don't offer niceties, they can have the lowest commissions, usually $5 a trade or less. Leaders include the following:

>> **FolioInvesting** offers a variety of pricing plans so that investors can choose which one works best. FolioInvesting's Basic plan lets you trade stocks for a low price of $4 as long as you're okay if the trades aren't executed right away, but instead, during two "windows" during the day. If you'd like your trades to go through right away, you'll be charged $10. You also pay a $15 maintenance fee per quarter if you place less than three trades in the quarter. If you pay a $290-a-year subscription fee, though, you get free delayed trades and a discounted rate of $3 to have trades go through right away.

>> **Robinhood** offers the ultimate lure: Free commissions. It's different than other brokerages in that it is entirely focused on mobile devices. Instead of providing a website for investors to log into and place trades, Robinhood focuses on apps for smartphones and tablets. You won't find the rich data services available on the websites of other brokers — but you won't pay for them, either.

>> **SogoTrade**'s $4.88-a-trade is appealing not just for the low price. If you plan to be a serious trader, SogoTrade lets you download software to your computer — software similar to that provided by more expensive online brokers — which helps you track the market's daily movements. You must open an account with at least $500, but you do not need to maintain a minimum balance going forward. And the commission drops to $3 if you trade 150 times or more a quarter.

>> **Ally Invest** aims to give investors a few more bank-like niceties than other deep discounters, such as the ability to store cash balances in a high-yield savings account. Ally Invest, shown in Figure 4-1, also offers access to some company news and research reports, and a straightforward flat-fee commission of $4.95. The brokerage is a capable complement to what was primarily an online bank but is most appealing to existing bank customers. This broker isn't for the advanced trader.

No minimum account balance is required, but you'll be charged a $50-a-year fee if you have less than $2,500 in your account and don't trade at least once a year. You can view some of the tools Ally Invest offers to options investors in Figure 4-1.

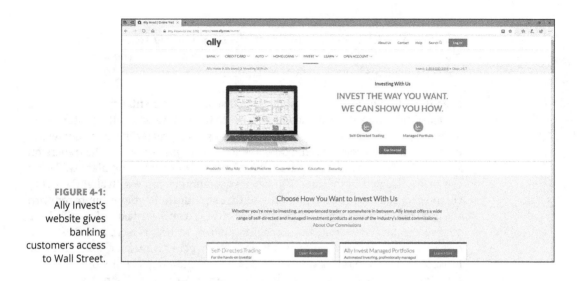

FIGURE 4-1:
Ally Invest's
website gives
banking
customers access
to Wall Street.

Table 4-1 sums up the main differences among the deep discounters.

TABLE 4-1   **Deep Discounters**

Broker	Web Address	Commission	Minimum to Open an Account
FolioInvesting	`www.folioinvesting.com/`	$4.00 to trade stocks on a delayed basis, $10.00 for immediate trades with Basic plan	None
Robinhood	`https://www.robinhood.com/`	$0	None
SogoTrade	`www.sogotrade.com/`	$5.00	$500
Ally Invest	`www.ally.com/invest/`	$4.95	None

TIP

Beginning investors always ask me how much money they need to begin and where they can get started investing online. You can start with next to nothing with brokers that have no minimum deposit requirements, which includes most of the deep discounters. If you're the kind of person who can't seem to save money until you've sent your cash off to a bank or brokerage, these are great places to start.

Get more with a discounter

If the thought of being completely on your own makes you nervous but you're not willing to give up low-cost commissions, the discount brokers sit in the sweet spot for you. These brokers suit most investors ranging from beginners to the more advanced because they generally offer some advice (if you ask for it), and many have offices in most major cities.

Even if you're not looking for advice, the discounters are still appealing because they load their websites with advanced tools to help do-it-yourself investors of all levels. Some provide access to advanced trading tools, real-time stock quotes, or special computer programs that let you enter trades just as fast as the traders on Wall Street. Top-notch apps that let you check your portfolio and place trades on the go are also part of the deal. These extras sometimes come with slightly higher commissions, but the difference isn't all that significant anymore compared with the deep discounters, and it might not be a deal-breaker for you. Price wars have yanked commissions from the discounters down to between $4 and $10. Most discounters also offer price breaks if you're a hyperactive trader. Most of these brokers also offer services where you can invest in a premade mix of diversified investments, rather than picking your own stocks or funds. The names to know here are

>> **Bank of America** might not be what you think of as a stockbroker, but it's one of the large banks aggressively boosting its brokerage services. Traditionally, banks have targeted the well-heeled with personal bankers who pick out investments like personal shoppers pick out ties for rich executives. But Bank of America's Merrill Edge unit has added self-service brokerage fees with commissions starting at $6.95. And you can get 30 free trades a month if you keep at least $20,000 with the bank in a deposit account, such as a Bank of America savings account. As your account grows, you have access to the wealth management services offered by the bank. Bank of America makes its connection with Merrill Lynch clear on its website, as shown in Figure 4-2.

>> **Charles Schwab** tries to be the Toyota Camry of brokers: not flashy or exotic in any one area but practical and pleasing to the bulk of investors. Schwab lowered commission to $4.95 in 2017, keeping it competitive among the other discounters. Schwab's commissions are still among the cheapest, and for that price, the broker adds services that might be valuable, whether you're looking for help or want to be left to your own devices. For instance, you can buy hundreds of exchange-traded funds for no commission. Do-it-yourselfers might like Schwab's Equity Ratings, a computerized system that evaluates stocks and assigns them letter-grade scores from A to F. It also provides access to Wall Street research and a full suite of banking services, including high interest rates paid on cash sitting in your account. But if you decide later you need more help, Schwab offers mutual funds designed to fit specific needs in addition to making consultants available to give you personalized advice. If you're not going to use all these extra services, though, the higher commission might not be worth it. You can see the site in Figure 4-3.

FIGURE 4-2:
Bank of America's
Merrill Edge aims
to win over
investors looking
for a bank and
broker.

FIGURE 4-3:
Schwab tries to
provide access to
the tools that
most investors
will need.

>> **E*Trade** has a reputation as being an innovator in the industry and seems to be always looking for ways to separate itself from others. E*Trade has long targeted active traders with computer software such as Power E*Trade, which is software that lets you find stocks and other investments that meet your criteria or test how trading strategies would have worked in the past. But

E*Trade has things for beginners, too, such as access to stock research from several providers and the capability to shift cash to a checking or high-yield savings account. There's an advanced smartphone app and a more basic one, too. The commission is typically $6.95 but can be lower based on your account balance and how often you trade.

» **Fidelity** consistently gets good marks for making its website easy to navigate and getting trades through quickly. Fidelity has also been a leader in adding functions outside of just plain-old U.S. stock trading, including an advanced online system to buy bonds, invest in initial public offerings, and trade stocks outside the United States. It's also well designed and a good value. For years, Fidelity was a premium-priced online brokerage, but after slashing its commissions to $4.95, it's competitive if not on the low end. In addition, Fidelity is offering commission-free purchases on select ETFs from Fidelity and also iShares, which is one of the largest providers of these investments.

» **Interactive Brokers** is looking for the pros — or people who want to be. This isn't the brokerage for casual investors. You'll find advanced trading tools and software designed for sophisticated and rapid-fire trading strategies. The company maintains two pricing structures, both designed to reward frequent traders or those with relatively large balances of $100,000. If you're serious about trading, this is a broker worth considering.

» **Motif Investing** is best for investors who want to pick trends or themes, not necessarily individual stocks. Customers can choose from dozens of premade investing Motif Thematic Portfolios, which are broad ideas for investment, such as companies working on biotechnology developments, called Biotech Breakthroughs, or companies that get most of their revenue from the U.S., called All American. Investors can buy the Motif Thematic Portfolios, and then Motif Investing will invest the money in a group of up to 30 stocks fitting the theme.

This brokerage is convenient for investors who don't want to choose individual stocks but aren't happy with the current selection of mutual funds or ETFs. Motif Investing charges a $9.95 commission to buy or sell a Motif Thematic Portfolio. You can also buy and sell individual stocks for $4.95 per trade. The company has been adding additional features, such as the ability to invest in themes that reflect your personal values and also new stock sold by companies for investors for the first time.

» **TD Ameritrade's** earliest customers were active traders looking for low commissions. But the brokerage's low-cost roots are eroding, as its $6.95-per-trade commission is now more than what most of its major rivals charge. But TD Ameritrade tries to make up for its higher commission by offering a variety of high-tech digital tools and services that might save you money. Investors who trade frequently during the day also like TD Ameritrade's bonus PC software trading tools, such as thinkorswim, which let you see second-by-second stock price movements or test trading strategies and analyze how they would have done. The broker also offers solid mobile apps to keep tabs on your portfolio and to make trades.

TD Ameritrade is also a leader in offering consumers free trading in ETFs. Customers can choose from hundreds of ETFs from several leading providers, including iShares and State Street, and pay no commission as long as they are held more than 30 days. Keep in mind that Vanguard's uber-popular ETFs are not included. If you want to buy those, you might look elsewhere, including at Vanguard. (See Figure 4-4.)

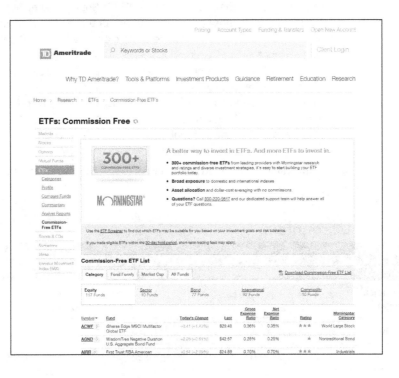

FIGURE 4-4: TD Ameritrade allows you to search all the ETFs it will allow you to buy and sell for no commission on its website.

>> **Vanguard** wins fans for its speed, the quality of customer service, and availability to help in navigating the site and making investment decisions. The company, best known as a mutual fund provider, is taking brokerage more seriously. Vanguard's commission structure, though, is a little more complex than at other brokers. For stocks, the first 25 trades you make in a year are a competitive $7 if you have less than $50,000 in your account. After you trade 25 times, trades jump to $20. If you keep more than $50,000 in your account but less than $500,000, you can get unlimited $7 trades. If you have more than $500,000 in your account, trades are discounted to $2, and trades are free if you have more than a million bucks in your account.

Here's one key selling point for Vanguard: It provides free unlimited trading to all investors in its own family of well-regarded ETFs. Remember, Vanguard's stock brokerage offering is separate from the account that lets you buy and sell Vanguard mutual funds, which I cover later. Vanguard is also top-notch in putting any uninvested cash in your brokerage account automatically in a safe, interest-bearing investment. This is a huge advantage, as you'll read about later in this chapter. Some investors may be charged a $20 annual account service fee unless they sign up to get account statements only online.

>> **Wells Fargo** is another bank that follows the model of using brokerage services to tempt customers to put more money in its hands. Wells Fargo's self-service stock commissions start at $8.95. But if you keep at least $25,000 in your deposit accounts, you can cut that to $2.95 without paying the monthly service charge of $30. Wells Fargo also gives you 100 trades a year with no monthly service fee if you keep $50,000 with the bank and its brokerage. But falling short of the $25,000 deposit balance or $50,000 total can be costly, resulting in a $30 a month fee. If you're a Wells Fargo customer with a decent sized portfolio, it's worth considering. The company's mobile app is capable but not fancy. And its website provides helpful planning information, especially pertaining to taxes and dividends.

Check out Table 4-2 for an overview of what the different discounters have to offer.

TABLE 4-2   ## Discounters

Broker	Web Address	Commission	Minimum to Open an Account
Bank of America (Merrill Edge)	www.merrilledge.com/	$0 if requirements are met; otherwise $6.95	None
Charles Schwab	www.schwab.com/	$4.95	None
E*Trade	www.etrade.com/	$6.96	$500
Fidelity	www.fidelity.com/	$4.95	None
Interactive Brokers	www.interactivebrokers.com	Varies	None
Motif Investing	www.motifinvesting.com/	$9.95	$1,000
TD Ameritrade	www.tdameritrade.com/	$6.95	None
Vanguard	www.vanguard.com/	$7.00	$3,000
Wells Fargo	www.wellsfargo.com/	$2.95 if requirements are met; otherwise, $8.95	$1,000

ARE FREE TRADES REALLY FREE?

When anything claims to be "free" in online investing, your defenses should go up instantly. Robinhood and Bank of America's Merrill Edge promise free trades to investors. Several brokers offer free commissions on ETFs, too. Be on guard and evaluate all the stipulations, though, before assuming that these free offers are best for you. (See the section on hidden fees later in this chapter.) Keep three things in mind:

- **"Deal flow" is a hidden money maker.**
- **Consider cash.**
- **Free commission ETF deals have a big catch.**

First, some firms, including those that offer free trades, such as Robinhood, do it in part by selling your orders to market makers. *Market makers* (firms such as Two Sigma, Citadel, and Virtu), compete with the exchanges (such as the New York Stock Exchange) to process orders. These market makers then pay the broker for the business with a rebate. You want to make sure your broker is getting you the best price on your trade, not looking for the best rebates for itself. Robinhood's Founder Vlad Tenev says the firm doesn't consider rebates when choosing which market maker to give the order to.

Second, the interest rate you get from uninvested cash left in the account is an important factor. This is especially true if you're required to have a certain amount of cash on deposit to get the free trades, or if you tend to leave lots of cash in the account. Not paying attention to interest rates could wipe out any savings you think you're getting from free trades.

Suppose you trade ten times a year and normally leave about $10,000 of uninvested cash in your account. If trades are free, it's true that your commission costs would be zero. But you still could be overpaying if you're not getting a rate of return on your uninvested cash. In fact, you'd be $150 better off paying $9.99 a trade if you get 2.5 percent interest on cash sitting in your account. If interest rates rise, the real cost of free commissions could be higher, still.

I've come up with a formula that takes the guesswork out of "free" trades:

1. Multiply the number of trades you do each year by the commission. Write down this number.
2. Multiply the amount of uninvested cash you expect to keep in your account by the interest rate you will collect. Divide this number by 100 and write down the result.
3. Subtract the answer in Step 2 from the answer in Step 1.

(continued)

(continued)

This formula helps you calculate the true cost of the broker's offering. You'll see how much the commissions are costing you after adjusting for the rate of return you'll get on your cash: The lower the number, the better. If you're choosing between a couple of brokers, crunch this formula and choose the broker with the lowest (or negative) number. When rates rise, savvy investors should pay close attention to this hidden cost of free trades.

Finally, free ETF commission offerings from many brokers are compelling, popular, and something most investors should consider. ETFs are a fast and easy way to build a diversified portfolio. And free commissions can save you money. Just remember that the broker you choose is important. You'll have to stick to the menu of ETFs your broker has selected, which may or may not be best for you. TD Ameritrade, for instance, removed all Vanguard ETFs from its lineup of free ETFs. If you want to buy Vanguard ETFs, you have to pay TD Ameritrade's regular commission. ETF investors might decide which ETFs they want and then see which brokers offer those with no commission.

Full-service traditional

Because you're reading *Online Investing For Dummies*, chances are good that you're a do-it-yourself kind of investor or one looking for minimal handholding. But maybe after reading the preceding descriptions, you're looking for even more help. That's when you might consider a full-service traditional broker.

Full-service *broker-dealers* pride themselves on being part of your team of people whom you call on routinely for advice, such as your real estate agent, housekeeper, and mechanic. The top full-service traditional brokerages are the Wall Street firms you've probably heard of, such as J.P. Morgan Securities (www.jpmorgansecurities.com), Bank of America's Merrill Lynch (shown in Figure 4-5), Morgan Stanley (www.morganstanleyclientserv.com), Edward Jones (www.edwardjones.com/), Goldman Sachs (www.goldmansachs.com/), and UBS (www.ubs.com/us/en.html). Merrill Lynch, through Bank of America, competes with the discounters. But Merrill Lynch (www.ml.com/) also provides full-service brokerage services as part of its wealth management offering, geared for wealthy investors.

And by now, most full-service traditional brokers can legitimately call themselves online brokerages because they have websites that let you view your accounts. Services that these firms provide include

>> **Constant stock recommendations:** Most big Wall Street firms have well-known strategists and analysts who think big thoughts and come up with stock tips. The brokers then spread those tips to you.

FIGURE 4-5:
Merrill Lynch provides web-based tools to investors as part of its online service.

>> **Access to initial public offerings:** When companies go public, they first sell their shares to large Wall Street investment banks. Those shares, especially if the initial public offering (IPO) is expected to be popular, are often a sought-after commodity because they have the chance to rise in value the first day. If you're an active customer with these firms' brokerage divisions, you might get a shot at buying these shares at the IPO price. (You find more on IPOs in Bonus Chapter 2 on the website associated with this book.)

>> **Availability of other financial services:** If you're a customer with a full-service traditional brokerage, you might get extra financial services, such as help with your taxes or estate planning.

But before you get too excited about the extra services that traditional full-service brokers may provide, you also have downsides to consider, such as

>> **Relatively high cost:** Wall Street firms have to pay somehow for those fancy offices you're enjoying. The fees tend to be higher, and you might pay a lofty commission for each trade or pay a percentage of your assets.

>> **Uneven treatment:** Remember that it's unlikely you'll end up being Goldman Sachs's best customer, so don't expect to get the real goods. For instance, when shares of the next truly promising IPO are doled out, if you're not a top customer or famous, you probably won't get shares anyway. (Fees and rates can vary, too, which is why I didn't even bother coming up with a table comparing fee structures for the full-service traditional brokerage crowd.)

>> **Potential for conflicts:** Because brokers are often paid by commission, they might have an incentive to urge you to trade more frequently than you might like.

TIP

There are broker-dealers and then there are investment advisors. They both offer financial advice and call themselves advisors, but they are registered with regulators differently and have unique standards of conduct. *Broker-dealers* must sell you investments that are suitable. They are regulated by the Securities and Exchange Commission (SEC) and the Financial Industry Regulatory Authority (FINRA). *Investment advisors*, which are typically independent and not associated with giant Wall Street firm, are regulated by the SEC. They must act as *fiduciaries*, putting client's interests first. Typically investment advisors offer their own websites or use specially gated areas for clients at Schwab, Fidelity, or TD Ameritrade.

WARNING

Be skeptical if a friend or family member recommends a broker to you. Many brokerage firms give customers bounties of $50 or more or dozens of free trades if someone they refer signs up. I'm not telling you that you can't trust your friends. Just know that people who recommend their broker might have a motive other than telling you which broker is best for you.

Avoiding Hidden Fees

The stock trade commission is likely the fee you'll pay the most often, so it's wise to pay the most attention to it. But don't think it's the only fee. Brokers often charge a host of other fees, which, depending on your circumstance, can add up fast. These extra fees are increasingly important for online investors to monitor as brokers' trading commissions get more comparable. You should look for a page that discloses these fees, like the one shown in Figure 4-6.

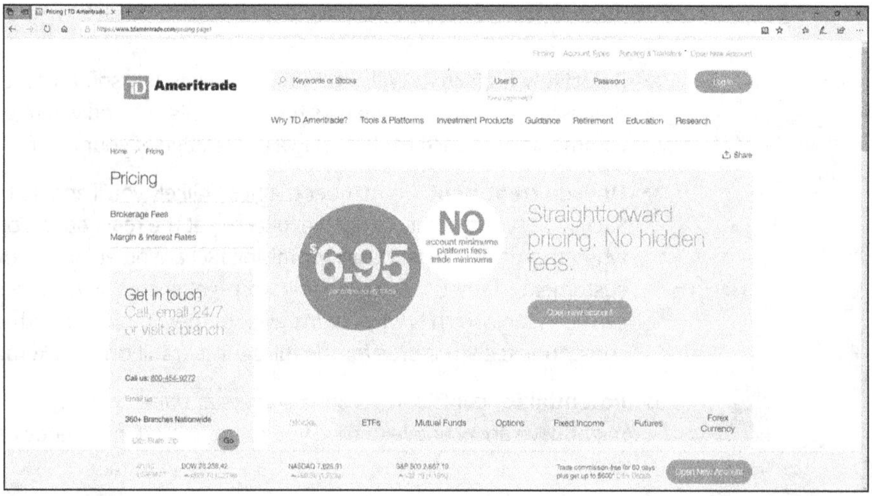

FIGURE 4-6:
TD Ameritrade discloses all its miscellaneous fees on a Brokerage Fees page.

Here are some common hidden fees you should be aware of:

>> **Maintenance fees** are monthly, quarterly, or annual fees that some brokers charge you just to have an account with them. Don't pay maintenance fees. Period. If you're paying them, you're probably at the wrong broker. Most brokers exempt you from paying maintenance fees if you meet certain requirements. If you can't meet them, switch to a different broker.

>> **Inactivity fees** are the ugly cousins of maintenance fees. A brokerage might charge these fees if you don't gin up enough commissions for the brokerage by trading. Don't allow these fees to push you to buy and sell stock more than you're comfortable with. Most brokerages that charge such fees offer exemptions for customers who meet other criteria. Sogo Trade, for instance, charges $50 a year for investors whose balance drops below $100. But Sogo Trade won't charge this fee, if you trade at least once in a 12-month period.

>> **Transfer fees** are charged when you want to part ways with your broker. Expect to get nicked with a $50 or higher fee, which brokers charge supposedly to cover their cost of shipping all your stock holdings and transferring cash to your new broker. One way to avoid this charge is to transfer only some of your holdings. Some brokers will do this for free. You could also sell all the stocks in the old account and then transfer the cash to the new broker drawn on your old account. But this might not work. Keep in mind that you'll incur commissions for every stock you sell, and tax considerations might cost you well over $50. Refer to Chapter 3 for a refresher on capital gains taxes. Some brokers will pick up the transfer fee tab if you move the account to them.

>> **IRA fees** are sometimes assessed when opening a new retirement account. Fortunately, most brokers have done away with this fee.

>> **Certificate fees** are charged if you want your broker to mail you the physical stock certificates you own. It's usually a $500 or higher charge. Some online brokers won't help you get paper certificates at all.

>> **Check-writing or debit-card fees** range dramatically from broker to broker. Some charge you an annual fee to have the privilege to make payments against your account. Others give you a certain number of free checks and charge only if you write checks that bounce.

>> **Special orders** are added fees if you trade more than a set number of shares. Most brokers also charge extra for placing *limit orders* — trades in which you set the price you're willing to accept. Limit orders are covered in more detail in the next chapter.

>> **Margin fees** are interest charges that result from borrowing money from the broker to buy investments with. Buying on margin is only for the most risk-ready investors, and I explain why in Chapter 5.

Finding Out What Reviewers Think

It can be overwhelming to parse through all the brokers' commissions because there appear to be more moving parts than in a Swiss watch. Minimum requirements and fees vary, and it's hard to know how fast a broker's website will be until you actually sign up and try it. Luckily, some professional reviewers have kicked the tires for you. Different rating services and publications that evaluate brokers each year include

>> **StockBrokers.com:** This site puts all the major brokers through the paces. You'll find "best of" lists that name the top brokers based on a number of factors such as the quality of their online tools and apps plus service and commissions. You can also look up specific brokers for summaries of their capabilities and requirements. The site, shown in Figure 4-7, also has a comprehensive section that ranks the reviews of online brokers and summarizes their findings.

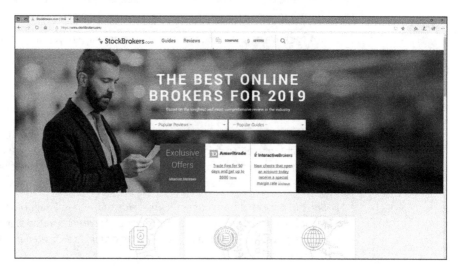

FIGURE 4-7:
StockBrokers.com summarizes the key value of online brokers.

- **J.D. Power:** Although it's best known for rating cars, J.D. Power also evaluates both online and full-service traditional brokers every year. It rates brokers based on several criteria, including cost, customer service, how quickly trades are completed, website design, data that's provided, and overall satisfaction. Read the latest reviews at www.jdpower.com/business/press-releases/jd-power-2018-us-self-directed-investor-satisfaction-study.

- **Barron's:** A Wall Street fixture since the 1920s, Barron's keeps an eye out for online brokers that serve sophisticated investors best. You'll have to subscribe, though, to read the stories online. An online subscription costs $120 a year and includes access to its entire site, which contains more than just broker ratings. Barron's Online is available at www.barrons.com/, and you can read the most recent brokerage ratings for free: www.barrons.com/articles/who-are-2019s-best-online-brokers-51550882807?refsec=best-online-brokers.

- **Investor's Business Daily:** IBD is primarily a source of business and markets news, but it annually rates investors' impressions of their brokers, too. The findings can be useful because they tell you how happy other investors are with their brokers. Subscriptions to IBD cost $269 a year, but you can read the broker ratings here: www.investors.com/news/best-online-brokers/broker-survey-methodology-reveals-top-online-brokers/.

INNOVATION IS BLURRING ONLINE BROKERAGE LINES

Classifying brokers is getting increasingly difficult. Big cuts to commissions by discounters such as Schwab and Fidelity put them into closer price competition with the deep discounters (and each other). Meanwhile, new commission-free ETF offers are putting online brokers in competition with mutual-fund companies. Meanwhile, a number of online brokers are also offering advice and even helping investors find live financial advisors, putting them head-to-head with full-service brokerages.

New technology is also disrupting the online brokerage scene. New brokerage business models defy categorization. Consider brokerage firm Acorns (www.acorns.com/). Rather than paying a per-trade commission, you pay a monthly fee starting at $1. In exchange, the brokerage firm will round-up purchases or allow you to make small contributions and invest the money in ETFs. It's a novel spin on investing, in which a computer essentially builds a portfolio for you using ETFs and handles all the buying and selling. Because the process is so automated, these types of brokers are called *robo-advisors.* You can read more about Acorns and other robo-advisors in Chapter 11.

Is Your Money Safe? Checking Out Your Broker

When you're about to hand over your life's savings to a broker, especially one with no offices, you want to make sure that it's a reputable outfit. As investors in the epic Bernie Madoff investment scam in 2008 learned the hard way, it's up to you to make sure that you're dealing with a legitimate broker. Unlike bank savings accounts, brokerages have no government guarantee. But you still have some safeguards.

Your first layer of protection comes from the Securities Investor Protection Corporation (SIPC). SIPC was formed by Congress in 1970 to protect investors by promising to help recover and return cash to investors if their brokerage closes due to bankruptcy. If cash or stock mysteriously goes missing in your account, the SIPC might help you recover the funds. The SIPC has provided $2.8 billion in funds and helped in the recovery of $139 billion in assets for 773,000 investors since it was formed in 1970 through 2017. If a brokerage fails and doesn't have enough money to repay customers, the SIPC covers up to $500,000 (including up to $250,000 in cash) per customer. You should always check whether a broker is an SIPC member by logging on to www.sipc.org/. In addition, some brokers carry additional insurance to protect customer assets beyond $500,000. All the brokers mentioned in this chapter are SIPC members.

Next, make sure that your broker has the appropriate approval from regulatory bodies to buy and sell investments. You wouldn't let someone who isn't a doctor remove your appendix, right? You should also make sure that your broker is registered to be a broker. You can do this using the Financial Industry Regulatory Authority (FINRA) BrokerCheck at https://brokercheck.finra.org/. Broker-Check tells you whether the brokerage is registered with this important regulatory body and whether the registration is current. If you're dealing with an investment advisor, BrokerCheck will point you to their information at the SEC. Each state also keeps tabs on brokerages serving customers in its region. State regulators are coordinated by the North American Securities Administrators Association, which provides access to the public at www.nasaa.org/.

Lastly, you want to know whether the broker you're considering has been disciplined recently. You can access this info from FINRA's BrokerCheck by downloading the broker's regulatory report and checking the section that spells out disciplinary action. Information is also available from a system maintained by the New York Stock Exchange's Disciplinary Action database at www.nyse.com/regulation/disciplinary-actions. And the ultimate watchdog on Wall Street is the U.S. Securities and Exchange Commission, which maintains records on brokers at `www.sec.gov/` and provides tips to investors looking to check out their brokers at `https://sec.gov/investor/brokers.htm`. The SEC leaves tracking routine disciplinary actions to FINRA, but does provide information when it pursues legal action against brokers. You can track SEC's legal actions by using the search function at `www.sec.gov/`. For an in-depth look at how to make sure your advisor is on the up-and-up, see my article on the topic on Motley Fool at `www.fool.com/investing/2019/02/17/3-ways-to-avoid-financial-advisors-who-have-scamme.aspx`.

Cutting the Cord: Mobile Trading

If the idea of checking up on your portfolio and placing trades while sipping margaritas by the pool appeals to you, get a life. Well, okay, sometimes you *do* need to check up on your account even when you're not sitting behind a computer at your desk. To help, plenty of brokers are providing wireless access to account information so that customers can access their portfolios at any time, be it from a device running Google's Android operating system, Apple's iOS, Microsoft's Windows 10, or other wireless devices. You have several ways to accomplish this:

>> **From a laptop:** If your laptop is set up for wireless access, you can get online at thousands of locations that offer wireless Internet connections, called Wi-Fi hotspots. Go to a Starbucks and you can get online. Keep in mind, though, that Wi-Fi connections are risky because they're not private. Read the sidebar "A Word about Wireless Security" for tips on keeping yourself safe when your checking stocks and sipping a latte.

>> **From a smartphone or tablet (or computer) using an app:** Nearly all major online brokers offer one or more apps that you can download to your smartphone or tablet and use to check stock quotes or trade stocks. After you download and install these apps, you start them and can enjoy a decent online trading experience. TD Ameritrade, for instance, offers two apps: TD Ameritrade Mobile for most users and TD Ameritrade Mobile Trader for more advanced traders. If mobile trading apps are important, you will want to check with the online broker before signing up to make sure the app meets your needs.

A WORD ABOUT WIRELESS SECURITY

Security is a serious concern when dealing with your money, and I discuss how to keep your money safe in more detail in Chapters 2 and 18. But when you access your stock data wirelessly, especially from a public Wi-Fi network, you need to pay special attention to security. Here are four ways to do just that:

- **Avoid using public Wi-Fi for financial matters.** Free Wi-Fi is great but is not secure. Your brokerage username or password could be hijacked, so don't use public Wi-Fi connections when checking your financial accounts. When at the coffeehouse, hotel, or airport, fire up your smartphone instead and make sure you're connected to the cellular network. Use the brokerage's app on your phone if you can.

- **Make sure that your data is encrypted.** If you must use your laptop, be aware of the risks. Most Internet browsers let you know whether the data is being *encrypted* — scrambled, in other words. If you're using Microsoft's Edge browser, the padlock icon is a signal to you that the data is being scrambled to make it harder for the guy sitting next to you at Starbucks to read your information. The data is then decrypted, or unscrambled, by the website. You can click the padlock icon to get more information about the website's security. Be sure to look at the text in the pop-up window to confirm that the site's certificate, or identification, lists the name of your brokerage firm. If the padlock doesn't appear, the site might use a different method of securing data, which is something you should ask your broker about.

- **Consider virtual private network (VPN) software.** A *VPN* is technology used to protect your data from snoops over the Internet. Some Internet service providers (ISPs) offer this service to customers; if you're using your work laptop, a VPN might be installed already. You might also consider installing VPN software on your computer. Some VPN software is free, such as Hotspot Shield (www.hotspotshield.com), which you can download from the Windows app store. Most other VPNs charge annual fees.

- **Consider tethering with your smartphone.** You're on the hotel's Wi-Fi and need to look at your portfolio on your laptop. You don't have a VPN installed. Please, resist the urge to log on to your brokerage account. Instead, connect your laptop to your smartphone with the USB cable or a similar cable and enable tethering. Back on your laptop, your smartphone appears as a wired network connection. Connect to it just as you would any other wired network.

Be sure to ask your broker what kind of protection it gives you if a hacker gets into your account. E*Trade and TD Ameritrade, for instance, will cover the entire loss. Also, TD Ameritrade (www.tdameritrade.com/security/index.html) provides a detailed guide to all the things you can do to protect your computer when investing online. You don't need to be a TD Ameritrade customer to use the site.

Pay Attention to Where Your Cash Is Parked: Money Market Funds

You're an online investor, right? So why would you care about money that you haven't invested? It turns out that one of the biggest secrets in the brokerage world is what happens to cash sitting in your account that's not invested. Brokers often collect interest on your money for themselves and you get nothing.

Don't underestimate how important this is. If you have $10,000 in cash in your account waiting to be invested, that's worth $200 a year at a 2 percent interest rate. And while rates have been historically low, if they rise to more normal levels, the interest rates earned by uninvested cash will be even more important.

This is my way of telling you that, before choosing an online broker, you want to be sure what rate of interest your uninvested cash will get and how it's handled. Ideally, you want a sweep account. With a *sweep account*, idle cash is automatically scooped up and put into a savings or money market account. You don't have to do anything, and you're certain that your money is working for you. Just make sure that your money is being swept into a savings account or money market that pays an interest rate that is competitive with the going market rate. Some brokers won't automatically sweep your uninvested cash into a money market fund, so it's up to you to ask about having it done.

Since interest rates have been at historical lows since around 2009, don't expect to get rich off your savings held at a brokerage site. Still, there's usually no additional charge for sweeping cash to a money market fund, so it doesn't hurt.

WARNING

A dirty little secret in the brokerage industry is that uninvested cash gets about 0 percent interest at nearly all brokers. Even many brokerage firm's sweep accounts pay next to nothing on uninvested cash. Don't leave cash sitting in a brokerage account for a long time. Most brokerages allow you to transfer cash in and out of your account from an outside bank by using automated clearing house (ACH) technology. You can create an ACH link between your brokerage account and savings account so money earns interest when it's not invested. Be sure to set up a savings account outside the brokerage that pays a decent amount of interest. Check `https://bankrate.com/` to find banks offering decent interest rates, about 2 percent in 2019.

Buying Stocks and Mutual Funds without a Broker

Can you be an online investor without an online broker? Sure. Some investors want to buy stocks but don't want to bother with opening an account with an online brokerage firm. There's nothing that says you need to have a broker to buy and sell stocks or mutual funds.

Stocks: Direct investments

Direct investments are where you buy the stock straight from the company. Many large companies, such as Coca-Cola, Procter & Gamble (P&G), and Walt Disney, allow you to buy and sell your stock with them and avoid a broker. Many direct investment programs are connected with dividend reinvestment plans (DRIPs), where the companies let you use dividend payments to buy, or reinvest, additional shares.

If you're interested in going with a direct investment program, you can visit the investor-relations section of the company's website to see whether it offers one. Many companies allow you to participate in direct investment programs through their *transfer agent* — a company with the responsibility of tracking ownership of shares.

Coca-Cola, for instance, has an elaborate shareholder investment program that lets you buy as little as $500 in stock — they'll even reinvest the dividends. You can read about this program, offered through the transfer agent Computershare (shown in Figure 4-8), at `www-us.computershare.com/Investor/#DirectStock/Index`. EQ by Equiniti, at `www.shareowneronline.com/UserManagement/WFIndex.aspx`, is another provider of direct stock purchase plans for many companies.

The other way to find direct investment programs is through directory services, such as The Moneypaper's Directinvesting.com (`www.directinvesting.com/`). The site provides a search function so that you can see whether a company you're interested in sells shares directly to investors. Just enter the symbol of the company you're interested in, and you can see whether the company offers a direct investment plan.

Here are the upsides to direct investing:

>> **Potential commission savings:** The fees charged by direct investment programs can be lower than what some brokers charge. Coca-Cola, for instance, charges $3 if you pay for it using an electronic transfer from your bank, and $2 if you set up a recurring order to buy the stock.

>> **Dividend reinvestments:** Dividends can often be reinvested for free. If you're with a broker, you would often incur a commission to reinvest a dividend into the company stock.

FIGURE 4-8: Computershare allows investors to buy shares of many companies directly from its website.

As you might suspect, direct investing has some downsides:

>> **Not free for all transactions:** Some companies even charge commissions that exceed what deep discount brokerages charge for certain services. For instance, Coca-Cola charges $25 if you want to sell the shares immediately. There may be loads of additional fees, including quarterly maintenance fees. Be sure to check the company's website, usually in a document called a direct stock plan *prospectus,* and understand all the fees that are charged.

>> **Setup fees:** Although opening an online brokerage account is usually free, some direct investment plans charge a fee to get started. Some plans also have minimum initial deposits. Coca-Cola, for instance, requires a $500 investment for a new account. Some charge setup fees.

>> **Limited universe:** By using direct investment plans, you're narrowing your universe of possible investments to the hundreds of the largely older, blue-chip companies that offer these programs. That means you miss out on younger or smaller companies.

>> **Administrative hassles:** With direct investment plans, you need to manage all your separate accounts, which could be a pain if you have ten or more investments. You also won't get access to any of the tax assistance or research the brokers provide.

Mutual funds: Straight from the mutual fund company

Mutual funds gather money from many investors and use the cash to invest in a basket of assets. When you buy a mutual fund, you're joining a pool with other investors that own assets, rather than owning the assets yourself. You can read more about mutual funds in Chapter 10.

Nearly all brokers let you buy and sell mutual funds in addition to stocks and other investments. And sometimes trading in mutual funds can make sense, especially if it's free. Most brokers have a list of transaction-free mutual funds you can buy and sell for no charge. Schwab, for instance, lets you buy and sell thousands of mutual funds that are part of its OneSource Select program at no cost (`www.schwab.com/public/schwab/investing/accounts_products/investment/mutual_funds/no_load_mutual_funds`).

However, if you're not going to buy from the transaction-free lists, you're wasting your money buying mutual funds this way. Schwab, for instance, charges $50 to buy a mutual fund not on its list (selling is free). Don't let your broker's commission schedule determine which mutual funds you buy.

REMEMBER

One of the best things about mutual funds is that you can buy them with no transaction fee if you deal directly with the mutual fund company. This feature can be a tremendous advantage, especially if you're making frequent and regular investments into a fund. After you figure out what fund you want to buy, log on to the mutual fund company's website, open an account, and buy it. You'll save yourself some cash.

WARNING

When opening an account with a mutual fund company to buy a mutual fund, be sure to open a *mutual fund* account, not a brokerage account. Several mutual fund companies, including Vanguard and Fidelity, offer brokerage accounts in addition to mutual fund accounts, and the fees are completely different.

Opening and Setting Up Your Account

After you've made the decision about which broker to go with, the hard work is done. All you need to do to get started is open an account and get your cash to the broker. You can do this online or through the mail. If you're comfortable doing this online, which I imagine you are because you're reading *Online Investing For Dummies,* the online route is definitely the way to go because the cash can be transferred from your bank account and you can be up and running in a few hours or days. Signing up by mailing in a check and application, on the other hand, could take weeks.

TIP

Don't be shocked by the seemingly endless number of questions you'll be asked when setting up a new account. It's common for the broker to ask for your social security number and other personal information. Given the sensitivity of the information you'll be sharing, that's all the more reason to make sure that you understand online security by reading the previous sections. Please don't use the Wi-Fi connection at your local park when setting up your account.

The checklist of what you need to know

The biggest button on most broker's website is the Open an Account or Start Now button, so you won't have trouble finding it. Typically, that's all you need to click to launch the area of the website that can set up your account. (If you want to sign up through the mail, click a link to download the necessary forms.)

Typically, you need to know three things to complete the application:

>> **The kind of account you want to create:** This is usually a cash account or margin account. I cover margin accounts in more detail in Chapter 5.

>> **The number of people associated with this account:** Is this just for you or for you and a spouse? This determines whether you create an individual or joint account. You can review this in Chapter 3.

>> **The tax status of the account:** Is this a taxable account or a tax-deferred account, such as an IRA or a fund for college? You can review the differences in Chapter 3.

TIP

If you're opening a retirement account, make sure the broker you're considering doesn't charge a monthly, quarterly, or annual maintenance fee. Most brokers waive maintenance fees if you're opening an IRA account because they figure you'll keep your money with them for quite some time. Many also waive the minimum deposits. For these reasons, if you're just starting out with online investing, you might consider opening a retirement account first.

The checklist of what you need to have

You need these bits of info if you want to set up an account:

>> **Identification:** You need ID such as a driver's license or a government-issued ID card.

- » **Social Security number:** If you're creating a joint account, you'll also need the Social Security number of the person you're setting up the account with. This information is used for tax reporting.

- » **Bank statement of the financial institution from which you'll transfer money:** The statement contains the account and bank routing numbers you'll need to instruct the broker to get your cash. Keep in mind that some brokers won't let you open an account with electronically transferred money if you're depositing less than $500. In those cases, you need to mail a check.

- » **Address of your employer:** This information is necessary if you're an officer, director, or large shareholder of a publicly traded company.

See, that wasn't hard. And here's the best part: Now that you've entered all your information and funded your account, you're all set to start investing.

IN THIS CHAPTER

» **Understanding the different ways your broker can hold your shares**

» **Differentiating between different types of orders**

» **Knowing the potential rewards and risks of buying on margin**

» **Appreciating the upsides and downsides to trading after hours**

» **Using put and call options**

» **Finding data about options**

Chapter **5**

Getting It Done: How to Enter and Execute Trades

All the theory in the world about online investing won't do you a bit of good if you can't seal the deal and execute your trades. *Trade execution* is the process of logging on to your online broker and buying or selling investments. You might be wondering what's so hard about buying a stock: Just log on to the online broker's website and click the Buy button. And in some cases, you're right. But sometimes you want to be more exacting. You have ways to tailor your buys and sells so that your broker carries out the transaction precisely how you want it to be handled. For instance, you might want to buy a stock only if it falls below $25 a share, or you might want your broker to automatically sell shares if they fall below a certain price.

In this chapter, I start at the beginning and go over all the ways you can hold your stock and how that decision affects how your trades are executed. Then, I cover the main ways to enter orders — ranging from market orders to limit orders — and talk about the advantages and costs of each. For the adventurous types, this chapter examines buying investments using borrowed money, called buying on *margin*, and also discusses the risks and returns of trading after hours. I then discuss the basics of options, which present unique ways for you to boost your returns or cut your losses, depending on how you use them.

Understanding How Stock Trades and Shares Are Handled

When you buy or sell a share of stock online, you click a few buttons and everything is done. In a few seconds, if even that long, you'll often have a confirmation sitting in the messages section of your online broker's website or in your email box. The *confirmation* is a memo that shows you what stock you bought or sold, the number of shares involved, and the price at which the trade was executed.

But perhaps unbeknownst to you, after you clicked the Buy button, your trade wiggled its way through countless computer networks where buyers and sellers competed for your order to buy stock until it was ultimately *executed*, or filled. You might never need to know how the process works, much like you might never need to know what's going on under the hood of your car. However, the process is an important part of investing online, so the following sections describe a day in the life of a trade that's on its way from being an order on your computer screen to a done deal.

Ways you can hold your investments

The biggest factor that influences how your investments make their way to Wall Street depends on how you hold your shares. The three main types are as follows:

>> **Street name ownership** is the most common with most online brokers. It's so common that unless you tell your online broker to do otherwise, your broker will assume that you want your shares owned in street name.

>> **Holding paper stock certificates** is the old-school way of owning stocks. This form of stock ownership was glamorized in the 2019's film, "Mary Poppins Returns." Even so, it's generally not a good idea for the reasons I outline in the section "Paper certificate ownership," later in this chapter. If you insist on paper certificates, let your online broker know so that they can be mailed to you.

>> **Direct registration** is when the company that issues the stock holds your stock for you but lists you, not your broker, as the owner. This form of ownership is common if you buy stock through a direct stock purchase plan, as I discuss in Chapter 4.

Street name ownership

If you're not sure how to hold your shares, street name ownership is probably your best bet. For most investors, the advantages of this form of ownership outweigh the few negatives.

Shares kept in street name are listed on the books of the company in your broker's name, not yours. The broker then lists you as the owner of the shares on its books. That might seem scary, I know, but you do have safeguards against broker fraud, as I describe in Chapter 4.

Street name ownership has several advantages:

>> **Easy handling of dividends:** Dividends paid by companies you own stock in are sent directly to your online broker, which then deposits them to your account. For online investors used to doing almost everything on a website, this feature is a huge advantage and saves you from having to deposit dividend checks with your bank or broker.

>> **Central source of company documents:** If you're like most online investors, you probably own shares of several companies. When you own the stock in street name, all the paper correspondence sent out by the companies first goes to your broker. The broker then forwards it to you. This situation has a giant advantage, especially if you move often: You can just let your broker know where you live and not worry about missing important documents. If you've asked to only hear from companies electronically, rather than on paper, your brokerage will email you links so you can read the materials.

Your broker can also help make sure that you get everything that's due to you. Periodically, a company you invested in years ago is sued or forced by regulators to make payments to past investors. If you own the stock in street name, you can be certain to receive these old payments, even if you're living somewhere else, because your broker knows where to find you.

>> **Security:** It's up to the brokerage to safeguard your stock. And that's a good thing because getting paper stock certificates replaced, if you lose them, can be a hassle and an expense.

>> **Easy to sell:** If your online broker has your shares on hand, you can sell them anytime you want without having to mail in a paper certificate first. That saves you time and postage, as well as the worry about sending an important document through the mail.

Sounds great, right? But, street name ownership does come with a few disadvantages:

>> **Potential delays in dividend payments:** Some brokers are quicker about crediting dividends to your account than others. You might have to wait a few days to receive a dividend after it was paid by the company. Delays, however, are pretty rare now that much of these accounting matters are handled electronically.

>> **Hassle if your broker fails:** Getting stock certificates transferred back to your name might be harder if your brokerage becomes insolvent. Some victims of the Bernie Madoff financial scam have found this out the hard way.

Paper certificate ownership

Maybe the cons of street ownership are enough to make you consider Route No. 2 — the paper certificate option. The advantages to paper certificate ownership include the following:

>> **Cutting out the middleman:** Company materials come straight to you, which can reduce the time it takes to get some documents.

>> **Using certificates as loan collateral:** When you have the actual certificates, you might have a little easier time using the stock value to secure a loan.

>> **Having actual certificates makes it easier to give them as gifts or for display:** A paper certificate can be framed and given to young investors as a present. There's something nice about having an item to wrap.

>> **Being in control:** With the certificates in your possession, you know where they are and can decide who can have them.

In all honesty, though, I have to tell you that the main disadvantages to paper certificate ownership far outweigh the advantages. The disadvantages of paper certificate ownership include the following:

>> **Difficulty in selling:** You might not be able to sell the stock as quickly as you'd like. Paper certificates must be mailed to your broker or to the company or a firm it hires to handle such matters so the stock can be sold. Nearly all online

brokers charge significantly more to process paper certificates and strongly discourage investors from using them.

>> **Burden of keeping your contact information current with the company:** It's up to you to make sure that the company has your current address.

>> **Responsibility for safekeeping the certificates:** It's up to you to keep the paper certificates safe. You'll probably have to spend money to get a safe deposit box or at least lock the paper stock certificates in your home somewhere. And when you send them through the mail, you will need to insure them in case they get lost. Some financial institutions recommend insuring mailed certificates for 2 percent of the market value, for reasons I explain later in this chapter.

If you decide to hold paper certificates rather than listing them in street name, don't lose them. Getting lost paper certificates replaced can be a hassle and somewhat costly. If the unfortunate event does occur, though, here's what to do to try to make it right:

1. **Call or email your broker or the company's transfer agent and explain what happened.**

   Transfer agents are firms that companies hire to handle the processing of shares. The transfer agent will likely ask you to say how you lost the shares in a written report.

2. **Buy an indemnity bond with the help of your transfer agent.**

   An indemnity bond protects the company that issued the lost stock in case someone tries to cash it in later. Indemnity bonds usually cost up to 2 percent of the market value of the stock you lost.

For more details on what to do if you lose a stock certificate, the Securities and Exchange Commission maintains advice at www.sec.gov/answers/lostcert.htm.

Direct registration

If all my talk about the hassles of losing paper certificates makes you long for another way of owning stock, you can always go for direct registration. You get several advantages from having direct registration, including

>> Company correspondence coming straight to you

>> Being able to sell shares without mailing certificates to your broker

>> Not having to worry about keeping the certificates safe

BUYING PAPER STOCK CERTIFICATES ONLINE

Because of the disadvantages listed elsewhere in this chapter, it doesn't make much sense to hold paper stock certificates for the shares in your portfolio. Paper stock certificates, as a result, are quickly becoming extinct (some companies don't even offer them). But the scarcity makes paper certificates even more attractive to some. A few investors still like to buy paper stock certificates for gifts. Yet other folks collect old stock certificates much like you'd collect stamps or coins. There's even a word for the practice of collecting stock certificates: *scripophily*. If this interests you, check out these online services that let you buy paper stock certificates:

- **GiveAShare** (www.giveashare.com/) and **Frame A Stock** (http://uniquestockgift.com/) are single-share sales sites that understand the lost art and beauty of many stock certificates. Both let you buy a share of stock in companies which have certificates that are popular with individual investors. Both of these services even frame the certificates for you. The sites make it easy to find the perfect stock for the need. You can sort through the available certificates based on the occasion, recipient, or interest. For men, GiveAShare recommends Harley-Davidson and Boston Beer, and for women it suggests Tiffany and Starbucks. Some certificates are also popular because of the artwork on them, with Disney being the best example.

  Just be forewarned that you'll pay much more to acquire stock this way than through an online broker. In addition to the share price and framing fees, you also pay up to a $25 transfer agent fee to acquire the stock. A $38-a-share stock might easily cost more than $100 by the time all the fees are added.

- **eBay** (www.ebay.com/), not surprisingly, is a source for paper certificates. But because eBay isn't licensed to sell securities like stocks, it has to be careful about what kinds of certificates its members sell; otherwise, eBay risks running afoul of securities law. Only two types of stock certificates may be sold on eBay. The first type concerns old or collectible certificates of defunct companies, such as old railroads or Internet companies. The other type that may be sold on eBay are single-share stock certificates packaged as gifts and marked as being nontransferable. eBay requires that these certificates sell for at least twice the current market value of the stock as evidence that they're priced based on their keepsake value.

- **Scripophily.com** (www.scripophily.net) and other certificate collection sites provide prices on some hard-to-find certificates. Even if you're not a collector, it's interesting to see what some of the certificates go for when they're popular with collectors. Some Standard Oil stock certificates, personally signed by John D. Rockefeller, for instance, sell for $1,500 or more. Pixar stock certificates, decorated with characters from *Toy Story* like Buzz Lightyear, were a hot commodity when the company was bought by Disney. Old shares of *Playboy* were popular for their, um, artwork, because the company's certificates used to display some, let's say, assets. The old certificates have become even more sought after since *Playboy*'s new certificates were changed to be more PG. The old shares sell for $400 or more. And some infamous companies, like Enron, also have collectible value even though the companies themselves have largely vanished, as shown in the following figure.

Direct registration has two main downsides:

>> **Inability to sell shares immediately:** Selling shares you hold in direct registration almost always takes longer than you might think. You may instruct the company to sell the shares, but your request is generally put into a pool and executed at set times in the future, such as later in the day, week, or month. You may also sell your shares by instructing the company's transfer agent to electronically send the stock to your online broker. (A *transfer agent* is a firm hired by a company to track its shareholders and record transactions.) The transfer process can take a few days, so the price might change by the time you're able to sell the stock.

>> **Pool of stock choices is somewhat reduced:** Most companies offer direct registration, but not all. Many of the stocks you want to buy might not offer direct registration.

A second in the life of a trade

When you buy or sell a stock on your online broker's site, your order is usually filled in a fraction of a second. But before that transaction is completed, in milliseconds your order snakes its way through an advanced security trading system that has taken decades to build. Just a few years ago, it could take about 12 seconds for a trade to go from your desk to the floor of the New York Stock Exchange and back. Now that most of the steps have been computerized, the process takes less than a second. Using NASDAQ as an example, here's what happens in the one second it takes to execute an online trade:

1. You enter your order with your online broker.

2. The order is placed in a database.

3. The database checks all the different markets that trade the stock and looks for the best price. The different markets might include the NASDAQ and New York Stock Exchange in addition to electronic communications networks (ECNs). ECNs are computerized networks that connect buyers and sellers of stocks.

4. The market that successfully matched the buyer and seller sends a confirmation to both parties' brokers.

5. The order and the price are reported to the regulatory bodies that oversee trading activity so that they can be displayed to all investors.

6. NASDAQ stores a record of the trade in case regulators want to study past transactions.

7. NASDAQ sends a contract to the broker who sold the shares and the broker who bought them.

After all that is completed, the brokers have three days, called T+3, to exchange the cash and shares in a process called *settlement.* Then the money or shares are officially in your account.

When you buy or sell, most online brokerages will check the prices everywhere to see where they can get the best price. If you can get a better price through an electronic network rather than through a traditional exchange, that's where your trade will occur. Some brokers let you choose where you want your order filled through something called *direct routing.* If your account is set up for direct routing, you can instruct the broker to execute at the exchange or electronic trading venue of your choice.

WARNING

Direct routing is a bad idea for most online investors. Online brokers have computers that shop your order to all the top markets automatically. They're required by regulators to get you the best available price. If you direct-route your order, you lose this advantage and could wind up paying more.

Getting It Done: Executing Your Trades

If you're buying something, such as a new computer, from a regular store, you can either buy it or not. End of discussion. But in more casual marketplaces, such as flea markets or garage sales, where prices are fluid and changing, there's a strategy to buying and selling things. It might surprise you that buying stock is more like a flea market than shopping at your local Walmart, where prices are set. Because investments are priced in real time through active bidding between buyers and sellers, there are techniques to buying and selling.

Types of orders

When dealing with investments, you have five main ways to buy or sell them online:

>> **Market orders** are the most common types of orders and the ones you will probably use the most. This is where you tell your broker to sell your shares at the best price someone is willing to pay right now or buy shares at the price currently being offered. Because these orders are executed almost immediately and are straightforward, they typically have the lowest commissions. (In Chapter 4, where I discuss different online brokers' commissions, I concentrate on market orders because they're the most common.)

>> **Limit orders** let you be pickier about the price you're willing to take for a stock you're selling or the price you're willing to pay if you're buying. With a limit order, you tell your online broker the price you're willing to take if you're selling stocks and the price you're willing to pay if you're buying. The order will execute only if your price, or something better, is reached.

For example, imagine you own 100 shares of ABC Company, which are trading for $50 a share. The stock has been on a tear, but you're convinced it will fall dramatically soon, by your estimate to $30. You could just sell the stock outright with a market order, but you don't want to because you're a bit opportunistic and don't want to miss out on any gains in case you're wrong. A limit order could be the answer. Here, you'd instruct your broker to sell the stock if it fell to $45 a share. If you're right, and the stock falls to $45 a share, your online broker will sell as many shares as possible at that price. You can also set a time limit on limit orders and tell your broker to let them expire after a few days or weeks. Limit orders can also protect you during market malfunctions. If there's a *flash crash* — or a quick and dramatic drop in stock prices due to rapid-fire trading — a limit order can save you from getting a disappointing price. Rather than entering a market order to sell (which would be executed at a depressed price during a flash crash) putting in a limit order could avoid selling during the tumult.

The precision of limit orders can be a shortcoming, too. Limit orders are filled only at the price you set. If the stock falls further than the price you set, the broker might be able to sell only some of the shares, or none, at that price. If that happens, you're stuck with the stock. In the preceding example, if ABC Company opened for trading and plunged straight to $25, never stopping at $45, you will still be holding the stock. This is a serious limitation that can give you a false sense of security.

>> **Stop market orders** are similar to limit orders in that they let you set a price you want to buy or sell shares at. They have an important difference, though, that addresses some of the shortcomings of limit orders. When a stock hits the price you designated, the order converts into a market order and executes immediately.

Imagine again that you have 100 shares of ABC Company, which are trading for $50 a share. But this time, you enter a stop market order for $45. And again, you wake up to find the stock plunged instantly to $25. This time, though, all your stock would have been sold. But, maybe not at $45. Your online broker will sell the shares at whatever the price was the moment your order converted to a market order, which in this case could have been $25.

>> **Stop limit orders** are like stop market orders, but they're designed to cure the danger that your shares will be blindly unloaded when a stock is moving. Stop limit orders are customizable. First, you can set the *activation price.* When the activation price is hit, the order turns into a limit order with the limit price you've set.

Okay, ABC Company is trading for $50 a share when you enter a stop limit order with an activation price of $45 and a limit price of $35. It would work like this: Again, you wake up to find that the stock plunged instantly to $25. This time, your broker would turn your order into a limit order after it fell below $45. When the stock fell to $35, the broker would try to fill orders at that price if possible. Most likely, though, you'd still be stuck with shares. But unlike with the stop market order, you would not dump the shares when they fell as low as $25.

>> **Trailing stops** are a way to keep up with the times. With regular limit orders, they're either executed or they expire. Trailing stop orders get around this problem by letting you tell your broker to sell a stock if it falls by a certain number of points or a percentage.

If you're buying and selling individual stocks, trailing stops can be a good idea. Even before you buy a stock, you should have an idea of how far you'll let it fall before you cut your losses. Some investment professionals suggest never letting a stock fall more than 10 percent below the price you paid. If this sounds like a good idea to you, a trailing stop could work for you.

Costs of different orders

Market orders are the most straightforward orders, so it shouldn't be that surprising that they're also usually the least expensive. Limit orders, though, can help save investors from volatile markets. During the Flash Crash of 2010, prices of several stocks, including giants such as Procter & Gamble, plummeted for about 15 minutes for no reason other than a system malfunction. Had you entered a market order to sell P&G during those 15 minutes, you would have sold at the current market price, which was 20 percent below where it was supposed to be. However, if you used a limit order that was close to the accurate market price, your order would not have been executed. An increasing chorus of market experts are urging investors to use limit orders to protect themselves from such market malfunctions. Luckily, such events are rare.

WARNING

A few brokers charge extra for limit orders, so check the commission fees before you start trading.

Tailoring your trades even more

When you enter an order for a stock, you have a few other levers you can pull, including

>> **Designating lots:** Many people buy the same stock many times. Each time you buy, that bundle of stock is called a *lot*. When you sell, your broker will assume you'd like to sell the lot that you've held for the longest time for recordkeeping purposes. This method, called *first in, first out,* or FIFO, is the standard and what the Internal Revenue Service expects. If, for tax reasons, you'd like to sell a specific lot that's not the oldest, you can tell your broker which lot you'd like to sell.

>> **Setting time frames:** You can enter an order for a stock that is active only for the day you place the trade. If it's not filled — perhaps a limit order for the price you ask for isn't reached — the order expires. That time frame is called *day only*. You can also enter orders and let them stay active until you cancel them. That time frame is called *good till canceled*. Good-till-canceled orders are generally active for up to six months after you enter the order, but that limit varies for each broker.

>> **Placing rules:** When you issue an "all or none" restriction on your trade, your broker must completely fill the order or not fill it at all. Say you want to sell 100 shares of stock at a limit price of $45, but the broker can find buyers for only 10 shares at that price. If you stipulated all or none, none of your 100 shares would be sold.

Going off the Beaten Path with Different Trading Techniques

If all you could do was buy and sell investments, traders would get awfully bored. Investors looking for a little more excitement can dabble with some more advanced ways to enter online trades that go beyond everything I have discussed in this chapter so far. The most common ways to get a little fancier with your trades are

>> **Selling stock short:** This method lets you make money even if a stock declines in value.

>> **Buying stock on margin:** This method lets you bet big on a stock you think will go up. You borrow money to buy stock, which can magnify your returns if it rises in value.

>> **Trading after hours:** Perfect for night-owl investors who aren't satisfied with the 9:30 a.m. to 4 p.m. EST regular trading hours of the NYSE and NASDAQ.

Cashing in when stocks fall: Selling stock short

Most investors are pretty optimistic folks. When they go to a restaurant, see long lines, and enjoy the food, they rush home to buy stock in the company that owns the restaurant. These types of investors, who hope to profit from a company's good times and rising profits, are called *longs*.

But there's another class of investors, called *shorts*, who do just the opposite. They search the Internet for news stories about diners getting food poisoning at a restaurant, for instance, and look for ways to cash in on the stock falling.

Investors looking to *short a stock* do it through four steps:

1. They borrow the stock they want to bet against.

   Short sellers contact their brokers to find shares of the stock they think will go down and they request to borrow the shares. The broker then locates another investor who owns the shares and borrows them with a promise to return the shares at a prearranged later date. The shares are then given to the short seller. Don't think you're getting to borrow the shares for nothing, though. You'll have to pay fees or interest to the broker for the privilege.

2. They immediately sell the shares they've borrowed.

   The short sellers then pocket the cash from the sale.

3. They wait for the stock to fall and then buy the shares back at the new, lower price.

4. They return the shares to the brokerage they borrowed them from and pocket the difference.

Here's an example: Shares of ABC Company are trading for $40 a share, which you think is way too high. You contact your broker, who finds 100 shares from another investor and lets you borrow them. You sell the shares and pocket $4,000. Two weeks later, the company reports its CEO has been stealing money and the stock falls to $25 a share. You buy 100 shares of ABC Company for $2,500, give the shares back to the brokerage you borrowed them from, and pocket a $1,500 profit.

REMEMBER

When you short a stock, you need to be aware of some extra costs. Most brokerages, for instance, charge fees or interest to borrow the stock. Also, if the company pays a dividend between the time you borrowed the stock and when you returned it, you must pay the dividend out of your pocket. You're responsible for the dividend payment, even if you already sold the stock and didn't receive it.

Tracking the short sellers

You might be interested to find out how many investors are shorting a stock you own, a statistic known as *short interest*. Some investors even incorporate tracking short interest in their strategies by seeking stocks that are heavily shorted, on the theory if the shorts are wrong the stock might surge higher in a *short squeeze*. A short squeeze is what happens when the short sellers get nervous that a stock they're betting against will rise and they rush out and buy the stock back so that they can return it to the brokers they borrowed it from. Short squeezes can cause a stock to skyrocket as the shorts buy shares.

Exchanges release short interest data on stocks on the third Monday of each month. You can easily get the data online. A helpful source I've found is NASDAQ. com, shown in Figure 5-1. You can look up the level of short interest on many stocks, including some that trade on other exchanges such as the New York Stock Exchange. Here's how:

1. **Point your browser to** www.nasdaq.com/.

2. **In the Search field, enter the stock's name or symbol, and then click the name of the company when it pops up or click the Search button.**

3. **Choose Short Interest from the menu on the left side of the screen.**

You see a detailed list that shows you the number of shares being shorted, as shown in Figure 5-1. That number in itself doesn't tell you much because different companies have different numbers of shares trading, or *shares outstanding.* So, to put the level of short interest in perspective, you also get to see the *average daily share volume* — the number of shares that usually trade hands in a given day. Lastly, you see *days to cover,* which is the number of days it would take, on average, for the number of shares that are being shorted to trade. Days to cover is calculated by dividing the number of shares shorted by the average daily share volume. The bottom line? The higher the days to cover, the greater the amount of real short interest in the stock.

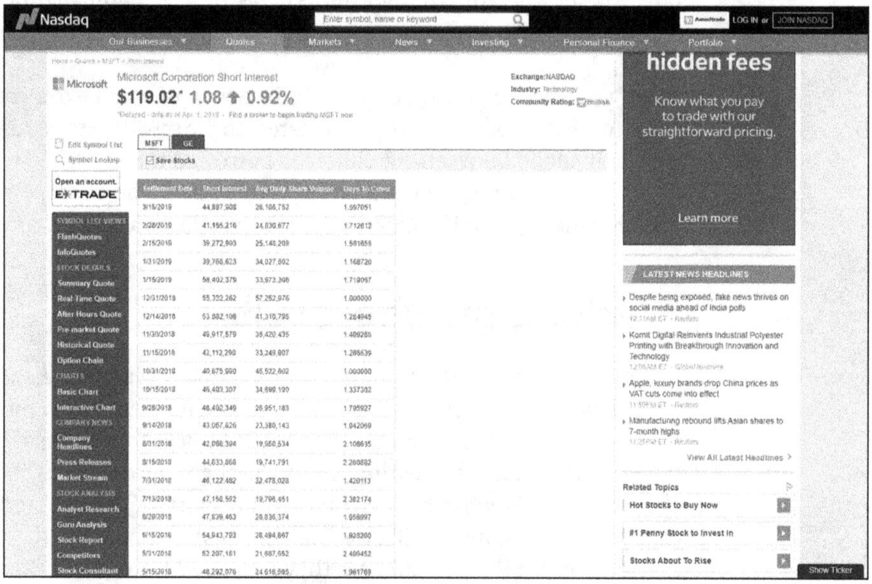

FIGURE 5-1: NASDAQ.com lets you track how many investors are betting against the company by providing data on short interest.

Living on borrowed time: Buying stock on margin

The standard brokerage account is called a *cash account.* That's where you deposit cold hard cash with the broker and use that pooled money to buy stocks. But when you set up your account, as I describe in Chapter 4, you can also request a *margin account.* This is an account type that lets you borrow money you can use to buy stocks.

Buying stock on margin isn't for the faint of heart. Remember, if you borrow money, you must not only pay interest on that cash but also pay back the money you borrowed even if the stock goes down. Buying on margin is generally a good idea *only* if you're a highly risk-tolerant investor. You can determine your taste for risk by reading Chapter 1.

As is the case anytime you borrow to invest, buying stock on margin can boost your profit when you're right and sting badly when you're wrong. When you buy a stock that goes up, using margin, you can boost your returns. But if you bet wrong and buy one that goes down, margin magnifies your loss. To understand why, take a look at the following example.

Imagine buying 100 shares of a stock that goes from $15 a share to $32 a share. Your investment of $1,500 turns into $3,200. Assuming that you paid a $5 commission to buy and sell the stock, your rate of return, as explained in Chapter 1, is 112.3 percent and your profit is $1,690.

It's calculated like this:

1. **Subtract the commission of $5 from the sale proceeds of $3,200. Write this down.**

2. **Add the commission of $5 to the amount paid of $1,500. Write this down.**

3. **Subtract the answer in Step 2 from the answer in Step 1. Divide that answer by the answer in Step 2. Multiply by 100.**

That's not bad. But if you bought on margin, your return would be even greater. Here's what I mean. Say your broker has a 60 percent *margin requirement,* meaning that you must put up 60 cents of every $1 you invest. In this case, you'd have to put up $900 of your own cash because that's 60 percent of the $1,500 purchase price. You then borrow the remaining $600 at 10 percent interest. Your gain, thanks to margin, goes from 112.3 to 180 percent.

Here's how your rate of return when using margin is calculated, using the previous facts as an example:

1. **Subtract the commission of $5 from the sale proceeds of $3,200.**

   Write this down: $3,195.

2. **Add the commission of $5 to the amount paid of $1,500.**

   Write this down: $1,505.

3. **Multiply the amount you borrowed, $600, by 0.10 to calculate the interest you owe.**

   You use 0.10 because that is 10 percent converted from percentage to decimal form. You get $60.

4. **Subtract the answer in Step 2 from the answer in Step 1.**

   Subtract that difference by the answer in Step 3. You get $1,630.

5. **Divide the answer in Step 4 by $905, which is the amount of your own money you put up plus the commission you paid to buy the stock.**

   Multiply by 100. The answer is 180.1 percent.

TIP

If the preceding is too much math for you, do it online. Most online brokers' sites calculate your margin requirements. If you're interested in buying on margin, make sure that the broker has margin-tracking capabilities. Figure 5-2 shows Fidelity's Margin Calculator.

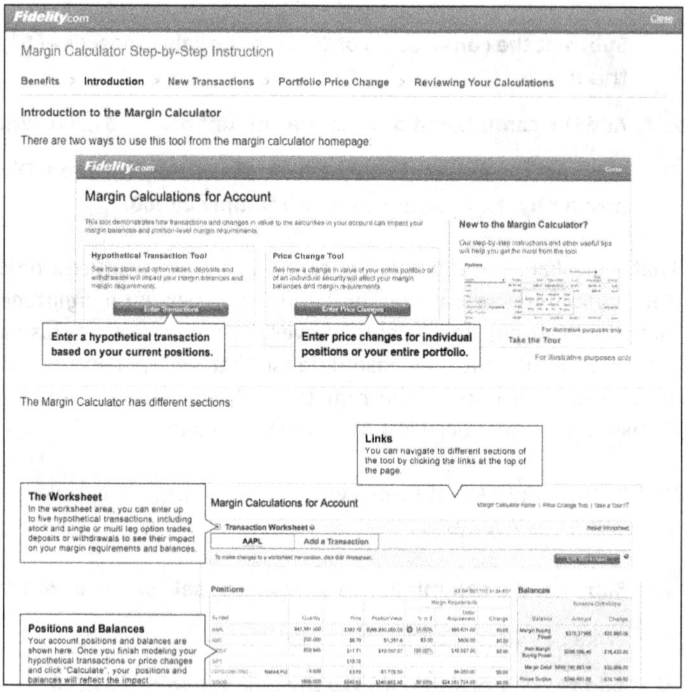

FIGURE 5-2:
Fidelity's Margin Calculator helps you measure how much stock you can buy with borrowed money and estimate the costs.

The call you don't want to get: The margin call

Most online brokers require investors to maintain a certain percentage of ownership of stocks relative to what has been borrowed. This is called the *maintenance margin,* and it's typically 30 percent or higher at most firms. If a stock rises, this isn't a problem because the value of the loan becomes a smaller slice of the position. But if the stock falls in value, the shareholder's stake shrinks. If it falls below 30 percent, the broker requires the investor to put up more cash, or the shares will be sold.

Imagine that, when you bought the previous $15-a-share stock, you borrowed 40 percent or $6 a share, meaning that your ownership stake is $9 a share or 60 percent. But say the stock falls to $7 a share. Because you borrowed $6 a share, you own only $1 of the $7-a-share price. That means you own just 14 percent of the stock, violating the 30 percent margin requirement.

If you still have questions about investing on margin, Dummies.com provides an easy-to-follow description of margin at `www.dummies.com/how-to/content/buying-stock-on-margin.html`.

WARNING

Some online brokers can crunch the numbers for you automatically and let you know when margin calls will kick in. And you can be certain that online brokers won't waste any time contacting you for a margin call. But if the preceding math seems too complicated to do yourself, you might want to steer clear of using margin.

The nightshift: Trading in the extended hours

One of the great things about stocks and bonds is they're usually easy to sell. Unlike real estate, which usually requires hiring a Realtor who sprinkles air freshener through the house and invites prospective buyers to an open house, you can sell stocks pretty much instantly. The main stock exchanges are open every business day, for *regular trading hours,* from 9:30 a.m. to 4 p.m., EST.

But you can trade before 9:30 a.m. in what's called *premarket trading* and after 4 p.m. in *after-hours trading.* Here are several reasons why some investors pay attention to after-hours trading:

>> **A chance to react to late-breaking news:** Some active traders believe they can use after-hours trading as a way to profit from news companies that might report *after the close.* It's common for companies to release important

information, either good or bad, after 4 p.m. to give investors time to digest. But investors don't have to wait and can place trades after hours.

>> **An indication of how late-breaking news might affect the stock when regular trading hours begin:** You don't have to be a high-profile online trader to get access to after-hours quotes. Most online brokers' sites and apps as well as financial websites discussed in Chapter 2, including Yahoo! Finance (`https://finance.yahoo.com/`) as well as search engines such as Bing (`www.bing.com`), let you see how stocks and indexes are trading after hours. Many of those sites — as well as Google Finance (`https://finance.google.com/`) — also show you the after-hours *volume,* which is the number of shares trading hands. Volume is important when looking at after-hours trading because the more shares that are trading hands, the more reliable the price is.

WARNING

Trading after hours isn't a good idea for most online investors for several reasons:

>> **Lower participation:** Fewer buyers and sellers participate in after-hours trading, so there's a chance you'll get a lower price for a stock you're selling or pay more for a stock you're buying than had you waited for regular trading to begin. After-hours trading attracts little interest. Only a small portion of the trades placed each day on the NYSE are conducted after hours.

>> **Limit orders are required:** Most online brokers accept after-hours trades only if they're entered as limit orders. Limit orders present their own shortcomings, as explained in the "Types of orders" section, earlier in the chapter.

>> **Unpredictable pricing:** Sometimes stock prices set after hours aren't necessarily harbingers for how things will open the next day. They can be a poor indicator of the next day's trading if the after-hours volume is low.

Knowing Your Options: Basic Ways to Best Use Options

If you've ever put down a deposit so that someone would hold something for you, you know what an option is. For instance, you might pay a landlord a $100 non-refundable deposit to hold an apartment so that it'll be available for you if you decide to rent it. If you don't rent the apartment, you're out the $100.

Options are the financial version of that idea. If you own an *option*, you have the right, but not the obligation, to buy or sell an investment, including shares of stock by a certain preset time in the future. Options can be powerful in the right hands, and they can either help you boost your returns or reduce your risk, depending on how you use them.

I often describe options as the financial version of dynamite. If used prudently and safely, options can remove perils in the way of your financial goals. But if abused, misunderstood, or used recklessly, options can blow your financial plan to smithereens.

When you own an option, you have the power to make someone follow through on a trade for an *underlying asset,* such as a stock, no matter what happens to the price. Options expire on the third Friday of every month.

Need an example? Say that ABC Company's stock is currently trading for $30 a share, and you own an option to buy it for $20 a share on its *expiration date* in one month. That option is worth $10 a share, the difference between $30 and $20, which is its *intrinsic value.* If you own an option like this that lets you buy a stock for less than its current value, it's *in the money.* But if the price you can buy the stock at, known as the *exercise price,* is higher than the current price, the option is *out of the money.*

The different types of options

Option strategies can get pretty complex. If you're serious about trading them, you can find out all the gory details in *Trading Options For Dummies,* by Joe Duarte (Wiley). But I'm perfectly willing to give you the basics.

Two types of options exist:

>> **Calls** give their owners the right to buy a stock at a certain price (called the *exercise* or *strike price*) at a certain time (called the *expiration date*) in the future. One call contract gives you the right to buy 100 shares of the underlying stock.

>> **Puts** give their owners the right to sell a stock at a certain price at a certain time in the future. One put contract gives you the right to sell 100 shares of the underlying stock.

Basic options strategies

The real beauty of both call and put options kicks in because you can either buy or sell them to other investors. That gives you four distinct strategies:

>> **Buying a call:** When you buy a call, you have the right to force someone to sell you the stock at the exercise price you agreed upon ahead of time. You make money on a call when the stock price rises above the exercise price. This strategy is for investors who are convinced a stock will rise and want to bet big. Buying a call isn't free. You must pay the seller for the option, in what's called the *premium.*

Nothing says you must exercise an option. But, not exercising an option that's worth something would be foolish. So foolish, in fact, that most online brokers will automatically exercise options that are worth something, or in the money.

» **Selling a call:** When you sell a call, you're on the other side of the option strategy of buying a call. You get paid the premium and pocket the money. And it gets better: If the stock falls, you keep that money free and clear. But if the stock rises, you're in trouble because you've agreed to sell the stock for the lower price. If you don't already own the stock, you're what's called *naked*. That means you'll have to go out and buy the stock you've already sold, no matter the price.

You should never sell a call unless you know what you're doing. If you sell a call and don't own the underlying stock, that's called *writing a naked call.* If the stock rises, your losses are unlimited because in theory the stock could rise hundreds of points.

If a call sounds like something you'd like to trade, here are places online where you can find out more:

- *The Chicago Board Options Exchange's Options Institute* (www.cboe.com/LearnCenter/cboeeducation/Course_01_02/mod_02_01.aspx)

- *The Options Guide* (www.theoptionsguide.com/call-option.aspx)

» **Buying a put:** When you buy a put, you have the right to make someone buy a stock from you for a prearranged price. You're betting that the price of the underlying stock will fall. And like buying a call, it lets you make a big gamble with little up-front money. It's another way to bet against a stock, similar to shorting a stock, as described earlier in this chapter.

» **Selling a put:** This strategy places you on the other side of the person who is buying the put. When you sell a put, you're usually betting that the price of the underlying stock will rise. But you might also sell a put if you're willing to buy the stock at the current price but think it might go lower in the short term. That way, if the stock does fall, you must buy the stock at the higher exercise price but get to keep the premium.

Selling a put can be extremely risky. If the stock falls, you keep losing money until it hits $0. Don't sell a put unless you know exactly what you're doing.

BUYING TROUBLE BY BUYING CALLS

Buying calls is the best way to maximize returns if a stock is about to go up. And that's why they're perfect tools for investors who use *illegal insider information* about stocks for personal gain. Illegal insider information is important information the public doesn't know about yet but will move the stock when the news gets out. It's illegal to trade using important and confidential information you got from working for a company or being connected to people with such secret information. For just a little cash, these investors can post giant gains when the market-moving news — news they already know about — hits the market.

Regulators are aware of this, too, though. Options activity is one of the first things the Securities and Exchange Commission (SEC) looks into following a big move of a stock, especially on news that a company is being acquired. A classic case came in August 2005, when the SEC uncovered a ring of nine investors who allegedly made more than $6 million in illegal profits largely by buying call options ahead of the August 3 announcement that athletic apparel maker Adidas was buying Reebok. The case included lurid details of the illegal traders meeting with an exotic dancer to exchange tips as well as secret meetings inside Russian spas. A few members of the ring worked for investment banks and knew the deal was coming, giving them time to make the options trades. You can read all about it in one of the SEC's complaints at https://sec.gov/litigation/complaints/2006/comp19775.pdf. Another high-profile example came in 2011 connected with Walt Disney's purchase of comic book empire: Marvel Entertainment. The SEC accused an individual of investing in call options on Marvel's stock in 2009 based on a tip from a girlfriend who worked at Disney, and gaining 3,000 percent on the allegedly illegally obtained information (www.sec.gov/news/press/2011/2011-166.htm).

Table 5-1 explains the four main option strategies and describes the basics of how they work.

TABLE 5-1   The Four Basic Option Strategies

	Calls	Puts
Buy	A bet that the stock will go higher. If you're right, you can make a large profit with little investment.	A bet that the stock will fall. If you're right, you can make a large profit with little investment.
Sell (or *writing*)	A bet that the stock will fall. It's risky because your loss is unlimited if you're wrong.	A bet that the stock will rise. It's risky, but your losses are limited because a stock can fall only to $0.

How to get option prices online

Most of the leading stock quote sites provide options prices. They're usually called *options chains* because they show data on options for many exercise prices and for different expiration dates. Two helpful places to get options chains are NASDAQ.com (`www.nasdaq.com/`) and Yahoo! Finance (`https://finance.yahoo.com/`). Options quotes are also provided by most online brokers.

No matter where you look up options chains online, most providers give you a chart with the same basic information, including

>> **Premiums (or prices) of both call and put options at all price levels:** The *bid* is how much you will get for selling the option, and the *ask* is how much you'd pay to buy one.

>> **Volume:** This shows you how many contracts are being bought and sold.

>> **In the money and out of the money:** You can see which options are in the money and which are out of the money. Remember, a call option is *in the money* if the stock price is higher than the option's strike price. A call option is *out of the money* if the strike price is higher than the stock's price.

>> **Prices for different dates:** You can see how much options with different expiration dates are trading for.

INSURANCE TO PROTECT YOU FROM LOSING MONEY INVESTING ONLINE

You can buy insurance to cover yourself in case your house burns down or your car is stolen. But what about your online stock portfolio? Can you buy insurance to protect yourself from losing a catastrophic amount of money from investing online? Yes, you can, but instead of buying a policy from an insurance company, you can buy a put option.

Buying a put is normally a way to bet against a stock. But if you buy a put for a stock you already own, you have what's called a *protective put.* Say you own 100 shares of ABC Company. The stock is trading for $30 a share, and you're worried about a market meltdown. You can buy a put that would give you the right to sell ABC Company for $30. Even if the stock crashes and falls to $15 a share, you can still sell it for $30. You've essentially bought catastrophic insurance.

>> **The trading symbol of the option:** Stocks have ticker symbols, which are abbreviations to help investors communicate with each other and brokers. Options also have symbols that serve the same purpose. For more than 25 years, options had five-letter symbols. But that changed in 2010 when the Options Clearing Corporation, which handles the behind-the-scenes processing of options, changed the way options are given symbols. Now, options symbols have four sets of data in a long string of letters and numbers. First you'll see the security's ticker symbol, say IBM. Next, comes the expiration date, followed by the strike price, and then a letter *p* or *c,* depending on whether it is a put or call option. Investopedia provides an in-depth description of these symbols for investors (www.investopedia.com/ask/answers/05/052505.asp).

How to buy options online

Most of the mainstream online brokers allow you to buy and sell options. Some of the brokers are specialists with options and can help you calculate your gains and losses. Those specialty firms are listed in Chapter 4. You also need to pay a commission to buy or sell options, just as you pay to buy or sell stocks. The fees vary by broker. Table 5-2 lists a few examples.

TABLE 5-2

Some Online Brokers' Options Commissions

Broker	Commission per Contract
Ally Invest	$4.95 plus $0.65 per contract
E*Trade	$6.95 plus $0.75 per contract
TD Ameritrade	$6.95 plus $0.75 per contract
Charles Schwab	$4.95 plus $0.65 per contract

Entering an option order is similar to placing a trade for a stock. You must follow these steps:

1. **Go to the option-trading section of the online broker's site.**

2. **Enter an order to buy or sell a call or put option.**

3. **Enter the number of contracts you want to trade.**

   One options contract controls 100 shares of the stock.

REMEMBER

4. **Enter the option contract symbol.**

5. **Select an order type, such as a limit or market order.**

   For more on limit and market orders, see the "Types of orders" section, earlier in the chapter.

Discovering more about options online

Options aren't complicated, but they can be a little bewildering to novices. You need to make absolutely certain that you know what you're doing before trying to play with options. These online resources can help:

>> **Your broker's website:** Most brokers have an education section, where options are explained in detail. Brokerages that offer special tools for options traders, such as Ally Invest (www.ally.com/invest/self-directed-trading/options-trading/), have comprehensive tutorial information.

>> **The Chicago Board Options Exchange (CBOE) Options Institute (**www.cboe.com/LearnCenter/Default.aspx**):** Online tutorials, courses, and educational webcasts step you through the options process before you risk inflicting some major damage on your portfolio. You can also find an OptionQuest game that attempts to make options fun. You can see the kinds of options tutorials CBOE provides in Figure 5-3.

FIGURE 5-3: The CBOE provides tutorials to help you understand options before you dive in.

>> **The Options Industry Council** (www.optionseducation.org/en.html): The organization that processes much of the data that powers the options market offers investors free training and education. You find online courses for beginner, intermediate, and advanced options investors.

>> **The Options Guide** (www.theoptionsguide.com/): Here you'll find detailed descriptions on the basics all options investors need to know.

Stepping Through Placing a Trade

This chapter has a lot of information to digest. But you probably just want to know how to enter a trade. You've come to the right place. In this section, I step you through the process of entering an order to buy a stock using a broker. In this case, we'll use TD Ameritrade to buy 100 shares of Microsoft. (Note that this is not an endorsement of TD Ameritrade.) The process is largely the same no matter who your broker is.

I also show you how to enter the order by using the broker's online site, the mobile app, and the downloadable PC software. Don't worry, you'll find plenty of screen-shots so you can follow along.

Using the brokerage's website

More times than not, you'll probably use the broker's website when entering an order. The website is the to-go option for many investors because it contains all the capability you need and doesn't require you to download additional software. If you have a browser you're good to go.

1. **Go to the broker's site and log in.**

   Point your browser to the broker's site, in this case www.tdameritrade.com/, and enter your username and password. (I hope you're keeping that information safe by using a password vault, as discussed in Chapter 2.) If the site asks if you want to "trust this device," do so only if you're using your own personal equipment (as opposed to a friend's).

   For security purposes, you should always use your own equipment when signing onto your broker's site.

TIP

2. **Choose the trade type.**

   To place a trade with TD Ameritrade, hover your cursor over the Trade option at the top of the screen. Because you're buying Microsoft stock, select Stocks & ETFs.

3. Enter the trade details.

TD Ameritrade requires you to enter or choose five pieces of data to execute the trade, as shown in Figure 5-4:

a. *Choose the action, which in this case is Buy.* This is also where you would indicate if you wanted to sell or sell short the stock.

b. *Enter the quantity.* This is the number of shares you want to buy in this case, which is 100.

c. *Type the stock symbol.* Microsoft's symbol is MSFT.

d. *Enter the order type.* There are market orders, limit orders and other options. Here you should choose a market order, because you want to pay the current market price.

e. *Choose how long the order stays active, or time-in-force.* This option is more important with limit orders, but you must select it for market orders, too. Choose Day, meaning the order is active for a day.

FIGURE 5-4:
TD Ameritrade's web-based stock order screen is straightforward.

4. Click the Review Order button.

You get one last look at the order before you commit.

5. **Click the Place order button and you're done.**

   In about a second, you'll see a confirmation screen showing you the trade went through and at what price.

Congrats. You're now a proud owner of 100 shares of Microsoft!

Using the brokerage's mobile app

If you're traveling, in a coffeehouse, or staring at your phone looking for something to do, you might decide instead to use the mobile app to buy your 100 shares of Microsoft. Mobile apps are an increasingly popular way to check on stocks on the go as well as to enter trades. Here's how to do it:

1. **Download and install your broker's app.**

   Visit the app store on your phone and download the app, if you haven't already. TD Ameritrade is a little different in that it has two mobile apps: the main TD Ameritrade app and the TD Ameritrade Trader app. For most people, the main app is just fine.

2. **Log into the app.**

   Enter your username and password information. Use the same credentials you used to sign into the brokerage website. Most mobile apps have a helpful party trick in that they will identify you in the future by using your fingerprint or face. After you sign in the first time, you rarely, if ever, need to enter your username or password again.

3. **Enter your trade as follows:**

   a. *Activate the trading portion of the app by tapping Trade.*

   b. *Enter the symbol of the stock you want to buy, MSFT, in this example.* A series of drop-down boxes appears.

   c. *Choose the action, which is Buy.*

   d. *Choose the type, which is Market.*

   e. *Enter the number of shares, which is 100.*

   f. *Enter the expiration, which is Day.*

   g. *Enter any special instructions, which you should most likely leave blank.*

   The completed screen is shown in Figure 5-5.

4. **Click the Review Order button to review your order.**

5. **Place the order by clicking Place Order.**

   The order is filled in less than a second, and a confirmation appears. Wasn't that easy?

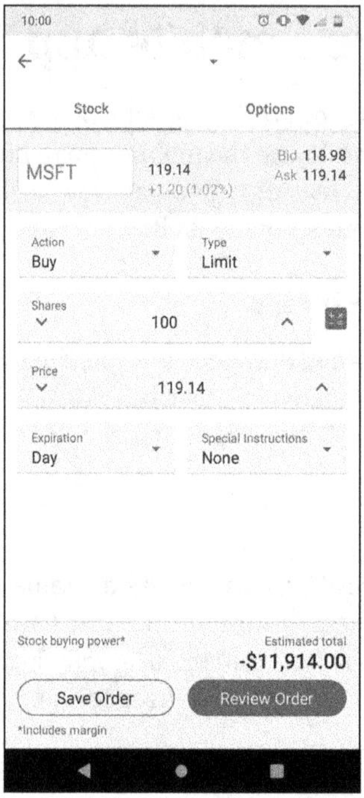

FIGURE 5-5:
Easily trade stocks from anywhere by using a mobile app, in this case, from TD Ameritrade.

Using the brokerage's PC software

Some online brokerages, including TD Ameritrade, offer additional software that you install on your computer for entering trades, as shown in Figure 5-6.

Typically, this software is for more advanced traders who want additional control and power than what's available on the website or app. Sometimes these downloads give users additional features, especially pertaining to complicated trades. If this sounds like your kind of thing, follow these steps to use the TD Ameritrade version:

1. **Download the software to your computer.**

   Log on to the regular TD Ameritrade website, and choose Trade ⇨ Thinkorswim. Click the Download Thinkorswim button and follow the directions to install the software on your computer. Why TD Ameritrade doesn't put its thinkorswim software in the Windows app store is beyond me.

2. **Log into the software:**

   a. *Find the thinkorswim software in your computer's Start menu and launch it.*

   b. *When asked, enter your username and password.* You can place trades on your actual account or with a paper trading simulation. (Read more about the value of testing your investing skills by using simulations in Chapter 2).

   c. *You want to use your real account, so make sure the Live Trading option is selected.*

3. **Enter your trade:**

   a. *Choose the Trade tab.*

   b. *Enter the stock's symbol, MSFT, in the entry blank.* You see all sorts of detail on the stock ranging from news and the options chain.

   c. *Click the arrow to the left of Underlying in the list.* You see details about the stock including the bid and ask price.

   d. *Click the Ask X price.* An Order Entry blank opens at the bottom of the screen.

   e. *Change the order type to Market and choose a quantity of 100 (which is the default).*

   f. *Although you can choose which trading marketplace will execute the order, in most cases it's a good idea to keep Best chosen.* This way, TD Ameritrade will find the best price for you automatically.

   g. *Click the Confirm and Send button.* You're done!

FIGURE 5-6:
TD Ameritrade's thinkorswim PC software puts a professional-level trading system on your desk.

2

Using Online Investment Resources

Find out what drives stock prices and how to track those forces by using online calculators and communities on the Internet.

Measure the risk and return of stocks and your portfolio, one of the most important, and most ignored, skills that all online investors need.

Find out how to use the Internet to design an asset allocation, a (boring-sounding) step that determines your success as an online investor.

You also get tips on how to research and buy mutual funds and exchange-traded funds online.

Chapter **6**

Why Stock Prices Rise and Fall

nvestors often wonder why bad things can happen to shares of "good companies." It's common for a company to report seemingly solid news, such as sharply higher profit, and its stock will fall anyway. It doesn't seem right to many investors who expect markets to be logical. Sometimes, especially in the short term, markets don't do what you'd expect them to. This chapter answers the burning question you and many investors might have: "Why do stocks rise and fall?" It's a two-part answer because one set of forces causes stocks to move in the short term, and another set influences stock prices in the long term. I explain what moves stocks and show you online tools that can help you track market-moving events.

How Stocks Get into the Public's Hands

If you've ever seen the screen of a stock trader's computer, on most days, it looks like a Christmas tree. Ticker symbols are flashing red and green, indicating that stock prices are moving up and down during the day. But why are the stocks moving up and down so much? To understand that, it's helpful to see how and why companies decide to sell stock to the public, allowing you to become an online investor. The following sections take a look at how the process works.

Step 1: An idea becomes a company

Clever entrepreneurs with an idea for a product or service form a company. Young companies usually pay for the equipment and materials they need by using private money. Let me clarify: They use *their* money. But, if it's a promising concept that could sell on Wall Street, the entrepreneurs might hit up venture capital investors for cash. *Venture capital (VC)* investors are specialized investors who buy stakes in young companies, most of which will fail, on the hope they hit just one future Facebook or Google and make a bundle. You can track trends in the VC industry at The National Venture Capital Association (www.nvca.org) and PriceWaterhouseCoopers' MoneyTree Report (www.pwc.com/us/en/industries/technology/moneytree.html).

Step 2: The company expands and grows

If the entrepreneur's hunch is right and a demand exists for what the company sells, the business takes off. At this point, the company needs more money to grow. The company might remain *private* by finding large institutional investors, such as pension funds, insurance companies, or companies that invest in private companies. These private placement investments aren't typically open to online investors. *Private placements* are selective sales of investments usually to a small and savvy group of money managers, such as the aforementioned pension funds or insurance companies.

But the Internet is quickly changing who can get in on buying ownership pieces of these nascent companies. The key ways companies find public investors for ownership — before hitting the big exchanges — include

>> **Direct public offerings.** Some private companies choose to raise money through direct public offerings so that they can sell their private stock to

investors. In a *direct public offering (DPO),* companies will often sell stock to their customers, who may end up being more patient than Wall Street. In a DPO, the companies raise money directly from investors instead of lining up a broker to dole out the shares. The regulatory hurdles and costs can be much lower with DPOs than with other forms of selling ownership to the public. These offerings are typically but not always for very small companies. Music-streaming service Spotify used a unique spin on the direct public offering in 2018. You can read more about DPOs at the following site on the topic, run by the regulator, North American Securities Administrator Association: www.nasaa.org/industry-resources/corporation-finance/scor-overview.

WARNING

Although some direct public offerings might work out, they're highly risky and are only for investors willing to lose their entire investment.

>> **Pre-IPO stock marketplaces:** Sites such as SharesPost (www.sharespost.com) and NASDAQ Private Market (www.nasdaqprivatemarket.com) are attempting to give investors a chance to buy shares of companies while the companies are still private. You can buy shares from other investors who own the private shares, usually employees or founders of the companies. There are strict rules on who can use these sites, though, as a buyer must be considered an accredited investor. Just to give you an idea, the SEC describes *accredited investors* as individuals with a net worth of more than $1 million or an annual income of $200,000 or more. These private exchanges are trying to broaden their appeal. SharesPost, for example, launched a mutual fund that allows investors to invest as little as $2,500 in a basket of companies that have not yet sold stock to the broad public.

>> **Equity crowdfunding sites:** If you've used sites such as Kickstarter, you have a pretty good idea about how *crowdfunding* works. The idea is that if lots of people donate a small sum to an inventor with a great idea (but not enough money), the total amount can finance the development of the concept and make it a reality. Kickstarter contributions, though, are essentially donations. Equity crowdfunding looks to take this idea further by allowing the masses to buy small slices of ownership in very young companies. The rules allowing such financing to happen were approved by the Securities and Exchange Commission in 2015. Hopes are high that this kind of funding will catch on and provide entrepreneurs with a source of funds. But it's in the early stages and still only for investors with money to lose. Some of the early players include WeFunder.com, AngelList, and StartEngine. You can read the nitty gritty of the rules passed by the SEC here: www.sec.gov/news/pressrelease/2015-49.html.

COMPANIES JOINING THE CROWD: CROWDFUNDING

Very young companies and entrepreneurs trying to raise money from the public have complained that the cost and regulations have made it onerous. The Jumpstart Our Business Startups Act, or JOBS Act, was signed into law on April 5, 2012 to address these complaints. The law includes a provision that loosens regulations surrounding companies looking to sell up to $1 million in securities to investors, in what's called equity crowdfunding. *Equity crowdfunding* is when a person or group of people with an idea for a business promotes it, usually online, and attracts financial backers to contribute money to the project. Originally, crowdfunding was a way for artists and philanthropists to raise money from backers to fund pet projects. But over time, sites such as Kickstarter.com (www.kickstarter.com) have increasingly been used by entrepreneurs to get financial backing for new products or services, not as owners, but as early customers. The JOBS Act will open up crowdfunding as a way for companies to raise money from investors, too. It's still an early concept and the risks and rewards aren't clearly understood yet. It's definitely something to watch. You can read what the SEC says about what crowdfunding means for investors here: www.sec.gov/divisions/marketreg/tmjobsact-crowdfundingintermediariesfaq.htm.

Step 3: The company goes public

To raise money, the company sells a fraction of itself in an *initial public offering*, or IPO. The shares are usually first sold mostly to large institutional investors, such as mutual funds, pension funds, and investment banks at the IPO price. When the large institutions and other initial investors sell their shares, they're available for you to buy online. I cover IPOs in more detail in Bonus Chapter 2 on the website associated with this book, but great places to start researching IPOs include

>> **Renaissance Capital's IPO Home** (www.renaissancecapital.com/IPO-Center/Stats) maintains all sorts of statistics about IPOs, ranging from how many there are to how well they do. You can also find research about upcoming IPOs and read their prospectuses.

>> **IPOScoop.com** (www.iposcoop.com) is a collection of data and commentary about the IPO market from long-time IPO expert John Fitzgibbon. You'll find what companies have sold stock to the public and how the shares are performing.

>> **Professor Jay Ritter's site at the University of Florida** (https://site.warrington.ufl.edu/ritter/ipo-data) is a bonanza of IPO data. Ritter, a professor of finance at the Warrington College of Business, has studied IPOs for decades and makes much of his research available to all.

When a company finally sells its shares to the public in an initial public offering, you can see which VC firms were investors in the prospectus. The *prospectus* is a legal document that explains everything about the company selling shares to the public.

Step 4: The new shares trade

After the IPO shares get into the hands of investors, the investors are free to buy and sell them at will on the exchanges. If you have a broker, as I describe in Chapter 4, you're free to participate and bid for stocks you want to buy. After you buy, you can sell.

TIP

This constant buying and selling of shares creates a dynamic way to determine stock prices. The process of how shares trade hands on the exchanges is described at length in Chapter 5.

Why Stocks Move Up and Down in the Short Term

Shares of large companies generally gain about 10 percent a year on average, as I explain in Chapter 1. Over the long term, individual stock prices are driven by several factors, including the movement of the broad market (which is controlled by economic growth and corporate earnings), the size of the company (smaller companies are riskier, so their stocks tend to rise more over time) and the price other investors are paying for the stock (stocks that are bid up already in price tend to underperform going forward).

But the road to a 10 percent average annual return is far from a smooth ride. The daily, monthly, or even yearly ups and downs of stock prices can be vicious as investors react to different news and corporate developments that trickle out randomly.

Stock prices are volatile in the short term because investors can either worry about or get excited about countless things. Stock prices reflect what investors know and expect from the company. But stock prices change the second there's a bit of unexpected news that alter investors' outlook for the stock. Investors instantly react to any news about the company, including the following:

>> **Movement by the rest of the stock market:** If the entire market goes up or down, most stocks move in the same direction.

>> **Earnings reports:** Such reports are released quarterly by companies to give investors a status report on the business. Investors usually react quickly and intensely to these reports.

>> **Industry developments:** What's happening to the industry as a whole can affect every company in the field. If one company, for instance, creates a new product that makes rivals' offerings obsolete, a swift reaction can occur.

>> **Management changes:** Who gets hired and fired at the top can be critical because such moves might signal a turn in the company's direction or a power struggle in the executive suite.

>> **Raw materials:** Changes in the price of raw materials can significantly affect companies that must buy basic ingredients to make their products. Higher raw material costs must be passed on to the company's consumer, or profits will suffer.

>> **Trading momentum:** When a certain stock gets its mojo going, it might seem as if there's no stopping it. Many times, companies become darlings with investors and can enjoy big rallies as everyone piles in.

>> **Merger chatter:** When the buzz tells you that a corporate wedding is in the offing, that can be market-moving information because companies are usually bought out for a premium to the existing share price.

>> **Bond yields:** The yield on bonds determines how much stocks are worth to investors, so a move in yields has a swift effect on stocks.

>> **Economic reports:** Official pronouncements about the state of the economy, including changes in short-term interest rates by the Fed, help investors decide whether they want to own stocks at the time.

>> **Legal insider buying or selling:** When corporate executives are doing a lot of buying or selling of their company's stock, that's worth watching closely. When companies' chief executive officers (CEO) are buying, for example, investors assume that they know what they're doing and might want to go along for the ride. (Don't confuse legal insider trading with illegal insider trading, which I discuss in Chapter 5. Illegal insider trading occurs when anyone with special connections to the company, including the management, uses important information not known by the public to unfairly make a profit.)

The preceding list just gives you a taste of all the things that can cause a stock that you own to go up or down in the short term. In the following sections, I expand on a few of these things and show you places online where you can track them insofar as they pertain to investments in your portfolio.

Tracking the market's every move

Perhaps the biggest factor in the short-term (and long-term) moves of stocks is the direction of the broader market. Investors generally watch stock market indexes — tools that track a basket of stocks — to find out what the market is doing. Popular indexes include the Dow Jones Industrial Average, Standard & Poor's 500 index, and the NASDAQ Composite index. You can find out how to track these indexes online in Chapter 2. Monitoring the broad market is telling because when market indexes are falling, it's not uncommon for investors to dump all stocks, including those of companies that are doing well. Traders describe this phenomenon with an old cliché: "Investors are throwing the baby out with the bathwater."

Getting in tune with earnings reports

Your stock's ultimate value will be determined by how profitable the company is in the long term. But even the best market forecasters are unable to measure a company's profits 10 years in the future, much less in 20 years. So, investors tend to overcompensate for their lack of long-term vision by focusing on how companies are doing in the short term. *Earnings reports* tell you how much the company made during the quarter. Earnings reports also contain all the vital financial results for the quarter, including the *net income* (or total profit) as well as earnings per share, which is how much of the company's profit you can lay claim to as a shareholder.

TIP

Investors and online databases usually use the shorthand term *EPS* when referring to earnings per share. If you see the abbreviation *EPS TTM*, that means earnings per share over the trailing, or past, 12 months.

WARNING

All public companies that trade on major exchanges, such as the New York Stock Exchange and NASDAQ, are required to tell investors how they did during the quarter. These earnings reports can be incredibly important to investors in the short term. But stocks that trade on other markets, including the Pink Sheets, are often not required to make these important disclosures, adding a great deal of risk if you choose to invest in them. You can read more about the risks of investing in stocks listed on the Pink Sheets in Chapter 2.

Getting the goods

Here are several ways to get your hands on earnings reports the second they're released:

>> **Financial news websites:** Nearly all the financial news sites described in Chapter 2, including Yahoo! Finance (https://finance.yahoo.com/), provide the earnings reports directly from the companies as soon as they're published.

Earnings releases are easy to find because in the list of news stories, they're usually tagged as being from one of two sources: PR Newswire (www.prnewswire.com) or Business Wire (www.businesswire.com). These reports are formal and written in almost legalese language. They describe how the companies did, in exhaustive detail, and provide the quarterly financial statements. (I cover how to analyze financial statements in more detail in Chapter 12.) If you don't want to take the time to pick apart the company releases, look for earnings stories written by the wire services, such as Reuters and The Associated Press. These stories are analyzed by reporters trained to look for the important things and put their findings in plain English. Wire stories are also available on most financial news sites.

>> **Press release distribution services:** Most companies hire one of two companies — either PR Newswire or Business Wire, mentioned in the preceding bullet — to electronically distribute their earnings press releases. Both these sites let you search press releases that might have been released by different companies.

>> **The regulators:** You can get earnings reports, called 10-Qs, directly from the Securities and Exchange Commission (www.sec.gov). The 10-Qs are the official reports, so they usually take a few weeks to be released following the end of the quarter. Prior to that, the company must file an 8-K report stating that it put out a press release with quarterly earnings information. If you're interested in getting the information this way, I show you how to do that in Chapter 2. You can find out how to dig into a company's regulatory filings in one of my other books, *Fundamental Analysis For Dummies* (Wiley).

>> **Earnings calendars:** Earnings calendars like the one maintained by Morningstar (www.morningstar.com/earnings/earnings-calendar.aspx) let you see what companies have reported their earnings most recently. You can also see which companies are due to report their earnings. For some companies, you can also read brief comments by Morningstar analysts on what investors should look for in the reports. (Figure 6-1 shows you what the Morningstar earnings calendar looks like.) Other sites maintain solid earnings calendars, too, including Yahoo! Finance's earnings calendar at https://finance.yahoo.com/calendar/earnings and Bloomberg at www.bloomberg.com/markets/earnings-calendar/us.

TIP

Stocks often react immediately to the release of earnings statements by companies. However, you might be surprised at the counterintuitive reactions such news sometimes provokes. This can be one of the greatest riddles on Wall Street, and it reveals just how deeply investors pick apart everything a company says to determine the price of the stock. Oftentimes, a company will release sharply higher earnings, but the stock will fall. Pure perversity? An Alice-in-Wonderland kind of world? Not necessarily. It's just a complicated world, as the next section makes clear. (Hey, if it were easy, everybody would be rich.)

What's so important about earnings reports?

To get into the heads of short-term investors and understand how they read quarterly earnings statements, ask yourself the following questions:

>> **Were the company's results better than expected?** When a company releases its earnings per share, investors instantly compare those results to what Wall Street analysts who follow the stock expected. Even if a company's EPS is just a penny short of expectations, the stock can get punished. But the stock can fall even if earnings per share are up, if they are not up as much as analysts expected. How do you find out how much the analysts thought the company would earn?

- **Financial wire stories:** Most of the wire stories from financial websites contain figures that detail what analysts were expecting and describe how the results compared with said expectations. Stories from the Associated Press, Reuters, and Bloomberg are especially good about this.

- **Zacks Investment Research's earnings surprise summary (**www.zacks. com/earnings/earnings-reports**):** Here you can see how much analysts were expecting companies to earn and whether the actual results were a positive surprise or a negative surprise. Morningstar's and Bloomberg's earnings calendars also show what analysts expected companies to earn.

Yahoo! Finance also has an entire section dedicated to tracking the analysts. Just enter the stock's ticker symbol in the search box at the top of the screen. Click the company's name to get the summary information. Click the Analysis link at the top of the page.

REMEMBER

When looking up analysts' expectations for earnings, be sure to find out how many analysts cover the stock and how many have provided an earnings estimate. If three or more analysts are on the stock, the estimate is more meaningful than if there's only one.

>> **What did the company say about the future?** What the company says about the just-completed quarter is practically ancient history. Investors spent all quarter anticipating the results and are usually pretty close in their estimates. But sometimes a company drops a bomb in its press release regarding what it expects in the future. Usually, though, companies make comments about the future in so-called *investor conference calls* — scheduled teleconferences or webcasts between Wall Street analysts and other investors with the company's top brass. During these calls management discusses how the quarter went and may explain what it expects to happen in the future.

You're not likely to be on the to call list for such investor conference calls, but you can still get the highlights from these calls from wire stories or earnings news stories. And, if you're really curious, you can often access such investor conference calls yourself online from a variety of sources, including

- *The company's website:* Start here. You can usually find an Investor Relations link that you can use to access the feed for earnings calls. Most companies let you click a link to hear the calls as they're being made, and many rebroadcast the call for 24 hours after it occurred.

- *Financial news sites:* Many major financial sites provide calendars of upcoming conference calls as well as the audio broadcasts from the calls themselves. EarningsCast (www.earningscast.com) offers an easy-to-use website that helps you see which companies had calls with investors and listen to what they said. Briefing.com (www.briefing.com) offers a similar service under the Conference Calls option under the Calendar tab. Briefing.com requires a subscription to listen to some of the conference calls. Reuters presents a list of what conference calls are coming up: www.reuters.com/finance/markets/conferenceCalls.

- *Seeking Alpha* (https://seekingalpha.com/earnings/earnings-call-transcripts) provides text transcripts of conference calls, which are handy because you can skim them without listening to a CEO drone on for an hour. The site also provides a calendar of companies with upcoming conference calls.

>> **Are analysts changing their opinions on the company?** The minute a company releases earnings, Wall Street analysts are already picking the results apart. They're looking for anything that changes their expectations for the company. Analysts publish their opinions on stocks in analyst reports, which I show you how to read and interpret in Chapter 15. But, for quick ways to find out whether analysts are changing their expectations, here are some sources:

- *Zacks Investment Research* (www.zacks.com) closely tracks analysts' opinions of stocks. If analysts change their opinion on a stock, you can find out immediately. Zacks helps you keep tabs on the analysts and closely track *analyst revisions,* which occur when researchers either increase or decrease their expectations for earnings.

  From the Zacks Investment Research home page, just enter the stock's symbol and click the Brokerage Recommendations link on the left side of the page. You'll see a chart that plots the stock's price and the Current ABR number, or *average broker recommendation*. This number averages all the recommendations made by the Wall Street analysts. A current ABR of 1 means that all the analysts covering the stock give it a "strong buy" rating, whereas an ABR of 5 means the analysts give it a sell. A 3 means hold. You can also see what the stock's ABR was in the past so that you can tell whether analysts are getting more bullish or bearish.

  Zacks also provides a Zacks Rank, which scores stocks from a low rating of 5 to a high of 1, which is located in the upper-right corner of the page. But unlike the ABR number, which looks only at analyst ratings, the Zacks Ranks considers four factors: how much the analysts agree, how dramatically estimates have been increased or cut, how quickly the average estimate is rising, and how much the recent financials have differed from the estimate.

REMEMBER

  You must subscribe to Zacks Premium to access all of the site's information; it costs $249 a year.

- *Reuters* (www.reuters.com/markets/stocks) has a comprehensive database of analysts' ratings on stocks so that you can see how Wall Street is reacting to an earnings release. Just click the magnifying glass at the upper-right corner of the screen, enter the stock symbol of the company you're interested in, press the Enter key, and click the company's name. Next, click the Analysts tab. You're greeted by a page that lets you look up what analysts have been expecting and also lets you track whether the company has the tendency to beat estimates in the past and by how much. You can view estimates for both revenue and earnings.

- *Estimize* (www.estimize.com) is taking a different approach to earnings estimates. The site will show you what the official Wall Street analysts expect a company to earn during a quarter or year. But the site welcomes you and other investors to enter guesses, too. Estimize summarizes these crowdsourced estimates, giving investors another look at what's expected.

TIP

In addition to tracking earnings reported by companies, it's valuable to see how earnings from all the companies in the Standard & Poor's 500 index are coming in. S&P 500 earnings are closely watched by the pros because it gives them an idea of how healthy companies are. S&P Dow Jones' S&P 500 page (https://us.spindices.com/indices/equity/sp-500) lets you see how much companies in the S&P 500 have earned each quarter for decades and also how much the companies are expected to earn. From the S&P 500 page, click the Additional Info button and then click the Index Earnings link. A spreadsheet pops up with a treasure-trove of earnings data.

Companies and the company they keep in their industries

Sweeping changes in an industry can have a tremendous influence on all the companies in it. A new product coming to the market can affect all the companies in its industry. Apple's iPhone, for instance, shook up other electronics companies, software companies, and music companies. Other times, good news for one company, such as a change in regulation, can help other players in the industry. If you're interested in keeping up with industry trends, here are several online sources:

>> **Specialized boutique research firms:** These guys closely track an industry or a collection of related industries called a *sector*. These firms usually charge large sums for their research. Sometimes, though, they provide useful industry data on their websites for free. You can usually find them by searching for "research" and the name of the industry in most search engines. Table 6-1 lists a few of the more prominent boutique research firms.

>> **Industry associations:** Can you say "lobbyist"? Industry associations are usually groups paid by companies in the industry to represent them on Capitol Hill. So, they're certainly biased in favor of the industry. Still, most release helpful information that can tell you about industry trends. Typically, the easiest way to find such groups is by just entering the name of the industry and *association* into a search engine, as I describe in Chapter 2, and see what that turns up. Table 6-2 lists a few of the larger industry associations.

TABLE 6-1   ## Boutique Research Firms That Track Select Industries

Industry	Research Firm	Address
Cars	Motor Intelligence	`www.motorintelligence.com`
Consumer goods	NPD Group	`www.npd.com`
Financial	IBISWorld	`www.ibisworld.com`
Technology	Forrester	`https://go.forrester.com`
Travel	PhoCusWright	`www.phocuswright.com`

TABLE 6-2   ## Large and Influential Industry Associations

Industry	Research Firm	Address
Finance	Securities Industry and Financial Markets Association	`www.sifma.org`
Real estate	National Association of Realtors	`www.nar.realtor`
Retail	National Retail Federation	`www.nrf.com`
Manufacturing	National Association of Manufacturers	`www.nam.org`

>> **Pay services:** D&B Hoovers (`www.hoovers.com`) provides full reports on a wide range of industries to subscribers. S&P Global Market Intelligence also publishes industry surveys (`www.spglobal.com/marketintelligence/en/?product=industry-surveys%23`), but be forewarned, they can cost hundreds of dollars.

>> **The U.S. government:** The U.S. Department of Labor's Bureau of Labor Statistics (`https://stats.bls.gov/iag/home.htm`) maintains a set of comprehensive industry data that's free to the public.

TIP

>> **Competitor information:** Sometimes the best way to find out about a company is to listen to what its rivals are saying about the industry. You can hear what companies are saying about each other with a two-step process online:

   a. *Find the competitors.* You can get D&B Hoovers (`www.hoovers.com`) to display the main rivals of any company. Just click the Search Companies link, enter in the blank field the name of the company you're interested in, and click the Search button. Next, click the name of the company and scroll down to the Competitor Profiles section of the page.

   You might also want to see which companies in the industry are planning an IPO or recently have gone public. Regulatory filings from newly public companies contain great details about the industry. Renaissance Capital (`www.renaissancecapital.com/IPO-Center/Pricings`) provides a detailed list of recent IPOs and what industry they are in.

b. *Find the competitors' filings.* Regulatory filings published by rivals can be revealing. Using the Securities and Exchange Commission's database, you can look up regulatory filings made by competitors. The annual reports, labeled 10-Ks in the SEC database, will usually have a section on the industry. And don't miss the registration filings made by companies planning to go public, called S-1s. You can usually find excellent industry information in those. (Chapter 2 tells you how to pull regulatory filings from the SEC's website.)

» **Reuters** (www.reuters.com/markets/stocks) provides statistics that allow you to easily compare a company's performance to that of its rivals. Click the magnifying glass in the upper-right corner, enter the name or symbol of the company you want to learn more about in the search field, and press Enter. After selecting the company from a list, click the Financials tab. When you scroll down, you'll see how the company sizes up in the industry based on everything from sales to profit, as you can see in Figure 6-2.

» **S&P Dow Jones Indices** (https://us.spindices.com/indices/equity/sp-500): This industry heavyweight provides detailed and free information on corporate profit growth of different sectors. Click the Additional Info button, and then click the Index Earnings. On the spreadsheet that pops up, check out the Estimates & PEs tab for data on the sectors (available on the Sector EPS tab of the spreadsheet).

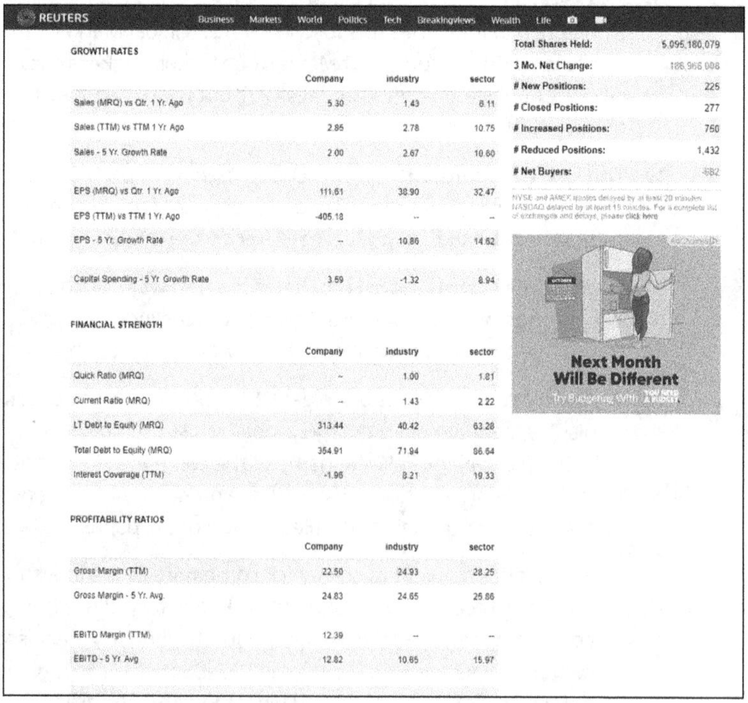

FIGURE 6-2: Reuters shows you how a company is performing in key areas relative to other companies in its industry.

Monitoring the big cheese

Investors usually have a strong reaction to management changes. Stocks might fall when the chief financial officer (CFO) resigns because it might make folks wonder whether the company's books are okay. But the opposite is also true — stocks might rise if a CEO who has worn out his welcome with investors decides to ride off into the sunset.

You can track management changes with the help of the following:

>> **Press releases:** Regulators require that such releases be put out the moment a company announces a significant personnel change. The news sources described in Chapter 2 all have this information.

>> **AFL-CIO CEO Pay Database** (https://aflcio.org/paywatch/highest-paid-ceos)**:** This website provides data on the comings and goings of corporate executives, with a keen focus on how much the people at the top are getting paid. Because the site is operated by labor groups, you find a not-so-subtle bias toward executive pay being too high. Even so, the data can be helpful.

>> **Chief Executive** (https://chiefexecutive.net/ceo1000-tracker) monitors the CEO ranks with great detail. You'll find articles highlighting things CEOs have said in addition to the CEO1000 Tracker, a database of CEOs' histories.

>> **Morgan Stanley Capital International (MSCI)** (www.msci.com/esg-integration)**:** This provider of indexes tracks trends and data on executives. Most of the data, though, must be paid for and the charges can vary. You can view some of the indexes MSCI has created to attempt to capitalize on data it has collected about companies' management.

Where it all begins: Tracking prices of raw materials

Companies can make more money in three main ways: Sell more products, raise prices, or reduce costs. Most companies must buy certain raw materials including *commodities* such as coffee, copper, or oil to make what they sell. When the prices of these goods rise, that can be bad for the companies' bottom lines. I have much more on how commodities are traded online in Chapter 11, but for just checking price information, you can track the pricing of key commodities at the following sites:

>> **Chicago Mercantile Exchange (CME) Group** (www.cmegroup.com/) is home for the trading of many financial instruments, including futures and options, making it a good place to see the prices of different foreign currencies. But it's also where much agricultural product trading goes on, including in pork bellies and live cattle.

RAW MATERIAL COSTS AND THAT MORNING CUP O' JOE

Never underestimate how rising raw materials costs can jolt a company. For instance, early in Starbucks' history, in June 1994, skyrocketing coffee bean costs posed a grave danger to the coffee retailer as it weighed how to handle the higher costs. Another price shock came in September 2004, after coffee and sugar prices spiked more than 35 percent in a year's time. Starbucks reacted by boosting prices by 3 percent for all its drinks. It was the first time Starbucks had raised prices since August 2000. Starbucks increased prices again in some states in early 2012, again citing higher coffee and energy costs, and again in 2015. But in a testament to the pricing power of some companies, including Starbucks, they can raise prices even when raw materials don't necessarily increase. When bumping up prices in 2018, Starbucks cited general inflation. Companies that can keep hiking prices show investors that demand for their product is strong.

The CME website has data on everything from corn to soybeans, from oats to gold. To see prices, hover your cursor over the Settlements tab at the top of the page, which will open a pop-up list of desired commodities.

>> **Bloomberg** (www.bloomberg.com/markets/commodities) maintains a relatively easy-to-read and understand table of most of the commodities you're likely to care about.

Getting with the mo'

Stocks, in the short term, often get what traders call *momentum*. There's always a handful of darling stocks that short-term speculators jump on due to the fact that they might have a hot product or simply because the stock is going up. Some speculators try to jump into these stocks and hope they can enjoy the ride higher and get out before the fall. Classic examples of stocks with momentum are the so-called FANG stocks during the late 2010s: Facebook, Apple, Netflix, and Google (which changed its name to Alphabet).

The following sites help find the high-octane stocks other investors are jumping into:

>> **BigCharts.com** (http://bigcharts.marketwatch.com/): This site has a BigReports tab that gives you access to all the stocks with the biggest moves, or those that are up the most or down the most over the past year. You can also see the stocks with the most short interest. *Short interest* is the number of

shares being sold short by investors and is an indicator of how many investors think the stock will go down. (I describe stock shorting in Chapter 5.)

>> **Investors.com** (`www.investors.com`): Scroll down on the home page of Investor's Business Daily, and you will see a section called Stocks on the Move. This feature shows you the stocks other investors are making heavy bets on that day, or, stocks investors are dumping.

>> **Morningstar.com** (`www.morningstar.com/markets.html`): This page of the Morningstar.com site provides an update on the market during the day. It shows you which stocks on all the major U.S. stock exchanges are rising or falling by the largest amounts. Bloomberg also provides a rundown of how 30 stocks in the Dow Jones Industrial Average are doing here: `www.bloomberg.com/quote/INDU:IND`.

Mania over merger chatter

If you own shares of a company being bought out, you likely just hit the Wall Street version of a lottery. There are exceptions, of course, but it's common for shares of a company being acquired to rise. That's why investors love trying to predict takeover candidates.

REMEMBER

Trying to guess what companies are buyout bait is not a great way to make money. Many of the merger-and-acquisition deals (M&A deals, for short) investors expect to happen *don't* happen. And even when the deals do happen, in rare cases, companies' shares can fall if investors expected a buyer to offer more.

Most of the leading trackers of merger activity, including Dealogic and Thomson Reuters, sell their data only to institutional investors able to pay large sums. But some other places track merger activity, including the following sites:

>> **mergermarket** (`www.mergermarket.com/`): These folks have comprehensive merger-tracking information, ranging from scuttlebutt on what companies are in play and some summary data about merger activity. You must subscribe to get most of the information, but you can find a few free tidbits.

>> **FactSet** (`www.factset.com/hubfs/mergerstat_em/monthly/US-Flashwire-Monthly.pdf`): This website provides some free data about the merger-and-acquisition market if you register. Factset's quarterly updates are informative and give you an idea about the wheeling-and-dealing going on in the market.

>> **Reuters** (`www.reuters.com/finance/deals/mergers`): Count on Reuters to summarize all its M&A news in one place.

Why bond yields aren't boring

Stocks can be highly sensitive to changes in the yield on debt sold by the U.S. government, called Treasurys. Investors keep a close eye on two types of Treasurys: Treasury notes that mature in ten years or less and Treasury bills that mature in less than a year. The yield on Treasurys is important because it indicates what return investors can expect in exchange for taking no or very low risk.

Stocks and Treasurys have an interesting relationship with each other. When Treasury yields rise, stocks often suffer because there's less impetus for investors to risk money on stocks. Why suffer the volatility of stocks if you can just buy a Treasury and collect your payments? I discuss the basics about tracking yields online in Chapter 2 and give more advanced tips in Chapter 16. These sites help show the relationship between Treasury yields and stocks:

>> **StockCharts.com** (www.stockcharts.com/charts/YieldCurve.html): This page of the website has a Dynamic Yield Curve function, which shows you, graphically, how the yields for short-term Treasurys, typically called *bills*, compare with yields for long-term Treasurys, called *notes* and *bonds*. This graph is called the *yield curve*. But more importantly, it plots the yield curve against the stock market so that you can understand the relationship between bond yields and stocks.

>> **Fidelity's Historical Yield Curve** (https://fixedincome.fidelity.com/ftgw/fi/FIHistoricalYield): This site plots the yield curve and also helps you understand it by explaining what it means if short-term rates are higher, lower, or equal to long-term rates.

The heartbeat of the economy: Economic reports

If you can picture a patient at the hospital with probes and sensors on every inch of his body, you get the idea of how closely investors monitor the health of the economy. Investors are looking for any sign the economy is speeding up, slowing down, or going sideways. They rapidly buy or sell stocks if their opinion changes even a little. You can look in countless places for economic indicators, but the key sites are

>> **Conference Board** (www.conference-board.org/): The Big Daddy of economic prognosticators, the Conference Board site, shown in Figure 6-3, measures everything from manufacturing activity to unemployment claims, from building permits to consumer confidence. Pay special attention to the *U.S. Leading Economic Index,* which falls when the measures it monitors predict an economic decline.

Although the Conference Board's leading index is widely watched, it's not always right. Investment pros like to joke that the leading index has predicted six of the last three recessions. For instance, the indicator fell in 1984 and 1987, but the economy didn't contract either time.

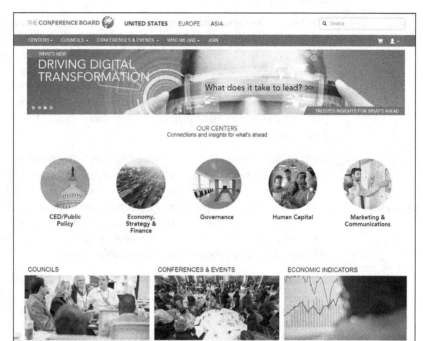

FIGURE 6-3:
The Conference Board makes a variety of important measures of the economy's health available on its website.

>> **U.S. Department of Labor's Bureau of Labor Statistics (**https://stats.bls.gov/**):** The U.S. government is also in the predicting business, tracking a vast majority of the indicators investors focus on, including the following:

- The *Consumer Price Index,* which measures how much prices for the things individuals buy are changing.

- The *Producer Price Index,* which tracks prices paid by companies that create goods. When prices are rising, both bond and stock investors pay attention because that affects the value of their investments. Stock investors typically don't like inflation because it drives up costs and makes their investments worth less.

- *Employee wages.*

- *Unemployment.*

>> **U.S. Department of Commerce's Bureau of Economic Analysis** (www.bea.gov/): More government predictors at work. The Bureau of Economic Analysis monitors how fast the economy is growing, generally using a measure called the *gross domestic product,* or GDP. You can also look up how much individuals are spending on average, what personal income levels are like, and how corporate profits are doing.

>> **The Federal Reserve Board** (www.federalreserve.gov/): Some investors are practically infatuated with the Fed. Investors watch the Fed and its moves closely for many reasons. First, the Fed sets short-term interest rates, which determine how much money is worth. Short-term rates affect every aspect of the economy, from how fast it grows to how much you have to pay to borrow money, and how much you earn from investments and savings. You can track the *intended federal funds rate* here: www.federalreserve.gov/fomc/fundsrate.htm.

REMEMBER

Don't confuse short-term interest rates and long-term interest rates. The Fed sets short-term rates to moderate or accelerate economic growth. When the Fed wants to slow the economy, it tightens credit by raising short-term rates, making it more expensive for companies and people to borrow and spend. It can loosen credit by cutting short-term rates, which boosts the economy. Long-term interest rates are set by traders who guess the direction of the economy. The difference between short- and long-term rates is known as the *spread.*

The Fed also publishes the Beige Book eight times a year. The Beige Book indicates the nation's economic health. You can view the results at www.federalreserve.gov/monetarypolicy/beigebook/default.htm.

>> **National Association of Realtors** (www.nar.realtor/): The fate of the housing market has a major impact on the economy as a whole. The National Association of Realtors' website releases closely watched data on both new- and existing-home sales, data that investors can use to get a better sense of the health of the economy as a whole.

>> **Yahoo! Finance's Economic Calendar** (https://finance.yahoo.com/calendar/economic): This calendar from Yahoo! is handy when trying to track important economic reports. You can see which reports are coming up each week, what they are, how important they are, and what analysts are expecting. It's all in one place, too, saving you the trouble of bouncing between all the sites in this list.

What they know that you don't — Insider buying and selling

Some investors closely watch what the top officers and directors are doing when deciding whether they should buy or sell a stock. This is *legal insider buying* or *selling,* which is very different from the *illegal insider trading* that I describe in Chapter 5.

Investors assume that when officers of a company are buying the stock, it's a sign the company is doing well. Some investors get bearish on a stock when executives are selling company stock.

When you see executives selling stock, it doesn't necessarily mean that they're bailing out. Executives might sell stock to buy a home, send a kid to college, or diversify their holdings. Diversification offers great benefits to investors, as I describe in Chapter 9, so it shouldn't come as a big surprise if higher-echelon types diversify as well.

Nevertheless, major sell-offs or a run on stocks by executives might actually be saying something significant about the stock. If you'd like to track what officers are doing, the following sites can help:

>> **NASDAQ's Ownership Summary (**www.nasdaq.com/**):** You get to this page on the NASDAQ site by entering a stock symbol in the Search text box and then clicking the name of the company or clicking on the search button. Scroll down the menu on the left side and then click the Ownership Summary link under the Holdings heading. You get a list of what all the big investors, including officers, directors, and mutual funds, are doing. The Insider Trades section shows how many officers are buying or selling stock, how much, and when. You can view insider-trading data for stocks listed on the major exchanges, including the NASDAQ and New York Stock Exchange.

>> **Morningstar (**https://insiders.morningstar.com/trading/insider-summary.action**):** The Morningstar Insider Trading Overview page lets you see trends of insider buying and selling over time. That's useful because you can see whether the officers have an uncanny ability to buy and sell at just the right time. The page shows you overall trends in trading. You can also search for specific insiders or companies by scrolling down and entering search information in the Insider Search box.

>> **InsiderTrading.org (**www.insidertrading.org/**)** is designed to be an efficient way to see what the insiders are doing. The site's design is sparse, but you can quickly search for insider buying and selling transactions and InsiderTrading.org pulls the data from the regulatory filings.

Many market pros who track insider trading don't get too interested if just a few executives are selling. After all, CEOs might want to sell stock for many reasons, such as for buying a house, diversifying their portfolios, or sending a kid to college. But if you see executives at many companies in an industry dumping shares, you might want to take a closer look.

Knowing how investors are feeling: Tracking market sentiment

The way investors are feeling about stocks at the moment can greatly influence the market's movements in the short term. Typically, during a brutal *bear market,* a period of time when stocks are falling in value, investors sour on stocks and want nothing to do with them.

TIP

When investors hate stocks, market sentiment is negative, and that can be a good time to buy them because you'll likely pay less. The market's downturn in the late 2000s was a classic example. Had you invested in the Standard & Poor's 500 in March 2009 when other investors were panicking, you would have scored a 65 percent gain that year. Investors who buy stocks when they're out of favor are called *contrarians.* It got even better. Those who held those stocks until early 2019 more than quadrupled their money.

When stocks enter a *bull market* and start rising, more investors pile in and push markets higher. Eventually, sentiment becomes overly positive, and anyone who wanted to buy stock already has. When there's a whiff of bad news, these investors bail out and send stocks lower. That's what happened during the tech-stock boom in the late 1990s. And, as you might remember, when investors were overly bullish in March 2000, that was a bad time to buy stocks. Investors, again, got overly optimistic in October 2007, just before the financial crisis that erupted in 2008 and 2009.

A number of online tools can help you monitor sentiment:

>> **Schaeffer's Investment Research** (`www.schaeffersresearch.com/`): This site is a haven for investors who want to know what the crowd is doing, and then do the opposite. The Markets News tab contains posts that help you pinpoint stocks the herd likes the most and the ones it hates. The idea is that buying stocks no one else wants can be profitable.

>> **Chicago Board Options Exchange** (`www.cboe.com/micro/vix/introduction.aspx`): This website maintains the CBOE Market Volatility index, a popular measure of how bullish investors are. (It's referred to fondly as the *VIX.*) It's also known as the "fear gauge" by investors because the higher the VIX, the more nervous investors are about the stock market, as defined by the Standard & Poor's 500 index. You can track the VIX much like you'd track any other index or stock, as I describe in Chapter 1. You can see what this page looks like in Figure 6-4.

The site also shows you the *put/call ratio,* an indicator of how bullish investors are. The higher the put/call ratio, the more bearish investors are. You can access such put/call ratio data at `www.cboe.com/data/mktStat.aspx`. Also, don't miss the description of what puts and calls are in Chapter 5.

FIGURE 6-4:
CBOE gives
you quick and
easy access to
the fear gauge.

>> **Investment Company Institute** (www.ici.org/): This site tracks how much
money investors are putting into mutual funds.

TIP

So what's the big deal about mutual funds? Wall Street pros closely watch *fund
flows* as a measure of what general investors are doing. The idea is that if tons
of cash surges into mutual funds, investors are getting overly optimistic, and it
might be a good time to sell. You can track fund flows at www.ici.org/
research/stats. As for how effective mutual funds are at pointing out what
not to do, check out Table 6-3. Basically, the market doesn't always work out
the way the mutual fund investors want. Investors essentially played one of
the most dramatic bear and bull cycles — completely wrong.

TABLE 6-3 **Don't Follow the Money**

Mutual Fund Investors	The Stock Market	Interpretation
Pour in $53.7 billion in February 2000 and $35.6 billion in March 2000, setting a record at the time.	Tanks. The S&P 500 index hit its then-record market high on March 24, 2000, and began a vicious decline that lasted until 2002.	Mutual fund investors buy at the top. They piled into stocks at just the wrong time.
Panic and pull out $7.6 billion in October 2002.	Rallies. The S&P 500 index hit its bear market low on October 9, 2002.	Mutual fund investors panic-sell, making a big mistake. They pull their money out and miss out on a powerful market rally.

(continued)

TABLE 6-3 *(continued)*

Mutual Fund Investors	The Stock Market	Interpretation
Pile back into stocks in early 2007, pouring $99.9 billion in stock mutual funds.	Falls apart. The S&P 500 index peaks in October 2007 and falls into one of the biggest bear markets in history.	Mutual fund investors didn't learn from the 2000s debacle and bought in just as the market was peaking, again.
Yank out $41.2 billion from stock mutual funds in the first three months of 2009.	Rallies strongly. The S&P 500 index surges from its March 2009 low and ends up returning 26.5% for 2009. The resulting rally was still alive and well in early 2019.	Mutual fund investors are fooled again. They sell just before the recovery that undid much of the bear market's damage.

Source: Investment Company Institute

WHAT DOESN'T MOVE STOCKS: STOCK SPLITS

For some reason, individual investors are fascinated by stock splits, perhaps because they think they're getting something for nothing. A *stock split* occurs when a company believes its stock price is getting so high it might scare off investors with sticker shock. Companies might consider a split if their shares get to $75 or higher. After a split, investors own more shares, but the stock price is cut. For instance, when a company does a 2-for-1 stock split, investors get twice the number of shares, but the stock price is cut in half. So if you had 100 shares of a $10 stock, worth $1,000, after the split, you'd have 200 shares worth $5. There's no change in the size of your stake; you still own $1,000 in stock.

Most financial websites show you whether a stock has split. Yahoo! Finance (www. finance.yahoo.com), for example, places a square on a historical stock chart to indicate when a split occurred. Here's how to do it: Enter the stock symbol you're interested in at Yahoo! Finance, click the name of the company when it pops up, and then click the Charts header at the center of the page. Choose the time period you're looking for, and look for the split icon under the chart. StockSplits.net (www.stocksplits.net/) also tracks splits and has a free newsletter for people who are interested.

The value of stock splits is controversial. Some academic research shows that stock splits are early signals a company will perform well in the future. The theory is a company's management wouldn't split the stock unless it was fairly certain that the stock wasn't likely to head lower in the future. Other research, though, finds splits to have negligible value for investors. Zacks Investment Research studied small and midsize companies going back to 1998 to see how splits of at least 1.5-to-1 affected the shares of companies up to 12 months later. Zacks found no discernible difference in the returns of companies that split their stock versus those that didn't over the following 12 months.

What Moves Stocks in the Long Term?

Almost anything can move stocks in the short term. Investors are so touchy on a minute-by-minute basis that they might even sell stocks if a Wall Street trader sneezes. Long term, though, the market is much more, well, sane. Several key factors affect stocks' returns over the long term:

>> **Company fundamentals,** such as how much the company generates in cash and earnings over its lifetime, is *the* major contributor to how its stock performs. I discuss how to analyze long-term financial performance in Chapters 12 and 13.

>> **Long-term economic trends** set the table for stocks. If a chronic problem with inflation or low economic growth exists, that can spell trouble for many investments.

>> **Valuations** refer to how much you're paying for a piece of a company. A stock's valuation is a measure of how expensive it is based on how much the company is expected to earn in profit. This topic is pursued in more detail in Chapter 12.

>> **Risk** is the price you pay for higher returns. If you own a piece of a risky asset, you should demand a higher return in exchange. Academic research discussed in Chapter 1 shows how shares of small companies and companies based in emerging markets tend to generate higher returns because they're riskier. I describe the relationship between a stock's risk and return in Chapter 3.

Going back to school with academic research

If you're curious about what moves stocks in the long term, spend time reading the research put out by academics. Because they're not pressured to sell investments, academics have the time to sit down, study markets, and search for patterns. Some of the work that has come from academia has revolutionized investing and has greatly enhanced the understanding of why stocks do what they do. I mention several critical sources of academic research in Chapter 1. Other online resources worth checking out include the following:

>> **Google Scholar (**https://scholar.google.com/**):** This particular arm of Google lets you search through millions of academic papers for those that match your search terms. You can follow the links to get access to view the research.

- >> **Microsoft Academic Search** (`academic.research.microsoft.com/`): You can use this site to quickly locate academic works. The site also allows you to browse academic research based on topic areas. Microsoft Academic Search allows you to search by keyword, but also based on the name of the publication, conference, or organization. You can see what the search page looks like in Figure 6-5.

- >> **Social Science Research Network** (`https://papers.ssrn.com/`): Here you can find the primary database for published works by academics. The database is fully searchable by keyword and author. You can view some of the research for free, but you have to pay for other parts.

- >> **Jeremy Siegel** (`https://fnce.wharton.upenn.edu/profile/siegel/`): Siegel, a professor at the Wharton School of the University of Pennsylvania, is best known for his exhaustive market research. Some of Siegel's data has led to important discoveries, including the concept that stocks become less risky the longer they're held. Siegel has also cofounded a company, WisdomTree (`www.wisdomtree.com/`), which sells investment products that take advantage of his research. I discuss Siegel's work in greater detail in Chapter 11, where I explain exchange-traded funds.

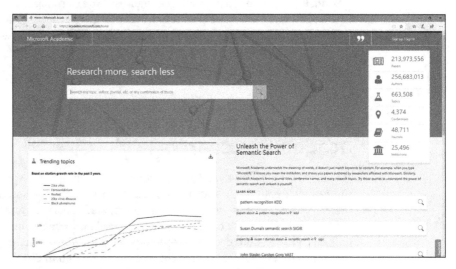

FIGURE 6-5: Microsoft Academic Search allows you to dig through piles of academic research online to find data that might help your investing.

Learning from the wise men

Some investors have so much experience with markets that they're worthwhile listening to. No, they're not always right, but you can learn from their mistakes. A few examples, in addition to those listed in Chapter 1, include

- » **Warren Buffett** (`www.berkshirehathaway.com/`): He's perhaps the best-known and most successful investor ever, so it's worth your while to listen to him. Each year Buffett, CEO of a holding company called Berkshire Hathaway, releases the company's annual report in addition to various letters to shareholders. Even if you're not a Berkshire Hathaway shareholder, Buffett's letters are some of the best reads in finance. Not only are they cleverly written and full of witty turns of phrase, but they also contain market insight you can't find elsewhere. Berkshire Hathaway's financial reports are available for free on the company's website, shown in Figure 6-6.

- » **Jeffrey Gundlach** (`www.doubleline.com/`): As chief executive officer at the bond fund management firm DoubleLine, Gundlach shares his insights on the economy and investments.

- » **George Soros** (`www.georgesoros.com/`): You may or may not agree with his outspoken political views, but George Soros, a long-time (and successful) investor, also offers his opinions on global markets and investing.

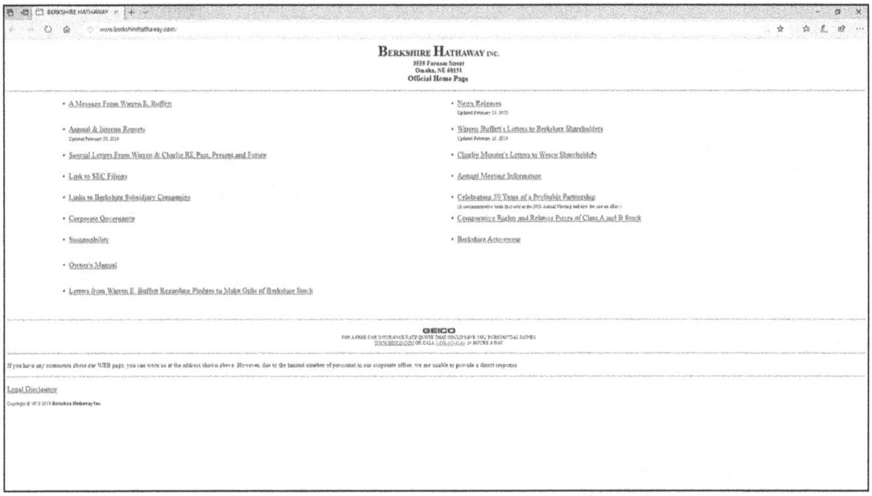

FIGURE 6-6:
Berkshire Hathaway's website provides free access to the company's annual reports, which contain sage advice from famed investor Warren Buffett.

TIP

Another great way to see what famous investors are doing is to check the forms they must file with regulators. Money managers who oversee $100 million or more must file a *Form 13F* with the SEC. These forms must disclose what the investors own, how many shares they own, and the value of their holdings. These Form 13Fs can provide revealing glimpses into what large investors like Warren Buffett and other professional investors are doing. The SEC tells you more about the 13F forms and how to access them at `www.sec.gov/answers/form13f.htm`. You can also find more information on digging up regulatory filings in Chapter 12.

IN THIS CHAPTER

» **Discussing stocks with others on stock message boards**

» **Understanding the dangers of penny stocks**

» **Joining investment clubs, both online and offline**

» **Taking advantage of general social networking sites such as Twitter and Facebook**

» **Sorting the valid information from the garbage**

Chapter **7**

Connecting with Other Investors Online

nvesting used to be a solitary pursuit. Investors would analyze stocks, bonds, and other assets to decide which ones to add to their portfolios. Sometimes a financial advisor or a broker might be summoned for help or advice.

But all that's changing as investors turn to the Internet for places to chat and compare ideas with others online. Online investors used to rely on *stock message boards*, often called *chat boards*, to trade stock tips, gossip, and hunches with each other. Stock message boards are still a way for some investors to connect, but they've become marginalized by new types of social media, including Twitter and Facebook. Social media turns out to be useful not just to watch cool skateboarding videos but also for investors. These sites have distinct advantages when it comes to monitoring what people are saying about stocks and companies, in large part because so many people use them. Many brokerages, too, are providing technology to allow investors to communicate with each other online.

In the first part of this chapter, I show you how to get online with stock message boards, including how to contribute to them and what to watch out for.

Later, I explore the dangers of penny stocks, which are some of the favorites on stock message boards and other online forums. And lastly, I explore the emerging area of using Twitter and Facebook for investing purposes.

Finding Kindred Investment Spirits Online

Whenever you're about to try something risky, or at least something you've never done before, it's comforting to talk to people with experience. That's why many investors attempt to connect with each other. You have several ways to do this: through stock message boards, investment clubs, and social networking or social investing sites.

Following are a few reasons why you might consider adding a social aspect to your investment strategy:

>> **Moral support:** Many beginning online investors are bewildered by the things they need to know to be successful. By connecting with other investors online who have already tried an investment strategy you are considering, you can gain firsthand knowledge of the risks and rewards.

>> **A new perspective:** You might think you know the best way to manage your money. But why not run your strategy by others first and make sure that you're not overlooking anything?

>> **New ideas for investments:** Members of online communities come from different professions and from all over the world. You can use this diversity to your advantage, and you might even find out about investments you've never heard of.

Getting the Message with Stock Message Boards

When you think of connecting with other investors online, you probably think of Twitter and Facebook first. And yes, social media is the primary way online investors connect with each other. But before jumping into social media, it's helpful to first check out stock message boards. These informal, anonymous boards were an early forum for investors to chat with each other online. They give you an instant venue to brag about your returns, promote a stock you own, or *flame* a stock you've sold for a loss. They're easy to jump into — giving you a quick flavor of what you might gain from sharing ideas with complete strangers.

Stock message boards aren't for everyone

Some investors, especially passive investors described in Chapter 1, might not care what other investors think about their stocks. They've carefully crafted their asset allocation — as I describe in Chapter 9 — and they're going to stick with that no matter what.

But if you're an active investor and you see online investing as a hobby or a sport, you might be interested in the chatter that surrounds stocks you're considering. Stock message boards are suited for you if you

>> **View investing as a form of entertainment:** Some investors buy and sell stocks not so much to accumulate a nest egg, but for speculation. It's almost like a trip to Las Vegas.

>> **Don't want to hassle with sign-up procedures:** You can be up and running with most stock message boards in just minutes and usually don't even have to identify yourself.

>> **Know the risks:** Investors who understand that many of the things said on stock message boards are exaggerations, manipulations, or just plain wrong have a better chance finding worthwhile nuggets of information.

WARNING

Blindly following what other investors are doing, generally speaking, isn't a good strategy and can be dangerous. If you're looking for stock message boards for stock recommendations, you'll likely be disappointed with your results.

Understanding the types of stock message boards

Stock message boards have been around essentially since the start of online investing, and arguably helped define it. However, these sites have morphed quite a bit through the past bull and bear markets. The following sections explore the various corners of the Internet where investors congregate to swap info.

WARNING

Using online stock message boards as the key to your investment strategy isn't a good idea. Listening to so many other opinions might cause you to second-guess yourself and prompt you to buy and sell stocks too often. But more importantly, you don't know whom you're chatting with, and such boards are havens for scammers. Consider Anthony Elgindy, an infamous stock picker who developed a strong following for some of his picks on the stock message board, Silicon Investor, as "AnthonyPacific," in addition to promoting stocks on his own website. Elgindy was convicted in 2005 in federal court on multiple counts of securities fraud and extortion. Remember, always consider the source when using stock message boards to pick stocks.

The investing areas of general Internet portals

As message boards get pushed aside by Twitter and Facebook, most of the portals have dropped them. The last holdout that still offers them is Yahoo! Finance (https://finance.yahoo.com/), which has become a top destination for casual stock message board participants. In the search box, enter the stock symbol of a company you'd like to hear about and click the name of the company when it pops up. Click the Conversations link at the top of the new page that appears. You can scroll through and read the messages, but if you want to reply to messages, you need a Yahoo! login ID and password.

Specialized stock message boards

Specialized stock message boards are often the most popular sites with investors who see themselves as being more advanced than those using the general Internet portals' boards. Examples include the following:

- » **The Motley Fool** (https://boards.fool.com/): Offers investors a robust place to chat with each other online. The Motley Fool community discussion boards organize everything investors might want to talk about into dozens of categories. You can find stock-specific groups where other investors chat about individual stocks as well as broader categories of discussion range from investing strategies to tips to get started investing.

- » **Silicon Investor** (www.siliconinvestor.com/): This site tends to attract investors primarily interested in large and midsize publicly traded companies.

- » **Investors Hub** (www.investorshub.advfn.com): Discussions here tend to focus on who's hot (and who's not) among smaller companies. The site also hosts discussions on highly speculative investments including *cryptocurrency*, such as bitcoin. All the previously mentioned warnings, and the ones you're about to read next, apply to online chatter on investments other than stock, too.

Knowing the ulterior motives of some online stock message board members

Although many of the people who use online stock message boards might be upstanding individuals just looking to help their fellow man, great caution is warranted. People can abuse online stock message boards for personal gain in several ways, including the following:

- » **Hyping stocks they own:** Some members might exaggerate or even make up good news regarding a stock they own, hoping to fool others into buying the stock. This behavior is commonly called a *pump-and-dump scheme* or *ramping*.

Scammers first *pump* a stock they own by doing whatever it takes to artificially inflate a stock price, usually by spreading lies. Then they *dump,* or sell the stock before anyone catches on.

>> **Disparaging stocks they're shorting:** Investors can profit from a falling stock by shorting shares, as I describe in Chapter 5. Some investors might spread false rumors about a company with the hopes that such misinformation will cause a panic and get others to sell.

>> **Promoting companies that pay them:** Questionable companies can hire legions of stock promoters to stoke enthusiasm for their shares. These promoters might float a stream of positive press releases online, trying to create the appearance that the company has lots going on.

STOCK MESSAGE BOARDS AND THE ENRON DEBACLE

Despite the many problems with stock message boards, sometimes they can contain valuable pieces of information. You should carefully monitor the boards for comments that appear to be from informed employees. The stock message boards, in fact, were one of the only places where investors were warned about the coming collapse of Enron in 2001 — an old example, but a noteworthy one, since the collapse of Enron was one of the largest bankruptcies in U.S. history. Even today, Enron stands as one of the biggest implosions for stock investors and a case study of what can go wrong in many ways. The energy firm, worth $60 billion at the end of 2000 and considered by many to practically be a must-own stock at that time, imploded in an accounting scandal which ultimately wiped out investors. It turns out the company was losing large amounts of money, which the audited financial statements did not reveal.

Between 1997 and 2001, ahead of Enron's fall, more than 129 detailed posts were found on Enron's stock message board on Yahoo!, according to James Felton and Jongchai Kim in their article "Warnings from the Enron Message Board." These posts, many of which appear to be from employees, indicated serious problems at the company, even while most Wall Street analysts rated the stock a buy or strong buy. In April 2001, for instance, an anonymous post read, "It will soon be revealed that Enron is nothing more than a house of cards that will implode before anyone realizes what happened. Enron has been cooking the books with smoke and mirrors. Enron executives have been operating an elaborate scheme that has fooled even the most sophisticated analyst."

That post appeared online four months before Enron employee Sherron Watkins wrote the famous warning letter to Enron CEO Ken Lay. You can read Felton and Kim's article at http://papers.ssrn.com/sol3/papers.cfm?abstract_id=918519.

Determining what exchange or market a stock trades on

If you're going to be using stock message boards, you need to know the difference between unlisted stocks and stocks listed on an exchange. Some of the most popular stocks discussed on stock message boards aren't listed on an exchange such as the NYSE or NASDAQ. Instead, they trade on informal and lightly regulated electronic markets such as OTC Pink or OTC Bulletin Board.

It's important for you to know whether a stock trades on OTC Pink, better known as Pink Sheets, or OTC Bulletin Board. If it's trading on either exchange, it doesn't have to meet the same listing standards that any stock on the exchanges needs to meet, so the stocks have less oversight. For instance, stocks on Pink Sheets aren't required to file audited financial statements. And many stocks on these exchanges are abandoned shell companies that can be used by fraudsters to create a pump-and-dump scheme. (These dangers are covered in greater detail in the next section of this chapter.) But for now, you want to know how to find out where your stock trades. The following list shows you how to find out the primary market for a specific stock:

1. Point your browser to NASDAQ.com (www.nasdaq.com) as shown in Figure 7-1.

2. In the search field, enter the company's name or ticker symbol.

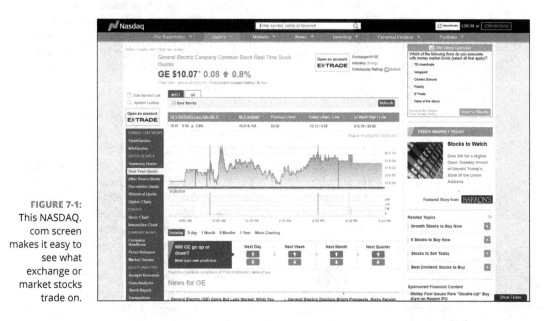

FIGURE 7-1: This NASDAQ.com screen makes it easy to see what exchange or market stocks trade on.

3. **Click the name of the company when it pops up.**

4. **On the left side of the page, click the InfoQuotes option.**

5. **View the company name and look at the market.**

   The entry under the Market heading — a link at the center of the screen — tells you the stock's primary market. (Table 7-1 tells you what all the abbreviations mean.)

TABLE 7-1   **Guide to Different Stock Markets Using NASDAQ.com**

Market Code	Market or Exchange
NASDAQ	NASDAQ (National Association of Securities Dealers Automated Quotations)
NYSE	New York Stock Exchange
OTCBB	OTC Bulletin Board (OTC stands for Over the Counter)
Other OTC	OTC Markets (including Pink Sheets)

A penny saved: Beware of penny stocks

If you spend much time looking at online stock message boards, you might notice that many of the messages are posted about stocks that trade for less than $1 — so-called *penny stocks.* That's partly because penny stocks, due to their tiny share prices, allow investors to buy large numbers of shares. Owning large chunks of stock is appealing to the same speculator types who flock to stock message boards to begin with.

But penny stocks can also be popular on stock message boards because they're easily manipulated. Unlike giant stocks such as Apple and Microsoft, which are so valuable that you'd need billions of dollars to budge the stock, penny stocks can be nudged with just a few hundred bucks. Just a small amount of hype or negativity can have a large effect on a penny stock's share price. A stock has to move only from one penny to two pennies to double a fraudster's money.

Many penny stocks also trade on the generally unregulated Pink Sheets and OTC Bulletin Board markets, considered to be the Wild Wild West of online investing. It's best to avoid investing in penny stocks, but if you can't resist the urge, be sure you have:

TIP

» **Read the warnings from regulators:** The Securities and Exchange Commission (SEC) has released multiple warnings to investors about investing in penny stocks, including this must-read guide: www.sec.gov/investor/pubs/microcapstock.htm. You should also search for the company's name and officers using the tools at the SEC's main site (www.sec.gov) to see whether prior problems have occurred. The SEC outlines the unique risks of investing in Pink Sheet stocks at www.sec.gov/answers/pink.htm.

>> **Checked the company's level of disclosure:** OTC Markets (www.otcmarkets.com) rates companies with one of three icons that indicate how much information they provide to investors. The highest-quality rating is OTCQX, followed by OTCQB and Pink. For companies that are especially questionable, a caveat emptor designation is added to the company's listing. You can find details about those ratings at www.otcmarkets.com/learn/faqs. (Part of the website page is shown in Figure 7-2.) Just enter the stock's symbol, and you can view its classification.

OTC Bulletin Board (www.otcbb.com) offers similar information on its stocks. The site, for instance, has a Delinquency/Eligibility list showing companies that haven't met its standards, which you can reference at www.finra.org/industry/otcbb/otc-bulletin-board-otcbb.

DON'T BE FOOLED: STARBUCKS WASN'T A PENNY STOCK

Some penny-stock investors claim many successful stocks such as Starbucks and Microsoft started out as penny stocks. To prove the point, they might present long-term charts, as I describe in Chapter 6, and say that those stocks started trading at less than $2 a share. That is simply not true, and it's worthwhile to understand why.

Consider Starbucks. Some investors look at a long-term chart and claim that the coffee-house chain's shares closed on their first day of trading on June 26, 1992, at $0.34 apiece. If you look at a chart, that appears to be true — but it's an illusion caused by stock splits. When a stock splits, as I describe in Chapter 6, the company cuts its share price and increases the number of shares. A stock split has no effect on the value of the stock or company, but changes historical prices because most charting services split-adjust historical stock prices. Starbucks' shares have had six 2-for-1 splits since they debuted on the NASDAQ, most recently in April 2015.

To find out what the actual closing price of Starbucks' stock was on June 26, 1992, you must undo the effect of the six splits that occurred after that date. You do that by multiplying the split-adjusted stock price in 1992, or $0.34, by each split amount. For Starbucks, that's $0.34 \times 2 \times 2 \times 2 \times 2 \times 2 \times 2 = \$2176$. That means Starbucks' actual price at the end of its first day of trading was $21.76, not 34 cents.

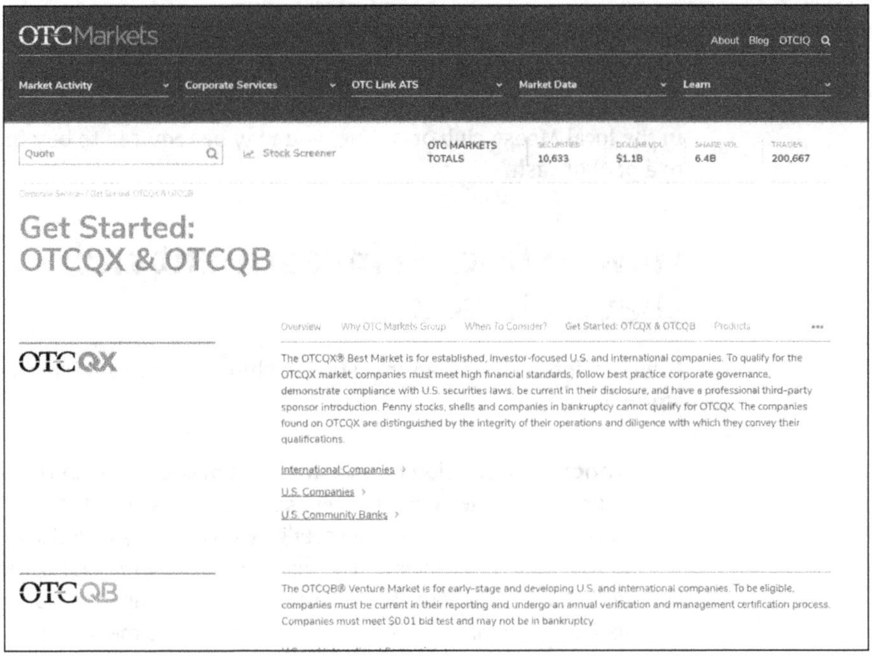

FIGURE 7-2:
OTC Markets
assigns one of
three easy-to-
understand icons
to stocks to let
you know how
much informa-
tion is available
about the
investments.

>> **Done your due diligence:** You should, at the very least, see whether the company has released any financial statements. (Chapter 2 has more on how to check for financial statements.) And if financial information is available, you should carefully analyze it using the guide in Chapter 12. Learning how to analyze financial statements is big enough to be the topic of its own book. In fact, I wrote *Fundamental Analysis for Dummies* (Wiley) to help investors dig into the numbers.

>> **Double-checked that you can't do better:** With thousands of stocks listed on the NYSE and NASDAQ, you should be able to find a listed stock you'd like to invest in.

Connecting with an Investment Club

If online stock message boards seem too wild and unreliable but you'd still like to connect with other largely anonymous investors, consider an investment club. Investment clubs are typically gatherings of investors in a certain geographic area who meet at a local restaurant or a member's house to shoot the breeze. Members pitch stocks they think the group should buy or sell. Investment clubs also have a bit of a party feeling to them, because they're usually designed to be fun, educational, and, oh yeah, profitable. If your city doesn't have an investment club, or if meeting with people in person doesn't fit your schedule, a few online investment clubs are cropping up. Whether the club you're interested in joining is held in the local Moose club or online, you may be required to buy in by adding money to a pool of cash.

How to find an investment club that suits you

If you're interested in an investment club, here are several (online) ways to get started:

>> **National Association of Investors Corporation,** also known as BetterInvesting (www.betterinvesting.org), is one of the top associations of investment clubs. BetterInvesting's website lets you find investment clubs in your area. You can also take online classes to work on improving your investing success. And if no investment club is near you, you can find out how to start a club of your own or join an online investment club.

>> **Bivio** (www.bivio.com) is perfect if you'd like the friendly and personal nature of an investment club but don't have time to attend monthly meetings. Bivio is a collection of online investment clubs. You can search through the club home pages and choose a club to join or even start your own.

>> **Value Investors Club** (www.valueinvestorsclub.com) is a selective group of members who pick stocks. You must apply to be accepted, and if you get chosen, you must submit two stock picks a year.

>> **Meetup.com** (www.meetup.com) provides an online way for people with common interests to connect in person. People interested in investing often create meetings, or meetups, and provide the time and location on the site.

Understanding the drawbacks of investment clubs

Before you rush out and join an investment club, be aware of the potential drawbacks:

>> **Bad decisions by others can cost you.** If the loudmouthed guy in the club talks the group into buying a stinker, you're going to take a bath, too.

>> **They give an incentive to tinker.** Many investment clubs consider themselves to be *long-term investors,* or shareholders who hang onto a stock for at least a year and usually much longer. But an investment club wouldn't be much fun if the members never bought or sold anything, so there's an incentive to be constantly buying or selling investments.

>> **Compromise can hurt.** Although nothing is wrong with agreement, having several people steering a portfolio sometimes means that there's no single and coherent strategy.

>> **A potential tax-time headache.** When an investment club buys or sells stocks, it might incur capital gains or losses. Dividends the club receives can also trigger tax events. Every year, you'll receive a K-1 tax form, which you'll need to report at tax time.

>> **Members' investing skill levels can vary.** Some investment club members are only there for the fun, food, and friends. That can leave much of the grunt work for the few members with the skill or desire to make money in the club.

Social Networking Comes of Age

Each year, Twitter and Facebook rapidly make message boards and other ways to connecting with other investors less relevant. Investors used to put up with the limitations of stock message boards because they had few other options. Investors who wanted to chat or trade ideas online had to deal with the ugliness of the anonymous forums in order to reach some legitimate investors online.

But both stock message boards and newsgroups are falling by the wayside as social networks have come to dominate online interactions. Online social networking sites, namely Twitter (www.twitter.com) and Facebook (www.facebook.com), allow anyone with an Internet connection to share news and information — or just worthless random musings — with others.

Social networking is just a fancy term used to describe computer systems that help you connect directly with other people online. So far, social networking is geared mainly for things other than investing, such as sharing family photos, trading news stories, or setting up weekend plans with friends. You can create a Facebook page and let all your friends see photos of your amazing skateboarding dog, for instance.

But believe it or not, there are ways to harness these social networks for the purposes of investing online. And in the following sections, I show you how.

What's the fuss about Twitter?

It's probably easiest to understand the power of social networking by examining one of its poster children: Twitter. Twitter is essentially an online service that allows people to create names for themselves and dash out mostly 280-character long statements, or *tweets*, about anything that's on their minds. Photos and links to websites can be included in tweets, too. You can view these messages on your computer by using a browser, or by using an app for your mobile device.

Twitter gets more powerful when people sign up to read and see all the tweets coming from people they're interested in, such as Bill Gates. You do this by *following* people on Twitter. If you sign up to get someone's tweets, you are a *follower*.

Usually, tweets are banal and not useful. The original use of Twitter was for people to dash out stream-of-conscience memos, such as, "I'm waiting in line for my cappuccino now." Who cares, right? But Twitter has grown up to such a degree that now investors are starting to use it as a source of information. What if you knew that the number of people waiting in line for coffee at Starbucks is up 10 percent this year compared with last year? Now, that's potentially useful information.

Ways you might use Twitter as an online investor include the following:

>> **Following the news:** All the major investing news organizations maintain Twitter feeds. The *New York Times, Wall Street Journal,* Reuters, CNN, and others routinely send out tweets immediately when they have a hot story. Best of all, these tweets usually include links that you can click to access the story or video feed. It's like having a real-time news service from the sources you trust. And you don't even have to sign up to view these tweets. Curious? You can read my online investing tweets without even signing up. Just go to www.twitter.com/mattkrantz, and you can see what I'm tweeting about.

>> **Keeping up with the regulators:** When regulators find new scams or scandals, they often send out tweets immediately. The Securities and Exchange Commission routinely sends out tweets with alerts and breaking news. You can read these at www.twitter.com/SEC_News.

>> **Monitoring developments at online brokers:** Most online brokerage firms maintain Twitter feeds, and they're a great source for news about the company. TD Ameritrade, Schwab, E*Trade, and Fidelity are all on Twitter and use the system to give investors information. Twitter is also a great way to open a public dialogue directly with an online brokerage or to get the brokerage's attention by sending a tweet about the firm. You can also send

your brokerage a *direct message*, which is a private message, almost like an email.

>> **Tracking trends as they're happening:** Some Wall Street traders and investment experts maintain Twitter feeds and make information available during the day. It's a great way to see what's on the minds of other investors as the day unfolds. Also, you might get some tidbits of information that are useful but would have been lost in the past because they weren't substantial enough for an article, blog post, or newsletter item.

Getting your tweet on

Before you can use Twitter, you first need to understand how to get access to the service. You can sign up using a mobile app or your computer. Because most online investors still count on their computers, the directions below are for the browser. It's really just a few basic steps:

1. **Go to** www.twitter.com **and sign up for Twitter (it's free) by registering your email address and choosing a Twitter name.**

   Your Twitter name is like your handle and is always displayed preceded by an ampersand. In other words, if your Twitter handle is TheBestInvestor, on Twitter you're @TheBestInvestor. It's like your email address on Twitter.

2. **Find people to follow.**

   Click the Notifications link at the top of Twitter.com and then select the Find People You Know option on the left. You can now search for people in your email address book. But if you already know the Twitter handle of a user, just enter www.twitter.com/*handle* in the address bar of your browser of choice. So to find me, for example, you'd type www.twitter.com/mattkrantz. You can also search for people or organizations you'd like to follow by entering their name into the Search Twitter field at the top of the page.

3. **Scan the Twitter feed and see whether you want to follow.**

   You can see on the page what kinds of things the person is tweeting about. If you want to get alerted whenever new tweets from that person are posted, click the Follow button.

4. **Monitor your timeline.**

   When you log on to Twitter.com from now on, the first page you'll see is your Twitter home, or a list of all the tweets being sent by the people you're following. Twitter home is your source of what's happening with people you're interested in. The same tweets will show up on your Twitter mobile app.

Being a good follower

Ready to start Tweeting? Now that you've created a Twitter account, the next thing you need to do to get going is to access the system. You can monitor your Twitter account in two ways:

>> **Twitter.com:** The easiest way to jump onto the Twitter bandwagon is to just use the Twitter.com website, as previously discussed. On the website, you can do everything you'd need to start tweeting and reading others' tweets.

>> **Mobile Twitter apps:** Some people get so addicted to Twitter, they can't bear to be away. And that's why some load Twitter apps onto their smartphones. You can download a version of Twitter for iOS, Android, and Windows 10 from their respective app stores.

Turning Twitter into an online investing tool

Because Twitter wasn't designed for investors, it takes a little effort for online investors to find useful information. The key to Twitter is finding people and news outlets that regularly tweet information you're interested in. You have several ways to do this:

>> **Use Twitter.com's search feature:** You can see a Search Twitter field at the top of the Twitter.com login page. You can search for people by their name or organization. A search by name is a great place to start, especially if you're interested in a certain investing source.

>> **Search Bing:** The Bing search engine has a nifty feature to help you find famous investors on Twitter. Enter the name of the investor in Bing (www. bing.com) and search. If the investor is on Twitter, there's a good chance a Twitter link will appear on the right side of the page. Click that link and you'll be taken to the investor's Twitter page.

>> **Utilize Twitter directory services:** Some websites try to corral Twitter into a more organized place by grouping people who tweet into topic areas or based on the publication they work for. Muck Rack (www.muckrack.com), for instance, categorizes all writers and reporters of major publications who tweet so that you can find them. StockTwits (www.stocktwits.com) searches for tweets related to investing. StockTwits, for example, presents at the top of the page a list of the ticker symbols being discussed most on Twitter.

>> **Understand hashtags and dollar signs:** Some tweets can easily get lost in the shuffle. To help tweets stand out, some include *hashtags,* or keywords

following a number sign. For instance, I might include #stocks or #investing in a tweet I send out. You can search for all tweets that have been tagged by typing **#stocks** or **#investing** in the search function on Twitter or the Twitter app. Similarly, it's become customary for investors to include a dollar sign followed by the ticker symbol of stocks they're chatting about. You can search $GE on Twitter, for example, and see all the tweets about General Electric that other investors have designated using the GE with the dollar sign.

Getting a read on the market with Twitter

Whether or not you sign up for Twitter, just know that millions of other investors are on the service and constantly chatting about stocks. Other investors might be sharing information about stocks you own, and if you're not part of the conversation, you might be missing out.

The problem with Twitter is separating the noise from truly useful information. That's why looking at *aggregate data* — or a summary of the bottom-line wisdom of the crowd — can be even more useful than following individual people on Twitter.

Luckily, new services are cropping up that allow you to get the bottom-line message on Twitter without doing much work.

StockTwits (www.stocktwits.com), for example, scours Twitter and reads the millions of tweets about stocks and companies — so you don't have to. See Figure 7-3. Using an algorithm that determines whether a tweet is bullish or bearish, Stock Twits shows you what the public is saying about a particular stock or market. The service even summarizes the stocks that the crowd on Twitter is talking about the most. You can also enter the name of a specific stock and get a rundown on what people are saying about it. You don't need to follow the crowd when investing — usually it's best if you don't — but it's handy to know what the vibe is.

Some online brokers, too, are trying to get into the action by adding tools that scan social media. TD Ameritrade (www.tdameritrade.com), for example, has a Social Signals tab on its website that displays recent tweets about stocks you own. TD Ameritrade's Social Signals feature also tells you if investors on Twitter are positive or negative about a stock and which of the company's brands are being discussed most.

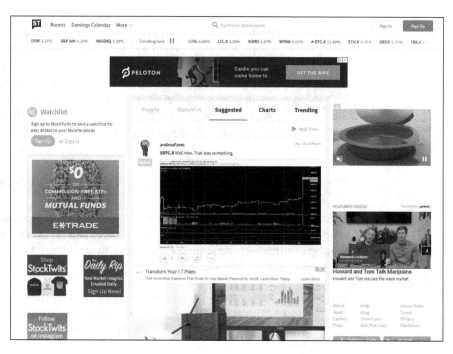

REMEMBER

Much of Twitter is just a bunch of nonsense. But increasingly, the market's banter, chatter, and discussion are moving to Twitter. (Heck, even politicians use it to make declarations to the world.) If you don't pay attention, you can miss out on some valuable insights. Investors in Twitter stock, ironically, got a head's-up on a disappointing earnings release over Twitter itself. In April 2015 at 3:19 p.m. ET, talk erupted on Twitter about the company accidentally releasing a disappointing profit report. Shares of Twitter were trading for $50.06 when talk on Twitter erupted. Less than ten minutes later, trading in the stock was halted as regulators realized the company's earnings release wasn't released properly. Trading in Twitter shares was reopened at 3:47 p.m. and the stock dropped to $38.38. That means investors who caught the early warning on Twitter — and sold — saved themselves from being part of a $7.6 billion loss.

Giving Facebook some face time

Like Twitter, Facebook is a general social networking site that was not designed to be an online investing tool. But as the site develops and grows, more resources valuable to online investors are finding their way on Facebook.

Facebook is essentially a place for people and companies to tell the world a little about themselves. Everyone on Facebook gets a *news feed*, which is a constantly updating list of notes, photos, and music sent out by your friends. You can *follow* other users on Facebook, or agree to share information, and then you'll be notified of any new developments with them or be alerted of things they find to be of interest. You might choose to follow other online investors so that you can trade tips and answers with them. You can also *like* different publications or companies such as online brokerages, which will put new information that might be useful on your news feed. You do this by clicking the iconic Like button, which looks like a thumbs up.

Getting your mug on Facebook

To get started using Facebook, go to their website (at, you guessed it, www.facebook.com) and sign up or follow the instructions on the app. Signing up is free.

After you sign up, if you use your regular email address, odds are that some of your friends have already extended you invitations to friend them on Facebook.

Using Facebook for investing online

Facebook might not seem like a place where much business is taking place, and you're largely right. Still, Facebook can offer some help to online investors, including the following:

>> **Keeping up with developments at your broker:** It's common for online brokerages to host a Facebook page, and if you indicate you like the brokerage, you'll get a glimpse of what's new at the firm. Some brokers make market commentary available to Facebook members who are its fans. Facebook pages are maintained by most of the major brokerages, including Charles Schwab, Vanguard, E*Trade, and TD Ameritrade.

It's easy to become a fan of a brokerage firm. After you're logged on to Facebook, enter the online brokerage firm's name in the search box at the top of the page and click the magnifying glass icon. You'll see a link to the firm's Facebook page. Just click the Like button (thumbs up icon).

>> **Communicating with your broker and other customers:** Sure, you could always pick up the phone and call your broker. But some online investors might want to connect in a more public and online way. For instance, you can either applaud or criticize items on the brokerage's Facebook page and see whether any other customers agree with you.

>> **Having a conversation with other fans:** Some online brokerages' Facebook pages become a virtual water cooler for investors, usually those who are customers of that broker. Just look over the broker's Facebook page, and you can see what others are chatting about, and even join the conversation.

The Brave New World: Social Networking Meets Online Investing

As the Internet grows up, it's becoming clearer that it's all about connecting people who might never have crossed paths in real life. Facebook has become the digital version of a backyard picnic and is the place for people to talk about what's in and what's not. Twitter allows everyone to share short bursts of information with a nearly unlimited number of people.

General social networking tools, such as the ones discussed previously, have some applications for investors. The technology of social networking continues to trickle into the investment world. You find websites and services that apply social networking specifically to investors, in sites I refer to as *social investing sites.* Social investing sites answer some of the shortcomings of stock message boards and investment clubs.

Social investing sites as a higher form of stock message boards?

Social investing is yet another way in which investors interface with each other. Unlike stock message boards, which cloak their users in anonymity, social investing is based on posting actual trades and often even investors' real names. And unlike simulations, which I discuss in Chapter 2, social investing sites are based on real trades with investors' real money. The main advantages of this exciting area of investing online follow:

>> **Show what's possible in the real world:** Anyone can get lucky picking winning stocks with funny money. Social investing sites take away the fantasy aspect of simulations by encouraging users to disclose actual stocks they own and when they bought and sold them. You can use that information to determine who's credible versus investors who talk a big game and those who might have ulterior motives.

>> **Separate the good from the bad:** Social investing sites often let you know how often different members are right about their picks.

>> **Allow investors to profit from others' expertise:** Social investing sites are designed to let investors who may not have the time to select investments to follow the moves made by investors who do.

>> **Provide some safeguards:** The brokers operating social investing sites are overseen by securities regulators. Fraudsters know this and might avoid

certain social investing sites because they could be easily tracked and monitored. It's similar to how a bank robber might not target a bank that's across the street from the police station.

Plugging into social investing sites

I discuss several social investing sites in the following list, but at their core they all work roughly the same. Follow these six steps to get involved in social investing:

1. **Choose a site.**

   Social investing sites are essentially gated communities of investors. You want to choose the site that fits you best and has a pool of investors you can identify with.

2. **Register.**

   Most social investing sites require you to give more details about yourself than some stock message boards do. That might be a slight burden at first, but it's also one of the ways these sites eliminate users who insist on being cloaked in privacy.

3. **Create a profile.**

   Here you describe yourself, only giving details you're comfortable sharing with the rest of the social investing site. Typically, you might say how long you've been investing, what kind of investor you are, and what types of stocks you prefer.

4. **Enter your transactions or portfolio.**

   The biggest thing that separates social investing sites from stock message boards is that other users can see your real trades if you give permission. You'll need to import your trades or give the site permission to share them. Trades may be imported several ways, either manually by you or automatically when you enter an order to buy or sell shares, depending on the site.

5. **Set your permissions.**

   Permissions are rules that tell the social investing site how much personal information you're comfortable with sharing. You can choose to use a pseudo-nym, or *handle,* or reveal your real name. You can decide whether you'll let other users look at your trades or send messages to you. This step is important. The more information you reveal about yourself, the more credibility you'll have on the site with other users.

TIP

   Be careful about listening to stock tips and recommendations by social investing users who reveal little personal information. These users might be cloaking themselves for the same reasons some investors are attracted to the anonymous world of stock message boards.

6. Look around.

After you're set up with a profile, you can peruse the community to find people you might want to be invest with. These are investors you think are worthwhile listening to. You can also read other investors' narratives on how they invest.

Starting to get social: Trying social investing sites

It's still early days for social investing sites, and many industry pioneers have been bought by larger firms or have given up. New players will certainly be showing up, so be sure to search for new social investing sites that have started since this book was published.

Here are a few to try:

>> **Interactive Advisors** (`https://interactiveadvisors.com`) is a robust social investing site that lets regular online investors follow the trades of experts. Interactive Advisors allows you to follow one of dozens of portfolio managers who are professional investors trading with actual money. Your money is invested along with the these portfolio managers', so if he or she is successful, you're successful. Be careful, though, because if your Model Manager hits a cold streak, your portfolio will suffer, too. Also, Interactive Advisors charges between 0.25 percent and 1.5 percent a year as a fee to participate.

>> **Motif Investing** (`www.motif.com`) got into the social investing game with its Thematic Portfolios feature. Here you can build your own *motif,* or collection of stocks that fit a broad objective. Examples include themes that help you invest in video games or in companies working on oncology research. You can offer your motif to other investors to buy, so they can own the same stocks you do in what are called community motifs. You can also invest in someone else's motif if they've identified a trend you're interested in.

>> **Collective2** (`www.collective2.com`) is like most other social investing sites in that it tracks and shares real trades. You can use the site to find a *strategy manager,* or one of dozens of investment managers who offer their investment strategy on the system. After you choose a strategy manager you're interested in, you hook it up to your actual online brokerage account. The system directly connects with a handful of brokers. When the traders running the system make trades, so do you. Fees vary wildly based on which system you choose and which brokerage you are using, but usually cost about $100 a month.

Chapter **8**

Measuring Your Performance

t's surprising how many investors keep buying and selling stocks online even when they have no idea whether they're beating the market. They'll brag at cocktail parties about the winning stocks they've bought. But if you ask them what their rate of return is, you get a blank stare. Many online brokers don't help either because they don't have tools that accurately measure your returns.

To me, investing online without knowing how you're doing is like driving with your eyes closed. As an online investor, it's pretty much up to you to calculate your own returns. To help you get back in control, this chapter first shows you how to manually calculate your returns and how much risk you've taken to get those returns. In case you want more handholding, I then discuss online sites and software that do all the calculations for you. Either method you choose, you'll be miles ahead of other investors who keep investing without knowing whether they're successful.

The Importance of Tracking Your Performance

From an early age, you learn to monitor your progress. In school, your progress was constantly monitored using letter grades and tests. And at work, annual reviews and pay often reflect the job you're doing and show what's working and what's not.

That's why it's so strange that many people don't monitor their investment performance. Investors often look through their portfolios, see a few stocks that are up since they bought them, and assume that they're beating the stock market.

Psychology plays a big part in investing. Many online investors get overly confident if they've recently picked a few lucky stocks. That prompts them to take more uncalculated risks in the future, which might cost them dearly. Investors also tend to wipe out painful losses from their memories, remembering only the winners. And other investors beat themselves up for losing money on a stock, blaming something that had nothing to do with the loss. By measuring your performance, you can try to remove some of the emotion from investing. (Morningstar, the independent investment research outfit, has a great lesson on how human nature can affect your success investing online; check out `https://news.morningstar.com/classroom2/printlesson.asp?docId=145104&CN=com`).

I suspect most folks don't bother monitoring their investment performance because it requires some math and a few scary-looking formulas that most investors don't understand. This chapter, though, demystifies how to track your portfolio's risk and return. I start by showing you how to do the calculations yourself.

It's important for you to understand how all the calculations are performed so that you don't blindly rely on websites to do it for you, but I also know that not everyone has the time or the willingness to crunch performance stats. That's why I include online tools that do the math for you. If you get confused at any point in this section about calculating performance manually, don't dismay. Just skip ahead to the section "Using Online Tools to Calculate Your Performance."

Why it's worth the trouble to measure your returns

Studies have shown that people who regularly weigh themselves tend to have more success reaching their fitness goals. It's similar with investing online. If you take the time to measure your results, you'll likely be a better investor. After all, even if your investments aren't doing well, you might be able to adjust your strategy if you track your performance. Some investors, for instance, might find that constantly buying and selling individual stocks isn't working for them. These investors can adjust accordingly and might find more success being passive investors. (You can review the difference between active and passive investors in Chapter 1.)

If you take the time to measure your performance, you'll be able to figure out whether you're going to do the following:

>> **Reach your financial goals:** When you invest, you typically estimate the rate of return you need to reach your goal, such as funding retirement or paying for college. By tracking your returns, you can see whether you're on the right path. And if you're not, you can consider ways to improve your results, including changing your *asset allocation*. I discuss how to design the right asset allocation for you in Chapter 9.

One of the first things you should do before you start investing is to decide how much risk you can tolerate and what rate of return you need to meet your goal. You can find out how to do this in Chapter 1.

>> **Hurt yourself more than help:** If you're an active investor who's constantly buying and selling the wrong stocks at the wrong times, you might be wasting your effort and hurting your portfolio. If you find that your returns are lower than what you could get by just buying a mutual fund, you might be better served by following a more passive approach.

>> **Find your mistakes:** You might have a good investment plan that's working, except for a few investments or stocks that are killing your performance. By tracking your results, you can find what's hurting you and make adjustments if needed.

Curious what the top mistakes investors make might be? Check out www. cfainstitute.org/-/media/documents/support/future-finance/ avoiding-common-investor-mistakes.ashx, where the CFA Institute has posted a list of the 20 most common mistakes individual investors make. It was compiled by professional money managers. You can also find my own take on the top ten mistakes made by investors in Chapter 17.

Why you want to measure your risk, too

I can't tell you how many investors ask me for "ten stocks to buy now." Investors get so obsessed with the potential return for winning stocks that they forget the other side of the picture: the risk. After all, you can get a great return by putting all your chips on black at the roulette table. But are you willing to risk it all? By measuring how much risk you're taking on with your investment, you'll know whether you are

>> **Getting adequate returns:** When you invest in a savings account, you're not taking any risk, so you shouldn't expect much of a return either. But if you invest in a risky stock, you should demand to be compensated with a bigger return. If you're not, you're being shortchanged.

>> **Invested properly:** Some investors aren't well matched with their investments. If you're risk-adverse and can't stomach it when your portfolio falls just 5 percent in value in a year, you shouldn't be invested in risky stocks that go up and down wildly. You might consider changing the types of investment you own so that you can smooth the bumps. You create a portfolio that matches your appetite for volatility by creating your asset allocation. (You find out how to use online tools to create a portfolio that fits your personality in Chapter 9.)

>> **Prepared for volatility:** If you know how risky your investments are ahead of time, you won't be surprised when the value of your account swings up and down. That foresight can help stop you from doing something in haste you'll regret, such as selling all your stocks in panic.

To get higher returns, you must accept more risk. Return and risk are tied at the hip. However, investing in a risky asset doesn't always mean that you'll get a higher return. As you find out in Chapter 9, many risky assets have generated poor returns over the years. You want to avoid these investments because they're bum deals.

Calculating Your Performance Yourself

If websites and software programs can calculate your portfolio's risk and return for you, why bother learning to do it yourself? I've found that many of the automated ways of calculating performance use slightly different methods, so you're not always clear what's going on. And with something this important, you don't want to rely solely on a website that might or might not be accurate. If you know how performance is measured and can approximate your performance yourself, you'll know whether you're getting the right information from the automated tools.

TIP

Still not convinced you need to dust off a calculator? If you don't care to know how portfolio returns are measured and just want to do it online, go to MoneyChimp's Portfolio Performance Calculator (www.moneychimp.com/features/portfolio_performance_calculator.htm). It automatically calculates your portfolio's return if you enter your portfolio's beginning and ending balance and indicate whether you deposited or withdrew money.

The easiest way to calculate returns

If you haven't deposited money into or taken any money out of your brokerage account, it's relatively easy to measure your rate of return for the year. Just follow these steps:

1. **Get your account balance at the end of the year and write it down.**

   You can get your year-end balance from your online broker's website or from a printed statement.

2. **Get your account balance at the end of the previous year and write it down.**

   Again, this information is available from your broker's website or from a printed statement.

3. **Subtract the answer in Step 2 from the answer in Step 1. Divide that difference by the answer in Step 2, and then multiply by 100.**

   Say your portfolio was worth $10,000 on December 31, 2018 and $12,000 on December 31, 2019. You would subtract $10,000 from $12,000 and get $2,000. Divide $2,000 by $10,000 and multiply by 100, and the answer is 20 percent. You earned a 20 percent rate of return in that year.

Don't worry about dividends and splits when using this approach. And don't concern yourself if you've bought or sold stocks. As long as your dividends and sale proceeds go into the brokerage account, this way of calculating your return reflects all these things.

An easy way to calculate returns if you've deposited or taken out money

You're probably already asking the logical question: What if you deposited money into or withdrew money from your brokerage account? Deposits or withdrawals complicate things a bit, they're still not hard to calculate. There's an easy way to calculate your return when you have deposits to or withdrawals from your account.

Say your portfolio was worth $10,000 on December 31, 2018, and $12,000 on December 31, 2019. But you made the withdrawals and deposits to your accounts follows:

Date	Action	Amount
Dec. 31, 2018	Account balance	$10,000
March 20, 2019	Deposit	$1,000
June 25, 2019	Withdrawal	$500
Oct. 1, 2019	Deposit	$1,000
Dec. 31, 2019	Account balance	$12,000

Okay, time to start crunching some numbers:

1. **Get your account balance at the end of the previous year.**

   Using the example, you'd write down $10,000, which was your balance on December 31, 2018.

2. **Get your account balance at the end of the current year.**

   You'd write down $12,000, which was your supposed balance at the end of 2019.

3. **Add all the money you've added to your account during the year.**

   In the example, you'd write down $2,000 ($1,000 from March 20 plus $1,000 from October 1).

   Only include fresh money you've deposited into your account. Don't include dividends that were paid.

4. **Add all the money you've withdrawn from your account during the year.**

   In the example, you'd write down $500. That's the only withdrawal you supposedly made.

   Include just withdrawals from the account or checks you have written on the account. Do not include stocks you've sold if you left the proceeds in your account.

5. **Subtract the answer in Step 4 from the answer in Step 3. Divide the result by 2 and write down the answer.**

   In the example, you'd write down $1,500. You'd get that by subtracting the $500 in supposed withdrawals from the $2,000 in supposed deposits. Divide the answer, $1,500, by 2.

6. **Add the answer in Step 5 to the number in Step 1.**

   You'd write down $10,750. You'd get that by adding $750 to the number in Step 1.

7. **Subtract the answer in Step 5 from the number in Step 2.**

   You'd write down $11,250. That's $12,000 minus $750.

8. **Subtract the answer in Step 6 from the answer in Step 7.**

   You'd write down $500. That's $11,250 minus $10,750.

9. **Divide the answer in Step 8 by the answer in Step 6 and multiply by 100.**

   You'd get your 4.7 percent rate of return by dividing $500 by $10,750 and multiplying by 100.

You might want to calculate how your portfolio is doing before the end of the year. For instance, in June, you might want to get your mid-year performance. That's no problem. Just use the value of your portfolio at any date in the year in Step 2. All the formulas remain the same.

The hardest way to calculate returns

The methods of calculating your returns described in the preceding sections can get you accurate measures of your rate of return. But as you can imagine, there's always a way to measure returns even more precisely. Some mutual funds, for instance, use a complicated calculation called the *dollar-weighted return* or *internal rate of return.* This approach requires advanced computing that's beyond the scope of this book. I show you some websites in this chapter, though, that have computerized performance tracking tools that can measure your internal rate of return for you.

You can find out more about different methods of calculating portfolio returns at the following sites:

» **dailyVest** (www.dailyvest.com) provides performance calculation services for large investment companies — not for the unwashed masses, in other words — but the dailyVest website *does* contain an in-depth description of the different ways returns are measured. Be sure to click the Personal Rate of Return tab for details.

» **Microsoft Excel's NPV and IRR help page** (https://office.microsoft.com/en-us/excel-help/go-with-the-cash-flow-calculate-npv-and-irr-in-excel-HA010342558.aspx) provides instructions on how to use the spreadsheet software to perform sophisticated performance tracking.

>> **Breaking Down Finance** (https://breakingdownfinance.com/finance-topics/performance-measurement/modified-dietz/) provides a detailed explanation of how you can measure your returns by using advanced techniques.

Calculating How Risky Your Portfolio Is

The returns you get from investing online are only half of what you need to know. Just as important, if not more so, is how much risk you took on to get those returns. Measuring risk is a little more controversial. You find many ways to do it, and investors generally disagree on the best way.

Most investment professionals, though, acknowledge the value of measuring an investment's or portfolio's risk by studying the volatility, or *standard deviation*, of its returns. Yikes, that term is scary and might conjure up memories of statistics class. But by using readily available online tools, you can use standard deviation as a way to get a handle on how much risk you're accepting in investing. Standard deviation is a mathematical way to determine how much your portfolio swings in value from its average return.

Just know this: When your portfolio's standard deviation is a large number, you'll probably see some big ups and downs in your portfolio's value. And when the standard deviation is low, you have a good idea that your portfolio won't keep you up at night.

Statistics tell us that 68 percent of the time, your portfolio should not rise by more than its average return (plus the standard deviation) or fall more than its average return (minus the standard deviation). And 95 percent of the time, your portfolio shouldn't rise by more than its average return plus two times its standard deviation or fall by more than its average return minus two times its standard deviation.

For example, if you put your money in a five-year certificate of deposit that pays 5 percent interest, the standard deviation of your return would be 0. In other words, you will get 5 percent a year no matter what. But if you invest in a risky stock that returns 15 percent a year on average, your standard deviation might be closer to 40. That means 68 percent of the time you can expect your portfolio to return somewhere between a gain of 55 percent (the 15 percent average return plus the standard deviation) and a loss of 25 percent (the 15 percent average return minus the standard deviation).

A simple way of calculating your average return

Before you can measure how risky your portfolio is, you must first calculate its average yearly return. Earlier in the chapter, you found out how to calculate your portfolio's annual returns. Next, you need to use those annual returns to measure your portfolio's average annual return. You can do this easily by taking all your annual returns, calculated using the directions in the earlier sections, and analyzing them.

After you calculate your portfolio's annual returns for each year, you should write them down or put them in a spreadsheet. I use the returns listed in Table 8-1 as an example.

TABLE 8-1

Returns in a Sample Portfolio

Year	Return, %
2018	-4.4
2017	21.8
2016	12.0
2015	1.4
2014	13.7

Source: S&P Dow Jones Indices

If the returns above look familiar, they should. Those are the annual returns over the past five years of the Standard & Poor's 500 index, which tracks large company stocks. Just look at those numbers. Can you say volatile? The fact that the market goes up or down so much in a year is why investors look at long-term average returns to create a sane plan for their portfolios.

How do you measure your average return? You can't just take a simple average by adding all the returns and dividing by five. Doing that will give you the wrong answer. Instead, you must calculate the geometric mean. The *geometric mean* is the way to correctly measure stock return, trust me. I could explain the technical difference between simple averages and geometric means, but we'll both get headaches for no good reason. If you're truly curious, Deborah Rumsey does a nice job explaining it in her *Statistics For Dummies* (published by Wiley.).

If you don't want to go to the trouble of measuring geometric mean as I describe shortly, the Average Return Calculator at Hugh's Mortgage and Financial Calculators (www.hughcalc.org/calc/areturn.php) can do it for you. Just enter your returns for each year, and the site calculates the geometric mean or what it calls the "true average return." Easy Calculation (www.easycalculation.com/statistics/geometric-mean.php) can also calculate the geometric mean.

You can calculate geometric means using a financial calculator or a spreadsheet. But this is *Investing Online For Dummies*, right? So, I show you how to do it online by using the Horton's Geometric Mean Calculator that you see in Figure 8-1 (available at www.graftacs.com/geomean.php).

Horton's Geometric Mean Calculator

Revised 01/25/2018

Enter 2 to 100 values. Do not leave blanks between values.
NEED HELP?

POINT 1: 95.6	POINT 2: 121.8	POINT 3: 112	POINT 4: 101.4
POINT 5: 113.7	POINT 6:	POINT 7:	POINT 8:
POINT 9:	POINT 10:	POINT 11:	POINT 12:
POINT 13:	POINT 14:	POINT 15:	POINT 16:
POINT 17:	POINT 18:	POINT 19:	POINT 20:
POINT 21:	POINT 22:	POINT 23:	POINT 24:
POINT 25:	POINT 26:	POINT 27:	POINT 28:
POINT 29:	POINT 30:	POINT 31:	POINT 32:
POINT 33:	POINT 34:	POINT 35:	POINT 36:
POINT 37:	POINT 38:	POINT 39:	POINT 40:
POINT 41:	POINT 42:	POINT 43:	POINT 44:
POINT 45:	POINT 46:	POINT 47:	POINT 48:
POINT 49:	POINT 50:	POINT 51:	POINT 52:
POINT 53:	POINT 54:	POINT 55:	POINT 56:
POINT 57:	POINT 58:	POINT 59:	POINT 60:
POINT 61:	POINT 62:	POINT 63:	POINT 64:
POINT 65:	POINT 66:	POINT 67:	POINT 68:
POINT 69:	POINT 70:	POINT 71:	POINT 72:
POINT 73:	POINT 74:	POINT 75:	POINT 76:
POINT 77:	POINT 78:	POINT 79:	POINT 80:
POINT 81:	POINT 82:	POINT 83:	POINT 84:
POINT 85:	POINT 86:	POINT 87:	POINT 88:
POINT 89:	POINT 90:	POINT 91:	POINT 92:
POINT 93:	POINT 94:	POINT 95:	POINT 96:
POINT 97:	POINT 98:	POINT 99:	POINT 100:

submit reset

FIGURE 8-1: Horton's Geometric Mean Calculator can do much of the work for you.

Before you rush and type in the returns from Table 8-1 into Horton's Geometric Mean Calculator, you need to follow an additional step. Horton's Geometric Mean Calculator can't handle negative numbers. I know you don't think you'll ever have a negative return, but just in case, I show you what to do. Just add 100 to each of the returns, giving you what you see in Table 8-2.

TABLE 8-2

Returns Converted to Get Geometric Mean

Year	Plus 100 (Adjusted Return, %)
2018	95.6
2017	121.8
2016	112
2015	101.4
2014	113.7

Enter those returns into the blanks in Horton's Geometric Mean Calculator labeled Point 1, Point 2, and so on. After you have entered the returns, scroll to the bottom of the page and click the Submit button. At the top of the page, you see the geometric mean, from which you subtract 100. In this example, the geometric mean is 108.50. You just subtract 100 from 108.50, and you find out your portfolio has a geometric mean gain of 8.5 percent.

If you'd rather measure your portfolio's geometric return in a spreadsheet, Microsoft Excel has a GEOMEAN function that can do it for you. And if you don't have Microsoft Excel, you can download a fairly capable spreadsheet program for free called OpenOffice (www.openoffice.org/). Although it's not as slick as Excel, it's hard to argue with the price. (OpenOffice'sCalc spreadsheet program calls its function the GEOMEAN function as well.)

Calculating your risk

If you used Horton's Geometric Mean Calculator to measure your portfolio's average return, you've also measured your risk. At the top of the page, right below the geometric mean, is the risk, or standard deviation. In this example, the standard deviation of the portfolio is 10.39 percentage points, as shown in Figure 8-2.

Microsoft Excel has a function that measures risk. The STDEV function can measure the standard deviation of returns that you enter.

Standard deviation works best as a measure of risk if you have many years of data to study. If you've been investing for only a few months or years, you can convert your quarterly results into a yearly or *annualized* number. Investopedia (www. investopedia.com/articles/04/021804.asp) shows you how to do this. If all this seems like too much effort, just use the online risk-measurement tools that I describe a little later in this chapter.

FIGURE 8-2:
Horton's
Geometric Mean
Calculator
crunches your
portfolio's risk
(standard
deviation) as well
as the return
(geometric
mean).

Geometric Mean Calculator Results

Number of points	5	Arithmetic mean	108.90	
Geometric mean	108.50	Maximum value	121.80	Graphs are currently not available.
Standard deviation	10.39	Sum of points	544.50	
Minimum value	95.60	Equation is	y=1.58 x + 104.16	

What does it all mean? Sizing up your portfolio

You did it. You measured your portfolio's average return and risk. Now what? You can start by shopping for a new pocket protector. But after that, you can compare your portfolio's risk and return with another investment so that you can put it into perspective. You can see how your performance stacks up by comparing it with a benchmark called an index. An *index* is a basket of stocks used to measure your success. If your portfolio's risk is higher than the index's risk, make sure that you're also getting a higher return.

Chapter 2 describes most of the popular market indexes. The Standard & Poor's 500, due to its general acceptance and the fact it closely tracks the U.S. stock market, is the most common index used to size up investors' returns. If you want to compare your portfolio's risk and return to the S&P 500 for the same time period, you can download the S&P's annual returns from Standard & Poor's by first going to https://us.spindices.com/indices/equity/sp-500 and then clicking the Additional Info button. From the menu that appears, choose the Monthly and Annual Returns option. The site opens a spreadsheet. Click the S&P Markets Attributes Web File link and enter those returns in Horton's Geometric Mean Calculator. The result you get is the S&P 500's risk and return for the same years.

If you want an easier way to compare returns, you can see how your portfolio fared relative to the long-term returns of major types of investments, such as the ones shown in Table 8-3.

Are your returns lower than the long-term returns on the S&P 500? If so, make sure that your risk is lower too. You can read the definitions of different types of Treasurys — called Treasury bonds, Treasury notes, and Treasury bills — in Chapter 16.

TABLE 8-3

Long-Term Risks and Returns of Different Investments

Investment	Return, %	Risk (Standard Deviation)
Standard & Poor's 500	9.5	19.6
Treasury notes (loans to the U.S. government that come due in 10 years)	4.8	7.7
Treasury bills (loans to the U.S. government that come due in a year or less)	3.4	3.0

Source: Federal Reserve database via New York University, using data since 1928

Finding other things to compare your returns to

You don't have to compare your stock portfolio to the S&P 500. Investors commonly choose different indexes to compare their performance to. It's important to rank yourself against the right index to get a good understanding of how you're truly performing. For instance, if you want to know how fast your sports car is, you'd compare it with another sports car, not an economy car. You can benchmark your returns against

>> **More specific indexes:** If you're investing mainly in small-company stocks, you should compare your results against an index that tracks small-company stocks. Same goes with mid-sized company stocks or bonds. Russell's Asset Class Dashboard (https://russellinvestments.com/us/insights/asset-class-dashboard) is an easy-to-use and color-coded way to find out how specific areas of the market have performed in 12-month periods going back many years. You can track stocks of different sizes, sectors, industries, regions, countries, and commodities.

FTSE Russell's US Index Performance Calculator (www.ftserussell.com/index-series/index-tools/russell-index-performance-calculator) can also help you do this. You can view a series of annual returns from many types of investments, including large-company stocks (measured by the Russell 1000) and small-company stocks (measured by the Russell 2000) going back many years. You can then enter those returns into Horton's Geometric Mean Calculator and see how your portfolio stacks up.

Some investors choose to slice the market even more finely when selecting a benchmark. For instance, if you invest mainly in large, undervalued stocks, you would want to compare your performance to a large *value* index that holds similar stocks. Undervalued stocks have share prices that are below what a company is really worth.

>> **A basket of index mutual funds:** Index Funds Advisors (www.ifa.com/portfolios) has created a number of portfolios of index mutual funds that can be used as benchmarks. The IFA portfolios are excellent benchmarks because they are passive index funds designed to deliver the optimum return for the risk taken. You can see where your portfolio would fit on the risk-and-reward chart. You also find a risk-and-return calculator (www.ifa.com/portfolios/PortReturnCalc/index.aspx) that you can use to see what the IFA portfolios have done between specific time periods. If you're getting lower returns for higher risk, you might consider switching to a more passive investment strategy. Table 8-4 shows a sample of some of the returns over the past 20 years.

TABLE 8-4   ## Index Funds Advisor Portfolios

IFA Portfolio	Annual Return between Jan. 1, 1999 and Dec. 31, 2018, %	Risk (Standard Deviation) between Jan. 1, 1999 and Dec. 31, 2018
100 (riskiest)	8.09	16.7
85 (moderate)	7.5	14.1
5 (low)	2.5	1.6

Source: IFA.com

Using Online Tools to Calculate Your Performance

If you understand the inherent value of tracking your portfolio's performance but maybe the math involved is just too onerous, you've come to the right section of this chapter. Here, I show you automated tools that can crunch your performance numbers for you. You find three main advantages to letting your computer do the heavy lifting in measuring performance:

>> **Ease:** All you have to do is enter your trades, and the computer does the rest. You don't need to look up formulas. You also don't risk making a mistake in the calculations.

>> **Speed:** The calculations are already programmed in, so after the data is entered, the system can spit out your performance. You don't need to fire up a calculator.

>> **Customization:** You can tinker and have the system calculate what your performance would have been, for instance, if you didn't have that one stinker in your portfolio.

Completely relying on online tools to tell you something as important as your portfolio's risk and return isn't ideal. Different sites might use different method-ologies, and it might be difficult to find out what precisely is being measured. With that said, it's better to rely on online tools than to not measure your portfolio's risk and return at all.

Looking at online performance-measurement tools

Because many new investors are just now getting interested in tracking their performance, a flurry of new tools is now promising to do the job. They generally fall into these four categories:

>> **Financial software:** You install this software on your computer to crunch the math. Financial software includes personal finance software (discussed in Chapter 1), which contains performance-tracking capabilities. You also find specialized software designed just to track returns.

>> **Online stock simulations and social investing sites:** Most of the stock simulation sites (discussed in Chapter 2) and social investing sites (discussed in Chapter 7) have adequate performance-measurement capabilities. I single out a few in this chapter.

>> **Portfolio-tracking sites:** These services allow you to enter your stock holdings and help measure your returns. Portfolio-tracking sites are kind of like Swiss Army knives: They feature a variety of portfolio-tracking tools in addition to measuring your portfolio's returns. Many portfolio-tracking sites, for instance, alert you if a stock is about to pay a dividend or provide links to online news stories about stocks you own.

>> **Performance-tracking websites:** These websites are designed with the express purpose of tracking portfolio performance. Because performance-tracking sites focus on performance tracking, they tend to give a great deal of information on your portfolio's risk and return and are precise and exacting.

Using personal finance and performance-tracking software

If you choose to go the software route, it stands to reason that you're going to be buying or downloading software and installing it on your PC. This software runs on your computer and crunches your returns, and sometimes your risk, too. Examples include the following:

>> **Quicken** (www.quicken.com): A major player in the financial software field, Quicken has advanced investing functions that monitor all your portfolio returns. What makes Quicken unique is that it measures the expected risk, or standard deviation, of your portfolio in addition to returns. Quicken compares your portfolio's risk with the risk of different benchmarks, including small and large stocks. You can access this feature in Quicken by choosing the Portfolio Analyzer feature on the Investing menu option. You may have to activate Classic Menus first, which is located under the Edit menu option. See Chapter 1 for more information on Quicken. Another feature in Quicken lets you put your portfolio online so you can check it from any computer with an Internet connection.

>> **Quant IX Software's Investment Account Manager** (www.investment accountmanager.com): Quant IX's entrant in the financial software market is an advanced software program designed to meticulously track your portfolio's returns. You enter your transactions, and the software does the rest with a great level of precision. The software costs $99, which includes one year of online access to stock data.

>> **Analyze Now!** (www.analyzenow.com): Technically, Analyze Now! doesn't offer a software program; rather, it provides you with a collection of free spreadsheets that can help you calculate everything you need. The Estate & Investment Manager spreadsheet not only calculates your annual returns but also helps you optimize your tax strategy and pick the right type of brokerage account. The Free Return Calculator calculates your portfolio returns even if you moved money in and out of your account. Click the Computer Programs link on the left side of the website to download the spreadsheets.

>> **Spreadsheet plug-ins:** If you're already a spreadsheet jockey and want to track your performance that way, you need a way to pull current stock quotes into your spreadsheet. The QMatix XLQ plug-in (www.qmatix.com/index.htm) pulls both current and historical stock quotes into Excel. But the QMatix XLQ Lite software costs you $159, and other data-access charges might apply.

Using stock simulation and social investing sites

Most stock simulation and social investing sites offer performance-tracking tools. I describe stock simulations in Chapter 2 as a way to get your feet wet by choosing stocks and investing online. And I cover *social investing sites* in Chapter 7 as a way to connect with other investors. The *performance-tracking sites* have noteworthy capabilities, including the following:

- » **NinjaTrader** (www.ninjatrader.com): This site's trading simulator allows you to practice trading using digital funny money. But it also gives you access to the site's performance section, which lets you see how your portfolio did during different timeframes. It's definitely designed with advanced active traders in mind and could very well be overkill if you just want to see how your buy-and-hold portfolio is doing.

- » **InteractiveBrokers Asset Management** (https://interactiveadvisors.com/): In addition to helping investors find professional investors who have performed well, Covestor also has an impressive performance-tracking tool. It's one of the few social investing sites that measures both risk and return.

Online brokers are so competitive that they often look at what others are doing and match it. Be sure to check with all the online brokers to see whether they have added any portfolio performance-tracking tools.

Using portfolio-tracking websites

Just about all the sites that track market information, which I describe in Chapter 2, contain portfolio trackers. These *portfolio-tracking sites* allow you to enter your holdings or transactions and then sit back, waiting for them to tell you how much your stocks are up or down for the day and year. Several, including Yahoo! Finance, let you download your portfolio into a spreadsheet. Portfolio-tracking sites do many things in addition to measuring performance. Still, some of these portfolio-tracking sites can also have advanced capabilities, including the following:

- » **Morningstar.com** (www.morningstar.com): Morningstar has a standout portfolio tracker because it tells you more than just whether your stocks went up or down for the day or year. You start by signing into Morningstar and clicking the My Portfolio tab. Next, if you click the My Performance tab for your portfolio, you can see how its value has changed over the past 12 months, as well as in each of the past 10 years. Morningstar can also email you each day, telling you how your portfolio did, or send you alerts when a stock moves up or down 10 percent in a day or a mutual fund you own got a new manager. The Portfolio X-Ray feature applies advanced statistics techniques to see whether your portfolio fits your needs. Morningstar can import an existing portfolio you might have saved at your brokerage or by using personal finance software. The Portfolio X-Ray feature, though, is available only to subscribers to Morningstar's premium service, which costs $199 a year.

- » **Personal Capital** (`www.personalcapital.com`): Personal Capital attempts to give online investors the same powerful portfolio-tracking tools on the web that they've had in software, such as Quicken. In fact, Personal Capital was built by several former Quicken developers. You can sign up for the service for free, and it will import all your portfolio information from various brokerage firms. Personal Capital's performance-tracking tools are some of the most powerful on the Internet. There are also mobile apps if that's more your speed. You will, though, need to trust the site enough to provide your brokerage account's login information. Also, although the site is free, you may be contacted by a financial advisor who works with Personal Capital to inquire whether you're interested in paying a fee to get some financial handholding.

- » **StockSelector.com** (`www.stockselector.com`): A free portfolio service for the more active trader, StockSelector.com provides ample links to all sorts of company news and other data designed to help you buy and sell stocks. StockSelector routinely spotlights specific stocks its members are paying attention to, such as the Top Ranked Stock, which is available near the top of its main web page.

- » **Mint.com** (`www.mint.com`): Intuit's online Mint.com website is geared mainly toward helping consumers save money. But you also find a basic portfolio-tracking feature that can size up your portfolio and see how you're doing relative to the broad stock market. Mint's portfolio-tracking features aren't as powerful as Quicken's, but the site is free.

- » **Money by Envestment Yodlee** (`https://money.yodlee.com`): Yodlee is the company that provides the heavy-duty calculations that many online brokers use to power their sites. Money provides many of the same portfolio-tracking tools to you, no matter who your brokerage firm is or even if you don't have a brokerage. And it's free. If you are with an online brokerage firm, Money can automatically download your portfolio so that you don't have to type anything.

Using performance-analytics websites

Performance-tracking websites focus on measuring how your portfolio is doing. These sites provide much more detail about your portfolio's risk and return than general portfolio-tracking websites. They take the mathematics seriously and explain exactly how they're getting the numbers they are getting. But best of all, their computers do the work so that you don't have to. Sites to check out include the following:

- » **Macroaxis** (`www.macroaxis.com`): If you want to put your portfolio through the paces and really see how it's performing, this site is for you. The free site runs your portfolio through *mean variance optimization,* a complicated analysis that precisely measures how much risk you're taking and what kind of return you're getting as a reward. The site also tells you whether your portfolio is correctly constructed to make sure that you're getting the payback you deserve for the risk you're taking.

>> **Profitspi** (www.profitspi.com)**:** This site lets you enter your trades and quickly calculates your returns. You can sort your stocks to see which ones are performing the best and instantly compare your results to the Dow Jones Industrial Average, NASDAQ, and Standard & Poor's 500. You can also download the results to a spreadsheet.

>> **Icarra** (www.icarra.com)**:** Icarra is primarily a sophisticated performance-tracking site that has social investing aspects. It's one of the few free sites that can calculate your returns similarly to how mutual funds track their performance — by using the advanced internal rate-of-return method that I describe earlier in this chapter. Icarra.com also lets you benchmark your performance against several major market indexes. You can share your performance with other users if you choose.

By measuring your portfolio's risk and return, you're already miles ahead of many other online investors. You have the know-how to tweak and refine your investments to make sure that you get the optimal return for the risk you're taking.

Chapter **9**

Choosing an Asset Allocation

You wouldn't sail a ship without a map or bake a cake without a recipe, but so many online investors do the equivalent when they buy and sell stocks and other assets without understanding how they fit into a broader plan. That plan, in investment language, is called an asset allocation. Your asset allocation determines how much of your portfolio is placed into different types of *asset classes,* or types of investments — typically stocks, bonds, and cash. By following this plan, you can make sure that you get the maximum return for the amount of risk you're taking. One controversial study claims that more than 90 percent of a portfolio's swings, on average, are due to the asset allocation.

In this chapter, I show you how a well-designed asset allocation plan can improve your success investing online. You also find out how to build your ideal asset allocation by using online tools to help you find an allocation that's right for you.

The Recipe for Your Online Investing: Asset Allocation

Many investors make the mistake of chasing random stocks they hear about, buying them, and throwing them into their portfolios. They pick up stock tips online and neighbors and blindly invest. Some of these investors wind up owning so many stocks that they have an unmanageable portfolio, which generates disappointing returns. Others try to be more selective and invest in just a few stocks they think are promising, but they later find out that their portfolios are too risky for their taste.

The answer is simple: Approach investing like a chef with a recipe in hand. Rather than tossing all sorts of ingredients into your portfolio pot and guessing what it will taste like, it's best to know what needs to go into the pot to get what you want. In investing, this plan is called an asset allocation.

An *asset allocation* might be general and tell you what percentage of holdings to put in stocks, how much in bonds, and how much in cash. But it can also get more detailed and exotic, calling for a dash of large U.S. company stocks, a pinch of international stocks, and just a touch of emerging markets.

REMEMBER

Asset allocations are designed to let all the investments in your portfolio blend together into a stew that will be most likely to generate the highest possible return for the lowest amount of risk.

The advantages of creating and sticking with an asset allocation include

- >> **Diversification:** Hands down, diversification is the biggest advantage of having an asset allocation. An asset allocation calls for certain percentages of your portfolio to be in certain investments. For instance, you might put 70 percent in stocks and 30 percent in bonds. You want your investments to be spread into different investments that tend to move up and down at different times. This diversification will hold the value of your total portfolio steady — and reduce risk — over time.

- >> **Rebalancing:** A great way to boost your returns without taking on additional risk, rebalancing pretty much does what the term implies. Periodically, one group of investments in your asset allocation will fall in value. Stocks might fall and bonds rally, for instance. When that happens, the percentage of your portfolio in stocks will fall below your plan and the percentage in bonds will rise. To stick to your allocation and maintain the percentages, you need to buy more of the investments that have fallen in value and sell those that have gained. And when you do that, you'll be buying investments when they're cheaper and selling them when they get pricier, which isn't a bad strategy.

>> **Discipline:** Staying in control is priceless with online investing. Because trading online is so inexpensive and easy, it's tempting to chase after popular stocks that are in the news or new investments other investors are talking about. Many of those investments end up disappointing investors, though, because they're overvalued. I explain how to measure a stock's valuation in Chapter 13, but if you stick with your asset allocation, you can avoid this pain.

What's so great about diversification?

If you were to design the perfect portfolio, you'd certainly want the maximum returns for the least amount of risk. The way you do this is by *diversifying*, or spreading your risk over a wide swath of investments. This approach certainly can reduce *risk*, which I define in Chapter 8 as standard deviation.

REMEMBER

A high standard deviation means that the portfolio is riskier, and a low standard deviation means that it's less risky.

The first aspect of diversification is the idea of safety in numbers. As you add more stocks to your portfolio, you reduce the odds that a vicious decline in any one stock will depth-charge your portfolio.

REMEMBER

Before you rush out and buy thousands of stocks, though, you need to be aware of two things. First, your portfolio's risk falls by smaller amounts as you add stocks. For instance, the reduction of risk when you go from 30 stocks to 40 is less impressive than when you go from 1 stock to 10.

Also, before you start buying every stock you can get your hands on, remember that better ways exist for buying hundreds of stocks at a time: You can buy *mutual funds*, *index mutual funds*, and *exchange-traded funds*. These single investments are baskets that own hundreds of stocks. So with just one trade, you get the same benefit of an investor who spends hundreds of dollars in commissions building a massive portfolio of stocks. That's why for many investors, buying an index mutual fund or exchange-traded fund is the optimum strategy. (I talk about index mutual funds in Chapter 10 and exchange-traded funds in Chapter 11.)

Zig-zag: The second element of diversification

Diversification isn't just the result of owning many stocks. You can reduce your risk further by combining different types of assets that zig when the others zag. Stocks that move differently than each other are said to have little *correlation* with each other. Investors build asset allocations by piecing together investments from popular asset classes such as the following:

>> **Cash** is typically parked in funds that buy short-term IOUs, such as money market funds. Money market funds are discussed in Chapter 10.

>> **Bonds** are generally longer-term IOUs issued by governments and companies.

>> **U.S. stocks** are the shares of the thousands of companies that trade on U.S. stock markets.

>> **Foreign stocks** are shares in companies that trade on exchanges in other countries. Foreign investing is covered at more length in a bonus chapter on international and emerging markets at www.dummies.com/bonus/onlineinvesting.

>> **Emerging market stocks** own pieces of companies in up-and-coming economies. The risk is high, but the returns can be high over time, too.

>> **Real-estate investment trusts (REITs)** own commercial property such as strip malls, apartment buildings, or offices. They tend to have low correlation with other asset classes, making them attractive in many asset allocations. REITs also tend to pay dividends that are higher than companies in other industries.

Personal finance site NerdWallet provides a helpful primer on the different asset classes at www.nerdwallet.com/blog/investing/investing-101-overview-major-asset-classes-invest.

Smart asset allocations put the asset classes together in optimal ways. For instance, foreign stocks and U.S. stocks don't move in lockstep with each other, so they work together well in a portfolio. Bonds and stocks also move differently. Blending the right doses of these different investments together helps give you the appropriate portfolio and is the purpose of diversification.

TECHNICAL
STUFF

As mentioned, the degree to which investments move together is called the correlation. It's a complicated mathematical issue that is discussed at more length in *Statistics For Dummies,* by Deborah Rumsey (Wiley), and online at www.investopedia.com/terms/c/correlation.asp.

Just know this: When an investment moves identically to the market, it has a correlation of 1 with the market. When an investment moves exactly opposite to the market, it has a low correlation, or −1. If you can find investments with a low correlation and add them to your portfolio, you might be able to reduce your portfolio's risk.

The secret to creating a portfolio is a balancing act among three factors: expected returns, risk, and correlation. Most investors appreciate the importance of choosing investments with high returns and low risk. There's another aspect of investing, though, that you might not think about. You want assets that don't move in lock step with each other. The idea is this: If you own two investments, and if one is doing poorly at the time, it's nice if the other investment is doing better. That way, the investment that is doing well offsets the lagging investment. The end result is a portfolio that's a little more stable, giving you the best return and lowest risk possible. Designing a perfect asset allocation can require more higher math than a college physics final exam. To make things easy, later in this chapter I show you websites that can do the number crunching for you.

For now, just know that most asset allocations will recommend that you own a certain percentage of stocks, bonds, and cash. Some asset allocations, though, dissect some asset classes, especially U.S. stocks, with even more precision. U.S. stocks are generally sliced into the categories described in Table 9-1.

TABLE 9-1

Popular Ways to Categorize Stocks

Large value	Large core (core stocks are between value and growth)	Large growth
Mid-sized value	Mid-sized core	Mid-sized growth
Small value	Small core	Small growth

©2019 Morningstar, Inc. All Rights Reserved. Reprinted by permission of Morningstar.

Let me explain the categories in Table 9-1. Each box contains a *size*, such as large or small, and a *style*, such as value or growth.

Bigger isn't always better: Understanding size

You'll often see references to *large-cap, mid-cap, small-cap,* and *micro-cap* companies when you're researching asset allocations. Those terms are critical to asset allocations and are the basis of how online asset allocation sites work.

When you hear a reference to large-cap companies, for instance, it's a way to describe the company's total market value, or market capitalization. The *market capitalization,* or *market cap,* is the total price tag the stock market places on a company and is calculated by multiplying the stock price by the number of shares the company has outstanding. Market cap is a valuable way for investors to look at stocks because studies show that companies with similar market values have similar returns, risks, and correlations. For instance, small companies tend to have higher returns than large companies, but they're also riskier.

You might wonder: What's a small company and what's a large company? The distinction changes over time as the stock market rises and falls, but Table 9-2 gives you a general idea of where the lines are drawn.

TIP

Want to know whether a stock you own is a large or small company? Nearly all the quote services that I describe in Chapter 2 can give you the market value. You can type a stock's symbol in the Quote search box at MSN Money (www.msn.com/en-us/money), click the name of the company, and scroll down a bit. The market value appears on the right side of the page next to the Market Cap label. Then just see where that market value figure ranks in Table 9-2.

TABLE 9-2

What's Big and What's Small?

Asset Class	Market Value
Large	Greater than $8.2 billion
Medium	Greater than $2.4 billion but less than $8.2 billion
Small	Greater than $600 million but less than $2.4 billion
Micro	Less than $600 million

Source: S&P Dow Jones Indices based on February 2019

Picking investments with the right styles

Companies' market values aren't the only things that matter when it comes to asset allocations. Some investors also pay attention to stocks' *styles*, such as *value* and *growth*.

The definition of what makes a value or growth stock isn't as cut and dried as market value. You find ways to decide whether a stock is considered to be a value stock or a growth stock in Chapter 13, but for now, just know that *value stocks* are those that are generally bargain-priced. Value stocks tend to be cheaper relative either to their assets or the earnings and dividends they are generating than their rivals. Value stocks, though, are cheaper for a reason: They're perceived as being risky because they are in trouble or in a mature industry. *Growth stocks,* on the other hand, generally command lofty prices relative to their assets and earnings because investors expect them to grow rapidly in the future.

When you put together market value, style, and correlation, you have everything you need to construct a perfect portfolio. These building blocks help you get the highest return for the amount of risk you're taking on. Table 9-3 shows the long-term return, correlation, and risk of some of the types of investments suggested by asset allocation sites.

TABLE 9-3

Investments That Zig When the Market Zags

Asset Class	Long-Term Return, %	Correlation with Large U.S. Stocks (S&P 500)	Risk (Standard Deviation)
U.S. large-company stocks	9.3	1	18.0
U.S. large value-priced stocks	10.6	0.94	21.8
U.S. small-cap stocks	11.0	0.89	24.2
U.S. small value-priced stocks	12.4	0.86	28.3
International value-priced stocks	10.4	0.79	23.0
Emerging markets stocks	12.1	0.82	23.5

Source: IFA.com based on data since 1928 through Dec. 31, 2018

TIP

You can read more about how asset allocations balance the three factors at the following sites:

>> **Investopedia** (www.investopedia.com/managing-wealth/achieve-optimal-asset-allocation): This site provides a comprehensive explanation of how an asset allocation plan is created.

>> **Investor Home** (www.investorhome.com/asset.htm): This is yet another description of how asset allocation has become so important in investing today.

>> **Securities and Exchange Commission** (www.sec.gov/investor/pubs/assetallocation.htm): This section of the SEC site runs through all the benefits of having an asset allocation. (See Figure 9-1.)

WARNING

Investors commonly make the mistake of thinking their portfolios are diversified if they own shares of companies in many different industries, such as energy, financial, and technology. I hate to burst your bubble, but that's not how diversification works. If you own only shares of a *large* energy company, a *large* financial company, and a *large* technology company, you might not be truly diversified. For instance, you're missing out on international diversification and bond diversification.

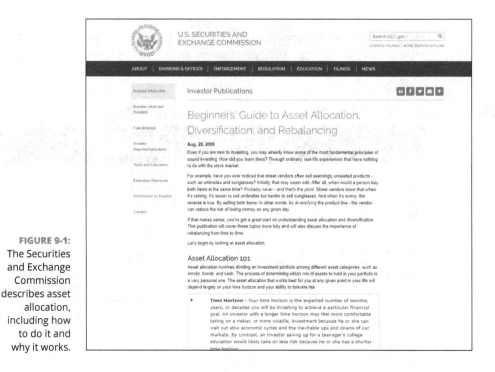

FIGURE 9-1:
The Securities and Exchange Commission describes asset allocation, including how to do it and why it works.

How rebalancing steadies your portfolio

When you have an asset allocation, you're given a recipe that you stick with. And doing this forces you to be a smart investor by buying more of certain asset classes when they're down in price. It may seem counterintuitive to buy investments when they're plunging in value. And, to be clear, buying individual stocks when prices are crashing can be hazardous. Individual stocks are a different animal, and are explained more fully in Chapter 12 and Chapter 13. But if you invest in mutual funds or exchange-traded funds that own large baskets of hundreds of stocks, buying when shares go on sale can be smart because you lower your cost. This approach, called the *rebalancing bonus* by respected financial historian William Bernstein, is described fully here: www.efficientfrontier.com/ef/996/rebal.htm.

WARNING

Rebalancing is advised only when you're buying diversified baskets of assets, such as mutual funds or exchange-traded funds, which track sections of the market. Buying individual stocks is a completely different animal. Buying when a stock is nose-diving is called "catching a falling knife" and can be hazardous to your financial health.

How discipline can save your portfolio from getting punished

When you have an asset plan, it gives you a playbook to stick to if the markets get choppy. Sometimes a plan can save you from yourself and help you resist the temptation to chase after the hot stock or an index your neighbors are talking about. And that's a good thing because investing in last year's winner is a good way to find this year's loser.

Chasing after hot asset classes is kind of like jumping between different checkout lines at the grocery store trying to find the shortest one. You end up spending lots of effort — and often end up in the slowest line anyway.

For instance, large U.S. stocks were the rage between 1995 and 1998 and were the top performers in each of those years, with gains of between 23 percent and 37 percent a year, according to IFA.com. But jumping into the hot asset class was a bad idea. Between 2000 and 2006, large U.S. stocks underperformed other stocks badly. And in 2009 and 2010, investors couldn't get enough of emerging market stocks, including shares of companies based in China and India. Emerging market stocks soared 100 percent in 2009 and 30 percent in 2010. However, investors who piled on in 2011 were left disappointed as emerging market stocks were poor performers and fell 23 percent that year. Emerging markets continued to lag, falling 3 percent in 2013, making them the worst major asset class that year. Emerging markets fell another 2 percent in 2014. Guess what happened in 2017. Emerging markets were the best asset class. Just shows you how random market returns can be. The IFA Style Drifters table (www.ifa.com/12steps/step6/) uses a color-coded chart that shows how asset classes rarely stay on top. Portfolio Visualizer shows you more details on how asset classes have performed: www.portfoliovisualizer.com/historical-asset-class-returns.

Using and Finding Your Perfect Asset Allocation

You have three main ways to design your asset allocation:

>> **Follow guidelines:** These simple rules, available on websites I point out, are great if you just want to keep things simple.

>> **Take a risk-based approach:** Calculate how much risk you can tolerate and select a blend of investments to give you the highest return for that risk.

>> **Take a return-based approach:** Work backward and measure how much return you need to meet your goal and design a portfolio that can get you there.

TIP

In this chapter, I help you choose an asset allocation, which gives you a road map of the types of investments you should buy to get the returns you're looking for. But an asset allocation doesn't do you any good if you don't act on it. In Chapter 10, I show you how to buy the investments your asset allocation calls for by picking the right mutual funds. Chapter 11 gives you the lowdown on exchange-traded funds, and in Chapter 13, I show you how to find individual stocks that match your asset allocation.

This chapter is dedicated to helping you figure out which types of assets you should own. Remember, though, asset classes aren't the same thing as investments. You can't directly buy an asset class, but you can buy an investment that represents an asset class, such as shares of a large company like General Electric, an exchange-traded fund that owns large-company stocks, or a mutual fund that owns large-company stocks.

If you're the kind of person who just wants to be told which investments you should buy, new online tools can do just that. A few online investing services, called *robo-advisors*, not only generate an asset allocation for you but also tell you which exchange-traded funds (ETFs) to buy. If that's what you're interested in, feel free to skip to Chapter 11, where these services are described.

Determining your current asset allocation

If you own any investments now, you already have an asset allocation. It just might not be what you think it is, and it might not be designed to give you the returns and risk you want. Understanding the types of investments you own currently and your current asset allocation is important.

To get this information, the best place to start is with your online broker's website. Some brokerages provide tools that tell you which asset classes you're invested in. TD Ameritrade's Portfolio Planner, available to customers of the brokerage, breaks down your holdings in granular detail, showing you how much is invested in large, mid-sized, and small U.S. stocks, as well as international stocks and bonds, for instance.

But there are also downsides to looking to your online brokerage to track your asset allocation. Your brokerage may not offer an asset allocation tool, or you may not like the ways that the brokerage classifies the asset classes. You may have investment accounts with other brokers or mutual fund companies and would like to see a complete view of your total asset allocation.

For those reasons, you might look to some alternatives to your online broker to track your asset allocation, such as the following:

>> **Personal finance software:** The last big player here is Quicken (now that Microsoft bowed out and no longer sells its Money software). It can classify all the stocks, bonds, and mutual funds in your portfolio and tell you what percentage of your holdings are in each. You can read more about Quicken (www.quicken.com) in Chapter 1.

>> **Morningstar's Instant X-Ray** (www.morningstar.com)**:** This free and handy tool is accessible on the My Portfolio tab of the Morningstar home page. (You might need to click the Tools menu option on the Portfolio Manager page to find the link for Instant X-Ray.) Just enter the ticker symbols of all your current holdings and the dollar value of each holding. Click Show Instant X-Ray, and your holdings are broken down into the major categories, such as cash, U.S. stocks, foreign stocks, bonds, and other. Cash is included in the analysis because some of the mutual funds you own may be holding cash that is not invested. You also see how much of your stocks are in value-priced or growth stocks and also whether they're large, mid-sized, or small companies. Also included is a breakdown of what industries your holdings fall in. The tool is free, but you need to register. (You can see a sample in Figure 9-2.)

FIGURE 9-2:
Morningstar's Instant X-Ray dissects your portfolio by looking for patterns in the types of stocks, industries, and regions you're invested in.

>> **Personal Capital** (www.personalcapital.com): If you want to find out how your assets are allocated and don't want to enter anything yourself, Personal Capital might be your friend. After you sign up for a free account, you enter your username and password for your brokerage firm. Personal Capital downloads all your stock transactions. Then, if you click the Investing tab and then the Allocation tab, Personal Capital will break down what percentage of your portfolio is in which asset class. If you're not comfortable giving your brokerage information to Personal Capital, you can also enter your brokerage transactions manually.

>> **David Grabiner's home page** (http://remarque.org/~grabiner/ assetalloc.html): Mathematics professor David Grabiner created an advanced spreadsheet that analyzes your current portfolio and tells you how it's currently allocated. What makes this spreadsheet unique is that it considers the effect of taxes on your portfolio. And it's a free download!

Using guidelines

If you're the kind of investor who wants to have an asset allocation but doesn't want to delve into all the complications, using guidelines might be for you. The resources covered in the next sections make asset allocation easy, either by suggesting a general-purpose asset allocation that can work for most people or letting you choose from simple but effective allocations.

Intuit's Quicken financial software

Quicken (www.quicken.com) has a helpful Asset Allocation Guide that lets you choose from several off-the-shelf asset allocations. You can look them over and decide which one gives you the level of return you're interested in at the amount of risk you can tolerate, such as conservative, moderate, or aggressive.

Efficient Frontier

Efficient Frontier (www.efficientfrontier.com/ef/996/cowards.htm) is a site managed by well-known and well-respected market scholar and advisor William Bernstein. He suggests a Coward's Portfolio, which he says is designed to be an easy way for investors to build a solid portfolio with international exposure. He also suggests which mutual funds to buy to match the portfolio.

AssetBuilder

Scott Burns, a former financial columnist for *The Dallas Morning News*, co-founded a website (www.assetbuilder.com) to help investors find simple asset allocations that they can stick with. For years, Burns recommended a Couch Potato Portfolio, the easiest-to-follow allocation you can find: 50 percent stocks and 50 percent bonds. Put half your money in an index fund that tracks the Standard & Poor's 500 index, which I discuss in Chapter 10, and half in one that tracks the bond market, and you're done. You can find the recipes for several of Burns's asset allocations on the site for free (www.assetbuilder.com/lazy-portfolios). Burns describes his Couch Potato system at AssetBuilder (see Figure 9-3) as well as offers to design an asset allocation tailored for you, for a fee.

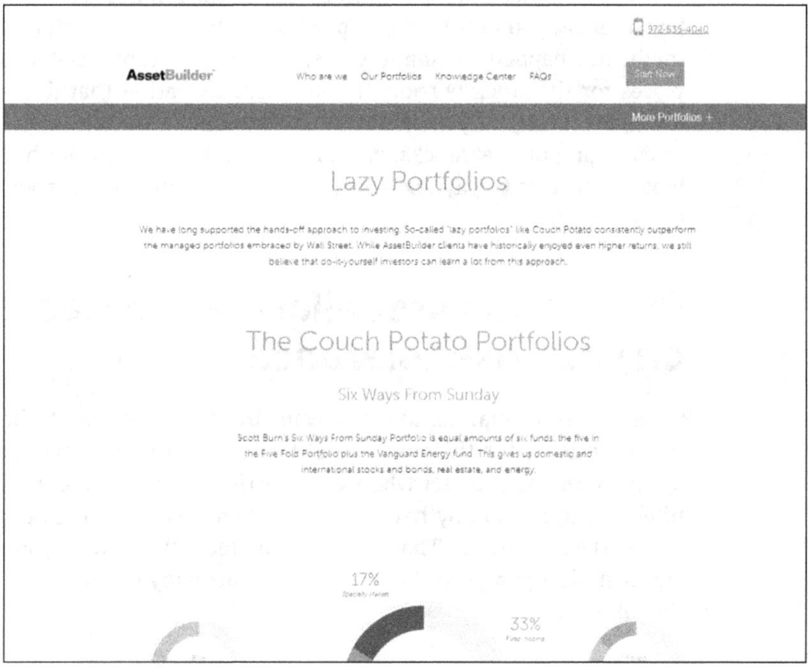

FIGURE 9-3:
AssetBuilder provides a number of off-the-shelf asset allocation plans that might work for you, including the easy-to-follow Couch Potato.

MoneyChimp

Okay, MoneyChimp isn't as big as Quicken, but the folks there know investing. The Asset Allocation page (www.moneychimp.com/articles/risk/portfolio.htm) gives you a general breakdown of what types of assets you should own with a simple calculator.

Iowa Public Employees' Retirement System

Manifesting some good Midwestern common sense, the folks at the Iowa Public Employees' Retirement System have set up a free and easy-to-use online tool that gives you an idea of what your dream allocation would be (`www.ipers.org/calcs/AssetAllocator.html`). You tell the system how old you are, how much you have, how much you save, your tax rate, and your risk tolerance by moving a series of sliders back and forth. It then spits out your asset allocation.

TIP

Most people mentally separate their taxable and retirement accounts when looking at their asset allocation. It's better, though, to think of all your accounts as a whole. You don't need one asset allocation for your 401(k) and another one for your taxable brokerage accounts. In fact, if your asset allocation plan calls for bonds, you could own them in your retirement account. That way, when the bonds pay interest, you don't have to pay the tax until you withdraw the money, which might not happen for many years. Meanwhile, your taxable accounts are good places for the stock portion of your asset allocation that doesn't generate large dividends. Lastly, if you own risky investments with large expected returns, such as emerging market stocks, you should put them in your Roth IRA. That way, you may never have to pay tax if you score big returns in exchange for the large risk you've taken on.

Picking an asset allocation based on your risk tolerance

Some investors may decide they want to tailor their asset allocation with a bit more precision for their individual taste. And if you're like most investors, the disappointment you feel when your portfolio falls more than you'd like is definitely greater than any happiness you might feel at eking out a slightly better-than-expected return. That's why online tools that assess your appetite for risk, and then design a portfolio, make sense for many investors. A few to try include the following:

>> **IFA.com** (`www.ifa.com/SurveyNET/index.aspx`): The folks at Index Fund Advisors offer a Risk Capacity Survey — which I mention in Chapter 1 — as a way to determine what kind of investor you are. The survey asks you a battery of questions to assess how much risk you can take, which is the way it recommends a portfolio to you. The Quick Risk Capacity Survey has just 5 questions, and a longer survey has 25 questions. After you answer the questions, the website suggests one of several portfolios. The most risk-tolerant investors are pointed to Portfolio 100, and risk-adverse investors to Portfolio 5.

IFA's asset allocations are much more detailed than some of the sites that provide guidelines. For instance, rather than suggesting owning large-cap stocks, IFA.com distinguishes between large-cap stocks and large-cap value-priced stocks. The portfolios also recommend specific index funds sold by asset management firm Dimensional Fund Advisors, which you can buy through a financial advisor licensed to sell them.

>> **Vanguard's Investor Questionnaire** (https://personal.vanguard.com/ us/FundsInvQuestionnaire): This section of the Vanguard site, shown in Figure 9-4, asks you ten questions in an attempt to figure out how much risk you can stomach. At the end, the site recommends that you own certain mixes of short-term reserves, stocks, and cash. You can view all the recommended portfolios at https://personal.vanguard.com/us/insights/ saving-investing/model-portfolio-allocations. (Short-term reserves aren't risky investments because they mature in a short period of time.)

>> **CNNMoney** (https://cgi.money.cnn.com/tools/assetallocwizard/ assetallocwizard.html): CNNMoney steps you through four questions designed to figure out what kind of risk taker you are. It then generates a fairly basic asset allocation mix.

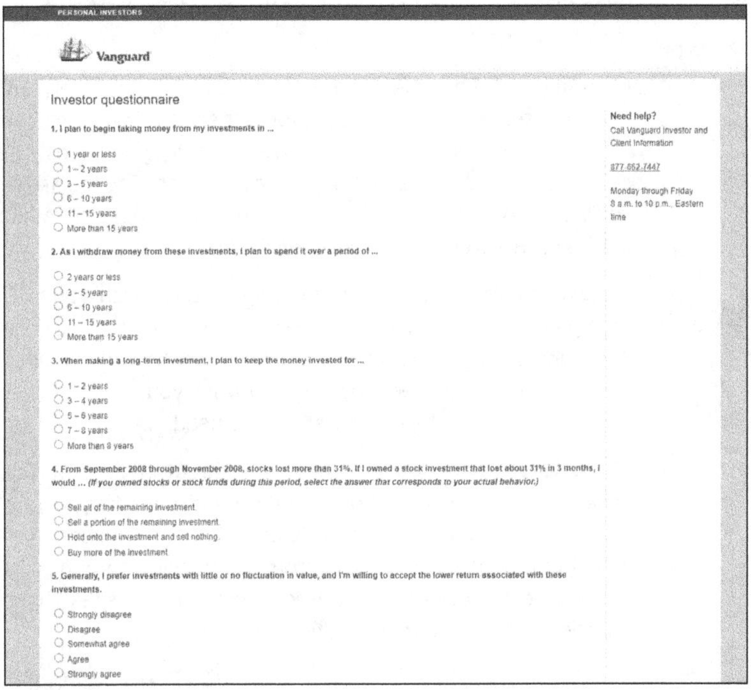

FIGURE 9-4:
Vanguard's Investor Questionnaire can help you decide how to construct a portfolio that fits your needs.

TIP

If you're constantly worrying about your portfolio when the stock market falls, your asset allocation is most likely wrong and you're probably taking on more risk than you can handle. This situation makes you a prime candidate to use the tools in this chapter to make sure that your portfolio is right for you.

Picking an asset allocation based on your goals

The other way to figure out how to allocate your portfolio is to first determine what kind of rate of return you need to reach your goal and then choose an asset allocation designed to get you there. Several of the asset allocation sites take this approach:

>> **Fidelity.com's Planning & Guidance Center** (www.fidelity.com/calculators-tools/planning-guidance-center) helps you plan for a wide array of goals, ranging from retirement and education to more specific things such as a vacation, a wedding, or wealth accumulation. The Portfolio Review also studies how much risk you can tolerate. The site can analyze your current portfolio and make suggestions on ways to improve and suggest an asset allocation. You don't have to be a Fidelity account holder to use the system; you can sign up for a free membership instead.

>> **Morningstar's Portfolio Planner** (www.morningstar.com/Cover/Tools.html) is a serious asset allocation tool for serious investors. The Portfolio Planner examines your financial goals and helps you choose the blend of cash, stocks, and bonds that will make it happen. The tool isn't free, though, so you'll have to pony up for a subscription to Morningstar Premium, which costs $199 a year. A free 14-day trial is available.

TIP

Want to calculate the rate of return you need to reach a goal? Try Money Chimp's Return Rate Calculator (www.moneychimp.com/calculator/discount_rate_calculator.htm). Just enter how much money you have now, how much you need to have, and when you need to have it, and the calculator tells you the rate of return you need.

>> **TIAA's Asset Allocation Evaluator** (shared.tiaa.org/public/publictools/assetallocationevaluator/submitquestions) designs your allocation based on your goal, as shown in Figure 9-5. The third question it asks is what your investment goal is, ranging from just hanging onto the money you have or trying to get the biggest financial score you can. The site then asks additional questions relevant to that specific goal.

REMEMBER

Some brokers and mutual fund companies provide asset allocation tools to their customers. Mutual fund company T. Rowe Price, for instance, offers tools that analyze your portfolio and generate asset allocations to customers.

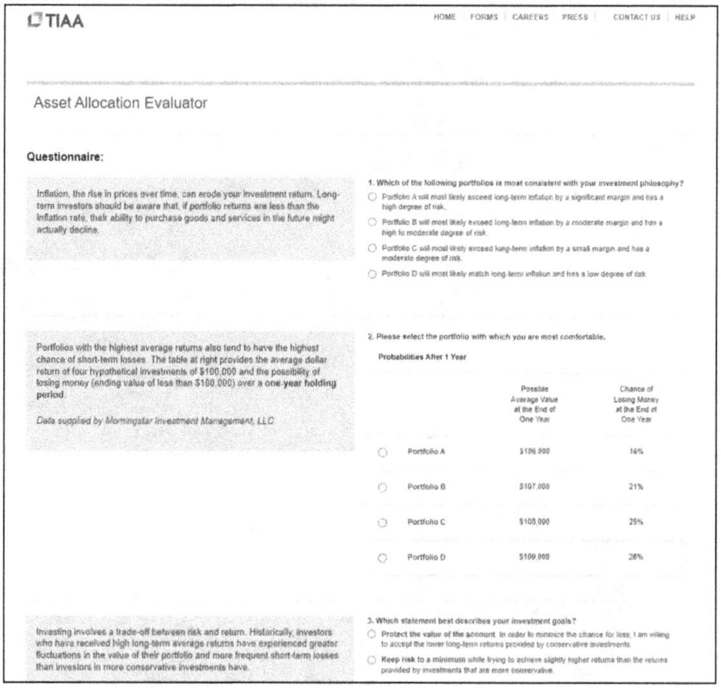

FIGURE 9-5:
TIAA's Asset Allocation Evaluator helps you determine what kind of portfolio can help you reach your financial goals.

IN THIS CHAPTER

» Seeing the advantages — and disadvantages — of mutual funds

» Finding mutual funds online that fit your needs

» Finding out where to buy and sell mutual funds online

» Understanding funds' risks and returns

» Determining the best ways to buy mutual funds

Chapter **10**

Finding and Buying Mutual Funds

Online investing isn't just for individual stock pickers. The Internet can also be used to pick, track, and monitor investments in *mutual funds* — funds that pool money from many investors so that it can then be invested in stocks, bonds, or other assets. By pooling money, mutual funds give many investors some of the benefits that larger investors enjoy, especially the ability to spread money over multiple investments, or diversify. Mutual funds are the way most people invest. More than 100 million individual investors, and nearly half the nation's households, own a piece of mutual funds either directly or through a retirement plan like a pension fund. U.S. mutual funds hold more than $22 trillion in investor assets, which they pool together and use to buy stakes in investments.

In this chapter, I explain how online tools can maximize your success investing in mutual funds. I also show you how to use online tools to pick the right investments for you and walk you through the process of setting up an account to buy or sell the funds.

The Feeling Is Mutual: Understanding Mutual Funds

If all the work it takes to pick individual stocks, which I describe in Chapters 12 and 13, sounds exhausting, mutual funds might be for you. By their design, mutual funds give investors what they're looking for with minimal work. Most mutual funds own large baskets of stocks, giving investors the benefit of diversification (as I describe in Chapter 9) right off the bat. And mutual funds come in many flavors, allowing investors to buy exactly what they want, such as specific types of stocks or industries. Want to own small value-priced stocks? No problem — you can buy a mutual fund that takes care of it. Passive investors can also buy *index mutual funds*, which match market indexes and charge low fees. Active investors can choose from *actively managed mutual funds* that rely on human stock pickers who try to beat the market (although few do).

There's just one problem. The sheer number of mutual funds is so enormous that it's hard to know where to start. There were 18,746 mutual funds at the end of 2017, according to the latest data available from the Investment Company Institute (`www.icifactbook.org/ch2/18_fb_ch2`). That's greater than the 5,745 stocks that trade on major U.S. stock exchanges, including the New York Stock Exchange and NASDAQ.

Considering the pros of mutual funds

Just because mutual funds are so popular, though, that doesn't mean they're right for you. You might decide that buying individual stocks is more your speed. Even so, it's worth first considering what you gain and lose by investing in mutual funds. First, what you gain:

>> **Instant diversification:** If you buy just one mutual fund, you own a piece of dozens, if not hundreds, of stocks, bonds or other investments. Buying a share of a fund is more cost-effective than buying and managing hundreds of stocks yourself.

>> **Easy asset allocation:** As I explain in Chapter 9, it's important to have an asset allocation that helps guide you in what kinds of stocks you should buy to get more return for the amount of risk you're taking on. Some of these asset allocations get specific, calling for a certain percentage of your portfolio to be in small value-priced stocks or large stocks. You can easily gain the right exposure by buying mutual funds dedicated to these *sizes* and *styles.* Buying just five or more mutual funds can give you an easy-to-manage and completely diversified portfolio. Some mutual funds are designed to help you

meet goals, such as growing the value of your portfolio or generating income. You can just buy the fund and leave it up to the manager to find investments that will help you meet your goal.

>> **Low fees:** By pooling your money with many other investors', you often gain significant cost savings. Large mutual fund companies can save money on trading commissions, research, and other fees, which means that they pay less than what you would if you were doing all this on your own. Mutual funds must also disclose the fees they charge you, so you can quickly find those that are the most efficient. The Securities and Exchange Commission (`www.sec.gov/investor/tools/mfcc/mfcc-int.htm`) describes how fees can eat into your returns.

REMEMBER

If you're interested in keeping your costs down, index mutual funds have extremely low fees, sometimes less than 0.1 percent a year. If a fund charges 0.1 percent and you have $1,000 invested, you pay just a $1 fee that year.

Drawbacks of mutual funds worth considering

Despite mutual funds' advantages, they have some significant drawbacks that might be deal killers for you:

>> **Lack of control:** When you buy a mutual fund, you're putting your investment in the hands of an investment company. If you invest with an actively managed fund, which hires a professional portfolio manager to select stocks for the fund to buy, you don't have much say in investment decisions. If the manager sells a stock — one you think is a good long-term hold, for instance — you can't do anything about it. This is the case with index mutual funds, too. If a stock is added to the S&P 500, for instance, your S&P 500 index fund will buy the stock, too.

>> **Tax inefficiencies:** When mutual funds buy and sell stocks during the year, their actions can often result in tax bills you weren't expecting. The most unfortunate type occurs when a fund sells a stock for a gain.

REMEMBER

Yes, you have to pay tax when you sell an individual stock for a gain. But *you* can decide when to sell that stock. Mutual funds may sell stocks for gains anytime, including a time that's not good for you. That gain is then distributed to you, the mutual fund owner, and you must pay tax on it. *Capital-gain distributions* often come with no warning and can spoil a well-thought-out tax plan. This tends to be much less of an issue with index mutual funds because the *turnover,* or number of stocks bought and sold, tends to be lower than with actively managed funds.

CAPITAL-GAIN DISTRIBUTION NIGHTMARE

Capital-gain distributions are one of the biggest drawbacks of actively managed mutual funds. These distributions can be large and unexpected, two things you don't want when it comes to managing your taxes. Consider the whopper of a capital-gain distribution paid by Fidelity's once hugely popular Magellan mutual fund in 2006. After the fund changed portfolio managers, the new manager cleaned house and sold off giant chunks of stocks owned by the fund under the previous manager. That resulted in 19 percent of the fund's assets, or more than $22 a share, to be distributed to shareholders. If you owned 100 shares of the fund in a taxable account, you might have owed capital gains tax on $2,200. The result? An approximate $330 tax hit many investors weren't expecting. Making things worse, if a portfolio manager sells stocks owned for a year or less for a gain, shareholders who own the funds in a taxable account can get hit with high short-term capital gains taxes. It's important to note that this applies to only taxable accounts. Distributions made in tax-deferred accounts such as a 401(k) wouldn't trigger an immediate taxable event.

Capital gains taxes are explained in detail in Chapter 3. They're a serious issue for mutual fund investors. CapGainsValet (www.capgainsvalet.com) is dedicated to forecasting and warning investors of mutual funds that are in the doghouse for massive capital gains distributions. You can see the list of funds in the doghouse at www.capgainsvalet.com/in-the-doghouse. Some of these funds included the Artisan International Small Cap and Goldman Sachs Rising Dividend Growth funds in 2018.

>> **Index shadowing:** The most deceiving actively managed funds are those that pretend to be adding value by picking winning stocks but are actually just tracking or shadowing the market. It's unfortunate when this happens because investors are paying for the expertise of a fund manager but not getting anything in return. These investors could get the same results, and save money on fees, by investing in low-cost index funds.

Types of Investment Companies

Investment-fund companies are usually structured in one of two ways. The structure dictates how the value of the fund is determined and how you buy and sell your shares. The main types of structures are as follows:

>> **Open-end investment companies:** These folks are all mutual funds, all the time. *Open-end* investment companies — also known as *fund* companies — buy baskets of stocks and then sell pieces of the portfolios they've assembled to outside investors. The price of a share of a mutual fund is set at the end of each day when the fund company adds up the value of the shares it owns and divides by the number of shares outstanding. The result, called the *net asset value* (NAV), is what one share of the mutual fund is worth. The NAV is how much the mutual fund company would pay you if you redeemed, or sold, your shares. You can redeem or purchase shares through most online brokers or directly from the fund companies.

How do you find a mutual fund's NAV? Nearly all the sites that provide stock quotes, described in Chapter 2, provide the mutual fund's NAV if you enter the fund's symbol. Some sites provide additional information about the fund. For instance, Morningstar also tells you

- *Performance* of the fund compared to other similar funds and the closest benchmark

- *Long-term returns* going back three and five years

- *Total assets invested with the fund,* a tally of how much investor money is invested in the fund

- *Portfolio managers' names*

- *Dividend yield,* if any

- *Expense ratio,* which is an important area that's discussed more fully later in this chapter, in the section "Deciphering the morass of mutual fund fees"

- *Purchase information,* with a link to the fund company to help you find out how to invest

>> **Closed-end investment companies:** These are part mutual fund, part stock. Like open-end investment companies, *closed-end* funds buy portfolios of stocks. But closed-end funds don't redeem shares held by investors directly. Instead, shares of closed-end funds trade on the stock market just like a regular stock. That means the price is set differently than with mutual funds. Investors study the value of the stocks in the closed-end portfolios and decide how much the basket is worth. The price of the fund moves during the day as buyers and sellers agree on a price. The fact that investors set the price on closed-end funds often creates an interesting situation where the price of the closed-end fund is less than the value of the stocks owned by the fund. When that happens, that means the closed-end fund is trading at a *discount.*

TIP

You can find all the closed-end investment companies that are trading for a discount by logging on to Morningstar's closed-end fund center (https://news.morningstar.com/CELists/CEReturns.html?fsection=CELists) and clicking the Premiums/Discounts column twice to sort by funds trading for a discount.

You can also find out more about closed-end funds in general at the Closed-End Fund Association (www.cefa.com).

Categorizing Mutual Funds

There are more mutual funds than stocks, so it's probably not too surprising that you also find many types of mutual funds. Mutual funds at their most basic level come in four basic flavors: those that invest in stock funds, bond funds, money market funds, and hybrid funds. But if you drill down, you find even more categories. The following sections give you a sense of how categories and subcategories branch off from each other.

Stock funds

Stock funds invest in shares of publicly traded companies. These funds typically go for large gains by pursuing one of a number of strategies:

WARNING

>> **Growth funds** are filled with shares of companies that investors generally expect to expand their earnings the fastest. Portfolio managers of actively managed growth funds are typically willing to pay higher valuations for *growth* stocks because they think the companies are worth it. Growth index funds buy shares of companies that have the highest valuations, often measured by the price-to-book ratio, a concept I explain in more detail in Chapter 13.

If you're young and retirement is still years off, many experts advise to invest in growth funds. The trouble, though, is that academic studies have shown growth funds, including growth index funds, tend to own the most overvalued stocks. That means they tend to have lower future returns and higher risk than value funds that own less glamorous stocks.

>> **Value funds** own companies that Wall Street generally considers to be out of fashion or ho-hum and mature. Actively managed value funds are constructed by portfolio managers trained to look for *undervalued* stocks, or stocks that sell for less than what they're truly worth. Value index funds generally own stocks that have the lowest valuations or, in other words, appear to be relatively inexpensive.

>> **Income stock** funds seek to invest in companies that pay fat dividends, such as utilities and real estate investment trusts (REITs). Income stock funds aren't looking for stock price appreciation alone but also a gravy train of cashflow.

>> **International funds** invest 80 percent or more of their money in companies located outside the United States. Some international funds concentrate on specific areas of the world, such as Europe or Japan. Yet others, called emerging market funds, focus on up-and-coming parts of the world.

>> **Global funds** invest in companies in any part of the world, including the United States.

>> **Sector funds** pick specific industries investors often like to invest in, such as technology, energy, and utilities.

Bond funds

Bond funds own diverse baskets of fixed-income investments, which usually have similar characteristics. Bond funds are generally seen as a way to reduce risk because they collect income from a variety of borrowers. If one borrower defaults on the loan, you own many other bonds and aren't wiped out. You find many types of bond funds, which I discuss in more detail in Chapter 16. The main ones to know about follow:

>> **Government bond funds** tend to invest in debt issued by the U.S. government. These funds usually invest in Treasurys that mature in the short term, intermediate term, or long term, or a blend of each.

>> **High-yield bond funds,** nicknamed *junk bond funds,* generate higher returns by investing in debt issued by companies with shakier finances. Investors get higher interest payments from these types of investments to compensate for the greater risk that some of the borrowers will default. The overall risk, though, is reduced by spreading the investment over many companies' debt.

>> **Corporate bond funds** own bonds issued by large companies. Their yields are generally higher than those paid by government bonds but less than high-yield bonds.

>> **Municipal bond funds** invest in debt issued by state and local governments. These bonds can be attractive because they're usually not taxed by the federal government, and sometimes not by states, either.

Money market funds

Money market funds can be an option for cash you might need at short notice. They invest in very low risk short-term Treasurys issued by the federal government or

IOUs from banks. Money market funds can be great places to get a decent return on cash you've set aside for emergencies. The SEC (www.sec.gov/answers/mfmmkt.htm) provides more information about money market funds.

TIP

Money market funds are supposed to be super-safe places to park cash, and they usually are. The price of a money market fund is supposed to be rock solid and always $1 a share. But like many things that were supposed to be true but weren't, the financial crisis that erupted in 2007 and 2008 called into question the safety of money market funds. In September 2008, the Reserve Primary Fund, one of the largest and oldest money market funds, became the only mainstream money market to "break the buck," or lower its price below $1 a share. The fund's shocking problem resulted from its investment in Lehman Bros. debt, which crashed in value during the crisis.

Reforms were created in July 2014 to tighten the rules on what money market funds can invest in, but as a result, their yields are lower than they were, too. Some investors continue to question whether money market funds are relevant when interest rates continue to be very low well into 2019. Investors know money market funds don't offer much higher interest rates — and sometimes lower — than what's available from a high-yield savings account from a bank.

Hybrid funds

Hybrid funds blend aspects of all the types of funds in the preceding sections into a unique package that suits some investors. Some examples include the following:

- **» Balanced funds** split their portfolios into a preset mix of bonds and stocks. Investors who want to diversify their holdings between stocks and bonds can in theory just buy one of these and leave it up to the portfolio manager.

- **» Target date funds** are an increasingly popular type of investment where you tell the mutual fund company how old you are and it determines the right mix of investments for you. You don't have to do anything. These types of funds automatically split your money into a preset blend of stocks and bonds. As you age and your appetite for risk declines, the funds automatically shift your portfolio to be more weighted toward bonds and away from stocks. The Securities and Exchange Commission (www.sec.gov/investor/alerts/tdf.htm) provides additional information about these types of funds and can help you find some that might fit your needs.

- **» Fund of funds** are mutual funds that buy other mutual funds. The idea is that these funds can assemble a collection of mutual funds so that you don't have to.

What to Look for in a Mutual Fund

When you're shopping for a fund, you want to have a checklist of all the fund characteristics that are important to you. Pay attention to the following:

>> **The fund's style:** If your asset allocation calls for investing in large value-priced stocks, you want to go with a fund that invests in large value-priced stocks. Sounds easy, right? Watch out, though, because the name of a mutual fund might make it sound like one thing, when in reality it's something else.

How could this "what's in a name" business affect you? Say you're debating between two mutual funds that claim to invest in small stocks. Both have the words *small stock* in their names, but the funds might define small stock differently.

Finding out which one owns smaller stocks is easy. Log on to the site of mutual fund tracker Morningstar (www.morningstar.com), enter the first mutual fund's ticker symbol, click the name of the fund, and then click the Portfolio tab on the top of the new page that appears below the fund's name. Scroll down and you'll see the fund's average market value, labeled Avg Market Cap USD, which measures how much the average stock held by the fund is worth. Do the same for the other fund and compare the results. If you want a small-cap fund, make sure that the average market value falls in the small range in the chart in Chapter 9. Figure 10-1 shows you what happens when you check the Vanguard 500 Index Investor portfolio.

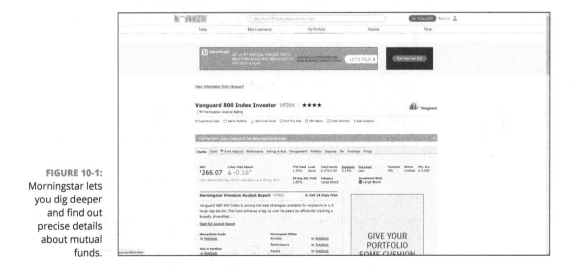

FIGURE 10-1: Morningstar lets you dig deeper and find out precise details about mutual funds.

>> **Long-term performance:** It's tempting to chase after mutual funds that did the best last year or in the last decade. But studies have shown explosive mutual funds are rarely able to maintain their streaks. You should concentrate on a fund's five- or ten-year track record, at the least. If you can get performance data going back further, that's even better. And always compare a mutual fund's performance to the comparable index. If you're looking to buy a mutual fund that invests in large value-priced stocks, you should compare its performance to a large value index.

TIP

>> **Turnover:** The amount of buying and selling a fund does is called its *turnover*. It's important to keep turnover low because when your fund sells stocks, you can face serious tax consequences if it causes capital-gain distributions (see the preceding Fidelity Magellan story).

>> **Ratings:** Mutual fund trackers Morningstar (www.morningstar.com/) and Refinitiv (www.lipperleaders.com) rank mutual funds based on many dimensions of their performance. Although you can't rely solely on these rankings, they're worth paying attention to. Plus, they're easy to understand.

>> **Size:** You have a dilemma when shopping for actively managed mutual funds. When they get too large and have huge chunks of money to invest, performance can suffer as they struggle to find enough investments to plow the money into. A general guideline on this is if you own an actively managed fund that invests in large companies, it might be getting too big when it has $50 billion in assets. Other considerations include how quickly money is pouring in, the size of the companies the fund invests in, the number of holdings, turnover, and cash holdings.

You can find out how much money is invested in a fund by logging on to Morningstar.com, entering the fund's symbol, clicking the name of the fund, and checking out the default Quote page. The amount invested in the fund is at the top of the page below where it says Total Assets. Morningstar offers research on when a fund's size is a detriment here: www.morningstar.com/articles/902120/when-are-stock-funds-too-big.html.

TIP

Popular funds attempt to stop themselves from getting too bloated by *closing* to new investors. When this happens, if you were already an investor in the fund, you can add money, but you can't buy the fund if you're not already an investor.

Being too small can be a problem, too. If a fund doesn't attract enough assets, it might be shut down.

>> **Fees:** The fees are how much the fund charges you every year to invest your money. The fees charged by your fund are typically taken annually no matter what. That means even if the fund falls in value, you pay fees. That's why fees are one of the most important data points to pay attention to. They're so important that the next section is dedicated to understanding them.

Actively managed mutual funds sell investors with the idea that their portfolio managers are so smart that they can beat the market. The reality, though, is that very few beat the market consistently, and they wind up charging investors fees for a promise that's never realized. A look at history shows how the odds are stacked against active mutual fund managers. Of the 355 funds that existed in 1970, only 32 percent were still around by 2009, according to information from John Bogle. Bogle is the founder of Vanguard, which pioneered the low-cost index mutual fund. The other 68 percent of mutual funds no longer exist, most of which were shut down due to poor performance. Even if you picked one of the survivors, you didn't necessarily score. Of the funds that lasted, 37 percent lagged the stock market, and 42 percent turned in performances that nearly matched the market. That means just 7 percent of the funds that existed in 1970 beat the stock market by more than 1 percentage point a year.

Newer data came to the same conclusion. More than 60 percent of active large-cap mutual funds failed to beat the Standard & Poor's 500 in 2018, says S&P Dow Jones Indices. It gets worse. Nearly 80 percent of actively managed funds underperformed in the past three years and more than 80 percent underperformed over the past five! That's why investing in a low-cost index fund, for many investors, is often the best option. S&P updates the statistics on how active funds are doing versus the S&P 500 at https://us.spindices.com/spiva/#/reports.

Deciphering the morass of mutual fund fees

Mutual fund performance swings up and down, along with the stocks and bonds the fund is invested in. But one thing's for sure: The mutual fund company will make sure to collect its fee.

If you're not careful, mutual funds can sting you with all sorts of charges. However, all fees must be disclosed ahead of time, so you can avoid expensive funds if you know what to look for. Following is the short list of the types of fees to be on the lookout for:

>> **Front-end loads** are charged to investors immediately when they buy a fund. These fees are the most difficult to overcome because a bite is taken out of your portfolio even before you get started. Investors often don't like front-end loads and are voting with their feet. Mutual funds with front-end loads saw $221 billion in net new cash outflows in 2017, while funds that don't charge loads saw $447 billion in inflows, says the ICI (www.icifactbook.org/ch6/18_fb_ch6). Regulators don't allow funds to charge more than 8.5 percent for front-end loads. You can read more about how the regulators oversee fees from the

Securities and Exchange Commission (www.sec.gov/answers/mffees.htm). You can usually spot a fund charging a front-end load because it sells what are called *Class A shares.*

>> **Back-end loads** are essentially commissions charged when you redeem shares. They're also called *contingent deferred sales* and are sometimes waived if you own the mutual fund shares long enough. For instance, you'll be socked with a 5 percent fee if you redeem shares in a year or less and 4 percent if you redeem in two years, and the fee keeps falling until it vanishes after you own the fund for five years. Back-end loads include so-called 12b-1 fees that the fund company charges shareholders to promote its fund. These fees cannot exceed 0.75 percent of the fund's net assets per year to pay for marketing costs. Funds that charge back-end loads are designated as *Class B shares.*

>> **Redemption fees** are charged when shareholders redeem, or sell, their shares. Redemption fees are technically different from back-end loads because the fees go to paying the costs that arise from your redemption. But they sting just the same. Regulators prohibit redemption fees from exceeding 2 percent of the amount sold.

>> **Purchase fees** are charged when shareholders buy shares of a fund. This fee might not be called a front-end load fee, but it is still a fee you must pay up front.

>> **Management fees** are the ongoing fees the mutual fund charges you to run your money.

>> **Other fees** include exchange fees if you shift money into a different fund owned by the same mutual fund company, or an account fee if you, for instance, don't meet a minimum account balance.

Although it might seem like the number of charges levied by mutual funds are limitless, mutual fund fees have been falling. The average fees and expenses collected by stock mutual funds were 0.59 percent in 2017, down from 0.99 percent in 2000. And the fees of bond funds have fallen to 0.48 percent from 0.76 percent during the same time period.

WARNING

No-load mutual funds don't charge front- or back-end load fees. But that doesn't mean they're free. Even no-load funds can charge redemption, purchase, exchange, and management fees.

You can easily find out online how much a fund charges in fees. Enter the symbol at Morningstar.com and click the Expense link on the top of the new page that appears just under the fund's name. The site shows you both the initial (front-end load) and deferred (back-end load) fees plus all other fees — including 12b-1 and management fees — on a screen like the one shown in Figure 10-2. Morningstar also shows you how much the fees will eat from your portfolio over the next three, five, and ten years.

FIGURE 10-2:
Morningstar.com
helps you find out
which funds
charge high fees
or low ones.

Quote	Chart	Fund Analysis	Performance	Ratings & Risk	Management	Portfolio	Expense	Tax	Purchase	Filings

NAV	1-Day Total Return		TTM Yield	Load	Total Assets	Expenses	Fee Level		Turnover	Status	Min. Inv.
$266.07	↓ -0.16%		1.79%	None	$ 479.6 bil	0.14%	Low		4%	Limited	$ 3,000
USD	NAV as of 08 May 2019	1-Day Return as of 08 May 2019	30-Day SEC Yield		Category		Investment Style				
			1.81%		Large Blend		▦ Large Blend				

Before paying a load, be absolutely certain that you can't find a less expensive mutual fund or index mutual fund that will accomplish the same thing. The Securities and Exchange Commission (`www.sec.gov/investor/tools/mfcc/mfcc-intsec.htm`) provides a fee calculator that shows just how costly fees can be. Personal Fund (`www.personalfund.com`) can also analyze mutual funds' fees and calculate how much they will cost you.

Finding mutual funds that work for you

With so many mutual funds to choose from, you need your computer's help to find the ones best suited to you. You can use computerized *screening tools*, which scour a database of all mutual funds, looking for criteria you select. Several websites provide such screening tools, including the following:

>> **Morningstar** (`www.morningstar.com`): That Morningstar is on the list shouldn't come as a surprise. To pinpoint the types of funds you're looking for, just click the Funds tab on the Morningstar home page. Next, click the Basic Fund Screener link under the Tools heading on the right side of the page. You can screen mutual funds based on everything from the type of fund, such as large-value, to funds with expense ratios below certain levels, low turnover, average market values of specific amounts, and ten-year returns that you choose. You can even exclude funds that charge loads or only view funds that have received Morningstar's highest ratings. When you've finished entering all your criteria, click the Show Results tab, and you get a list of all the funds that meet your standards.

It's generally a good idea to stick with mutual funds that charge total fees well below 1.5 percent — preferably much lower.

>> **Lipper** (`www.lipperleaders.com`): The other big-name mutual fund tracker, Lipper, lets you begin a search by clicking the Fund Screener link on the right side of its home page. You can narrow your search by type of fund (such as stock or bond) or classification (size and fund family, for instance). A fund's family is the company that offers the fund, say Vanguard or Fidelity. You can also limit your search to funds that receive Lipper's top rating in five categories: total return, consistent return, preservation, tax efficiency, and expense.

>> **Reuters Fund & ETF Screener** (https://funds.us.reuters.com/US/screener/screener.asp): If mutual funds found themselves on the *Survivor* reality show, they would be similarly winnowed down by failing to meet tests of their skill. Think of Reuters' Fund screener as the *Survivor* of mutual funds. The system gives you a count of all the funds that meet your criteria — and you can watch the number drop as you narrow your search.

REMEMBER

Many of the discount online brokers provide free access to mutual fund screening tools, most of which are based on either Morningstar or Lipper data.

Buying mutual funds with an online broker

You have two main ways to buy mutual funds: directly from the mutual fund company or through a broker.

Nearly all the online brokers that I discuss in Chapter 4 let you buy mutual funds. Buying this way is convenient because your mutual fund holdings are listed on your account statements next to your stock investments.

To buy a mutual fund through an online broker, log on to your account, enter the mutual fund's stock symbol, and proceed to buy it just as you'd buy a stock. The online broker's site then gives you the NAV from the previous day. (After the stock market closes, the mutual fund determines the NAV for the day. That NAV, measured after the market closes, determines the price you pay for the shares.)

WARNING

Some online brokers charge exorbitant commissions for buying and selling mutual funds. Table 10-1 shows you some sample commissions from a few top online brokers.

TABLE 10-1

Mutual Fund Commissions

Broker	Regular Online Commission
Charles Schwab	$76.00
E*TRADE	$19.99
Fidelity Brokerage	$49.95
Scottrade	$17.00
TD Ameritrade	$49.95 for no-load funds, $0 for load funds
TradeKing	$9.95 for no-load funds, no commission to buy or sell load funds

Online brokers often offer a number of transaction-free mutual funds that you can buy and sell for no commission. Just be careful, though, because these online brokers also usually hit you with a *short-term redemption fee,* even on a transaction-free mutual fund, if you sell the fund too quickly after buying it. These fees are usually around $50.

How to buy mutual funds without a broker

You might not want to fuss with getting a broker, or perhaps you hate limiting yourself to the transaction-free mutual funds to avoid a broker's high commissions on other funds. You might be a candidate for buying shares directly from the mutual fund companies. This approach might save you money because mutual fund companies typically don't charge commissions.

If you're interested in buying a fund that isn't one of the transaction-free choices that uses a broker, it's best to buy directly from the fund company to avoid paying commissions. It's especially a good idea if you plan to periodically make small investments, which could ring up hefty fees if you use a broker.

To buy mutual funds from a mutual fund company, you need to set up an account, which you can do pretty quickly online. After you decide which fund you'd like to buy, just log on to the fund company's site and click a link that's usually labeled Open an Account. You have to answer the same questions needed to open an online brokerage account, described in Chapter 4, including your address and type of account (individual or joint). You also need to tell the mutual fund company whether you want dividends deposited to your account or used to buy additional shares of the fund. You can fill out the application online in about 20 minutes or print it and mail it in.

Most mutual fund companies offer automatic investment plan (AIP) programs. If you sign up for an AIP, the fund company automatically takes money from your bank savings or checking account each month. It's a good way to make sure that you're regularly saving money. Some funds even let you start with a smaller initial investment if you sign up for the AIP.

Table 10-2 is a directory of some of the larger mutual fund companies.

Some mutual funds can't be bought directly by individual investors. A few mutual fund companies, including leading index fund provider Dimensional Fund Advisors, sell their funds only through certified financial planners.

TABLE 10-2   **A Few Leading Mutual Fund Companies**

Mutual Fund Company	Website	Minimum Deposit for Regular Account
American Century	www.americancentury.com	No minimum, but $100 a year maintenance fee if balance less than $10,000.
Dodge & Cox	www.dodgeandcox.com	$2,500 per fund.
Fidelity	www.fidelity.com	$2,500.
Oakmark	www.oakmark.com	$1,000 per fund.
Royce	www.roycefunds.com	$2,000 on many funds, and $1,000 if part of AIP. Other funds require $50,000 or more.
T. Rowe Price	www.troweprice.com	$2,500.
Vanguard	www.vanguard.com	$3,000 for most funds. $10,000 to avoid $20 annual fee. You can avoid the fee also if you manage your account only online. Be sure to sign up for a mutual fund account, not a brokerage account.

Comparing Mutual Funds

When you're choosing a mutual fund, it's always a good idea to compare several similar funds to each other to make sure that you're getting the best one for your needs. You want to consider the funds' characteristics and risks.

Putting funds' characteristics side by side

Morningstar offers many useful tools that let you compare mutual funds. For instance, it shows you the average price-to-earnings ratios of all the stocks a fund holds.

The price-to-earnings ratio, discussed at more length in Chapter 13, is one way to see how pricey stocks are. Just visit the site and from there, enter the name or symbol of the fund in the Quote field, and click the fund's name when it pops up. Select the Portfolio heading below the name of the mutual fund, which takes you to the portfolio page. Next, click the Holdings link, on the right of the summary link below the name of the fund. You'll see a list of the fund's top holdings and all key information, including the P/E ratios. Morningstar also offers a feature that allows you to compare two mutual funds side-by-side. This Fund Compare feature is located on the Funds tab under the Screeners option. You can compare several funds based on a number of key criteria. The Fund Compare feature is free if you register with the site.

Analyzing a mutual fund's risk

Understanding the potential returns you might enjoy from a fund is just half of the equation. It's equally — if not even more — important to know how much risk you're taking on to get the return. Many of the same online tools used to measure your portfolio's risk, which I explain in Chapter 9, can be used to gauge your mutual fund's risk, too.

Online mutual fund investors, though, can get additional information about risk from Morningstar. Enter the mutual fund's ticker symbol at Morningstar.com in the Quote field in the upper center of the page, and click the name of the fund when it pops up. Next, click the Ratings & Risk tab on the new page that appears, just under the name of the fund. Scroll down a bit and you will see all the vital measures of the fund's risk, including the following:

>> **Standard deviation:** As I explain in Chapter 8, standard deviation is a way to measure an investment's risk. All you really need to know is that the higher the standard deviation, the higher the fund's risk.

>> **Sharpe Ratio:** This measure gives you, at a glance, an idea of how much bang you're getting from the mutual fund for the risk you're taking. The higher the Sharpe Ratio — named after Nobel Laureate William Sharpe — the more return you're getting for the risk.

>> **R-Squared:** This measure helps you figure out how much of a fund's movement is due to the judgment of the portfolio manager and how much is due to the movements of the stock market. The closer R-Squared is to 100, the more the fund mirrors what's going on in the stock market. An index fund tracking the S&P 500 index, for instance, would have an R-Squared very close to 100.

Don't pay a mutual fund manager high fees for just investing in an index. You could pay much less and just buy an index fund. To know whether your manager is shadowing the market, look at R-Squared. If an actively managed fund you own has an R-Squared close to 100, consider dumping it and buying an index fund.

>> **Beta:** This measure tells you how sensitive your fund is to movements by the rest of the stock market. A fund with a beta of 1 moves up and down by the same order of magnitude as the stock market. A beta of 0.75 shows that the fund tends to underperform by 25 percent when the market gains but declines 25 percent less when the market falls. If you want less wild swings in your financial life and can accept lower returns as a result, look for a fund with a low beta.

» **Alpha:** Definitely one of the best statistics out there for measuring mutual funds, this single number tells you whether the portfolio manager is adding value or destroying value. When a fund has a negative alpha, it performs worse than it should, based on the amount of risk that's being assumed. When the alpha is positive, the manager is adding value by getting a better return than would be expected for the risk being taken. Always look for mutual funds with positive alphas. In measuring alpha, Morningstar compares all funds not only to the market (S&P 500) but also to the index that most closely matches a fund's investment objective.

Getting the Full Story: Reading a Mutual Fund's Prospectus

Mutual fund companies are required by regulators to clearly explain to investors, in writing, everything an investor would need to know. This information is contained in a regulatory filing called the *prospectus.* These documents are detailed and worth reading before you invest in a fund.

TIP

Nearly all the most vital data contained in mutual fund prospectuses are captured by mutual fund websites described in the preceding sections. You don't need to dig through a prospectus to get information such as fees or investment objectives. But a section of the prospectus that's often left out of the websites is the Risks section, which outlines all the things that could go wrong. That section is worth checking out. Also, the SEC provides guidelines on what to look for in the prospectus at www. sec.gov/answers/mfinfo.htm.

You have several ways to get the prospectus online, including the following:

» **The mutual fund provider's website:** The mutual fund company's website almost always has a link to the prospectus.

» **Sources for regulatory filings:** Mutual fund prospectuses are regulatory filings, so you can retrieve them from many of the same places you can get companies' filings, as I describe in Chapter 2. The Securities and Exchange Commission's website (www.sec.gov) provides the information for free. (Figure 10-3 shows the SEC's Search for Mutual Funds Prospectuses page at www.sec.gov/edgar/searchedgar/prospectus.htm.)

FIGURE 10-3:
The SEC's
website makes
mutual fund
prospectuses
readily available
to online
investors who
know where
to look.

Getting More Information about Funds

The funny thing about mutual funds is that investors can take an extremely hands-off approach or turn them into an addiction. On the one hand, you can buy a target date mutual fund, set up an AIP, and never think about your mutual fund again. But you could also read about the ins and outs of mutual funds and keep up on all the new developments. If you're interested in studying funds, check out the following sites:

>> **MAXfunds.com (**www.maxfunds.com**):** MAXfunds features a blog that constantly presents news developments regarding the mutual fund world.

>> **John Bogle's website at Vanguard (**www.vanguard.com/bogle_site/ bogle_home.html**):** A collection of Vanguard founder John Bogle's speeches, this page is an invaluable source of investing insights for everyone, not just mutual fund investors.

>> **MarketWatch (**www.marketwatch.com/investing/mutual-funds?link=MW_ Nav_INV**):** A destination for all things pertaining to investing, MarketWatch maintains a center that features news and data on mutual funds.

>> **The Mutual Fund Education Alliance's Mutual Fund Investor's Center (**www. mfea.com**):** This site has helpful information on everything from how to get started with mutual funds to help with asset allocation and retirement saving.

>> **U.S. News and World Report (**https://money.usnews.com/funds/ mutual-funds**):** U.S. News dedicates an entire website to ranking the best mutual funds. You can find the best-of-breed in categories such as long-term bond funds or large growth.

Chapter **11**

Finding and Buying Exchange-Traded Funds

A still relatively new type of fund called an exchange-traded fund, or ETF, is exploding in popularity. Like index mutual funds, most ETFs invest in baskets of stocks tied to a stock market index. ETFs have proven to be so popular that new types are constantly being created, including variants that own investments in commodities or stocks picked by human money managers. ETFs differ from mutual funds in several key ways, including that they trade during the day just like an individual stock and have potential tax advantages over mutual funds. These important differences give ETFs an edge over mutual funds for some investors. ETFs have lured more than $3.4 trillion of investors' cash since they started to catch on in the early 1990s. In this chapter, I explain how online tools can maximize your success investing in mutual funds and ETFs. You see how to use online tools to choose the right investments to set up an account to buy or sell the funds.

Getting to Know ETFs

Exchange-traded funds have been one of the biggest developments in the world of finance since banks started giving customers free toasters. Their popularity continues to amaze the financial industry. Although the $3.4 trillion invested in U.S. ETFs trails the $18.7 trillion in mutual funds, ETFs are growing fast. The value of assets invested in ETFs has jumped more than 150 percent in just five years through 2017, says the Investment Company Institute.

Exchange-traded funds are baskets of stocks, much like mutual funds, that trade like stocks. You can buy and sell them using your online broker just like you would with other stocks. All ETFs have trading symbols and qualify for the low commission rates from online brokers. Several online brokers, including Charles Schwab, Fidelity, and TD Ameritrade, even let you trade some ETFs for no commission. You can get price quotes by using your favorite stock-tracking websites, including those listed in Chapter 2. And ETFs are the instruments that are being used by the increasingly popular robo-advisors, in which a computer picks an optimized portfolio for you.

REMEMBER

You can buy and sell ETFs by using the online broker you're already signed up with. Just enter the ETF's trading symbol, and you can buy and sell just like you would shares of a company's stock.

Investors like ETFs because they're easy to buy. There's no hassle of signing up for accounts with different mutual fund companies. Unlike mutual funds, which update their prices once a day after the market closes, ETF prices are constantly updated during the trading day. That means investors can just buy ETFs and sell them whenever they want during the day, which explains why the number of ETFs has taken off, as shown in Table 11-1.

ETFs have some of the same advantages of mutual funds, as I describe in Chapter 10. Some of those advantages are diversification and access to specific corners of the stock market, including certain sizes of stocks or industries. ETFs, though, offer several advantages over mutual funds, including the following:

>> **Intraday trading:** Mutual funds price once a day, meaning that you don't know how your portfolio has performed until the markets close and the fund companies get around to publishing the net asset value (NAV) for the day. In contrast, the prices of ETFs, like stocks, constantly update during the day.

TABLE 11-1

ETFs Everywhere

Year	Number of ETFs
2009	797
2010	923
2011	1,135
2012	1,195
2013	1,295
2014	1,412
2015	1,595
2016	1,716
2017	1,835
2018	1,988

Source: Investment Company Institute

>> **Access to tougher areas of the market:** Investors interested in buying commodities, bonds, and currencies can buy them easily, just like buying a stock, thanks to ETFs. And because ETFs are priced during the day, speculators can get in and out of risky positions anytime they want. ETFs are a great way to add foreign exposure to your portfolio, as I explain in the "Broadening Your Horizons: International Stocks" bonus chapter on the website associated with this book at www.dummies.com/bonus/onlineinvesting.

>> **Low fees:** Fees on index mutual funds are low, but ETFs in many cases are even lower. It's not unusual for ETFs to charge lower maintenance fees than mutual funds that mirror the same stock index by owning all the stocks in the index. The average expense ratio of ETFs is roughly 0.21 percent, well below the 0.59 percent charged by mutual funds.

>> **Tax advantages:** Due to their structure, ETFs rarely stick investors with capital-gain distributions. That helps investors plan tax strategies. Keep in mind, though, many ETFs still pay dividends, which are usually taxable.

>> **Offer advanced trading options:** Most ETFs offer *options*, specific trading vehicles I discuss in Chapter 5. That feature is attractive to investors who want to do more than just buy or sell the investments. ETFs can also be *shorted*, a technique used to bet that an investment will decline in value that I also explain in Chapter 5.

Invest in Popular Indexes with ETFs

So far, most ETFs track a market index much like an index mutual fund. That's not a bad thing because indexes often outperform actively managed mutual funds and usually have lower fees.

Most of the oldest and largest ETFs, not surprisingly, track the most popular stock and bond market indexes. Some of the largest ETFs that track widely followed indexes include those listed in Table 11-2.

TABLE 11-2   **Popular ETFs**

ETF Proper Name	ETF Nickname	ETF Symbol	Index Tracked
SPDR S&P 500	Spider	SPY	Standard & Poor's 500 (large companies).
Diamonds Trust	Diamonds	DIA	Dow Jones Industrial Average (large companies).
Invesco QQQ Trust	Cubes	QQQ	NASDAQ 100 (100 largest, nonfinancial stocks that trade on the NASDAQ).
iShares MSCI EAFE Index	N/A	EFA	MSCI EAFE index, with stocks from *Europe, Australia,* and the *Far East,* as the EAFE acronym makes clear. (The MSCI part reveals the fund's beginnings as part of *Morgan Stanley Capital International.*)
iShares Russell 2000 Index	N/A	IWM	Russell 2000 (small companies).
iShares Core U.S. Aggregate Bond	Barclays Agg	AGG	Bloomberg Barclays Aggregate Bond index, a broad measure of the value of bonds. It tracks government and highly rated corporate bonds.

How to Find the Right ETF for the Job

As with mutual funds, one of the toughest things about ETFs is finding the right ones for you amid the hundreds of choices out there. But as with mutual funds, online screeners can help you scour through the universe of ETFs and find the ones that fit your needs. The following list gives you a representative sampling:

>> **ETF Screen** (www.etfscreen.com): This site allows you to search for an ETF by using a keyword or by selecting a type of ETF, such as those that track bonds or stocks. You start with the Traditional ETF Screener. Searching by keyword is especially handy if you're looking to invest in a somewhat offbeat

type of stock, type or commodity, or part of the world. Just enter the keyword in the Filter Based On Name field. Want to invest in an ETF that invests in natural resources stocks, for instance? Just type **natural resources** in the search field, click the Search button, and you get a list.

» **ETF Database** (`https://etfdb.com/screener`): ETF Database is another online system that helps you pinpoint just the right ETF for you. You can search ETFs based on a number of criteria, including the all-important expense ratio. The site shows you how many ETFs make the cut as you tweak your requirements.

» **ETFGuide** (`www.etfguide.com`): ETFGuide is a useful site that provides breaking news and developments in the ETF world. It's a good place to check for new ETFs or find out about ETFs that are being closed because they failed to attract enough investors to make them viable.

» **ETF.com** (`www.etf.com`): This site provides data, news, and information connected to investing in ETFs. Investors can find loads of data that compare different ETFs against one another.

» **Morningstar** (`https://screen.morningstar.com/ETFScreener/Selector.html`): Yes, Morningstar does ETFs, too. This section of the site provides a complete screening tool, with detailed search capabilities that help you quickly find the ETF that meets all your criteria. Morningstar's ETF screening tool is free, but you need to register with the site, which is also free.

TIP

Some investors seek ETFs that track specific asset classes or industries. Morningstar makes it easy to find them. The preceding link takes you to Morningstar's basic ETF Screener. Then you can choose an ETF's fund group, such as Domestic or Bond. Morningstar's basic ETF screen also lets you screen on asset class, or Morningstar Category, such as Large Value or Small Growth. Morningstar also has a more advanced ETF screener, which is also free if you register, here: `https://screen.morningstar.com/etfselector/etf_screener_version1.aspx`. This advanced ETF screening tool lets you screen on many more variables than the basic screener does. Just click the Add Criteria button located in the center of the screen. Here you can also choose industries from the Morningstar Sector Weighting category in the screening tool. Similarly, you can filter on a specific asset class from the Style Box option in the Portfolio Style category of the advanced screening tool.

» **Online brokers:** The big players often provide tools that help you find the right ETFs for you. For instance, TD Ameritrade (`https://research.tdameritrade.com/grid/public/screener/etfs/overview.asp`) offers a site that studies your investment objectives and suggests ETFs that might help get you there. You don't need to have a brokerage account with TD Ameritrade to use the system.

» **ETF providers' websites:** The largest ETF providers — iShares (`www.ishares.com/us/index`), Vanguard (`https://investor.vanguard.com/etf`), and

State Street (https://us.spdrs.com) — provide detailed information about their families of funds.

You can find some interesting features digging into ETF sites, including ETFReplay's ETF Correlation calculator (www.etfreplay.com/correlation.aspx), which can tell you how correlated different ETFs are with each other. (Investments are said to have low correlations with each other when they don't move in lockstep with one another.) Buying ETFs with low correlations, as I explain in Chapter 9, is attractive because it can lower your portfolio's total risk.

REMEMBER

Curious which stocks an ETF owns? All the online resources I mention here provide ETFs' *top holdings*, which are the stocks that have the largest positions in an ETF.

Tracking ETFs' every move

Because ETFs are priced during the day just like stocks, they can be useful tools to tell you what types of stocks and industries are moving each day. NASDAQ's ETF center (www.nasdaq.com/investing/etfs) provides in-depth analysis of the ETFs that went up and down the most in value each trading session. ETF center also shows you the most popular ETFs, ranked by trading activity, or volume. (*Volume* is a measure of how many times shares of a stock or ETF trade hands.) Another way to look at ETFs is finviz's ETF heatmap (https://finviz.com/map.ashx?t=etf), which uses a color-coded grid to show which ETFs are moving the most.

ETF fees can vary

Using screening sites like the ones I describe in the preceding section, you can easily find and compare the fees charged by ETFs. Here's how you do it using Morningstar, for example:

1. **Point your browser to** www.morningstar.com.

2. **In the search field at the center top of the page, enter the symbol or name of the ETF for which you want to check fees.**

3. **Click the name of the ETF when it pops up.**

4. **Look over the ETF Quote page.**

   The screen shows all the vitals about the ETF, including its price, the fund company that sponsors it, when it was created, what it invests in, and what its top holdings are. You also see the breakdown of industries it owns and how it has performed relative to major market indexes.

5. **Look at the Expenses area to the right.**

   The ETF's expense ratio appears on the right side of the page.

THE MOST POPULAR ETFs MIGHT NOT BE THE BEST

When you buy an ETF, you're most frequently buying a basket of stocks that mirrors a stock index. And when shopping for index funds, you typically want to find the ones that either best track the type of stocks you're interested in or have the lowest fees.

Ask yourself the same questions you consider when buying an index mutual fund:

- **How large is the ETF?** An ETF's popularity is somewhat of an advantage at least in one aspect. In the case of an ETF, the more assets under management, the better. You don't want to invest in a small ETF that doesn't attract enough investors and ends up being shut down. This issue is becoming more prevalent as more ETFs are rushed to the market. In 2016 and 2017, for instance, 97 and 114 ETFs, respectively, were shut down and the holdings given back to investors or transferred to another fund, says the Investment Company Institute. More ETFs are expected to shut down as the market gets overly crowded with more funds than investors can buy. During 2017, for instance, an additional 241 ETFs were created, the most since 258 were created in 2015.

  To find out how large an ETF is, go to the Morningstar site (`www.morningstar.com`), enter the ticker symbol of the ETF in the Quotes field, and then press Enter. The new page that appears is the Quotes page. The total assets number is found on the top of the page near the right side.

- **What index does the ETF track?** Some small-cap indexes, for instance, track the Russell 2000, and others track the Standard & Poor's 600. Both track small stocks, but differences exist between the indexes themselves. Make sure that you're tracking the index you prefer.

  Imagine, if you will, that you want to buy an ETF that invests in small companies. It's a good idea to check the website of the ETF company and check the average market value of the stocks held by the ETF and compare it with the competition.

- **What are the expenses?** If everything else is equal, nothing is wrong with looking at the price tag and going with the ETF that's cheapest. Vanguard, a low-cost leader in mutual funds, has emerged as a low-cost leader in ETFs as well. Vanguard almost always deserves serious consideration for that reason. The rampant competition in the ETF business has dramatically driven down fees, so it's worthwhile to use one of the screening tools mentioned in this chapter to see what fee the fund charges and compare it to other options.

REMEMBER

The expense ratio is an important number that tells you the annual fee the ETF provider will charge you for owning the ETF. If you invest $1,000 in an ETF with an expense ratio of 0.5 percent, you'll pay an annual fee of $5. You want to compare this ratio with other ETFs you might be considering. You can see a sample in Figure 11-1.

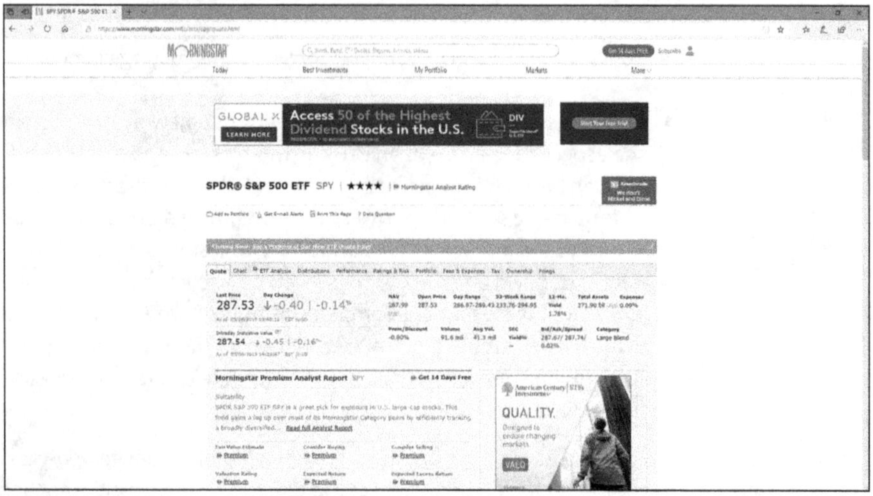

FIGURE 11-1:
You can find all sorts of particulars about ETFs at Morningstar's ETF information page, including the all-important management fee.

Finding out how pricey an ETF is

Stock investors commonly look at the *price-to-earnings ratio*, or *P/E ratio*, of an individual stock to find out how expensive it is. The higher the P/E ratio, the more richly valued the stock is, as I explain in detail in Chapter 13. But ETF investors can also use P/E ratios to find how cheap or expensive the stocks held by the ETF are.

Several websites provide P/E ratios for ETFs. Using Yahoo! Finance (https://finance.yahoo.com/), enter the ETF's symbol in the search field on the top of the page. Click the name of the ETF when it pops up. You'll see the ETF's P/E ratio listed on the right side of the quote box, next to the label P/E (TTM), which stands for price-to-earnings ratio for the trailing (or last) 12 months.

TIP

Yahoo! Finance also provides risk and performance measures for ETFs. The risk measures, such as standard deviation, help you determine how much the ETF will give you indigestion by swinging up and down in value. (I explain these risk measures in detail in Chapter 1.) The performance measures tell you how well the ETF has performed. After entering an ETF's symbol, just click the Performance link on the right side to get the ETF's returns. Click the Risk link on the right side to get the ETF's risk.

To get the P/E ratio of an ETF from Morningstar (www.morningstar.com), enter the symbol of the ETF you're interested in and click the name of the ETF when it appears. In the new page that opens, click the Portfolio link at the top of the page under the ETF's name. Scroll down quite a ways until you see the Value & Growth Measures heading. Below that heading, you can find the ETF's P/E ratio, labeled Price/Prospective Earnings, and see how it compares with the relevant benchmark index, such as the Standard & Poor's 500 index. You can also find lots of other details on the Portfolio page, such as other valuation ratios and which industry sectors the ETF's holdings fall into.

Using ETF-Recommending Robo-Advisors

Perhaps you're on board with this ETF revolution and like the advantages ETFs have over mutual funds, but you're overwhelmed. It's normal to be a bit bewildered on how to start an ETF portfolio, given the vast number of ETFs out there.

Meanwhile, even if you have a solid asset allocation plan, it's up to you to find the right ETFs to match your objectives. For instance, consider that your asset allocation calls for 20 percent of your portfolio to be in large U.S. company stocks. You might not want to do the research to figure out which large U.S. company ETF to buy.

Enter the ETF recommendation service. These online services attempt to turn ETFs into a turnkey operation not only by designing your asset allocation but also by telling you specifically which ETFs to buy. The services have unique approaches, but the idea is the same. You just indicate your investing goals and risk tolerance, and the website handles the rest.

What the heck is a robo-advisor?

If you have a droid that vacuums the floors, you know what wonders a robot can do. Robots can mow your lawn — although that sounds a little scary, frankly. Robots are entering the financial world, too. So-called *robo-advisors* are essentially online tools programmed to pick the perfect portfolio for you. You log in to the robo-advisor and tell the computer how much risk you can stomach and your financial goals. The algorithm spits out a recipe of what ETFs you should own. Some robo-advisors can even buy the ETFs for you.

TIP

Robo-advisors are trying to serve investors who have simple investment needs but are still looking for help. Robo-advisors charge fees, but they're a fraction of what it would cost to hire a human financial advisor. However, you can still save yourself tons of money, especially over the long-term, if you pick your own ETFs and buy them yourself.

The term robo-advisor is more applicable to some providers than others, because with some of these services you don't have to do much more than sign up and put in money. Many younger investors with simpler portfolio needs have gravitated to these services because they're quick, simple, and online.

Robo-advisors that hold your hand

If you would like to tap the wisdom of a financial robot but are not willing to hand over the keys completely to HAL yet, robo-advisors that make recommendations might be for you. With these robo-advisors, you enter your portfolio goals and then receive a recommended portfolio of ETFs. It's up to you to make the decisions and execute the trades.

Following are a few examples of robo-advisors that make recommendations but don't carry them out:

>> **MarketRiders** (www.marketriders.com) is aiming to not only design your asset allocation but also to choose the specific ETFs that can put the plan in motion. You enter some basic information about yourself and your financial goals, and the site generates an asset allocation plan and recommends ETFs. If your asset allocation falls out of balance — say if one type of investment does better than the others — the site tells you which ETFs to sell and which ones to buy to get back in balance. You still need to log on to your brokerage account and do the buying and selling as suggested by MarketRiders' instructions, though. You also pay a fee, $14.95 a month.

>> **Invest-it-Yourself.com** (www.invest-it-yourself.com) brings an à la carte approach to ETFs. You can choose from three menus of portfolios: standard, advanced, and premier. The standard portfolio recommends four asset classes and four corresponding ETFs, the advanced portfolio recommends eight ETFs, and the premier recommends nine ETFs. The system is free, but you'll be offered additional advisory services that do cost money. Just as with MarketRiders, you need to log on to your brokerage account and do the buying and selling of the ETFs recommended by Invest-it-Yourself.com, unless you sign up for more personalized assistance.

>> **Morningstar Model Portfolios** (www.morningstar.com/content/morning starcom/en_us/model-portfolios.html) is like a giant cookbook of recipes for which ETFs to buy. You'll find model portfolios complete with a list of ETFs to buy if you're a retiree or a saver. Morningstar also modifies the allocations for aggressive or conservative investors.

Robo-advisors that are completely automated

If you're comfortable with the idea of handing over your portfolio to a machine, you can choose among the completely autonomous robo-advisors, which pick your ETFs and buy them. These services are designed to completely automate the process of picking ETFs, buying them, and keeping them in balance. There are some catches, namely the fees and the lack of control, but for beginning investors or people who want to hand over the keys to someone, they can be great options. Some examples include the following:

>> **Schwab Intelligent Portfolios** (`https://intelligent.schwab.com/`) isn't the first turnkey robo-advisor, but it is certainly the one making the biggest impact. When one of the largest online brokers in the world — and one that caters to the do-it-yourself investor — unveils a robo-advisor, the world takes notice. Schwab's system assesses your taste for risk and then builds a portfolio of up to 20 different asset classes. Even more stunning: The service is free. It doesn't charge advisory fees or commissions. The service also helps you sell losers at tax time, giving you tax losses that can be used to cut your taxes.

WARNING

Does Schwab Intelligent Portfolios sound too good to be true? A couple of drawbacks exist. First, you'll need to trust the machine's selection of ETFs. But a more important consideration is a hidden fee. One of the asset classes Schwab Intelligent Portfolios can choose is cash. That's right, part of the money you've invested in the portfolio can be held in greenbacks, on which you get no return. As discussed in Chapter 4, allowing cash to sit in your brokerage account collecting no interest and not appreciating can be pretty costly. This hidden fee is something investors need to be aware of — and a big reason why you can still beat the Intelligent Portfolios by choosing your own investments.

>> **Personal Capital** (`www.personalcapital.com`) is best known for its great account tracking tools, but it's also a robo-advisor. You find out how to use Personal Capital to monitor your spending and portfolios in Chapter 1. But the site will also help you build an appropriate portfolio crafted from ETFs as well as individual stocks where appropriate. The site's account tracking service is free, but the ETF recommendation service costs 0.89 percent annually up to $1 million invested.

>> **E*Trade Prebuilt Portfolios** (`https://us.etrade.com/what-we-offer/investment-choices/prebuilt-portfolios`) is another example of a model where an online broker recommends a portfolio and suggests specific

ETFs that can work. Portfolio Builder recommends three portfolios: conservative, aggressive, and moderate. The system doesn't charge a commission but does park some of your portfolio in cash at no return.

>> **Wealthfront** (www.wealthfront.com) is targeting investors who want to enjoy the benefits of ETFs but want to leave most of the work to someone else. Simply answer a few questions on Wealthfront's website, including how much you have to invest and your age, and the site not only will choose ETFs for you but buy and manage them, too. However, this service comes a cost. Wealthfront takes a cut of your portfolio to the tune of 0.25 percent of your assets a year. That amount is less than the 1 percent charged by many human advisors, but you're not getting the personal touch, either. Then again, this service is for investors who don't want a personal touch.

>> **TD Ameritrade's Managed Portfolios** (www.tdameritrade.com/investment-products/managed-portfolios.page) is another major broker's entrance in the robo-advisor race. The brokerage, best known for its tools for active investors, provides off-the-shelf tools for people who just want to automate everything. The Essential Portfolios are the simplest way to build an ETF portfolio and the service costs 0.3 percent a year.

>> **Betterment** (www.betterment.com) is another site trying to appeal to ETF investors who want someone else to choose their ETFs and are willing to pay for the convenience. The site has added features to give more control to people who want to be a little more hands-on as well. To use Betterment, you answer questions about your financial goals, and the site creates a collection of ETFs deemed to be ideal for you. The site will then buy and manage those ETFs for you. Depending on the size of your initial deposit, Betterment takes anywhere between a 0.25 percent and 0.4 percent cut of your portfolio a year as a fee. Need more help? If you pay the 0.4 percent fee, you get access to a team of investment professionals to help you.

WARNING

These automated robo-advisors might seem appealing. They can be a great solution if you've decided you're not interested in managing your money yourself because you don't have the time or interest. These robo-advisors are better than doing nothing — and can be perfect if they urge you to get started. But because you're reading this book, you're probably more than a little interested in optimizing your return. And frankly, you can do better yourself. Most investors can set up an account at a brokerage account with no-commission ETFs, buy the ETFs themselves, and save at least 0.1 percent a year, if not more. That savings adds up over time. Robo-advisors also aren't right for investors who are looking for exposure to some off-the-beaten-path corners of the market, like the ones discussed later in this chapter.

A WORD ON EXCHANGE-TRADED NOTES, OR ETNs

With the success of ETFs, it was just a matter of time before Wall Street cooked up new-fangled variants. One of the latest cousins to ETFs are *ETNs*, or *exchange-traded notes*, or *ETNs*. The goal of ETNs is similar to that of ETFs, which is giving investors a way to easily and cost-effectively buy a basket of investments. And like ETFs, ETNs trade just like a regular stock on a stock exchange, usually the NYSE Arca exchange. However, investors should be aware of a big difference between ETFs and ETNs. ETFs are funds that own the underlying assets. For instance, if you buy an S&P 500 ETF, that fund controls a port-folio of the 500 stocks in the index. ETNs are based on a promise that the issuer of the fund will pay shareholders according to the terms spelled out in the prospectus. So, rather than owning the 500 stocks in the S&P 500, an S&P 500 ETN would be an IOU to investors from the issuer promising to buy and deliver the 500 stocks in the S&P 500 at some date in the future.

Like ETFs, ETNs trade constantly, so investors can buy or sell at any time and don't have to wait for the ETNs to be closed out in the future. The jury is still out on the effectiveness of ETNs versus ETFs. Some ETNs may be able to better mirror the value of the assets, and the costs can be competitive with ETFs. However, some ETNs come with complicated terms that may be too convoluted for most investors. Meanwhile, remember that ETNs are payable by a promise, which you may not be able to count on in the future.

ETFs That Go off the Beaten Path

Most ETFs are typical and closely track their designated indexes. But ETFs are so new and easy to create that some companies, including the following, have experimented with some interesting concepts:

>> **WisdomTree** (www.wisdomtree.com) lets investors bet on academic research from Wharton Professor Jeremy Siegel. Rather than following the lead of most ETFs and index mutual funds, which hold bigger chunks of stocks that have the greatest market values, Siegel suggests that it's better to own bigger chunks of companies that pay large dividends. You can find an entire set of WisdomTree funds, enough to satisfy any asset allocation, based on this theory.

>> **Invesco ETFs** (www.invesco.com/portal/site/us/investors/etfs) provides ETFs that track just about any industry you can imagine, ranging from biotech to companies working on nanotechnology, as well as specialized portfolios that include companies that pay large dividends or buy back their stock.

>> **Direxion** (www.direxioninvestments.com) is best known for its ETFs that allow investors to either amp up or dial back their risk. The company offers a family of 3x ETFs designed to gain in price by an amount that's three times greater than the market. Similarly, it offers ETFs designed to gain in value when the stock market falls.

>> **ProShares** (www.proshares.com) is attempting to make advanced trading strategies more accessible. For instance, its Short QQQ ETF (PSQ) goes up when the NASDAQ 100 goes down, giving investors a way to bet against technology stocks. Similar funds let investors bet against other indexes such as the Russell 2000 and Dow Jones Industrial Average. And here's a fun one: an ETF with the symbol PAWZ. What does this ETF invest in? The petcare industry.

WARNING

During a bear market, ETFs that let you bet against investments such as stocks and bonds became popular. These inverse ETFs rise in value when the investment you're betting against falls in value. So if you're betting against the Dow Jones Industrial Average, and the Dow falls 2 percent during the day, your inverse ETF gains 2 percent. Some inverse ETFs even let you goose returns by *leveraging*, or using borrowed money, to increase your gain when you correctly bet that an investment will fall in value. Confused yet? Well, these funds have some big-time issues to be careful of. First of all, they tend to have high expense ratios, largely because they may use borrowed money. Also, these ETFs are reset daily and are not extremely effective in betting against an investment over the long term. That means if the investment you're betting against has wild daily swings, you might not get the long-term performance you're expecting.

ETFs Have Issues, Too

ETFs are great for many investors who are looking for ways to keep their costs down and simplify their lives. After all, you can buy all your stock and ETF investments from the same brokerage account. But ETFs have drawbacks, too, as the following list makes clear:

>> **Commissions:** Unlike mutual funds, which can often be bought with no commissions through online brokers or directly from fund companies, ETFs are treated like stocks, so your online broker's standard stock commission applies (unless the ETF is on a list of funds that can be bought or sold for no commission). That can be a deal-killer if you make frequent and small investments. Unless you use an online broker with free trades, such as those I discuss in Chapter 4, you might be better off with an index mutual fund.

- >> **Temptation:** The capability to trade in and out of ETFs is too irresistible for some investors — the kind who can't keep their fingers off the mouse button. If the constant pricing of ETFs encourages you to trade too much and veer off your asset allocation course, you might be better off with mutual funds.

- >> **Invisible cost — the spread:** ETFs come with an invisible but costly fee. Just as with stocks, ETFs have a bid price and an ask price. The *bid* is the price other investors are willing to pay for the ETF, and the *ask* is the price the seller will take. The difference, called the *spread,* costs investors money.

  For example, say you bought 100 shares of an ETF at the ask price of $100. Most likely, you'd only be able to sell it for $99.90 or less, costing you in effect 10 cents a share. The less popular an ETF, the wider the spread becomes, and the greater this cost becomes. Are you curious about an ETF's bid and ask prices? They're available from the same places you get stock quotes.

- >> **Premiums and discounts:** ETFs are priced based on what buyers and sellers are willing to pay for the basket of stocks they hold, so the price of an ETF might be greater or less than the value of the stocks it owns. When the ETF's price is greater than the value of the stocks it holds, the ETF is trading at a *premium.* When the opposite is true and the ETF is worth less than the value of its stocks, the ETF is said to be trading at a *discount.* You can look up the size of the premium or discount for an ETF at www.morningstar.com by using the previous directions in the "ETF fees can vary" section to find the expense ratio.

TIP

Don't get overly concerned with the premium or discount. Premiums and discounts are rather small for most ETFs and practically nonexistent for popular ETFs. It's yet another reason to stick with the largest and most established ETFs from the biggest players.

A Few Final Things to Consider about ETFs

One of the reasons ETFs have been so popular is that they make it easy to invest in assets that were difficult to invest in before. By buying a single ETF just as you'd buy a stock, you can instantly invest in a basket of companies working on alternative energy or in financial commodities such as gold, for example. Because ETFs have made it much easier to invest in a wide array of investments, it's more important than ever for investors read the prospectus so that they know how to find out exactly what they're buying when they purchase an ETF. The following sections show you how.

Using ETFs as a way to invest in themes

Investors might periodically want to get a stake on a trend they feel will be important in the future. Some investors, for instance, feel global warming is a serious issue and want to invest in stocks that are finding new sources of energy that generate less pollution. Other investors can't bear to invest in companies they feel contribute to social ills, so they focus on socially responsible ETFs. Such ETFs are often called *ESG*, for environmental, social, and governance. ETFs are perfect for this kind of thing because you can invest in an index that tracks a basket of stocks involved in the theme you're interested in. You can invest in the trend by just buying one investment and spreading your risk over several companies.

WARNING

ETFs that invest in specialty areas of interest generally charge higher expense ratios and may not generate large returns to warrant the costs. Before investing in an investing theme, make sure that you're not getting caught up in a fad. Also, make sure that you're not spending money on management fees that could have been better spent just donating directly to a charity.

A few examples of specialty ETFs are listed in Table 11-3.

TABLE 11-3 ## Green Investing Options

Investment Name	Symbol	Invests in Companies That Are
Vanguard ESG U.S. Stock	ESGV	Viewed as being socially responsible
SPDR MSCI ACWI Low Carbon Target	LOWC	Global and looking to reduce carbon emissions
Invesco Solar	TAN	Positioned to benefit from the demand for solar energy
iShares MSCI USA ESG Select	SUSA	Based in the U.S. and follow socially responsible principles

WARNING

Investors who buy an ETF that tracks a theme might feel they've reduced their risk by owning many companies, not just one. Although you are spreading your risk over many different companies, you're still at risk if the trend falls apart.

Betting on commodities and currencies with ETFs

Even today, buying commodities such as oil, gold, and steel isn't as convenient as you'd think. You usually need to establish a special account with a broker that specializes in commodity trading if you want to invest in commodities directly.

Buying and selling currencies can be a hassle, too. That's why ETFs are a boon for stock investors who would like to add some commodities and currencies to their portfolios.

Most of the major commodities and many currencies can be invested in through ETFs. Table 11-4 provides several examples.

TABLE 11-4   **Ways to Play Commodities with ETFs**

Investment Name	Symbol	Commodity the ETF Tracks
iShares Gold Trust	IAU	Gold
iShares Silver Trust	SLV	Silver
iShares S&P GSCI Commodity-Indexed Trust	GSG	A basket of many types of commodities, measured by the Goldman Sachs Commodity-Index Total Return Index
Invesco Energy Fund	DBE	Energy commodities ranging from oil to gasoline, heating oil, and natural gas
Invesco DB Precious Metals Fund	DBP	Gold and silver
Invesco DB U.S. Dollar Bearish Fund	UDN	Gains in value when the U.S. dollar loses value
Invesco DB U.S. Dollar Bullish Fund	UUP	Gains in value when the U.S. dollar gains value
Invesco DB Commodity Tracking Fund	DBC	Crude oil, heating oil, gold, aluminum, corn, and wheat
iPath S&P GSCI Crude Oil Total Return Index ETN	OIL	Oil
VanEck Vectors Steel Index ETF	SLX	Steel

WARNING

Just because you *can* invest in commodities doesn't mean you *should.* Despite what the infomercials say, gold, for instance, has been a poor long-term performer that has generated subpar returns and greater risk. Be sure that you understand the risks of commodities before jumping in.

Reading the fine print: The prospectus

Like mutual funds, an ETF must be fully described to investors in a *prospectus.* This document describes the ETF's structures, investing objectives, fees, and all other details to investors — and is filled with legal mumbo-jumbo. But looking at the prospectus is worthwhile if you're going to invest in an ETF.

You have several main ways to get the prospectus online, including from the following sources:

>> **The ETF provider's website:** If you log on to the website of the company that provides the investment, you can almost always find a link to the prospectus. This method is typically the easiest way to find a prospectus.

For example, say you're interested in investing in the SPDR S&P 500 ETF, Log on to State Street's ETF website (www.spdrs.com), enter the ticker symbol of **SPY** in the search field in the upper-right corner of the screen (by clicking the magnifying glass icon), and click the ETF's name. On the new page that appears, you see a Prospectus link on the right side. Click it to check out the prospectus.

>> **Sources for regulatory filings:** ETF prospectuses are regulatory filings, so you can retrieve them from many of the same places you'd use to get a companies' filings, as I describe in Chapter 2. Due to the structure of ETFs, though, it's easier to download prospectuses directly from the ETF provider. Many ETF families, such as iShares, make it easy to click a link and download the prospectus. Figure 11-2 shows the Prospectus link at us.iShares.com. (The link is in the upper-right side above the Ready To Buy? button.)

FIGURE 11-2:
The Prospectus link at the top of the iShares page lets you get regulatory filings.

3

Maximizing Investment Knowledge

Dig in deeper and take on more advanced topics that savvy investors rely on when choosing investments and constructing their portfolios.

Use online tools to closely examine companies' earnings, cash flow, and financial statements so that you can get a clearer picture about whether a stock is for you.

Make your computer do much of the hard work for you by building online screens that unearth stocks and investments from thousands of candidates.

Find out whether certain experts and analysts are worth listening to by using online tools that evaluate their performance.

For investors looking for more stability, learn about bonds and other fixed-income investments.

Chapter **12**

Putting Companies Under the Microscope

I f you're the kind of online investor looking to buy the next home-run stock such as Facebook, this chapter offers tips that might help you. I show you how to use online tools to unearth details about companies that aren't picked up by general investing websites. I explain how you can glean insights about companies by dissecting *financial statements,* and I show you how to compare companies with their peers.

Just be careful. Consistently choosing winning stocks and buying and selling them at the right times are infamously difficult and time consuming. If you don't know what you're doing, you might make less money picking individual stocks over the long term than you would if you just bought a mutual fund or exchange-traded fund (ETF) that keeps up with the market.

Understanding Financial Statements

Most investors focus on companies' quarterly earnings reports. It's understandable. Stocks rapidly respond to whether a company topped, matched, or missed earnings expectations for the quarter. Stocks move by an average of 5 percent on the day the company reports earnings, says Bespoke Investment Group.

Online tools, which I describe in Chapter 6, also make it easy to instantly see how a company did during the quarter and decide whether that changes your opinion on a stock. When companies report earnings, though, they provide only the most basic and top-level information in a press release.

Short-term performance can cause stocks to swing momentarily, but *long-term investors* know that a company's true value is based on how it performs over the years, not just the most recent quarter. Examining a company's long-term performance requires a bit more effort and calls for digging into a company's financial statements. Grab your financial shovel!

Investors that study a company's financial statements are said to analyze the *fundamentals*. Fundamental analysis is the part art and part science of determining how much a company is worth. Warren Buffett, one of the most famous investors, uses fundamental analysis to choose investments. If, after reading this chapter, you're interested in finding out more about fundamental analysis, you can check out my *Fundamental Analysis For Dummies* (Wiley). You can find excerpts from the book at www.dummies.com/personal-finance/investing/fundamental-analysis-income-statement/.

Financial statements are detailed documents that show you all the important numbers from a company, ranging from how profitable it is to how financially secure it is. Most detailed financial statements are available online a few weeks after the company puts out its earnings press release. The financial statements must be contained in documents required by regulators, including the following:

>> **The 10-Q:** The official quarterly report that must be filed with the Securities and Exchange Commission (SEC), the main regulator for stocks. It gives an update for the just-completed three-month period. The report is due 40 days after the end of the quarter for companies that have market values of $700 million or more.

>> **The 10-K:** The official version of a company's annual report required by the SEC. After the end of a company's fiscal year, the company must provide an annual report called a 10-K. The 10-K, for most companies, is due 75 days after the end of the fiscal year, according to the SEC (www.sec.gov/answers/form10q.htm).

The 10-Q and 10-K statements are vital because they contain these three key financial statements:

>> **The income statement** measures the company's bottom line. It tells you how much the company earned during the quarter or year based on *generally accepted accounting principles*, or GAAP. (GAAP provides the rules that all companies and their accountants must follow so that investors know how to read the numbers.) This statement is provided also in the earnings press release, but with less detail.

>> **The balance sheet** tabulates the company's net worth. The statement shows you what a company owns and owes at the end of the period. Do you want to know how much cash the company has in the bank or how much debt it has? Both numbers are in the balance sheet. The balance sheet might also be provided with the earnings press release but with less detail.

>> **The cash flow statement** tells you how much cash came into and went out of the company during the period and is considered to be one of the most important documents provided by companies.

The cash flow statement is typically not included in a company's earnings press release, but it's worth waiting for in the 10-Q and 10-K. A company's cash flow is more difficult to manipulate using accounting tricks because it's based on the amount of cold hard cash that comes into the company.

REMEMBER

You can spend a great deal of time mastering the complexities of reading companies' regulatory filings and financial statements. If that interests you, SEC (www.sec.gov/investor/pubs/begfinstmtguide.htm) has a helpful article on financial statements. The kind *Dummies* folks are offering free access to my *Fundamental Analysis For Dummies* cheat sheet here: www.dummies.com/how-to/content/fundamental-analysis-for-dummies-cheat-sheet.html.

Downloading financial statements

Investors can get their hands on financial statements almost instantly. Numerous sites, listed in Chapter 2, let you download regulatory filings for free. The SEC (https://sec.gov/investor/pubs/edgarguide.htm) also provides a users' manual online to show you how to download regulatory filings. When you download a regulatory filing, you might be shocked at how it looks. They're typically seas of text and no pictures — they certainly aren't the colorful magazine-like document you recall when you think of an old school annual report for shareholders.

REMEMBER

The annual report to shareholders is a different document than the 10-K. The *annual report to shareholders* contains all the required financial statements and information in the 10-Ks, but it's presented in a colorful format. If you've read the 10-K, you probably don't need the annual report to shareholders. However, the annual report to shareholders might provide additional, mostly promotional information about the company, such as photos of new products or happy customers, and they can be fun to look at depending on what the company does. You can order these paper documents from the investor relations section of most companies' websites, if the company still produces print copies. Many companies, in an effort to save money, are printing only 10-Ks and making annual reports to shareholders available only online, if at all. You can obtain the electronic copies of annual reports to shareholders at most companies' websites. Many of these annual reports are also available from services such as AnnualReports.com (www.annualreports.com) and the Public Register's Annual Report Service (www.prars.com). Keep in mind, though, that annual reports from these services are often provided in Adobe's Acrobat format. The Acrobat format preserves the photos of the annual reports but is harder to download into a spreadsheet to analyze.

The SEC's Interactive Data initiative represents one of the best ways to download financial statements. The SEC is urging companies to make their financial results available by using the increasingly popular eXtensible Business Reporting Language, or XBRL. Although companies don't have to issue their reports in XBRL, for the hundreds that do, you can easily download their data into a spreadsheet. You'll know that a company offers its financial reports in XBRL if you see a blue button in the SEC site's Edgar search results that says Interactive Data, as shown in Figure 12-1.

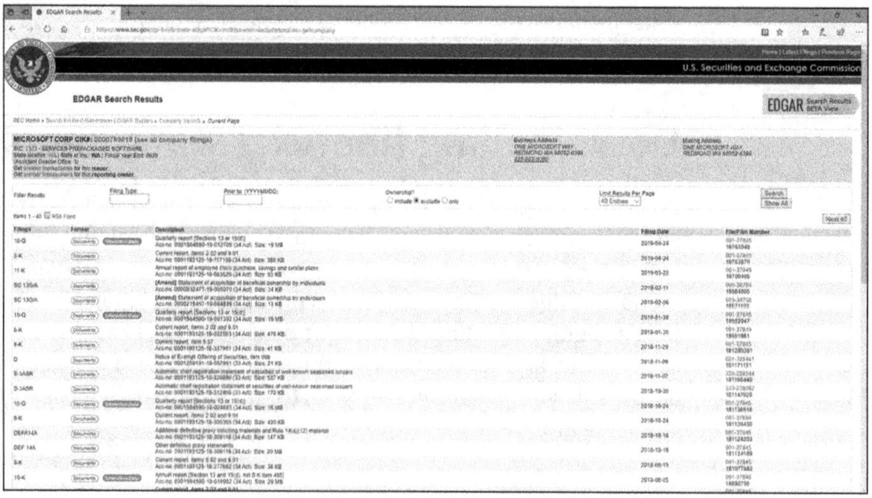

FIGURE 12-1:
The SEC's Edgar system lets you access and download financial statements in XBRL from participating companies, including Microsoft.

Reading the income statement

How much money did the company make? That common question is answered, in detail, by the income statement. The income statement begins with revenue, which is a measurement of the value of the goods and services sold by the company. The company's expenses are then subtracted from revenue to arrive at the company's profit. Making things a bit more complicated, though, is that profit can mean one of several things:

>> **Operating profit** measures how much the company makes after paying day-to-day costs, such as buying raw materials that go into the product, as well as paying salaries. Operating profit is closely watched by Wall Street analysts because it shows how much the company earns from its business and excludes distortion from one-time charges and gains.

>> **Net income** is also known as the bottom line. Net income shows you how much the company made after subtracting all its costs. If the company lost money, it's said to have a *net loss*.

>> **Diluted earnings per share** is what most investors should pay attention to. Diluted earnings per share converts a company's net income or net loss into a number that's more relevant to them: the investor's share of the profit. Diluted EPS is the earnings number most professional investors watch. Diluted EPS is measured by dividing adjusted net income by the number of *fully diluted shares outstanding* — that's to say the number of shares currently in shareholders' hands added to the number that could be in shareholders' hands if stock options were exercised. Monitoring dilution is important because when executives exercise stock options, they get additional shares in the company, so new shares are created. And more shares means the company's profits are cut into more slices, making your slice worth less.

>> **Basic earnings per share** is arrived at by simply dividing a company's net income by shares outstanding. It's a quick and dirty calculation that doesn't account for how exercised stock options can water down the value of your shares.

>> **Proforma earnings per share** is a controversial way to measure earnings that was designed to help investors. Proforma earnings allow companies to leave out certain expenses to help investors understand how the company did, excluding the effect of a big event, such as a merger. Some companies, though, have twisted proforma earnings in a way to leave out costs that made their results look better than they were. Proforma earnings drew such ire from regulators that companies are now required to detail step-by-step in their earnings press release what charges were left out of the proforma earnings calculation.

The first company accused by regulators of abusing proforma earnings was Trump Hotels (https://sec.gov/news/headlines/trumphotels.htm). Given the negative connection many investors have with proforma earnings, many companies are now avoiding the term and calling them adjusted earnings instead. Many Internet companies that sold stock to the public for the first time in 2011 and 2012, including online coupon site Groupon, online gaming site Zynga, and social networking company Facebook, all featured adjusted earnings in their first quarterly reports. Adjusted earnings *can* help investors better understand a company's results, but it's important to understand what's being adjusted and how.

Basics about the balance sheet

The balance sheet tells you what a company owns and what it owes. The company separates what it owns, called its *assets*, from what it owes, its *liabilities*. The difference between assets and liabilities is what portion of the company shareholders own, called *shareholders' equity*. The following list breaks it all down for you:

>> **Assets** are objects of value the company owns, including property, equipment, and machinery. Assets you can't see or touch (such as patents and trademarks) are called *intangible assets* and are also included. Assets are further classified as

   • *Current assets:* Stuff that will be turned into cash within a year.

   • *Non-current assets:* Stuff such as trucks and physical equipment that isn't expected to be turned into cash within a year.

>> **Liabilities** are the company's obligations. Liabilities include bank loans, IOUs given to suppliers, taxes owed, and promises to deliver products to customers in the future. Liabilities are further classified as

   • *Current liabilities:* Bills and other obligations due within a year. The current portion of long-term debt, for instance, is the chunk the company must pay off within a year.

   • *Non-current liabilities:* Long-term obligations the company doesn't have to pay back within a year.

>> **Shareholders' equity** measures the value of the investors' ownership of the company. It's like the corporate version of your net worth. Your net worth is the value of your assets minus your debt. Shareholders' equity is equal to a company's assets minus its liabilities.

One of the best things to pay attention to in the balance sheet is the company's *number of shares outstanding*, which is the number of shares in the hands of investors. A company's number of shares outstanding is important because it measures how many pieces the company's profits are sliced into and how big a piece each shareholder gets.

THE STOCK BUYBACK BLUES

When a company announces that it's buying back stock, you should monitor the number of shares outstanding. Sometimes companies use excess cash to buy their own shares. Investors often applaud stock buybacks because they can, in theory, reduce the number of shares outstanding. And that means each shareholder's slice of the pie gets bigger.

Sounds like a great idea, right? But stock buybacks aren't always what they're cracked up to be. Keep the following in mind when you hear that a company has announced a stock buyback:

- **Stock buybacks can distort earnings per share.** If you see a company's earnings per share rise, don't assume that's because the company is more profitable. If a company buys back stock, earnings per share can rise even if net income is flat. Be especially cautious if a company is using borrowed money to buy its stock back. Doing this may prop up a company's earnings per share but leave it in a weaker financial position.

- **No rule says that the company must follow through.** Just because a company announces it's buying back stock, that doesn't mean it will. Some academic research has found many companies that announced stock buybacks increased their shares outstanding as they issued additional shares to give to employees and executives. You can find out more about buybacks at The Buyback Letter (www.buyback letter.com).

- **Companies have a lousy track record of buying back their stock.** You'd think companies would be great investors when it comes to their own stock. That's not the case, though. Companies tend to buy back their stock when it's pricey and halt buybacks when the shares are cheap. Standard & Poor's 500 companies spent a record $172 billion on stock buybacks in the third quarter of 2007, just before the market peaked in October, S&P says. But then in 2009, when stocks were arguably dirt cheap, buybacks dried up. Companies spent just $24.2 billion on buybacks in the second quarter of 2009, the lowest level in at least a decade. And guess what? Stocks soared more than 120 percent in the following five and a half years. More recently, buybacks have worked out better. S&P 500 companies spent more than $100 billion a quarter on buybacks from June 2013 to hit more than $200 billion in September 2018. These buybacks accompanied a long bull market. We'll see how these purchases work out in the longer term.

Understanding the cash flow statement

Don't make the mistake of ignoring the cash flow statement. This statement cuts through all the smoke and mirrors of accounting to show you how much cash came into or went out of a company. The statement is divided into the following three parts:

>> **Cash from operating activities** tells you how much cash the company used or generated from its normal course of business. This portion of the cash flow statement adjusts net income by adding back expenses that didn't cost the company cash, most importantly an expense called *depreciation* that accounts for the cost of wear and tear on equipment.

>> **Cash from investing activities** shows how much cash a company uses to invest in new property and equipment, also known as *capital expenditures* or *Cap Ex*. The section also shows how much cash the company generates selling assets.

>> **Cash from financing activities** illustrates how much cash a company brings onto its balance sheet, mostly by selling bonds.

Putting it all together

Some of the real power of financial statements occurs when you take elements of one statement and compare them with numbers on other statements.

The first thing many investment professionals do when they get an annual report, for instance, is to compare the cash flow statement with the income statement. If a company is reporting banner profits on the income statement but not bringing in as much cash, that's a potential red flag. Anemic cash flow can be a sign that the company has low quality of earnings. A company has *low quality of earnings* when it shows large profits on its financial statements due to accounting gimmicks, not because it's selling lots of goods and services to actual customers.

TIP

Here's an easy way for you to analyze a company's cash flow: Just compare a company's free cash flow with its net income.

You can get the data by doing the following:

>> **Analyze the financial statements yourself.** A company's free cash flow measures how much cash it brings in the door after paying expenses to keep itself going. Free cash flow (FCF) is a cousin to cash from operating activities. FCF, however, is stricter than cash from operating activities in that it accounts for the

fact that companies use cash to buy new equipment and facilities. To calculate free cash flow, enter the stock's ticker symbol in the Enter Symbol, Name or Keyword field on NASDAQ's home page (www.nasdaq.com) and then click the name of the company when it appears. On the new page that opens, click the Income Statement link under the Fundamentals heading. On the next page that appears, click the Cash Flow tab at the top of the page, which brings you to a page similar to what you see in Figure 12-2. To get the company's free cash flow, scroll down the screen until you see the Capital Expenditures row. Subtract the number in that row from the number in the Net Cash Flow-Operating row. Compare that difference with the number in the Net Income row.

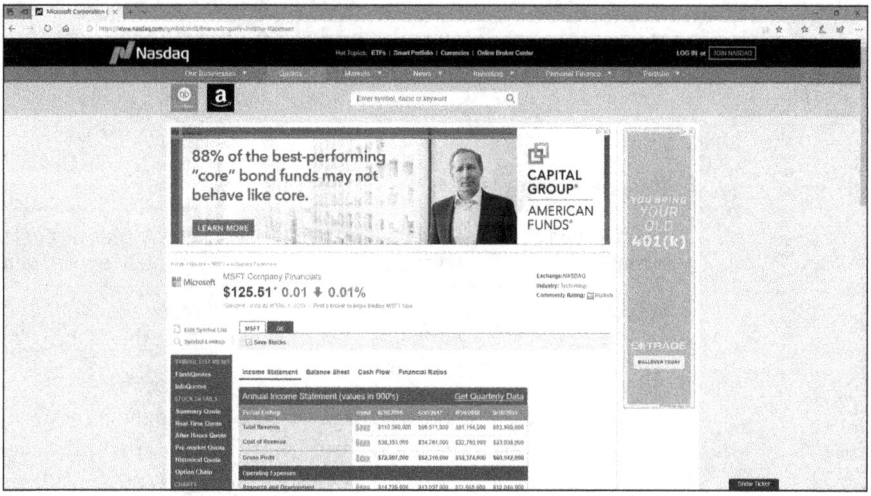

FIGURE 12-2:
You can look up a company's cash flow, capital expenditures, and net income all on one screen at NASDAQ.com.

>> **Get the data from a website.** Several sites, including Morningstar (www.morningstar.com), provide free cash flow data. On the Morningstar site, in the Quote blank, enter the stock's symbol or name (GE, for instance) and click the name of the company when it pops up. On the new page that appears, click the Key Ratios link at the top of the page. The company's free cash flow and free cash flow per share are listed in the new page that appears.

You have a company's free cash flow and net income. Now what? The following tells you how to interpret what you've found. It's the same thing many professional investors do.

If Free Cash Flow Is	It Means the Company
Greater than net income	Brings in more cash than it reports as profit. This situation is a good sign and can be an indication of high-quality earnings.
Less than net income	Brings in less cash than it reports as profit. This situation can be a red flag, so you should analyze the company more closely.

You can read more about free cash flow at Investopedia (www.investopedia.com/terms/f/freecashflow.asp) and Morningstar (https://news.morningstar.com/classroom2/course.asp?docId=2937&CN=COM&page=1&_QSBPA=Y&t1=1184108876).

Spotting trends in financial statements

When you're studying the financial statements, you should look for either patterns or changes to the company's usual trend. The following sections highlight a few of the aspects of trend spotting you should pay attention to.

A company's growth rate

When you get a raise from your boss, what's the first thing you want to know? How much of a percentage increase it is from your previous year's salary. The same goes for every item on a company's income statement and balance sheet. You could go through every item on the financial statements and calculate the change from last year by hand, but Reuters, shown in Figure 12-3, can do it for you. Here's how:

1. **Point your browser to** www.reuters.com/finance/markets.

   The Reuters Markets home page appears.

2. **Click the magnifying glass icon and enter the stock's ticker symbol in the search box.**

3. **Click the Search button and select the company you're interested in.**

   You see the Overview page for the company whose ticker symbol you entered.

4. **Click the Financials tab, and then scroll down to the Growth Rates section.**

   Here you can find the growth rates of sales and earnings per share (EPS) in the most recent quarter, called MRQ. Reuters also shows you the company's earnings growth rate in the trailing 12 months, called TTM. Lastly, you can view longer-term growth rates in earnings and capital expenditures over the past five years.

REUTERS	Business	Markets	World	Politics	Tech	Breakingviews	Wealth	Li

GROWTH RATES

	Company	Industry	sector
Sales (MRQ) vs Qtr. 1 Yr. Ago	13.99	49.75	-4.05
Sales (TTM) vs TTM 1 Yr. Ago	15.42	13.19	8.13
Sales - 5 Yr. Growth Rate	7.23	11.31	5.79
EPS (MRQ) vs Qtr. 1 Yr. Ago	19.42	-14.47	-11.62
EPS (TTM) vs TTM 1 Yr. Ago	17.98	--	--
EPS - 5 Yr. Growth Rate	8.51	10.38	13.10
Capital Spending - 5 Yr. Growth Rate	22.27	11.52	9.13

FINANCIAL STRENGTH

	Company	Industry	sector
Quick Ratio (MRQ)	2.93	1.93	1.90
Current Ratio (MRQ)	2.97	3.19	2.36
LT Debt to Equity (MRQ)	76.02	25.98	8.68
Total Debt to Equity (MRQ)	83.18	31.11	15.78
Interest Coverage (TTM)	--	287.79	13.78

PROFITABILITY RATIOS

	Company	Industry	sector
Gross Margin (TTM)	65.44	56.74	43.21
Gross Margin - 5 Yr. Avg	65.41	59.34	40.38
EBITD Margin (TTM)	42.85	--	--
EBITD - 5 Yr. Avg	39.17	24.88	26.43

FIGURE 12-3: Using Reuters to compare a company's sales and earnings growth rates with the industry, sector, and stock market rates as a whole.

A company's financial composition

Many professional investors compare each item on the income statement with revenue and each item on the balance sheet with total assets. This approach lets you find interesting trends, such as whether the company is increasing its spending on research and development or whether the company's debt is rising. You just need to divide each item on the income statement by revenue and each item on the balance sheet by total assets to perform this analysis, called *common sizing*. Investopedia teaches you how to common-size a balance sheet (`www.investopedia.com/terms/c/commonsizebalancesheet.asp`) and an income statement (`www.investopedia.com/terms/c/commonsizeincomestatement.asp`). NetMBA also explains why common-sizing financial statements is a good idea (`www.netmba.com/finance/statements/common-size`).

If you don't like dividing — no worries! Morningstar can common-size financial statements for you. After loading a company's financials at Morningstar.com, click the Financials tab and look to the bottom of the page. In the shaded bar, you'll see an All Financials Data option. Click it and a screen opens. Find the View option with a % toggle button. Click the toggle button — and presto! — the statement is common-sized.

Using financial statements to understand the company

Financial statements can help you understand the structure and objective of a company. Consider the following aspects of the company:

>> **Value:** Some investors try to figure out how much a company is worth by using its financial statements. If the company is worth more than the stock price would suggest, that tells these *value investors* the stock might be undervalued. One way investors determine how much a company is worth is by examining book value. Book value is an accounting principle. Just know that *book value* generally measures the value of the company's tangible assets recorded in the financial statements minus liabilities. If the company's market value is less than the book value, some investors see the company as being undervalued. The *market value* — the stock price times the number of shares outstanding — tells you how much the company is worth in investors' eyes. In Chapter 13, I show you how to use the price-to-book ratio to determine whether a stock is undervalued or overvalued.

>> **Growth prospects:** Some investors look for companies that post gigantic earnings or revenue growth, hoping to dig up the next market leaders. *Growth companies* generally don't pay large dividends and prefer to keep any extra

cash to invest in new products. Rapidly rising revenue and earnings are signs that a company has morphed into a growth company.

» **Links to broader economic cycles:** Some companies' earnings and revenue rise and fall along with swings in the broader economy. These companies are called *cyclical* companies because they follow economic cycles. Typically, industrial companies such as steelmakers belong to this category.

» **Protection from economic cycles:** Companies that don't follow the economy's ups and downs are often called *defensive* companies. These companies, such as utilities, hospitals, and grocery stores, tend to sell the same amount of goods no matter what the economy is doing. If there's a recession, you still need to eat.

» **Stability and sustainability:** Some companies generate steadily increasing revenue and earnings because they rely on several products with stable demand. Many large companies belong to this category. But companies involved in finding breakthroughs, such as biotech companies researching cures and oil companies looking for untapped reserves, have big ups and downs in their earnings based on their luck. Companies with volatile earnings are called *speculative* companies.

» **Debt load:** The balance sheet shows you how much money the company is borrowing. You can compare a company's debt load with its shareholders' equity to see how heavy the debt load is. Understanding how much debt companies had was critical during the financial crisis. Many companies that borrowed too much found themselves unable to pay back the banks and wound up in financial quicksand. In Chapter 14, I show you how to use computer screening tools to find companies with low debt levels.

Unearthing Details about the Company from Regulatory Filings

Many of the things you need to know about companies contained in quarterly and annual reports are pulled out for you by the financial websites I describe in Chapters 2 and 6. Nearly all the vital company information you need is easily obtained this way, including the following:

» Company descriptions, or *profiles,* which tell you what the company does

» Major owners of the stock, including large mutual funds and pension funds

» Names of the officers and directors, their ages, and their experience

- » Dividends paid by the company
- » Number of employees

But as helpful as the financial websites are, they're missing a great deal of textual information contained in companies' annual reports. It's up to you to read the company's regulatory filings to get the full picture. You can glean some interesting details about the company if you take the time.

Finding the nitty-gritty description of the company

Most 10-K filings contain a company overview section. This overview goes into exhaustive detail about the company's business, well beyond the quick snapshot descriptions offered on financial websites. For instance, a company can outline the countries in which it has facilities and employees. The company might also break out what parts of its business are the largest.

If you're investing in a large diversified company such as General Electric, which is involved in many businesses, you can get a grasp of the company's entire empire from the company overview in the 10-K. The company overview might also show you what parts of its business are the largest and most profitable.

Getting the details on company announcements

When a company has an important event — referred to by investment pros as a *material event* — the company is required to tell shareholders about it. Companies might inform shareholders by issuing a press release, which you can find out how to access online in Chapter 2. But it must also provide details of the announcement to regulators in the form of a Form 8-K. The SEC (www.sec.gov/answers/form8k.htm) explains all the corporate events that require companies to file 8-Ks. Companies have four days to provide an 8-K in most cases.

Finding out whether the company is being sued

When companies put out glowing press releases about their new products or services, they rarely bring up news about the lawsuits they might be facing. Although most lawsuits end up amounting to nothing, they're something you want to be aware of. Nearly all companies' 10-Ks contain a Legal Proceedings section that lists pending lawsuits and says how serious the company thinks they are.

WHEN DISASTER STRIKES: HEAD FOR THE 10-K

Getting sued is one of the certainties of business. It's typical for companies to list various lawsuits they face, both minor ones as well as potential landmines. If you read a company's 10-K carefully, you can find lurid legal details they probably aren't eager for the public to know. You might love your morning cup of coffee, but did you know that lawsuits over brewed coffee have vexed Starbucks for years? Back in April 2010, a group called the Council for Education and Research on Toxics filed a lawsuit against companies that make, package, distribute, or sell brewed coffee. The allegation is that brewed coffee products expose people to a chemical called acrylamide. The company explained that acrylamide is naturally occurring in trace amounts in roasted coffee. The suit has raged through the courts in through 2018. This information is not on the financial statements but is still important for investors to know. The company agreed that the matter was important enough to be called out in the filing. The filing says: "Starbucks believes that the likelihood that the Company will ultimately incur a loss in connection with this litigation is reasonably possible rather than probable. Accordingly, no loss contingency was recorded for this matter."

Electric car maker Tesla is another company that's been facing mounting lawsuits. CEO Elon Musk found himself at the center of legal hot water after making comments in 2018 over plans to take the company private. These comments resulted in civil penalties of $20 million, as spelled out in the 10-K. That's just one of a litany of legal matters the company has endured. Legal disputes surround the company's acquisition of SolarCity and the production of Model 3 vehicles. Perhaps nothing will come of these matters, but isn't it good to know about them?

TIP

Regulatory filings are typically giant seas of text. When perusing a filing online, you can quickly skip to different areas by pressing Ctrl+F and entering a search term, such as *legal proceedings.*

You can also check online whether a company is being sued as part of a securities class action lawsuit, where investors allege they were defrauded. The Stanford Law School Securities Class Action Clearinghouse (https://securities.stanford.edu/) is an excellent resource to see whether a company you're invested in is a party of one of these suits.

Getting the truth from management

CEOs and top management must include in their company 10-Ks a section called Management's Discussion and Analysis, or MD&A. This section is where the company must tell regulators and investors how the year went and give its honest assessment of how the business is performing.

Many professional investors read the MD&A section from the prior year before reading the one from the just-completed year and compare the two. It's telling to see what forecasts management made in the previous year and then find out whether they came true.

Seeing whether the company got into a tiff with its auditors

Companies must hire accounting firms to look over, or *audit,* their annual financial statements. Typically, the accounting firms study the company's results and sign off with a Good Housekeeping seal of approval. But periodically, the auditors find a problem, and that's something you want to know about as an investor.

You can find out about accounting problems by opening a company's annual report and searching for the word *restatement.* A restatement usually outlines any problems the company or its auditor has found with the accounting. Restatements can be a shock to investors because they mean companies might not have earned as much money as they previously said they did.

When a company finds problems with its financial statements, it's given a warning by the stock market exchange to fix the problems. During the time the company tries to fix its accounting, it's said to be *delinquent* in its filings. This can be a dangerous time to invest in a company's stock because it's unknown what the company's actual results will end up being. The easiest way to find out whether a company is delinquent is by going to Yahoo! Finance (`https://finance.yahoo.com/`), entering the stock symbol in the ticker symbol field, and clicking the name of the company when it pops up. If the company is delinquent, you can see a warning on the top of the quote page stating that fact. Additionally, if the stock has been delisted and trades on the OTC Bulletin Board market, its ticker symbol can tell the story. A fifth letter, an *E,* may be added to the stock's four-letter ticker symbol to indicate the stock is delinquent in required filings. The Securities and Exchange Commission (`https://www.sec.gov/divisions/enforce/delinquent/delinq index.htm`) also puts out notices to investors when a company is delinquent with its filings. If you see a stock on the SEC's list — run, don't walk, away from that investment.

Weighing the risk of failure

One of the biggest reasons to bother with reading financial statements is to look for red flags or warnings of trouble at the company. One of the easiest signs of trouble you might find, albeit late, is when auditors warn that they question whether the company can continue as a *going concern*. If you see these words in a company filing, take notice.

Seeing what the company is worried about

Companies must include a Risks section in their annual reports. These sections are stuffed with blanket statements about all the bad things that could happen. Sometimes the company will point out a risk it faces that you might not have thought of. Just search for the word *risks*.

Assessing how much the company's management is getting paid

When you're searching through the company filings, don't overlook the boring-sounding DEF 14A. These reports, more commonly called *proxy statements,* are about the juiciest reading you can get about a company. These statements are among the most frank documents released by a company because they disclose how much the company executives get paid. You can download them by using the same steps used to download other regulatory filings, but the SEC (www.sec.gov/answers/proxyhtf.htm) explains how to download company proxy statements.

Search the proxy for the compensation table. Typically, you see each top executive's pay broken down into the following categories:

>> Salary

>> Bonus

>> Stock awards

>> Stock option awards

>> Pension value

>> All other compensation

>> Total compensation

The proxy statement also contains details about what other perks executives receive, such as paid-for apartments and personal use of the corporate jet. How do you know whether the company executives are being overpaid? A few websites help you analyze executives' pay packages, including the following:

>> **AFL-CIO** (`www.aflcio.org/corporatewatch/paywatch`): Big Labor has a stake in what Fat Cat executives make, so it shouldn't come as a surprise that the AFL-CIO provides a free Executive Paywatch, which shows you how much executives were paid and how they rank. Just enter the stock symbol into the Ticker Symbol field and click Go.

>> **Salary.com** (`https://swz.salary.com/execcomp/layoutscripts/excl_companysearch.asp`): This site offers a free salary wizard that breaks down how much all the top dogs at publicly traded companies earn.

>> **Equilar** (`www.equilar.com/press-releases.html`): This is a consulting firm that helps monitor how much executives are getting paid. The company charges for its services but does provide some data at no charge. Equilar routinely releases data on executive pay in its press releases.

Determining the independence of the company's leadership

A company's *board of directors* is supposed to be the shareholders' champion in the board room. The board is a group of business experts, elected by the shareholders, to represent them at important company meetings. All pay packages and strategic decisions must be approved by the board, so you want to make sure that the board represents the best interests of the shareholders.

The proxy statement is an excellent source of information about the company's officers and board members. You almost always find a Related Party Transactions section, where the company must disclose any insider dealings between the company's officers, directors, and the company itself. For instance, if a board member's firm has a business relationship with the company, you'd want to know because it could skew the board member's judgment. With the proxy statement loaded on your screen, just search for the terms *related party transactions.*

IN THIS CHAPTER

» Measuring the potential risk and return of a stock

» Valuing a stock by using a discounted cash flow analysis

» Determining the valuation of a stock, including price-to-earnings ratios

» Using online stock selection tools to study investments

» Comparing a company to its peers and industry

Chapter **13**

Evaluating Stocks' Prospects

W hen investors say they bought a stock because "it's a good company," you should automatically become skeptical. As you find out in this chapter, one of the biggest mistakes investors make is confusing a company and its stock. They're not the same thing.

A *company* is a business that sells things to customers and tries to make a profit. A company's success is measured by its revenue and earnings growth, which I discuss in Chapter 11. But a stock is a different animal. *Stocks* are essentially pieces of ownership in a company. Stock prices are determined by how much investors are willing to pay to own a piece of a company. If too many people think a company is good, they might pay top dollar for the stock and drive up its *valuation*. And when a valuation rises, your potential future return decreases. Valuations are the root of one of the most perverse realities in investing: Good companies can be bad stocks. If you overpay for a stock, even if the company delivers great earnings growth, you can still lose money. Savvy investors know the price they pay for a stock is one of the biggest factors that determines how much they could profit.

This chapter shows you how to find good stocks with reasonable valuations. Although measuring valuations can get math heavy, I spare your calculator a workout by showing you online tools that can do much of the work for you. You also discover the ins and outs of the price-to-earnings ratio, one of the most commonly used — and misunderstood — ways to measure a stock's valuation. I show you stock tools that step you through the process of picking stocks and ways to compare a company's valuation with its peers.

Finding Out How to Not Overpay for Stocks

Even if you find a great company with a top-notch management team and popular products, it doesn't mean you should buy the stock. Why not? The sad truth is you're probably not the first or only person to know about the company's bright future. And if other investors bought the stock already, they likely have pushed the stock price higher. When a stock price has already risen in anticipation of good news, the good news has been *priced in*. That means even if the good news you're expecting pans out, the stock price might not budge — or may even fall — because it already nosed up previously in anticipation of the good news.

IN SEARCH OF LOW RETURNS

Investors figure if they buy the stocks of "good companies," they'll get great returns. But research has shown that's not always true. Companies that are growing and have popular products but are so trendy with investors that their shares have lofty valuations tend to be poor investments.

It's not just theory. In Tom Peters' landmark 1982 book *In Search of Excellence,* Peters, a management expert, extolled companies he determined to be the best. Had you bought $100 worth of stock in these excellent companies in 1981, your investment would have grown 82 percent to $182 through 1985, according to research by market strategist Michelle Clayman. But here's the funny part: Clayman created a portfolio of "unexcellent" companies that were missing all the things that made the excellent companies great. The same $100 invested in these unexcellent companies outperformed the excellent ones by a wide margin. The same $100 invested in the unexcellent companies jumped 198 percent and turned into $298. The counterintuitive idea that the best companies are often not the best stocks is described at length at Damodaran Online (pages.stern.nyu.edu/~adamodar/pdfiles/invfables/ch6new.pdf), a site dedicated to stock valuations maintained by Aswath Damodaran, Professor of Finance at New York University.

The difficulty of evaluating a stock's valuation is one reason why investing in individual stocks is more complex than buying and holding index mutual funds and exchange-traded funds (ETFs). Before I show you how to measure a stock's valuation, I run through the things you should ask yourself before you decide to buy a stock:

>> **Does the stock fit into your asset allocation?** If your portfolio is already stuffed with small companies, you might not want to add shares of another small company. Instead, you should invest in different types of companies that better fit your asset allocation plan. (I talk about asset allocation plans in Chapter 9.)

Morningstar (www.morningstar.com) provides an easy way to find out where a stock would fit in your asset allocation plan. Just type the stock symbol in the Quote box and click the name of the company when it pops up. Scroll down quite a bit and you can see the Company Profile section. In the Company Profile section, you'll find the Morningstar Style Box in the middle of the page — right there under the Stock Style heading. (The Morningstar Style Box is small, so it's easy to miss, but it's a big help.) The box uses a nine-by-nine grid (see Figure 13-1) to show you whether the stock is large, mid-sized, or small. (The grid also tells you whether the stock is value priced or is a growth stock.)

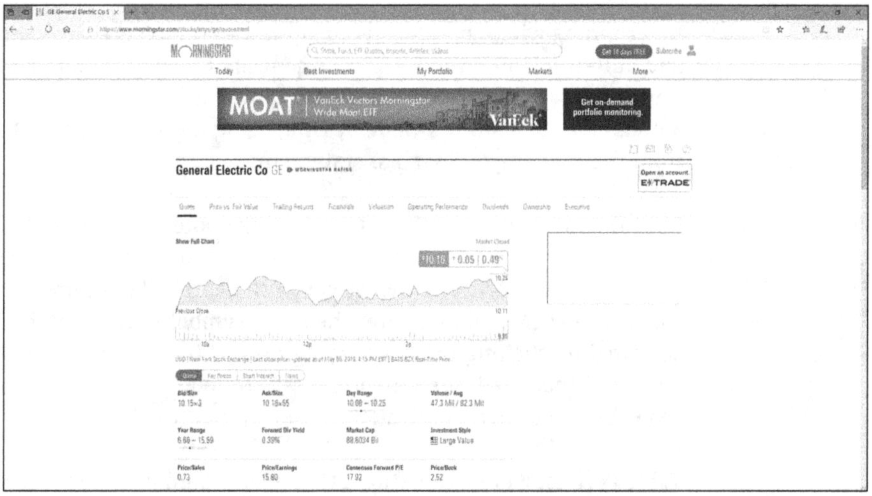

FIGURE 13-1: Morningstar shows you whether a stock is large, mid-sized, or small, and value-priced, growth, or somewhere in between. Here's an example with General Electric.

© 2019 Morningstar, Inc. All Rights Reserved. Reprinted by permission of Morningstar.

>> **Does the stock have solid fundamentals?** When you pick apart a company's financial statements, as I describe in Chapter 11, you're doing what's known as *fundamental analysis.* Essentially, you determine how fast the company's

revenue and earnings are growing and examine the management. (Much of what you need to know about fundamental analysis can be found in Chapter 11.)

>> **Does the stock stack up favorably against the competition?** Companies that have a defendable edge against rivals — typically thanks to a strong brand name — can remain more profitable over time. (I show you how to find a company's competitors in Chapter 6.)

>> **Is the price for the stock reasonable?** You should study how much other investors are paying for the stock before you jump in. Overpaying for a good company is just as bad as overpaying for a bad one. You might lose money in both cases. You see how to measure a stock's valuation in the next section of this chapter.

TIP

A stock's price alone doesn't tell you how expensive or cheap a stock is. Just because one company's stock price is $100 and another company's stock is trading for $1 doesn't mean the $1-a-share company is cheaper or a better deal. The stock's share price must be compared with something else, such as earnings or revenue, to determine its value.

Quick ways to determine how pricey a stock is

Determining whether a stock is cheap or overvalued is an arduous process that can be a full-time job, even for investment pros. Luckily, there's one quick way you can get an idea of how pricey a stock is: valuation ratios. *Valuation ratios* give you a rough idea of a stock's value by comparing the stock price with a measure taken from the company's financial statements.

TIP

Most financial websites that provide stock quotes, including the ones discussed in Chapter 2, provide several valuation ratios. Reuters (www.reuters.com/finance/markets), for instance, provides you with nearly all the important valuation measures on one screen. Just enter the stock symbol in the search text field, which is activated by clicking the magnifying glass. Find and click the name of the company and then click the Financials tab. If you scroll down, you find more ratios than you can shake a stick at.

Table 13-1 lists a few valuation ratios you should pay the most attention to.

The P/E ratio is the rock star of valuation ratios and gets most of the attention. The P/E ratio is popular because it's easy to understand. Imagine a stock price is $30 a share, and the company earned $1.50 a share. That means investors are paying a price that's 20 times higher than the company's earnings. If the price of earnings, or P/E, is high, the earnings are very valuable to other people, usually because they expect the company to grow rapidly.

TABLE 13-1   Guide to Valuation Ratios That Matter

This Valuation Ratio	Tells You How Much Investors . . .
Price-to-earnings (P/E)	Are willing to pay for each dollar in earnings the company generates. The *price-to-earnings (P/E)* ratio is measured by dividing the stock price by the company's annual earnings. A high P/E ratio tells some investors that the stock is overvalued, and a low P/E ratio shows it's undervalued.
Price-to-sales	Are paying for each dollar the company brings in as revenue. The *price-to-sales* ratio is the company's stock price divided by its annual revenue. This ratio is typically used to value *early-stage* companies, such as biotech firms, that lose money, so they don't have a P/E ratio.
Price–to–book value	Are paying for each dollar of the company's assets, minus money owed to others. The *price–to–book value* ratio is the stock's price divided by the company's book value per share. A company's book value measures the value of what it owns (assets) minus what it owes (liabilities). The price–to–book value ratio is very important and is a key measure used to determine whether a stock is a value-priced stock or a growth stock. A low price–to–book value ratio, typically 1 or lower, might signal an undervalued stock.
Price–to–tangible book value	Are paying for each dollar of physical assets owned by the company. The *price-to-tangible book value* ratio is the stock price divided by the company's book value per share, excluding assets you can't touch or feel.
Price-earnings-to-growth (PEG)	Are willing to pay for the company's earnings growth. The *price-earnings-to-growth (PEG)* ratio compares a company's P/E ratio to its expected growth rate. The PEG ratio is calculated by dividing the stock's P/E ratio by its expected growth rate. The expected growth rate is forecasted by analysts who follow the company. A PEG ratio of 2 or higher tells investors that the stock is either expected to grow very rapidly or that the stock is overvalued. Reuters doesn't give you the PEG ratio, but it gives you the P/E ratio and the growth rate, so you can easily figure it out.
Price-to-free cash flow	Value each dollar of cash that flows into the company as part of its doing business. The *price-to-free cash flow* ratio is the stock price divided by free cash flow.
Dividend yield	Receive in dividends relative to the stock price. The *dividend yield* is the company's annual dividend payment divided by the stock price. If a $30 stock has a dividend yield of 5%, that means it is paying $1.50 per share every year in dividends ($30 × 5% = $1.50). Stocks with high dividend yields are seen as potentially being undervalued.

Still confused about what a P/E ratio means? Imagine that a company put all the money it earned per share during the year in a box, promised to add more money if it was profitable in the future, and auctioned it off. Say the company earned $1 a share, so $1 was in the box. If investors paid $1 for the box, the stock would have a P/E ratio of 1. But if a bidding war ensued and someone paid $20 for the box that contained a dollar of earnings, the stock would have a P/E ratio of 20.

REMEMBER

P/E ratios can get more complicated because different people measure earnings differently. A *trailing* P/E ratio divides the stock price by the company's earnings over the past four quarters. A *forward* P/E ratio divides the stock price by what the company is expected to earn over the next four quarters. Both ways to measure P/E ratios are correct; just know which one you're talking about.

Morningstar (www.morningstar.com) gives both the trailing P/E ratio and the forward P/E ratio. Just enter the stock's symbol in the Quote box and click the name of the company when it pops up. Next, click the Valuation tab. Scroll down and you will find the stock's trailing P/E listed as Price/Earnings under the Current Valuation section. Look down a bit further and you'll find the Forward Valuation section. The Forward Price/Earnings ratio is the forward P/E ratio.

WARNING

Be careful. Some sites such as Google Finance (www.google.com/finance) provide a P/E ratio but don't indicate whether it's a forward or trailing P/E ratio, making it too ambivalent to be useful.

Ways to interpret valuations

If you took a look at Chapter 1 and figured out from my discussion there that you're a passive (as opposed to an active) investor, you're pretty sure that the stock price measures what one share of a stock is worth, or its *fair value*. If the market is willing to pay $20 for a stock, the stock is worth $20 at that time based on publicly available information. Passive investors believe markets are *efficient* over the long term and set stock prices that reflect all available public information. But *active investors* (including bargain hunters known as *value investors*) believe the stock market is *inefficient* and tends to overpay or underpay for stocks from time to time. These investors try to find out whether a stock is too expensive or cheap by studying its valuation ratios and comparing them with the following:

>> **The rest of the market:** Some investors compare valuation ratios, such as the price-to-book value ratio and dividend yield, with the Standard & Poor's 500 to get an idea of whether the company might be undervalued. If the valuation ratios are lower than the S&P 500's, that tells some investors that the stock might be undervalued.

S&P Dow Jones provides data on its index's valuation at https://us.spindices.com/indices/equity/sp-500. Concentrate on finding out the following:

- *Dividend yield:* First, click the Additional Info button on the left side of the screen. From the menu that pops up, choose Indicated Rate Change. A spreadsheet opens on your screen. The spreadsheet displays the dividend yield of different stock market indexes, including the all-popular Standard

& Poor's 500. You can also see the dividend yields of different sectors and different periods of time. It's a little tricky to find, but Figure 13-2 should help you.

● *P/E ratio:* Follow the same directions as in the preceding bullet, but instead select Index Earnings. The spreadsheet gives you the S&P 500's P/E ratio over several years. Scroll down and look for the As Reported Earnings P/E column, which lists the S&P's P/E ratio at the end of each quarter. Notice as well that the P/E ratio rises and falls as investors get bullish and bearish about stocks and the economy.

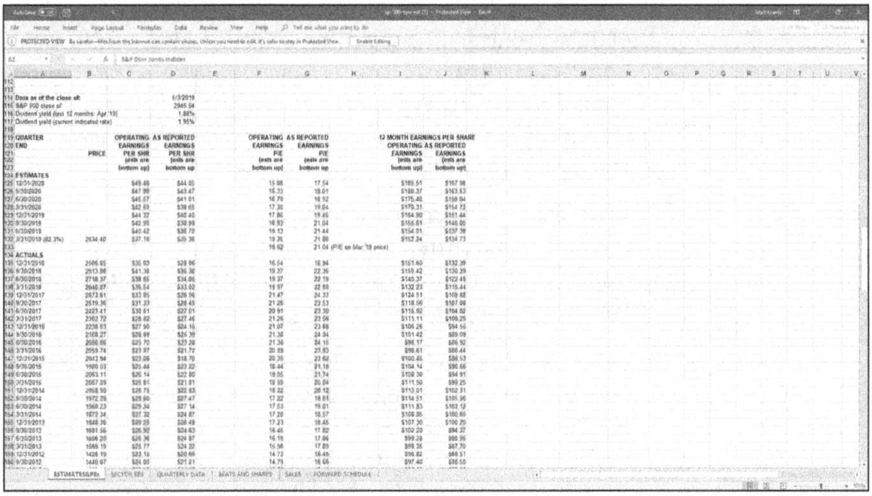

FIGURE 13-2:
S&P provides
in-depth data
about its
indexes —
including the S&P
500 — on its
website.

» **The industry:** It's also a good idea to compare a stock's valuation ratios with other stocks in the industry. Some industries tend to grow more slowly and almost always have a lower valuation than the stock market. The only way to know whether a stock's valuation is truly lower than average is to compare it with the ratios of similar companies.

Reuters' Financials pages, described in the previous section, give you valuation ratios for individual stocks in addition to the industry and stock market. Enter the stock's symbol in the Search Stocks text field, click the Search button, and select the name of the company. Click the Financials tab. Scroll down and you can see how the valuation ratios compare with the company's industry, sector, and the S&P 500. If you'd like to dig a bit deeper, Damodaran Online (pages. stern.nyu.edu/~adamodar/New_Home_Page/datafile/pbvdata.html) provides price–to–book value ratios for many industries.

REMEMBER

Some investors completely ignore P/E ratios because they figure that good companies are worth paying more for and deserve higher P/E ratios. In these investors' minds, a high P/E ratio is justified just as a Monet deserves a bigger price tag than a velvet Elvis painting sold at a flea market. These investors tend to pay more attention to how fast a company is growing as well as to patterns in its price movements. I discuss such investors in greater detail in the "Taking It Further: Technical Analysis and Initial Public Offerings" bonus chapter on this book's companion website at www.dummies.com/bonus/onlineinvesting.

» **Guidelines:** Investors typically have a general idea of what they think makes a cheap or expensive stock. Some investors, for instance, think a stock is reasonably priced if the PEG ratio is less than 2. You can calculate a stock's PEG ratio yourself by dividing the P/E ratio by the growth rate, or you can get it from Yahoo! Finance (https://finance.yahoo.com/) by putting the stock's symbol in the Enter Symbol field, clicking the name of the company, and then clicking the Key Statistics link on the left side of the page. You find the PEG ratio under the Valuation Measures heading.

As for other resources, check out MoneyChimp (http://www.moneychimp.com/articles/valuation/peg.htm) for its PEG ratios and Investor Home (www.investorhome.com/anomfun.htm) for some guidelines for you to follow regarding other valuation ratios.

» **Index membership:** Most of the major providers of stock market indexes categorize stocks as being value or growth. The index providers have sophisticated screens that rank stocks based on a number of valuation metrics. If you're not sure whether a company you're considering is a growth or value stock, you can see which index it fits in. For instance, if you want a list of the largest value-priced stocks, go to the area of S&P Dow Jones Indices' website dedicated to value and growth stock indexes (https://us.spindices.com/index-family/us-equity/style). When you're there, click either the S&P 500 Pure Growth or S&P 500 Pure Value charts. Next, a new page dedicated solely to the index you chose loads. Click the Constituents tab at the top of the chart. A list of the largest 10 stocks in the index appears. Below this list is a "Full Constituents List," which gives you all the stocks in the index.

If that's too much clicking around, you can add links to the index pages as Favorites using your browser. You can access the S&P 500 Pure Growth index at https://us.spindices.com/indices/equity/sp-500-pure-growth and the S&P 500 Pure Value index at https://us.spindices.com/indices/equity/sp-500-pure-value.

Studying stocks using automated tools

Is your head spinning with all this talk of P/E ratios, book value, and other ratios? Don't worry. Several online tools can hold your hand through the process of analyzing a stock's valuation. The following list highlights sites that are excellent places to start to get you thinking about what goes into evaluating a company's stock price and see whether it might fit in your portfolio:

» **BetterInvesting** (`www.betterinvesting.org`): BetterInvesting provides a Stock Selection Guide to its members that helps evaluate a company's valuation to determine whether the stock is a buy, hold, or sell. The Stock Selection Guide, or SSG for short, compares the company's expected P/E ratio with its P/E ratios in the past. The Stock Selection Guide is available as a paper form you must meticulously fill out, but is also found in different software programs you can buy from BetterInvesting, which pull down company data automatically. A free trial of an online SSG system called Core SSG is also available.

» **MarketSmith** (`https://marketsmith.investors.com`): MarketSmith pulls in massive amounts of data to help you figure out when a stock might be attractively priced. The system looks for patterns that have traditionally been associated with stocks on the upswing.

» **Trefis** (`www.trefis.com`): Ever want to have your own black box that would magically analyze stocks? Trefis tries to make that wish a reality. Enter a company name or symbol in the search box and click the name of the company when it pops up. You'll see a chart that breaks down the company's different lines of business and shows how important they are to the company's stock price. This site is so good it's mentioned again later in this chapter to help in a different type of analysis.

Shortcomings of studying stocks' valuation ratios

I don't want to leave you with a misconception many investors have: Just find a "cheap" stock with a low valuation, buy it, hold on to it forever, and you'll make money. Unfortunately, investing isn't that easy. Several problems exist with using valuation ratios alone to pick stocks, including the following:

» **Cheap stocks might be cheap for a reason.** Sometimes a stock has a low valuation because the company is poorly run, it's in a slow- or no-growth industry, or other companies or technologies are stealing away customers.

THE FOUR (HEADLESS) HORSEMEN OF THE INTERNET

Despite the problems with valuation ratios — problems described elsewhere in this section — they're still a good way to get a quick idea of how highly valued a stock is. When you start seeing stocks' P/E ratios going above 60, though, you should get suspicious. Few stocks are able to maintain such lofty valuations before getting their comeuppance, because investors realize they've been too bullish. Even if the company can boost its earnings by 100 percent for a year or two, eventually the industry or the company will stumble and bring its stock price back to earth.

Even today, the Internet stock bubble of the late 1990s and early 2000s remains the best recent example of the dangers of overvaluation. Valuations of Internet stocks were inflated as investors got caught up in the dot-com mania. Many investors rightly viewed the Internet as a huge phenomenon for society and business. But, unfortunately, these investors overpaid for Internet stocks in March 2000 and doomed themselves to lackluster returns. Many Internet stocks vanished completely, and those that didn't have been very poor investments for anyone who invested at the peak.

The valuations of Cisco, EMC, Oracle, and Sun, the leaders of the Internet nicknamed the Four Horsemen of the Internet, soared in March 2000. Their stock prices have since plunged, though, erasing tremendous amounts of shareholder wealth on the way. In fact, just two of the horsemen still exist as independent companies. Oracle bought Sun in 2010 for $9.50 a share, a fraction of its price of nearly $200-a-share in March 2000. Dell bought EMC in 2016.

Investors, though, seemed to have forgotten the lesson of sky-high P/Es again during the second tech mania that kicked off around 2010 with the boom of mobile devices and apps. When Snapchat — a maker of a digital photo-sharing app — sold its shares to the public for the first time in 2017, investors paid so much the company didn't even have a P/E. Investors paid nearly $25 a share, even though the company lost money. But logic quickly set in and shares of the company lost half their value by April 2019.

>> **You get what you pay for.** Sometimes a company might appear to be overvalued and have a high P/E ratio. But if the company's profits grow by a huge amount, the P/E ratio will fall and the stock price may skyrocket.

REMEMBER

If a company reports strong earnings, a stock's P/E ratio can suddenly go from looking high to looking low. The P/E ratio is the stock price divided by earnings. That means if earnings, the denominator of the fraction, rise rapidly, the P/E ratio plunges. Imagine a company trading for $40 a share that has posted earnings over the past four quarters of $1 a share. That gives the stock a pricey-looking P/E ratio of 40. But if the company's quarterly profit surges and pushes earnings to $2, the P/E ratio falls to a more reasonable 20.

>> **Dividends aren't a contract.** Some investors target companies with high dividend yields. They figure that these companies' stock prices are temporarily depressed. And, as a bonus, even if the stock doesn't go up, they get paid their dividend.

Watch out, though. Dividend payments aren't written in blood. Companies can cut or stop their dividend payments at any time.

The armchair investor's way to not overpay

If you want to buy cheap stocks, but studying P/E ratios and price-to-book value ratios makes your head swim, here's an easy shortcut: Buy an index mutual fund or an ETF that owns value-priced stocks. That way, you own stocks that are in value indexes. Generally, the companies that create indexes use many measures to determine whether a stock is value or growth. S&P Dow Jones Indices ranks companies by book value, cash flow, sales, and dividend yield to see whether a stock is a value stock. You can see how S&P Dow Jones Indices identifies value stocks (and they're experts), at `https://us.spindices.com/index-family/us-equity/style`. On the right side of the page are four charts. Below the S&P 500 Pure Value chart is a small, easy-to-miss Methodology link. Click that link and you'll see what it takes to pass muster with S&P Dow Jones Indices to be a value stock. If you're interested in finding index mutual funds that mirror value stock indexes, check out Chapter 10. For ETFs that do the same thing, check out the "Finding and Buying Exchange-Traded Funds" bonus chapter on the website associated with this book at `www.dummies.com/bonus/onlineinvesting`.

Evaluating Stocks' Potential Return and Risk

If you're taking a gamble on a stock, you'd better get an ample return to make it worth your while. I tell you how to measure your portfolio's risk and return in Chapter 8. It turns out that you can apply the same techniques to individual stocks. I show you how here.

Measuring a stock's total return

Past performance is no guarantee of future results, but studying how stocks have done in the past can help you get a crude handle on what to expect. To find how stocks have done previously, you need their *total return* in previous years. A stock's total return is the amount its price has gone up — its *price appreciation* — plus its dividend. You can get a stock's total return by the following methods:

>> **Checking the company's website:** Some companies include total return calculators in the Investor Relations section of their websites.

>> **Calculating it by using online stock price downloading services:** You can download a stock's annual stock price for different years using services described in Chapter 2. Add the company's stock price at the end of the year to the amount per share it paid in dividends during the year. Divide that sum by the stock's price at the end of the previous year and multiply by 100, and you have the total return for the year.

>> **Using Morningstar:** This method is a much simpler way to get total returns. The investment tracker (www.morningstar.com) provides stocks' total returns going back for five years. Just enter the stock's symbol in the Quote field, click the company's name, and then click the Performance tab at the top of the new page that appears. Ideally, you want more years of data than Morningstar gives you, but it's a start.

After you get the stock's total returns for many years, enter them into Horton's Geometric Mean Calculator at www.graftacs.com/geomean.php3. (If you're not sure how to do that, refer to Chapter 8.) Horton's Geometric Mean Calculator shows you how much you would have gained in the stock each year on average and also how risky it is. You can then compare the stock's returns and risk with popular indexes, just as you do with your portfolio in Chapter 8. If the stock's returns are lower than the stock market's and the risk is higher, it might not be a good fit for your portfolio.

TECHNICAL STUFF

A search engine makes comparing risk and reward super simple — and pretty interesting to boot. WolframAlpha (www.wolframalpha.com) may not be as famous as some other search engines, but it can pull off some cool tricks. Just enter the name of the company and either press the Enter key on your keyboard or click the search icon, which looks like an orange rectangle with two lines on it. Scroll down and you'll find a nifty chart that plots the stock's risk and reward compared with other companies in its industry and the S&P 500. If your stock is further to the right than the S&P 500 (meaning it's riskier), it had better be higher on the chart, too (meaning it delivers higher returns).

TECHNICAL STUFF

Before you decide a stock is too risky or the returns are too low, you should compare its movements to the rest of your portfolio. If a stock rises when the other investments in your portfolio go down, it might reduce your portfolio's total risk by offering diversification. Some online tools can show you whether a stock can diversify your portfolio. Macroaxis (www.macroaxis.com) provides an impressive tool that will compare one investment's moves with another's. After signing in, click the Portfolio Center option on the left side of the screen. From the screen that appears, choose Analyze Correlations. You'll see a color-coded matrix that displays how correlated all your investments are with one another. Hover your mouse cursor over a square and you'll see if the correlation is strong or weak.

Don't get bogged down with all the scary math terms. Just know this: If the correlation is negative, the stock you're considering compared with the other one in your portfolio are mirror images. That situation is good because it means if your portfolio sinks, this stock might rise and decrease your overall risk. You can also compare an individual investment to your entire portfolio. The site can be used for free, and it's free to register, but you can unlock more features by paying.

TIP

Many online stock quote services let you compare several stocks by graphing them on the same chart — an easy way to see which stock has done best with the help of a colorful chart. To try it out, go to Yahoo! Finance (https://finance.yahoo.com/), enter in the Quote Lookup field the symbol of the stock you're interested in, and click the name of the company. On the new page that appears, click the Chart tab that appears on the left side of the page under the Charts heading. Next, select the + Comparison menu option and either choose from the preset stocks to compare it with or click the blank field at the top of the box. If you clicked the blank field, enter the symbol of the stocks you want to compare and click the name of the company. A new chart appears, superimposing one stock with the other. Don't just compare the stock with other stocks, though; you should also compare it with market indexes such as the S&P 500 and ETFs that track narrow slices of the market.

Finding out more about risk and return online

If you're interested in finding out more about how a stock's risk and return are linked, you can consult several sites dedicated to the topic. The sites listed here are a good start:

>> **InvestorGuide.com** (www.investorguide.com/igu-article-558-asset-allocation-correlating-your-portfolio.html): This part of the InvestorGuide site describes why it's so important for investors to understand the correlation between the returns they're getting from stocks and the risk they're accepting.

» **Index Funds Advisors** (`www.ifa.com`): The IFA site helps you understand how individual stocks are often riskier than baskets of stocks in index mutual funds. Specifically, IFA features a section about the perils of stock picking here: `www.ifa.com/12steps/step3`.

Digging Even Deeper: Advanced Valuation Techniques

Valuation ratios are often the most popular ways to measure how pricey stocks are. But even proponents of valuation ratios acknowledge that such ratios *do* have problems. For instance, it's not unheard of for a stock with a seemingly high P/E ratio of 50 or more to go even higher.

REMEMBER

Investors use valuation ratios as general rules, but you have other, more involved ways to try to figure out whether a stock is a good buy. Some investors try to use advanced mathematics to figure out what a company is truly worth, or its *intrinsic value*.

Using the dividend discount model to see whether a stock is on sale

Sometimes investors get so wrapped up in the drama of online stock investing that they lose sight of what they're buying. As a stock investor, you're letting a company use your money to sell goods and services for a profit. If the company makes money, it will ultimately give back your fair share of the profits over time. Typically, that's done by paying a dividend. Even young companies that don't pay a dividend now eventually start to as their profits exceed their needs for cash.

And that's the basis of the *dividend discount model* approach to valuing stocks. The idea is that most companies pay a dividend, and those that don't will. The size of the dividend a company pays, and how quickly it grows, can help you figure out how much a company is worth. You can find an ugly formula for a dividend discount model, but I'll spare you the agony. If you can't resist finding out how the calculation is done, Motley Fool (`www.fool.com/knowledge-center/what-is-the-dividend-discount-model.aspx`) provides a helpful description.

Because this is *Online Investing For Dummies*, I just list a few handy places on the Internet where you can enter a couple variables and have your computer do the rest:

>> **Calculator Pro** (www.calculatorpro.com/calculator/dividend-discount-model-calculator): This page offers a free calculator that may appeal to you if you'd like more control of the assumptions being used in the model. The site can tell you how much a stock is worth if you enter just three variables:

- *The most recent dividends:* The value of the dividends paid by the company in the most recent four quarters. The web page calls this current dividend.

- *Dividend growth rate:* How rapidly you expect the company to boost its dividend. You can either use the rate the company has increased dividends in the past, or use its expected earnings or dividend growth rate.

- *Your required rate of return:* The return you're expecting from the stock. If it's a risky stock, your required rate of return might be 15 percent or much higher. And if it's a conservative stock, you might have a required rate of return of less than 10 percent.

The calculator spits out how much it thinks the stock is worth based on the data you entered.

>> **Damodaran Online** (pages.stern.nyu.edu/~adamodar/New_Home_Page/spreadsh.htm#valmodels): NYU Finance Professor Aswath Damodaran provides an entire page of financial spreadsheets to keep your computer more than happy crunching numbers. If you scroll down to the Focused Valuation Models area, you see a simple Stable Growth, Dividend Discount Model spreadsheet. Click the ddmst.xls link to open the spreadsheet. You need to enter data in the cells highlighted in yellow, and the spreadsheet does all the math for you.

The dividend discount model is clever and is used by many serious investment professionals. But the model has some big problems. It is extremely sensitive to your assumptions, especially the required rate of return or discount rate that you enter. The *discount rate* is the return you demand in return for investing your money in the company. If you enter a discount rate of 10 percent, you get a wildly different answer than if you enter 12 or 8 percent. And good luck determining what a company's growth rate will be. Still, the model is a useful tool to get a general understanding about a fair value for a stock.

The value hunter's favorite weapon: The discounted cash flow analysis

Ask someone who the best investor ever is, and you'll probably hear the name Warren Buffett. Buffett doesn't publish a playbook that tells the world how he picks companies. He offers some pretty good clues, though, through his Berkshire Hathaway's annual reports. In a nutshell, Buffett tries to measure a company's intrinsic value and buys shares of the company only when it's trading for less than the intrinsic value.

Many speculate that Buffett and investors like him use what's called the discounted cash flow (DCF) analysis. The DCF method works on the assumption that successful companies generate cash flow every year and will, we hope, generate more each year. The *DCF* model attempts to estimate how much cash the company will generate over its entire lifetime and tells you how much that cash would be worth if you got it today. If the company's intrinsic value is greater than the stock price, the company is a good deal.

It's time for a concrete example. Imagine that you were a lucky lottery player and had just won a million dollars. Say the state said you could either have the million now or wait 30 years for it. You wouldn't even have to think about it; you'd take the money now. You didn't realize it, but you just did a DCF analysis in your head. Because money received today is more valuable than the same amount received later, you know that a million dollars paid 30 years from now is worth less than a million dollars paid today.

The DCF analysis can get somewhat complicated. You must first estimate a company's free cash flow, as I describe in Chapter 11. Next, you have to determine how rapidly the company's free cash flow will grow over the years and how much it would be worth if paid to shareholders right now. If you're interested in the nitty-gritty of this analysis, Lyn Alden Investment Strategy (www.lynalden.com/discounted-cash-flow-analysis) offers a helpful and in-depth description of how the DCF model is crunched.

Luckily, you can use online resources and get the benefits of the DCF model without actually doing any math. Check out the following helpful sites:

>> **Trefis** (www.trefis.com): If you've been eager to start building DCF models but the math and terms turn you off, Trefis is for you. The site helps you build a DCF analysis by letting you make assumptions about how a company's products will grow. For instance, if you think sales of Microsoft's Xbox video games will increase, you drag a line on a chart and Trefis does all the cash flow analysis to see how higher Xbox sales will affect Microsoft's stock. You can also share your assumptions with other users and see what assumptions other users have made.

>> **MoneyChimp** (www.moneychimp.com/articles/valuation/dcf.htm): This site is definitely one of the easier DCF model sites to use. You need to enter only five pieces of information and the website generates the stock's value. You must enter the following data:

- *Earnings per share over the past 12 months:* You can also use the company's cash flow per share, which is probably more accurate.

- *Initial expected annual growth rate*

- *Number of years earnings will grow at that pace*

- *What the growth rate will fall to after the initial growth period*

- *The return you can get on a similar investment:* If the stock is a large-company stock, you would enter the 10.3 percent average return of the S&P 500 here.

MoneyChimp does all the math for you and tells you how much the stock is worth. If you're interested in the approach Buffett uses, MoneyChimp also provides a slightly different DCF model believed to be more similar to Buffett's approach at www.moneychimp.com/articles/valuation/buffett_calc.htm.

>> **Numeraire DCF Valuator** (numeraire.com/value_wizard): Here you find a page from the Global Value Investing site that offers all sorts of free valuation calculators. Read the Intro text and then click the Portal link to find the model that fits your needs.

>> **Expectations Investing** (www.expectationsinvesting.com): This site takes the DCF analysis and turns it on its head. The site owners, Alfred Rappaport, a professor emeritus at Northwestern University, and Legg Mason Capital money manager Michael Mauboussin, say investors should examine a stock's price first and then work backward. By dissecting the stock price, you can figure out what the majority of other investors expect the company's cash flow and growth to be. Then you can decide whether the market is expecting too much or too little. You can read about the approach in the tutorials section and also download all the spreadsheets you need to do the analysis yourself.

>> **Damodaran Online** (pages.stern.nyu.edu/~adamodar): In addition to spreadsheets to help you build dividend discount models (described previously), this site also offers dozens of advanced valuation models that use variations of the DCF model. The site even has a "right model" spreadsheet that tells you which valuation model to use.

>> **NewConstructs** (www.newconstructs.com): This site uses a sophisticated DCF model that does everything for you. It enters all the data from its database, adjusts the company's financial statements to the appropriate format, and crunches all the math. That's the good part. A basic free option is available for beginning users. Premium plans, which offer more capability, start at $49 a month. NewConstructs, however, provides some of its research reports for free through some online brokers such as TD Ameritrade.

IN THIS CHAPTER

» **Getting to know stock screens**

» **Discovering how stock screens can pinpoint stocks that meet your standards**

» **Locating and using online stock-screening tools**

» **Deciding which criteria to base your screens on**

» **Finding out what kinds of screening tools online brokers offer**

» **Using screens to compare a company with its peers and industry**

Chapter **14**

Finding Investment Ideas with Online Stock Screens

One of the most popular questions investors ask is, "What stock should I buy?" These investors figure that, amid the pile of thousands of publicly traded stocks, a handful of stocks will be the big winners for the year. They're right. There will be stocks that are big winners and big losers each year. The problem, though, is that no one knows ahead of time which ones.

No online tool can tell you what stocks will be next year's winners. But some online resources and databases can help you find stocks with traits you believe make them likely candidates.

This chapter shows you how online screening tools are your best friend when you're trying to sort through thousands of stocks for those you might want to own. *Online screening tools* scour Wall Street for stocks that meet criteria you set. I show you a few of the top online stock-screening tools and give you some pointers on how to use them. You also find out about many ways you can filter stocks and how to pick criteria for your screen. I also cover methods to compare companies with their peers or other companies.

Getting Familiar with Stock Screens

No one person can do in-depth analysis of the thousands of publicly traded stocks out there. There's just not enough time. Even large Wall Street investment companies, with giant teams of researchers, can only study so many stocks. But that doesn't mean you want to miss out on stocks that might belong in your portfolio.

Stock-screening tools are the answer. Online screening tools are systems that let you describe what kind of stock you're looking for, and then the screening tool returns a list of results to you. The screening tool searches through thousands of stocks in a database and finds the ones that match your parameters.

Stock-screening tools aren't all that different from online dating services. Say you're looking for a mate with dark brown hair and brown eyes who likes to run and follow the stock market. You can enter those traits into an online dating service and get a list of people who match. Similarly, stock screens are excellent tools to help you come up with a list of stocks that might be attractive. You enter a list of traits for the stock, such as the industry, growth rate, and valuation. After you get a list of the companies that fit your criteria, you have a smaller and more manageable list of stocks you can study more closely.

Investors who use online stock-screening tools benefit in three key ways:

>> **Less time wasted:** Screening tools keep you from wasting time studying companies that aren't appropriate. You can design your stock screen to throw out companies that are undesirable to you for certain reasons, such as having too much debt or too little profit.

>> **No stone unturned:** Screening tools can highlight stocks you might have overlooked. One of the best things about stock screens is that they're dispassionate and robotic. Screens don't get caught up in marketing hype — they look only at the numbers. That means screens might find stocks you've overlooked because you weren't familiar with the companies' products.

>> **Great head-to-head comparisons:** Screening tools are great when it comes to comparing stocks. Stock screens are built using specific financial metrics and ratios, which are calculated for all stocks. Online screening tools allow you to rank companies against each other based on these objective measures.

WARNING

The biggest gripe about stock screens is that they do only what they're told. If you filter stocks using meaningless variables, your results are only as good as the elements you're searching for.

Creating an online screen

You find many stock–screening sites, and they all work slightly differently. But the general procedure of getting into the screening game is essentially the same:

1. Choose a screening site.

   Later in this chapter, I discuss several websites that provide free or low-cost screening tools.

2. Decide what kind of stock you're looking for.

   Perhaps you're trying to find a stock that fits your asset allocation. Are you looking for a company that's being ignored by other investors and should therefore be considered value-priced? Are you trying to find a fast-growing company that will blow away earnings forecasts? Are you looking for a stable stock that pays a large dividend? You can find all these types of stocks by using screens.

3. Pick measurable traits shared by stocks and companies you're looking for.

   I show you general traits that you can include in your search, as well as premade screens where professionals have already created the search criteria so that you don't have to spend your time doing it.

4. Refine your screen.

   Screening for stocks is a bit of a trial-and-error process. At first, the list of companies that meet your standards might be too large. You can make the criteria more stringent or add additional criteria to help narrow the list even more.

Now that you understand how the screening process works, the fun part begins. The best screens are carefully designed to pinpoint stocks that have the traits you're looking for. When building screens, it's best to be as specific as possible so that you find stocks that are the perfect matches for your portfolio.

General characteristics you can use to screen stocks

The number of characteristics you can use to screen stocks is virtually unlimited. If you can measure it, you can screen stocks for it. Even so, most investors use the following primary measures in screens:

>> **Company information:** I'm talking basic elements of a company's location, size, or industry here. Common criteria you might use would include the number of employees, the stock market exchange the stock trades on, the industry the company is in, and what stock market index the company is part of. How much money the company brings in — its *revenue,* in other words — is also important.

>> **Trading characteristics:** This category deals with how the stock has been moving. You can search for stocks that tend to swing more or less than the general stock market, stocks that are close to their high or low during the past year, and stocks that trade hands between investors more often or less often. You can also find companies that investors are betting against by *shorting* the stock. (For more on shorting stock, see Chapter 5.)

>> **Market value:** This measure of how much a company is worth is used to determine whether a company is small, mid-sized, or large.

>> **Profitability:** The level of earnings and cash flow a company generates is of utmost importance to investors. Not surprisingly, you can search on both earnings and cash flow. You can drill down even further by looking for specific things about profits, including how quickly profit has grown over the most recent quarter, year, or over the longer term.

>> **Analyst ratings:** Analysts often evaluate stocks and rate them as a buy, hold, or sell. You can set up your screen so that it finds stocks with a certain rating. Analysts' ratings are covered in more detail in Chapter 15.

>> **Valuation ratios:** Investors pay close attention to how much they're paying for companies, or what's called a stock *valuation.* Valuations are covered at length in Chapter 12.

>> **Dividends:** These periodic cash payments made by companies to shareholders are important because they account for about a third of many large companies' total return. Dividends are also widely watched because they're an indication of a stock's valuation.

REMEMBER

Many stock screens use the cryptic terms TTM and MRQ to describe the time frame in which you'd like to base your search. TTM is *trailing 12 months,* which means the most recent 12 months. MRQ is the *most recent quarter.*

Choosing an online screening site

Before you can start screening, you need to pick an online screening site. Over the past years, several of the top screening sites have scaled back their free offerings or eliminated them. Even so, many investors will be more than satisfied with the remaining free screening sites that are still available, and I focus mostly on those sites. The vast majority of these sites provide premade screens that you can call up immediately, without programming in specific criteria. If using premade screens seems like your speed, I provide more details on how to do that with some of the screening sites in the section "Getting Started with Premade Screens," later in this chapter. You might decide, though, that you want to go off the beaten path a bit and build a screen exactly to your taste. I show you how to design a screen from scratch using a few of the sites as examples in the section "Designing a Custom Screen," later in this chapter.

No matter whether you decide to go with canned or custom screens, the screening sites you choose are important. For online investors, the first place to check is your online broker's website. Many of the leading online brokers, especially those I refer to as *discounters* in Chapter 4, offer high-quality stock-screening tools on their websites. Charles Schwab's stock screener lets you screen for many standard criteria, but it makes things a little easier by letting you click preset ranges. It also lets you find stocks that rank high or low with the Schwab Equity Ratings, discussed more fully in Chapter 15. TD Ameritrade, Fidelity, and several others provide screening tools as well. You need to have an account with the online broker, though, to use the full versions of most brokers' stock screeners, although some allow non-customers to use a stripped-down version.

After you check out what your online brokerage has to offer, you might also consider the following (but in no particular order):

>> **Reuters Stock Screener (**https://stockscreener.us.reuters.com/Stock/US/Index?quickscreen=gaarp**):** This stock screener puts part of Reuters' powerful corporate information database into the hands of individual investors. The screening tool allows you to narrow the universe of stocks based on companies' five-year growth rates, geographic region and sector.

>> **MSN Money's Stock Screener (**www.msn.com/en-us/money/stockscreener**):** MSN Money's Stock Screener feature is a slightly different take on stock screening. It attempts to hide the complexity by showing only the criteria you select. To get started, just click the + sign next to the Filters label. With this online tool, you place check marks in a series of boxes with characteristics that matter most to you, including a high grade for fundamentals, valuations, or dividends. The screener then looks at its database and shows you the stocks that make the cut.

>> **Zacks Investment Research's Screening tool** (`www.zacks.com/screening/stock-screener`): The Zacks tool is one of the most powerful free screeners left. It contains more criteria than what's offered by most of the financial sites. Zacks' tool, shown in Figure 14-1, lets you filter stocks using the standard criteria but adds some unique things, too. For instance, you can filter stocks based on estimate uncertainty, which finds stocks where analysts strongly disagree over how much the company will earn in the next quarter. You can also find companies that have surprised Wall Street the most with earnings over the past quarters.

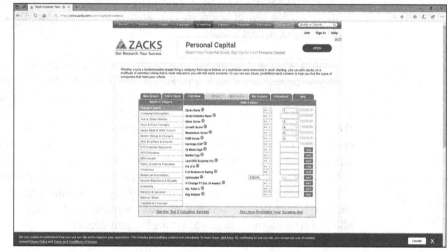

FIGURE 14-1:
Zacks Investment Research's screening tool lets investors choose from a wide variety of criteria when it comes to pinpointing stocks.

>> **Finviz.com** (`www.finviz.com/screener.ashx`): The Finviz screener is another one of the last remaining screeners that offer in-depth power for investors. The Finviz screener tries to give investors access to the critical criteria they need, but at the same time still keeps things simple. Unlike many other screeners that are sacrificing power for simplicity, Finviz still gives users a fair amount of control in building screens.

>> **Google Finance** (`www.google.com/finance`): Google Finance's screener might be missing some of the power offered by Zacks and Finviz but is worth checking out due to its interesting way of presenting the data. Google Finance's screener uses charts to show you how companies' ranks compared with others on various criteria. Access the screener by clicking the Stock screener link on the left side of the page.

- » **Kapitall** (`www.kapitall.com`): Screening for stocks might not sound like your idea of something fun to do on a Saturday night, but Kapitall is trying to change that. The site lets you prospect for stocks using a fun, colorful interface that looks more like a video game than a stock-screening tool. It's kind of fun. Really. You just need to register first to use the site. The site also provides contests and ways to invest real money.

- » **Morningstar's Stock Screener** (`https://screen.morningstar.com/StockSelector.html`): The Morningstar offering in the Stock Screener sweepstakes is designed to make it easier for beginning investors to design sophisticated screens. Rather than requiring you to pick through dozens of criteria you might not understand, you can just pick a growth grade, profitability grade, or financial health grade, based on a scale from A to F. After you're done, click the Show/Score Results tab, and you see all the stocks that made the cut. You'll need to sign up as a free member of Morningstar to use the stock screener.

- » **Portfolio123** (`www.portfolio123.com`): This site provides a number of premade screens that can help you find stocks with improving earnings or that are industry leaders. The site has a 15-day free trial; however, you need to pay a $38 monthly fee to use many of the site's features.

TIP

If you're interested in stock screening, most online brokers' sites offer a tour or tutorial of the tools they can provide. If screens are important to you, you might consider checking out the tools on various online brokers' sites to see whether they're good enough for you to open an account.

Knowing What You're Looking For: Popular Screening Variables

Investors can search for countless criteria by using screens, but I've noticed that certain variables routinely show up in stock screens because they're so useful. If you know what these variables are and why they matter, you can build some helpful screens.

The basics: Because you have to start somewhere

When you're first figuring out how to build screens, you want to start with some of the more basic variables. That way, you can get comfortable with the idea of building screens first and then add more advanced variables as you narrow your search. In this Basics category, I'd include the following:

>> **Valuation ratios:** These ratios include the price-to-earnings (P/E) ratio and the price–to–book value ratio. Valuation ratios are ways to compare a stock price with the company's value. If you're looking for potentially undervalued stocks, for instance, search for stocks with low P/E and price–to–book value ratios.

TIP

The P/E ratio and other valuation ratios are discussed at length in Chapter 13.

>> **Shares outstanding:** A company's *shares outstanding* measures the total number of shares in the hands of investors. It's related to a company's *float,* which is the number of shares that are available to be bought and sold by the public. When companies buy back their stock, shares are removed from the shares outstanding and float, and they sit on the sidelines. Those sidelined shares are called *treasury stock* and aren't included in shares outstanding.

>> **Market value:** The *market value* is a measure of the price tag the stock market puts on the entire company. The market value — usually called the *market capitalization* or *market cap* — is measured by multiplying the stock price by its number of shares outstanding. This measure determines whether a stock is large, mid-sized, or small.

>> **Earnings per share (EPS):** *Earnings per share* is the bottom line. It measures what portion of the company net income holders of each share of stock are entitled to. Investors generally use diluted EPS in screens. (The diluted EPS figure is a way to measure a company's bottom line that factors in the effect of companies issuing large amounts of stock options to employees.)

>> **Current ratio:** The *current ratio* measures how prepared a company is to pay bills that are due in a year's time. You can calculate the current ratio by dividing current assets (assets that can be turned into cash in a year or less) by current liabilities (bills due in a year or less). If the company's current ratio is 1, the company has enough assets to cover bills coming due in a year. The higher the ratio, the more solid the company's financial condition is.

>> **Revenue per employee:** The *revenue per employee* ratio shows you how efficiently the company uses its workforce. The ratio is the company's revenue divided by its number of employees. The higher the number, the more revenue the company derives from each employee.

Getting more particular: More advanced variables to screen for

Just using the basic screening variables is somewhat limiting. If you want to carve the list of stock candidates further, you can use some more advanced variables. Good choices here include the following:

>> **Gross margin:** One of many ways to measure a company's profitability, *gross profit* is how much revenue a company keeps after paying for things directly involved in the production of the good or service sold. A lemonade stand's gross profit is the dollar value of the lemonade sold minus the cost of things used in the lemonade, such as sugar and lemons. This gross profit divided by the company's revenue gives you *gross margin.* Gross margin tells you how much of every dollar in sales the company keeps after paying costs directly tied to making the good or service. The higher the gross margin, the more profitable the company is.

>> **Operating margin:** This method of measuring a company's profit includes more costs than gross margin. *Operating profit* is gross profit minus indirect costs, such as overhead. Overhead might include the cost of hiring a company to promote the business. *Operating margin* is the company's operating profit divided by revenue. The higher the operating margin, the more profitable the company.

>> **Net profit margin:** This particular margin compares the company's bottom line with its revenue. *Net profit* is measured by dividing a company's net income, which counts all company costs, by its revenue. It tells you how much of each dollar in revenue the company keeps as profit after paying all costs. The higher the net profit margin, the more profitable the company.

>> **Return on equity:** A great way to see how efficiently the company's management is using the money invested in the company, *return on equity* (ROE) is measured by dividing net income by shareholder's equity. Shareholder's equity measures how much money shareholders have invested in the company. So, ROE shows you how much profit the company generates per dollar invested in the company.

>> **Return on assets:** The *return on assets* shows you how much profit the company is able to squeeze out of its assets. The higher the number, the better the company is at making money from things it owns.

>> **Dividend payout ratio:** The *dividend payout ratio* tells you what portion of profit a company is paying out as dividends. You calculate this ratio by dividing a company's dividends by net income.

WARNING

If a company's dividend payout ratio gets high — paying 85 percent or more of its profit out as earnings, for example — it might be paying more than it can afford, depending on what industry it is in.

>> **Dividend yield:** The *dividend yield* tells you what kind of return you're getting as a dividend from the money you've invested in a stock. The dividend yield is a company's annual dividend paid per share divided by the stock price. A $100 stock that pays $2 a year in dividends has a 2 percent dividend yield.

>> **Institutional ownership:** This measure tries to show you whether the "smart money" is buying a stock. The *institutional ownership* ratio shows you what percentage of shares are in the hands of large mutual funds and pension funds, which presumably have large research units. Some investors look for stocks with low institutional ownership, figuring the stock will rise rapidly as these big investors discover the stock and buy shares.

>> **Debt-to-equity ratio:** The *debt-to-equity* ratio shows you how deeply in debt a company is. The ratio divides a company's liabilities by its shareholder equity. The higher the ratio, the more *leveraged*, or in debt, the company is. Remember, though, that different levels of debt are acceptable in various industries.

>> **Beta:** Most online screening tools use a measure called *beta* to gauge volatility. The higher beta is, the more volatile the stock is compared to the rest of the stock market. If a stock has a beta greater than 1, that means it's more volatile than the Standard & Poor's 500. If a stock's beta is less than 1, it's less volatile than the S&P 500. And if a stock's beta is equal to 1, it's equally as volatile as the S&P 500.

TIP

If you can't stomach stocks that swing as wildly as the stock market, you want to add a beta filter to your screens. Just look for stocks that have betas of less than 1.

>> **Short interest:** *Short interest* measures how many investors are betting a stock will fall. The measure is calculated by dividing the number of shares being *shorted* — or being sold in a complex maneuver by investors betting that the stock price will fall — by the number of shares that normally trade each day, or the *average daily volume.* (For more on shorting stock, see Chapter 5.)

Finding stocks using trading-pattern variables

Some investors are interested more in a company's stock than the company itself. These investors, generally known as *technical analysts*, believe stocks follow certain patterns. And if you detect the pattern fast enough, you can figure out where the stock is going and make money. Some screening variables are designed to find *technical stock patterns*, including

>> **Average daily volume:** When a stock rises or falls, some investors think heavy trading in the stock means more than a light trading volume. If a stock goes up, these investors look at trading volume to find out how many investors are buying. If the stock is rising and trading activity is strong, that tells these investors there's great demand for the stock and the uptrend might continue.

>> **Proximity to moving averages:** This indicator tells you whether the current stock price is higher or lower than where it has been in the past. The 200-day moving average, for instance, tells you what the stock's average price has been over the course of the past trading year. If the stock falls below the 200-day moving average, some see that as a bad sign because it means everyone who bought the stock in the past year, on average, is losing money and might be eager to sell.

>> **Proximity to a stock's price highs and lows:** You can use screens to find out whether a stock's price is close to its high price over the past year, called the *52-week high*, or its low price, the *52-week low*.

>> **Stock performance:** This simple measure shows you how much the stock has risen or fallen in a set period of time.

Getting Started with Premade Screens

If you've never built a stock screen before, you might want to first try out some of the premade screens available on various websites. The websites have done most of the work for you and entered all the variables, saving you the hassle. The following list highlights some of the better-known "canned" stock screens:

>> **Quicken's One-Click Scorecard** (https://investing.quicken.com/ research)**:** This Quicken tool takes a novel approach toward screening. You can find it by clicking the One-Click Scorecard tab at the top of the screen — after logging in (it's free to register). The site screens stocks for those that meet the criteria described by money manager Robert Hagstrom, author of *The Warren Buffett Way*, 3rd Edition (Wiley). The One-Click Scorecard seeks stocks with traits that Hagstrom says Buffett looks for, including a high return on equity, high net profit margin, and most importantly, a stock price that's lower than the company's *intrinsic value* — its true worth based on how much it's expected to earn in the future.

You must own a copy of Quicken that's three years old or less to access Quicken's website. Just click the One-Click Scorecard link at the top of the page under the Quotes & Research tab to access the system.

Just because a stock scores high in the Robert Hagstrom screen in the One-Click Scorecard doesn't mean that Buffett bought the stock or wants to buy it. The screen merely tells you what stocks have traits that match what Buffett looks for.

>> **NASDAQ's Guru Stock Screener** (www.nasdaq.com/investing/guru/guru-stock-screener.aspx): This particular NASDAQ canned stock screener uses preset criteria to help you determine whether one of several famous investors would buy a stock that you're interested in. On the page that appears, you can type the company's symbol and the tool tells you whether famous former Fidelity portfolio manager Peter Lynch, value investor Benjamin Graham, contrarian investor David Dreman, or growth investor Martin Zweig would be interested in the stock. You can also use the Find Stock Based on Guru Interest option to automatically screen for stocks these gurus might be interested in.

>> **Zacks Predefined Screener** (www.zacks.com/screening/stock-screener): The Zacks entry in the predefined screener market offers screens that focus on the key factors you'd expect, such as value and earnings growth. But Zacks' predefined screens also offer several criteria that highlight stocks on the move and those that enjoy the most positive or negative changes in analysts' recommendations. Access the predefined screens by clicking the Predefined tab.

You can run basic premade screens for free, but to do fancy things such as narrow all the screens to include small, mid-sized, or large stocks, you'll need to pay. Advanced screens are part of the Zacks Premium membership, which costs $249 a year.

>> **Morningstar's Stock Screener** (https://screen.morningstar.com/mstarScreens/chooseStockScreen.html): Morningstar offers not one but a number of helpful screeners with catchy and self-explanatory titles. A few of the screeners include Low-Priced Growth Stocks, Profitable but Unloved, Bargain-Basement Small Caps, Aggressive Growth, Blue-Blood Blue Chips, and Classic Appeal. You can also access some of these screeners by clicking the Stocks tab at Morningstar's home page and scrolling down the new page that appears.

>> **MSN Money** (www.msn.com/en-us/money/stockscreener): MSN Money gets down to business and heads straight to what many investors want to know: What are some top stocks. MSN Money shows a Popular Screens banner at the top of the page. You can choose from canned screens to find high dividend yields, bargain stocks, or tech giants.

TIP

Most of the online screening tools in this section let you customize canned screens. Tweaking an existing screen can be a good way to get started because you don't have to start from scratch. Instead, you can modify the variables to your tastes.

Designing a Custom Screen

After you start dabbling with stock screens, you'll probably start enjoying it. You can get a rush sifting through thousands of stocks for precise variables and get a list of candidates in a matter of seconds. Many investors, when they realize what stock screening is and how easy it is to do, can get kind of addicted to building screens. Screening shows the power of online investing.

The premade screens described in the preceding section cover most of the main searches investors would want to do. But sometimes, a canned screen isn't good enough. Many of the same sites that offer canned screens also let you create a screen from scratch. You might consider building a screen from the ground up if you encounter the following issues with a premade screen:

>> **The screen is too strict.** A premade screen might be so restrictive that you might miss out on stocks that just barely missed the cut. This situation is especially true when searching for value-priced stocks because investors' opinions on what makes a cheap stock vary. A canned screen might consider a P/E ratio of 8 to be cheap, but you might overlook some stocks with P/E

ratios of 8.5 or 9. Stocks with P/E ratios of less than 10 might be considered to be bargains, but not cheap enough for the screen.

» **The screen is too lenient.** A premade screen might not be as restrictive as you'd like. If you're looking for a company that's expanding rapidly, you might want to ratchet up what it takes to get into your screen. Many screens consider 20 percent annual earnings growth to be rapid, but you might want 30 percent or more.

» **The screen is not to your taste.** Some investors go after stocks that defy characterization. You might want to find stocks with high P/E ratios and low price–to–book value ratios, which are unusual things to look for at the same time. You need to build these personalized screens yourself.

Finding different industries' best companies by using Yahoo! Finance

If you're trying to figure out which companies in an industry are performing the best or worst, several of the sites mentioned previously can do the trick. Just for an illustration, I show you how using Yahoo! Finance's screening tool makes it easy:

1. **Point your browser to Yahoo! Finance's screening tool at** `https://finance.yahoo.com/screener/new`.

2. **From the Sector drop-down list, choose the industry you're interested in.**

3. **Increase your screening universe to define what you mean by a best company.**

   The definition of a best company is in the eyes of the beholder. You might, for instance, want companies with a return on equity that's higher than the industry's. To find companies with an industry-beating return on equity, you'd first click the plus sign to the left of the Add Another Filter link. Next, go to the Financial Highlights area and choose the Return on Equity % (LTM) option and then choose Close. You can then choose the level of return on equity you're looking for. Your screen should look something like Figure 14-2.

4. **Add more variables.**

   You can keep working your way down, adding different criteria if you choose. Just by clicking the Add Another Filer link, you can choose stocks that miss, match, or exceed industry averages on a variety of things, including price–to–book value ratio, price-to-earnings ratio, debt loads, and many other items.

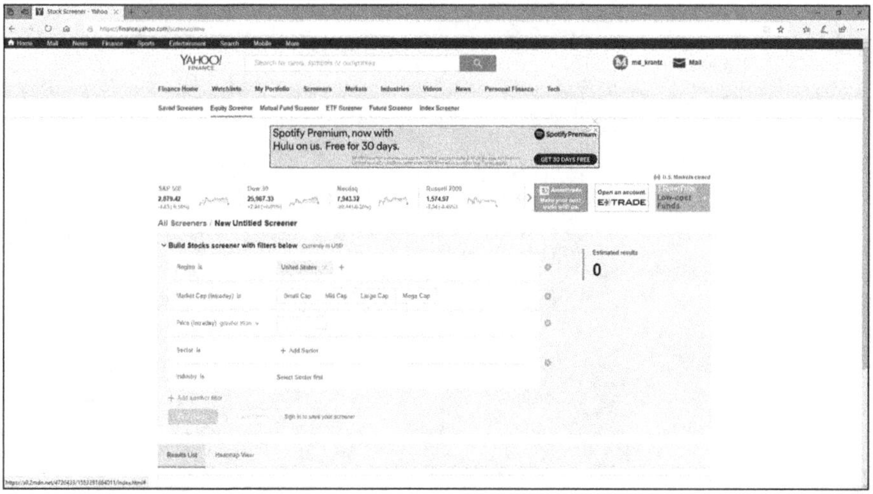

FIGURE 14-2:
Yahoo! Finance's
screening tool
allows you to see
how companies
and their stocks
compare with
industry peers.

Finding value or growth companies by using Morningstar's Stock Screener

You could go to the trouble of designing a convoluted set of criteria to find value and growth stocks. But why go to the trouble when Morningstar's Stock Screener has done the work for you? Morningstar's Stock Screener helps you design a custom screen, but with some helpful handholding. Here's how:

1. **Point your browser to Morningstar's screening tool at** `https://screen.morningstar.com/StockSelector.html?ssection=StockScreener`.

2. **If you haven't signed up for the free version of Morningstar, do so now.**

   The Stock Screener page appears in all its glory.

3. **In the Morningstar Equity Style drop-down list, choose your Growth or Value criteria.**

   You could go for Large Value, for example. That's the second item on the drop-down list from the top.

4. **Limit your search further if you want.**

   You can narrow your search further, based on growth or profitability grades and other items.

5. **When you're done, click the Show/Score Results tab at the top of the screener.**

   You get a lovely list of results.

Chapter **15**

Analyzing the Analysts and Stock Pickers

When you're looking to make a big purchase, such as a car, house, or big-screen TV, you probably ask other people questions before making your decision. You might ask a friend or family member for his recommendation or consult with a YouTube reviewer or website that ranks products.

Recommendations play an important role for some investors when picking stocks, too. Traditional brokers have long made it their business to recommend stocks for their clients to buy. And even before the hot dogs hit the grill, many family barbeques start sounding like an investment club meeting as everyone brags about his winners (and somehow fails to mention stocks he's lost money on). Many financial TV shows feature guests who can fire off stock tips.

Stock recommendations are impossible to avoid, so it's up to you to keep their value in perspective. There are smart ways to handle recommendations. In this chapter, I show you various online resources for stock recommendations, as well as how to interpret them. You get a chance to read about different stock-picking newsletters and sites and how to evaluate them. And I show you some new online sites that reveal how other individual investors rate stocks.

Picking Apart Professional Analyst Reports

Nearly all the major Wall Street brokerage firms have teams of research sell-side analysts. The *sell-side analyst's* job is to study companies and tell investors who are clients of the brokerage firm which stocks are attractive. You can also find *independent* research firms — research groups not connected with a brokerage firm that analyze stocks and sell their research.

TIP

Blindly following buy or sell recommendations is generally a bad idea. Smart investors know how to scan through research reports to pick out important insights on the company or industry. Later in this chapter, I show you how to quickly pull the most important information out of analyst reports.

Accessing analyst reports online

Before you can analyze research reports, you have to get your hands on them. Several techniques are available to do this online — some cost you money, but many don't. The following list highlights a few resources of both the free and not-so-free types:

>> **Online brokers:** You don't have to be a client of the full-service brokerage firms such as Credit Suisse or Goldman Sachs to get their analysts' research reports. Online brokers can sometimes get the goods for you. Charles Schwab, for instance, allows you to download reports from Credit Suisse, and Fidelity offers access to Barclays Capital's reports. E*Trade provides Credit Suisse's research to customers with more than $100,000 in assets. Most online brokers also offer access to independent research, including reports from Standard & Poor's Capital IQ, Argus, Thomson Reuters, and Morningstar. Getting research from your online broker is generally the best route because there's usually no charge.

>> **Research providers:** Some independent research providers sell their reports directly to investors. CFRA, for instance, sells reports on more than 5,000 companies. (See www.cfraresearch.com/individual-investors/ for a listing.) The reports include a forecast of what the stock's future price could be, called a *target price,* in addition to an analysis of the company's earnings. The reports often cost around $50.

CFRA reports also use an easy-to-understand rating system. S&P rates thousands of stocks using a star rating system where the most attractive stocks are given five stars and the least attractive stocks get one star. If your broker offers S&P reports, you can get the S&P ratings from the top of the reports.

TIP

Don't assume that stock research from an independent research firm is more accurate or better than research from large Wall Street firms. Sometimes research from Wall Street brokerage firms is very good. The quality of research varies greatly and largely depends on the strength of the specific analyst covering the stock. I show you how to track down the best analysts on various stocks in the next section of this chapter:

- *Yahoo! Finance* (http://finance.yahoo.com) has a comprehensive database of analyst recommendations. Enter a stock symbol in the search field at the top of Yahoo! Finance, click the name of the company when it pops up, and then click the Analysis link in the center of the new page that appears. You see how analysts, on average, are rating the stock and also the stock's *average price target* — what analysts, on average, expect the stock's price to be in a year or less. You can find out from Yahoo! Finance whether analysts raised their opinion on a stock, called *upgrading,* or cut their opinion, called *downgrading.*

- *Reuters* (www.reuters.com/finance/markets) provides analyst recommendations if you enter a stock symbol, click Search, and then click the name of the company. Click the Analysts tab and you'll find analysts' recommendations and how they've changed over the past month, two months, and three months.

- *Zacks Investment Research* (www.zacks.com) provides brokerage recommendations if you know where to look for them. Just enter a stock's symbol in the Quote text field, click the name of the company, scroll down, and click the Broker Recommendations link on the left side of the screen. Pay close attention to the average brokerage recommendation (ABR), a number that falls somewhere between 1 and 5. If the ABR is 1, that means analysts, on average, rank the stock a strong buy. If the ABR is 5, analysts, on average, rank the stock a strong sell. Zacks also ranks stock ratings by industry.

- *NASDAQ.com* (www.nasdaq.com) offers a handy guide to upgrades and downgrades for all stocks, not just those that trade on the NASDAQ. Scroll down quite a way to find the Recommendations section, where you can see how many stocks were upgraded or downgraded that day.

REMEMBER

Most summary sites convert stock ratings into numbers on a one-to-five scale, where 1 is a strong buy or outperform and 5 is a strong sell or underperform.

WHEN *HOLD* REALLY MEANS *SELL*

Research reports issued by Wall Street investment banks got a bad rap in the early 2000s — one they haven't completely lived down even to this day. That's when the former New York attorney general Eliot Spitzer began investigating a number of internal emails sent within several large Wall Street brokerage firms, and shook up the industry in ways still being felt more than a decade later. The emails allegedly indicated that sell-side analysts routinely issued glowing strong buy and buy ratings on stocks about which they had serious reservations. During the Internet boom, for instance, for every stock with a sell rating, there were 100 stocks with a buy rating, according to the University of Pennsylvania. Those ratings proved to be overly optimistic in many cases, and some investors who followed the research suffered large losses as a result. The regulators alleged analysts promoted stocks of companies the brokerage firms hoped to sell lucrative investment banking services to. The analysts, in turn, would receive bonuses resulting from the business that came from the companies they wrote positively about. The investigations resulted in dramatic reforms in the way investment banks handle stock research.

In 2003, ten investment banking firms agreed to a settlement with regulators in which they would pay roughly $1.4 billion in various penalties and fees in connection to issuing allegedly misleading research reports. (See the SEC page at www.sec.gov/news/press/2003-54.htm for more about the landmark case.)

Spitzer ran into legal troubles himself — allegations of misconduct led him to resign as governor of New York in 2008. But the settlement he helped strike with investment banks resulted in several changes to research that affect online investors. One of the significant outcomes of the settlement included the requirement that Wall Street investment firms make their analysts' ratings and price targets available to the public. By giving investors access to analysts' track records, investors gained the ability, thanks to several websites, to see which analysts might be worth listening to and which ones to ignore. Following the reforms, perhaps due to the greater accountability, analyst ratings improved in accuracy.

Determining which Wall Street analysts are worth listening to

Don't just assume that research from an independent analyst is better than research from a sell-side analyst. What really matters is performance. If an analyst is always wrong, independent or not, you probably don't want to listen to his or her advice.

But how do you find out which analysts are the best? These two online tools can help you find the best analysts:

» **Investars** (www.investars.com): Investars maintains an impressive database that shows which research firms and individual analysts are the most accurate and looks up ratings based on sectors and individual stocks. There used to be a free version of the site, but now access to Investars is sold only to professional money management firms. Once again, though, your online brokerage is your key. Some brokerages, including Fidelity, provide access to Investars data to customers, as you can see in Figure 15-1.

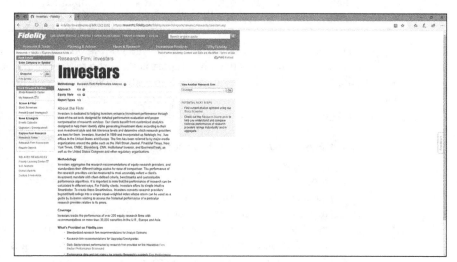

FIGURE 15-1:
Fidelity provides access to the Investars data to its customers, letting you track the quality of stock picks based on individual stocks, analysts, and research firms.

» **StarMine** (www.starmine.com): StarMine lets investors view lists that rank the top analysts. But like Investars, StarMine is made directly available only to money-management firms. Some brokerages, such as Fidelity, make StarMine data available to customers. You can get access to some StarMine data in another way: the company's awards. StarMine lauds the best analysts each year and makes the award announcements, available for free at www.analystawards.com. You can find the best overall analysts and firms and also find the ones that are the most accurate in specific industry sectors, such as financial, industrials, and utilities.

TIP

StarMine's own website is geared for professional money managers and Wall Street firms. If you're not part of that crowd, the easiest way to get StarMine and Investars data is through your broker. If this data is important to you, you'll want to ask if it is available when you sign up with a broker. This issue is yet another reminder of the types of services brokers are adding to their offerings to justify their commissions.

What to look for in an analyst report

Many investors who read Wall Street analyst reports tend to concentrate on the analyst's rating. These investors want to know instantly whether the stock is rated a buy, hold, or sell.

TIP

Savvy investors often skip past the analyst's rating on a stock. Much of the worthwhile information in an analyst report isn't in the rating but in the insights about the company, management, and industry. Dummies.com (`www.dummies.com/personal-finance/investing/online-investing/what-to-look-for-in-an-analyst-report/`) provides a useful guide in how to read analysts' research reports.

Pay the most attention to these portions of the report:

>> **Industry comparisons:** Many Wall Street analysts are assigned to cover companies in a specific industry. As a result, these analysts spend time going to industry conferences, meeting with employees, customers, and suppliers to build deep knowledge of industry trends. Industry information is one of the top things you should look for. Pay special attention to any signs that one company is taking market share from other competitors.

>> **Channel checks:** The better industry analysts take the time to see how much of the product that companies are shipping is actually making it into the hands of customers. The process of tracking the flow of goods from the company to warehouses to resellers and retailers and ultimately to consumers is called a *channel check*. If you get the feeling the company is shipping product that's just stacking up on retailers' shelves, that's a bad sign. A pileup of product might indicate the company is trying to boost its earnings in the short term and might suffer later as the glut of products is sold off.

>> **Price-target justification:** Analysts often use a variety of stock valuation techniques (explained in more detail in Chapter 13) to put a price target on a stock. A *price target* is the analyst's best guess at how much the stock might be worth in the future, usually one year from now. The most interesting part of the price target is often analysts' explanation of how they arrived at the number.

Pssst . . . understanding the whisper number

Many analysts put their MBAs to good use and pick apart the financial statements of companies to determine how much the stocks are truly worth. But some analysts take the lazy way out by blindly following the forecast given to them by the company. This presents a problem for online investors because companies can steer some analysts to lower their expectations for growth. And if the company is successful in lowering the earnings bar, it's easier for the company to beat the results. The opposite can happen, too. A company might convince analysts to go along with an overly optimistic view of the future, setting investors up for a disappointment.

That's where the earnings whisper number comes in. The *whisper number*, in theory, is the unofficial earnings number most investors honestly expect the company to report.

TIP

Whisper numbers gain even more prominence during strong bull markets when investors' expectations begin to soar. Whisper numbers were particularly popular during the dot-com stock boom, which even today, is one of the most overinflated markets investors have ever seen.

You can get whisper numbers for free online. WhisperNumber.com (`www.whispernumber.com`) is an easy way to see what the whisper number might be. Just enter the symbol of the stock you're interested in and click the search button, and you can view the whisper number for the current quarter. You can also look up the whisper number for the previous quarter and see how close it was to the number reported by the company. Lastly, you can see how the stock reacted in 1, 5, 10, and 30 days by following the company's last earnings announcement. The site is free, but you must register.

Estimize.com (`www.estimize.com`) has another approach to try to get a more accurate earnings estimate than the analysts, by measuring the wisdom of the crowd. The site allows members to enter their best guesses at what they think companies will earn. Estimize then tallies up the users' estimates and creates an Estimize estimate. You can use the site for free — both to look up estimates from other users as well as enter your own. Estimize attracts estimates and participation from big-time investors, too. The site contains a rich amount of data that will help you determine how much a company is really expected to earn, as shown in Figure 15-2.

Accessing and understanding credit ratings

Research analysts who study companies and their stocks get the most attention from many investors. But you find a second type of company analysts out there — debt-rating analysts or bond analysts. *Debt-rating analysts* study companies to determine how creditworthy they are. Debt-rating analysts are important because if they determine that a company is stable and trustworthy, the company can borrow money at lower interest rates. Debt-rating analysts give companies letter grades to measure their financial strength, with A being high and either C or D being the lowest grade possible.

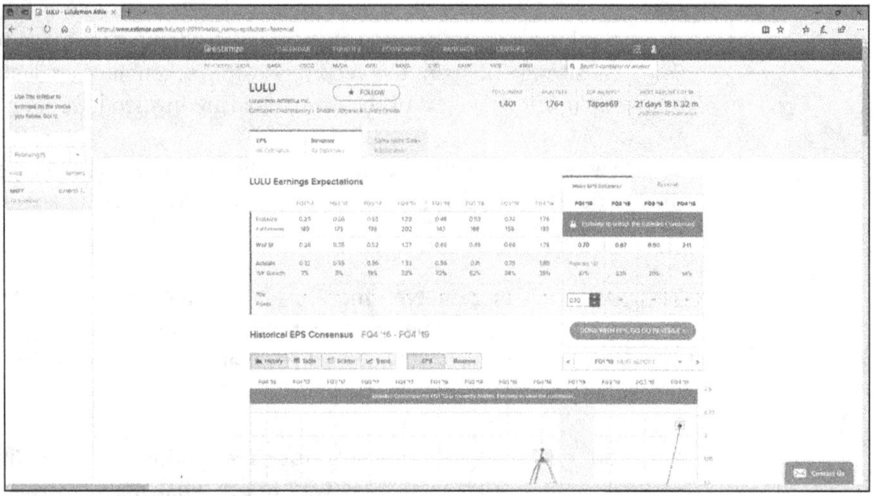

FIGURE 15-2:
Estimize.com harnesses the power of the wisdom of the crowd to try to get a good feel on what companies will earn.

You'll find three major debt-rating firms: Moody's, Standard & Poor's, and Fitch Ratings. The ratings used by Moody's vary slightly from the ratings used by the other two firms. The debt-rating firms employ armies of analysts trained to pick apart companies' financial statements looking for trouble. Although they miss problems from time to time, including both the Enron debacle and the subprime mortgage debt implosion, they're still a helpful source of information for investors.

Even if you're buying a company's stock, not its debt, credit agencies' ratings are important because they give you an idea of how solid the company's financials are. You find three leading credit agencies, but only the following two agencies make their ratings available for free online:

>> **Moody's Investors Service** (www.moodys.com): Moody's provides easy online access to its credit ratings. Moody's site is free, but you must register to get any information from it. Click the search box in the upper-middle portion of the screen. In the dialog box that appears, enter your login information or register for free and click the Log In button. Then enter the name or symbol of the company you want to research. After you click the name of the company you're interested in, Moody's ratings for the company will pop up on a new screen.

You might see several ratings for each company, but the rating of most importance to investors is the one called Long Term Rating. (See Figure 15-3.)

>> **Standard & Poor's** (www.standardandpoors.com): S&P lets you view its credit ratings for the thousands of companies it covers. Enter the company's name or symbol in the Find a Rating box on the left side of the page and click the Search button. After the page refreshes, scroll down until you see the company's name. After you click the company's name, you see S&P's credit rating for the company. The site is free, but you have to register to use it.

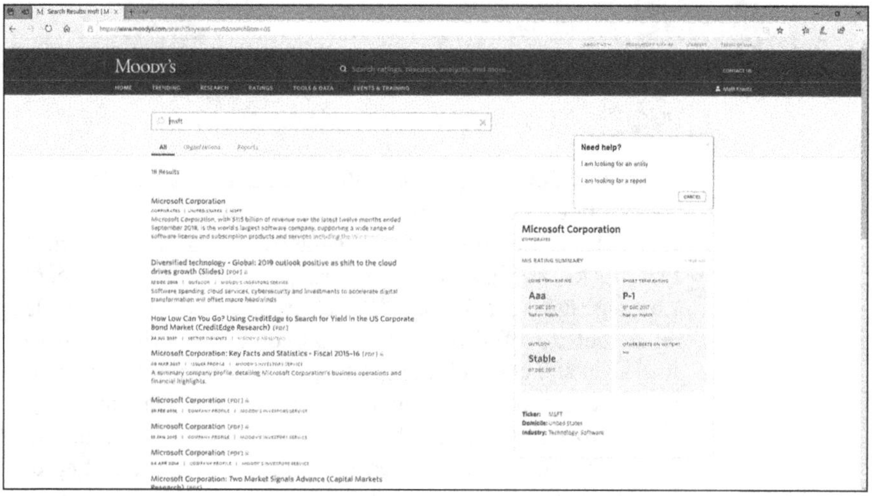

FIGURE 15-3: Moody's Investors Service lets you see its debt-rating analysts' ratings, which measure how secure they think a company's financial standing is.

CREDIT RATINGS LOST CREDIBILITY

Just as Wall Street stock analysts came under fire after the dot-com bust, credit rating agencies drew negative attention after the financial crisis of 2007. Credit rating agencies are supposed to be the watchdog for investors, carefully studying the strength of debt instruments. However, during the housing boom of the mid-2000s the credit rating agencies continued to give top credit ratings to financially shaky debt instruments tied to aggressive subprime mortgages. Investors who bought these instruments, assuming they were high quality, were sorely disappointed as the borrowers defaulted and the value of the instruments fell. The rapid decline in value of these mortgage debt securities stunned the financial system and was a big contributor in the financial crisis, which ultimately led to the failure and massive bailouts of some of the nation's largest financial institutions. Many critics of credit rating agencies felt that these companies should have alerted investors to the dangers of these debt instruments, which could have stemmed the financial crisis. Today, it's critical for bond investors to do their own due diligence and not blindly rely on credit agencies' ratings.

Connecting with Online Stock Ratings

Wall Street analysts aren't the only sources for ratings on stocks. You find a handful of online stock-rating services that let either a computer or other investors rate a stock. Some of these rating services are based on computer models, sometimes called *quantitative* (or *quant*) *models,* which analyze companies' financial statements and key ratios to decide whether the stock is a good buy. Other stock-rating services allow investors to share their ratings on stocks, with the idea that as a whole, the average of the crowd's opinions will be close to accurate. I cover both types of stock-rating services in the following sections.

Putting quant stock models to work for you

Research reports issued by Wall Street analysts and debt-rating analysts can be helpful, but they're not perfect. These analysts are human, too, and often fail to sound the bell before financial catastrophes occur — think the collapse of dot-com stocks, as well as the implosion of Enron and companies in the subprime mortgage industry. These missteps by human analysts have led some investors to think that it would be great if you could get ratings and recommendations on stocks yet somehow eliminate the potential of human error or lapses in judgment. That's where quant models come in. These models are programmed by market experts to analyze stocks by using a series of criteria and to rate them. Most of these systems are untouched by human hands after they're designed. Instead, they follow strict preset guidelines. A few online quant models include the following:

>> **Schwab Equity Ratings (**www.schwab.wallst.com/ser/perfMonitor/
public/?period=52wk**):** Schwab ranks thousands of stocks (using an A-through-F scale) based on companies' valuations plus the risk, valuation, and momentum of their stocks. Even if you're not a Schwab customer, you can get limited access to the Schwab Equity Ratings.

For instance, say you'd like to get a list of all the stocks that have been rated an A. Start by making sure that the Performance over Recent 26-51 Weeks tab is selected, as shown in Figure 15-4, and then choose the most recent period from the Select Performance Time Period drop-down list. You see a table underneath a few charts. In this table, you can click the time period, listed under the Performance for the Period header, and get a list of all the stocks that were rated A, and also B through F, 26 weeks ago.

REMEMBER

You need to be a Schwab customer to get access to current Schwab Equity Ratings for all stocks.

>> **Trefis** (`www.trefis.com`): If you're looking for a smart algorithm to give you a quick rating on a stock, Trefis is a nifty tool. The system, which is free to use, studies a companies' profitability and gives you an estimate of what the stock is worth.

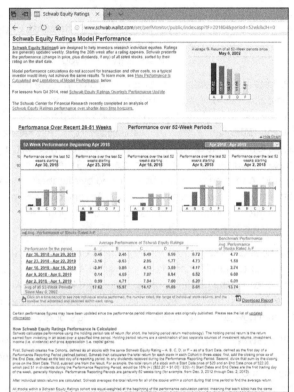

FIGURE 15-4:
Schwab makes its
Schwab Equity
Ratings available
on its website for
all web surfers.

Sharing stock ratings with other investors online

In his book *The Wisdom of Crowds* (Random House), journalist James Surowiecki argues that a crowd of regular people making decisions, on average, will get closer to the right answer as a whole than just a few experts. Collectively, a group of diverse and independent-thinking people will, on average, come up with an accurate guess.

Several online sites are trying to harness this wisdom of crowds and turn the masses' guess into information you can use to boost your returns. Some good sources for this collective intelligence are listed here:

>> **The Motley Fool CAPS** (https://caps.fool.com/)**:** This particular corner of the Motley Fool website allows members to enter their ratings on thousands of stocks. The ratings are then compiled into a single average rating that's available to all users of the website. You can access the CAPS database by clicking the CAPS Community tab. A stock with five stars is a strong buy, and a stock with a one-star rating is a strong sell. The site is free, but you must register first.

But CAPS gets more interesting the more you dive into the menus. After signing in, search for any stock. Scroll down on the stock information page until you see the stock chart. Click the On link located below the chart, next to where it says CAPS Rating. Now you can see how the CAPS rating has changed over the past few months, shown by the gold line on the chart. If you scroll down further, you can also read why certain CAPS members rated a stock the way they did. And even these blurbs are rated by members, so you can read the most highly rated comments on a stock. Anyone can view most CAPS ratings and information, but to rate stocks yourself, you need to register with the site, which is free.

And what does CAPS stand for? You're going to be sorry you asked. CAPS doesn't appear to stand for anything, but rather seems to be a play on the word *cap,* because the Motley Fool's founders are known for wearing jester hats. Participants in the CAPS system are assigned a color-coded hat, or cap, icon to signal how good they have been at picking stocks.

>> **PredictWallStreet** (www.predictwallstreet.com)**:** PredictWallStreet lets you start sharing recommendations with others pretty quickly and easily. From the front page, just enter a stock symbol in the search field and click the Up button if you recommend the stock or the Down button if you think the stock will fall. You can see the average recommendations of other users for other popular stock market indexes or popular stocks. One of the nice things about this site is that you can use it without registering.

WARNING

Following the crowd when it comes to investing can often be a bad idea. During periods of market manias, when investors become overly bullish about particular types of stocks, they often bid stock prices up too high and set themselves up for disappointments. Some investors, who call themselves *contrarians,* instead figure out what the crowd is doing and then do the opposite. If the crowd is bullish about a stock, a contrarian would assume that the group is wrong and be bearish about the stock. Exceptions exist, though, and sometimes the crowd can be right. A 2011 study by the National Bureau of Economic Research (https://www.nber.org/papers/w17298) found that picks submitted by investors in Motley Fool's CAPS system were "surprisingly informative about future stock prices."

Evaluating Stock- and Mutual Fund–Picking Newsletters and Websites

Whenever a crowd is trying to make quick money, there's no shortage of people happy to offer their expertise and skill . . . for a fee. Stock investing is no different. You can find dozens of stock- and mutual fund–picking newsletters, websites, books, and seminars. They all make great pitches for why you need to pay to subscribe to their wonderful services.

WARNING

By and large, many of the pitches you see for stock-picking newsletters and websites aren't worth much, and you should be skeptical before paying money for systems and programs that claim to be able to beat the market. A 1998 study by Jeffrey Jaffe and James Mahoney — available at `https://papers.ssrn.com/sol3/papers.cfm?abstract_id=937407` — found that stocks recommended by newsletters don't outperform the market. The study also found that newsletters tend to pile onto yesterday's winning stocks by recommending stocks that had done well in the recent past.

Before you sign up for a stock-picking service . . .

Before you pay a dime for any stock-picking newsletter or website, take the time to educate yourself about the specific service you're considering.

Your first stop should be a column written by Mark Hulbert (`http://hulbertratings.com/`). Hulbert is a well-known tracker of newsletter performance. Hulbert uses advanced performance-tracking methods to measure not only how well stock-picking newsletters perform, but also how much risk they've taken to get those returns. After all, a 30 percent annual return isn't that impressive if your portfolio swings up and down 80 percent a year.

Hulbert also writes a number of financial columns at MarketWatch that are worth reading because he tells you about trends among stock pickers. If you want to look up how a specific newsletter scores in Hulbert's ratings, you need to sign up for his Hulbert Financial Digest, which ranks many newsletters. You can sign up by clicking the promotional link on his online column. The service costs $50 a month, but you can get a free 30-day pass.

WARNING

If a newsletter or online stock-picking service you're considering isn't tracked by Hulbert, you should be skeptical. It might mean the service doesn't want its performance to be tracked — perhaps for shady reasons.

DON'T LET READING NEWSLETTERS BRING ON A JUNK-MAIL DELUGE

One potential peril of signing up for stock-picking services and newsletters is that some sell your name and address to other companies for profit. This might fill your mailbox or email in-basket with ads you don't want, including pitches for shady penny stock shams.

Here are two strategies to prevent you from getting slammed from junk mail:

- **Use a slightly different name when you sign up for the stock-picking service.** Instead of signing up as Joe Smith, use JoeD Smith or something like that. If junk mail starts showing up to that unique name in your mailbox, you'll know it's the stock-picking service that's selling your information. You can notify the service to stop selling your information.

- **Use an email alias.** Some email services, such as Outlook.com, allow you to create secondary email addresses. If your email address is joesmith@outlook.com, you can create a secondary email address, or alias, of joesmithnewsletter@outlook.com. You can use the alias when signing up for stock-picking newsletters. If email comes in addressed to the alias, you know where it came from. You can also instruct Outlook.com to direct email addresses to an alias to a separate folder in your inbox or even delete it if you don't want to receive it anymore.

- **Sign up for the Direct Marketing Association's Mail Preference Service** (www.dmachoice.org)**.** This service helps you take your name off of many lists used by companies to send out advertising and promotion material. You can fill out the form online at www.dmachoice.org/register.php.

Hulbert's data shows how few newsletters actually beat the market on a risk-adjusted basis. For instance, during the 10-year period ending in April 2019, only 28 percent of newsletters tracked by Hulbert during that time period beat the market. And you can be sure that the others still collected the subscription fees.

Using newsletters to your advantage

You might be wondering how the heck stock-picking newsletters could be at all helpful when they are often so wrong. Again, the contrarian approach might make sense, and it's a strategy used by many professional money managers.

The simplest way to see what newsletters are saying about stocks and doing the opposite is by determining how many newsletter writers are bullish and how many are bearish. When newsletter writers are nervous about the market and selling stocks, that's a signal to contrarian investors that now is a good time to buy stocks. And when newsletter writers are bullish and buying stocks, these contrarian investors start to take money off the table by selling stocks.

Investors Intelligence (`https://www.investorsintelligence.com/x/free_chart.html?r-1011`) provides some of the information you need to be a contrarian. Most of the company's data is available only to subscribers, but it does make a number of useful charts available for free. I like the NYSE Bullish % indicator, which tells you how bullish or bearish investors are about stocks. It's up to you to decide whether to jump into the market when other investors are giddy — or if that's your warning sign things are too good and it's time to get out.

Chapter **16**

Researching and Buying Bonds Online

B onds don't make very good cocktail party chatter. Just try to brag about your 3-percent-a-year bond return at a party. The only heads you'll turn will be the ones running away from you yawning. Bonds just aren't as exciting or glamorous as stocks, which can often gain more value in an hour than you'll collect from bonds all year.

But don't let the fact that bonds are boring discourage you from owning them. Bonds, often called *fixed-income securities,* are essentially IOUs issued by companies, cities, governments, and government agencies. These IOUs come with a promise to repay the lender by a specific time at a specific interest rate. These stable streams of cash flow can be very valuable if you choose bonds wisely. Bonds can help smooth out the ups and downs in your portfolio and help you reach your financial goals.

In this chapter, I explain what a bond is and how it differs from other investments, including stocks. I also show you ways to find out more about bonds and get up with the terms and lingo. You get a chance to discover websites that let you research bonds to find the ones that might fit your portfolio the best. And I show you ways to buy bonds online as well as a few alternatives to bonds you might consider.

Getting Acquainted with Bonds

If you've ever lent money to someone and set up a repayment program, you already know what a bond is. A bond is an IOU that entitles you to a stream of payments from the borrower. Companies, governments, cities, and government agencies often sell bonds so that they can raise money to build facilities, build bridges, or finance their operations. The money that was borrowed (called the *principal*) must be repaid over time at a predetermined *interest rate* and returned in full by a set period of time in the future (called the *maturity date*). This means that when you buy most bonds, you lend your money and then sit back and collect a stream of payments until the loan comes due. Not all bonds are alike, though. And with some bonds, called *zero-coupon bonds*, you lend money now but are paid back with interest in one big chunk in the future.

Bonds by their nature offer investors several benefits:

>> **Generally stable and predictable cash payments:** Investors who aren't looking for any big surprises tend to appreciate bonds' preset rate of return. When you buy a bond and hold it until maturity, you know ahead of time what your return will be. This predictability can be useful for reaching financial obligations.

>> **Repayment of principal:** When you buy a bond, you'll receive interest payments in addition to the money you loaned back, as long as the borrower can afford the payments and doesn't *default*. Investors who want to preserve their initial investment like bonds for this very reason.

>> **Liquidity:** You might be familiar with bank certificates of deposit (CDs), which also pay interest and return the original investments. But unlike most CDs, which you must hold for a set period of time or pay a penalty, you can sell your bonds to other investors, in most cases, at any time, just like you'd sell a stock. This characteristic of bonds means you can raise cash if you need to.

You have two ways to make money from a bond. You can hold it until it comes due, or *matures*. That way, you collect the interest as it's paid. Your other option is to sell the bond to someone else before it matures. However, when you sell a bond, you might not get back what you paid. The bond's price might fall if the bond becomes less desirable for reasons discussed later in the chapter.

>> **Diversification:** Bond prices tend to move up and down in a different pattern than stock prices. By owning stocks and bonds, you can smooth out the bumps in your portfolio. Table 16-1 shows you how bonds might not go up as much as stocks, but they don't usually fall as much either. It's not just theory, as the table shows. The worst-ever loss by long-term Treasurys was 14.9 percent in 2009, which is downright puny next to stocks' worst year, a 43.3 percent decline in 1931.

TABLE 16-1

Biggest Gains and Losses for Stocks and Bonds

Investment	Biggest Gain, %	Biggest Loss, %
Stocks (Standard & Poor's 500)	54.0 (1933)	−43.3 (1931)
Corporate bonds	42.6 (1982)	−8.1 (1969)
Short-term Treasury bills	14.7 (1981)	0 (1938)
Intermediate-term Treasurys	29.1 (1982)	−5.1 (1994)
Long-term Treasurys	40.4 (1982)	−14.9 (2009)

Source: Morningstar Inc., using data from 1926 through 2019

TIP

Typically, investors who need a more stable portfolio place most of their investments in bonds. But even if you're terrified of the thought of losing money, it's usually not a good idea to put your entire portfolio in bonds. Mixing some stocks in your portfolio can reduce your risk and increase your returns because bonds and stocks usually don't rise and fall at the same time by the same degree.

Knowing who issues debt

Before you can buy or sell bonds, you must understand the several types of bonds, based on who sold them. Each type of bond has unique traits and can be bought or sold online differently. The following is a quick rundown of the major issuers of bonds:

>> **U.S. government:** Debt instruments sold by the U.S. government are popular because they're backed by the full faith and credit of the United States, which stands behind these loans and promises that they'll be repaid. That greatly reduces, if not eliminates, the risk that you won't get paid. These fixed-income securities are often called *Treasurys,* and they come in three main varieties: Treasury bills mature in one year or less, Treasury notes mature in more than a year and up to 10 years, and Treasury bonds mature in more than 10 years. TreasuryDirect (www.treasurydirect.gov) provides in-depth information about Treasurys.

TIP

Even if you're not interested in buying bonds, the yield on Treasurys is a very important figure to keep in mind. Treasury yields tell you how much return you can get for taking little to no risk. If a risk-free Treasury pays 3 percent, you probably wouldn't be willing to buy a risky stock unless it would return considerably more than 3 percent.

WARNING

Treasurys are often called risk-free investments, but that's not really true. Even Treasurys face *interest-rate risk.* Say you buy a Treasury that pays 3 percent interest. If inflation rises, and interest rates rise to 4 percent as a result, your 3 percent interest rate isn't looking so hot anymore. If you sell the bond, you'll get less for it than you paid. And if you hold onto the bond, your 3 percent interest rate is lackluster.

>> **Government agencies and government-sponsored enterprises:** Individual government agencies can also borrow money. Debt issued by agencies is still considered safe, while perhaps not as safe as Treasurys. That means agency bonds may pay slightly higher interest rates than Treasurys.

Some examples of agency bonds include those sold by the Government National Mortgage Association, or Ginnie Mae (www.ginniemae.gov/), to provide financing to low- and moderate-income families to buy homes. Ginnie Mae loans are backed by several government agencies. Similarly, you find lenders called government-sponsored enterprises (GSEs) that, although closely tied to the government and often created by Congress, are private companies and are therefore not technically agencies.

The Federal National Mortgage Association, or Fannie Mae (www.fanniemae.com), is a GSE that buys and sells mortgage-backed securities that pass interest and principal payments made by homeowners to investors who own the securities.

WARNING

The rules regarding agency debt were turned upside down after the financial crisis linked with mortgage loans erupted in 2007 and 2008. Agency debt isn't technically backed by the federal government, so it's considered to be riskier than Treasurys. Fannie Mae is a company sponsored by the federal government that used to have its stock listed on the New York Stock Exchange. Investors long believed that the government would quickly step in and intervene if there was trouble. These investors were right in 2008.

As the mortgage market was seizing up in 2008, the U.S. government essentially took over Fannie Mae and Freddie Mac by placing them into conservatorship. Although the government took action in 2008, it wasn't obligated to do so. Since then, the company's stock was booted from the NYSE (although they still trade on the Over-The-Counter Bulletin Board marketplace, which is described in more detail in Chapter 2). Uncertainty about what the government will do in the future makes agency debt a question in some people's minds.

>> **Companies:** Bonds issued by companies, sometimes called *corporates,* allow borrowers to pay for equipment and services they need in order to expand or grow. Companies pay higher interest rates than the government because there's a larger chance they will default or hit hard times and have trouble paying back the money they borrowed. Bonds sold by rock-solid companies are called *investment grade.* Small companies or companies with shaky finances issue what's called *high-yield* or junk-bond debt. Investment-grade

bonds pay lower interest rates than junk bonds because investors are more certain they'll get their money back.

>> **Cities and municipalities:** Cities may borrow money by selling bonds, called *municipal* bonds, or just *munis*. The biggest attraction of munis to investors is the fact that their interest often isn't taxable by the federal government. And if you buy a muni bond issued by a government in the state or city you live in, the interest might also not be subject to state or city tax. Munis are often called tax-exempt bonds for this reason. You pay a price for this tax benefit, though. Munis often pay lower interest rates than bonds with similar risk. InvestorGuide.com (`www.investorguide.com/igu-article-575-bonds-municipal-bonds.html`) provides more information about munis.

TIP

Don't just look at the seemingly low interest rate offered by a tax-exempt muni bond when deciding whether you want to buy it. The actual interest rate is higher after you factor in the fact that the interest payments often aren't taxable. For example, if an investor in the 25 percent tax bracket buys a muni bond paying 5 percent interest, that's equivalent to a 6.7 percent interest rate from a taxable bond. And that's a good thing. One other thing to remember: Not all muni bonds qualify for the tax breaks, so be sure to check before you buy one.

Want to compare the interest rate on a tax-exempt muni bond with a taxable bond? The Investing in Bonds website provides a table that converts tax-exempt interest rates to taxable rates for different tax brackets at (`www.investinginbonds.com/learnmore.asp?catid=5&subcatid=24&id=206`). Bankrate's taxable-equivalent yield calculator (`www.bankrate.com/calculators/retirement/tax-equivalent-yield-calculator-tool.aspx`) is more customizable, allowing you to enter different yields and tax brackets.

INVESTING IN "BOWIE" BONDS

Bonds are usually sold by governments and companies, but some interesting exceptions have cropped up. One of the more famous and unorthodox sellers of bonds was rock star David Bowie. Bowie generated $55 million for himself in 1997 by selling "Bowie Bonds." Investors who bought the bonds were entitled to the cash stream generated by sales of Bowie's albums for a decade. Similar music-based bonds followed, allowing investors to buy the cash streams from James Brown and the Isley Brothers. Individual investors were unable to invest in Bowie Bonds. The Bowie Bond was the innovation of the Pullman Group (`www.pullmanbonds.com`). The future of music-based bonds is uncertain as more consumers buy and stream individual music tracks from online music stores, rather than purchase full-length albums from music retailers. So far, few artists have been able to pull off big bond sales.

Online resources to find out more about bonds

One of the toughest things about bonds is just figuring out the vocabulary. Investors who focus on buying and selling stocks often struggle with the different terms when they enter the brave new world of bonds. It's critical, though, for you to understand the lexicon of bonds before jumping in. Several websites step you through the bond world and can get you up to speed in no time. Here's the (relatively) short list:

>> **Investopedia's Bond Basics** (www.investopedia.com/university/bonds): This corner of Investopedia runs through everything you need to know to get started with bonds. The site covers the terminology and shows you how to calculate how much bonds are worth.

>> **Investing in Bonds** (www.investinginbonds.com): The name says it all. Check out the site, shown in Figure 16-1, for several well-written checklists and guides for beginning bond investors, and be sure to look on the right side of the page for the Learn More column. There you can find articles that cover bond basics and things you should know.

>> **Yahoo! Finance** (https://finance.yahoo.com/bonds): This corner of Yahoo! Finance provides all sorts of information on bonds, including an interest rate summary page and a bond screener to help you find bonds.

>> **The Bond Buyer** (www.bondbuyer.com): This site tracks new developments in the bond world. You can follow trends in bonds and find out about new offerings.

>> **Briefing.com** (www.briefing.com/investor/markets/bond-market-update): You'd expect Briefing.com to have a Bonds section, and you'd be right. It provides updates during the day on the direction of the bond market and also summarizes news that is affecting bond prices.

Common traits of bonds

Bond investors have their own language, and the Project : Invested site (www.projectinvested.com/markets-explained/bond-basics/#topic-glossary) provides a comprehensive glossary of terms. But before you get overwhelmed by all the terms, the following list offers a quick description of the most important ones you need to know. Nearly all bonds have the following characteristics:

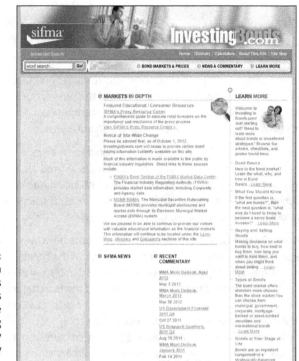

FIGURE 16-1:
Investing in Bonds answers most questions you might have when considering investing money in bonds of any type.

>> **Face (or par) value:** The *face value* is the amount of money you'll get back when the bond matures. For many bonds, the face value is the principal, or the amount that you've lent. The face value is also sometimes called the *principal.* There are some bonds where the face value is not equal to the principal, including zero-coupon bonds. You buy these bonds for less than the face value and get paid all in one lump sum in the future. Zero-coupon bonds have unique risks, as I discuss later.

>> **Interest rate:** The *interest rate* measures how much you'll receive as a payment in exchange for lending the money. Generally, the interest rate is a percentage of the money lent, known as the face value of the bond. Interest, often called the *coupon rate,* is often paid twice a year.

For example, suppose you bought a $1,000 bond that pays 5 percent interest, you would be paid $50 a year in interest or $25 twice a year. You would get your $1,000 back when the bond matured.

Interest rates can be *fixed,* meaning that the same rate of interest is paid to the investor for the life of the bond. Interest rates can also be *floating* and move up or down based on the direction of interest rates paid by Treasurys. Some bonds don't pay interest until the bond matures. These zero-coupon bonds are bought for less than their face value. Instead of receiving an interest payment twice a year as with many bonds, a zero-coupon bond pays nothing until it matures. When the zero-coupon bond matures, the investor receives the face value, which includes the interest.

Imagine an investor who pays $600 for a zero-coupon bond that matures in ten years, when it will pay $1,000. At the end of the ten years, the investor gets his $600 principal back plus $400. That $400 is the interest, which in this case amounts to an interest rate of more than 5 percent a year.

>> **Maturity:** A bond's *maturity* is the date by which it must be paid off. Debt maturities can range from days to 20 or more years. A fixed-income security's maturity is very important and determines what it's called. Table 16-2 shows you what different fixed-income securities (excluding Treasurys, which have their own naming convention, as explained previously) are called based on their maturities.

>> **Special provisions:** Bonds can be customized by the borrowers and contain unique privileges for either the seller or the buyer of the bonds. A *call provision* is especially important if you're interested in buying bonds. If a bond can be called, that means the borrower can repay the loan before the maturity date. You can expect a bond to be called if current interest rates fall below the interest rate on the bond. If you're collecting a fat 7 percent interest rate on a bond, and interest rates fall to 5 percent for similar bonds, the issuer will likely call the bond and end your gravy train. Similarly, some bonds have *put provisions,* which allow the bond buyers to force the bond seller to buy the bond back before the maturity date.

>> **Price:** You can buy bonds directly from the issuers, and when you do, you often pay the face value. But, you can also buy bonds from previous owners in the secondary market, and when you do, you'll pay the current price. A bond's *price* is determined by many variables, such as the current interest rates on similar bonds.

REMEMBER

When a bond's price is less than its face value, it's said to trade at a *discount.* Bonds trade at a discount when interest rates rise (say, to 6 percent), making the bond's interest rate (say, just 5 percent) less attractive. When a bond's price is greater than its face value, it's said to trade at a *premium.* This happens when interest rates fall (perhaps to 4 percent), making this bond's interest rate (still at 5 percent) look more attractive and the bond worth more.

>> **Credit ratings:** When you buy a bond from a company, one of the biggest dangers you face is the chance that the company won't be able to pay you back, or will default. *Debt-rating agencies* study companies' financial statements and rate them based on their ability to pay. The shakier the company, the more it needs to pay in interest to attract investors. Debt ratings are discussed more fully in Chapter 15, including instructions on how to access them. The three main debt-rating agencies, Moody's Investors Service (www.moodys.com), Standard & Poor's (www.standardandpoors.com), and Fitch Ratings (www.fitchratings.com), provide more details about their ratings online.

>> **Current yield:** The current yield tells you how much interest you'll receive from the bond based on the bond's price. You can calculate a bond's current yield by dividing the annual interest payment by the purchase price.

Example: You paid $900 for a bond with a $1,000 face value that pays 5 percent, or $50, a year in interest. The current yield is 5.6 percent, which is calculated by dividing $50 by $900 and multiplying by 100 to convert the answer into a percentage.

>> **Yield to maturity:** This tells you how much interest you'll gain as a percentage of the price you paid for the bond if you hold the bond until it matures. Yield to maturity is one of the best ways to measure the true return of a bond.

MoneyChimp's online Bond Yield calculator (www.moneychimp.com/calculator/popup/calculator.htm?mode=calc_bondytm) can calculate a bond's current yield and yield to maturity for you. You need to enter the bond's current price, face value, coupon rate, and years to maturity.

TIP

Remember that bond prices fall when yields rise, almost like a teeter-totter. Many beginning investors get hung up on this concept. Just think of it this way: If you own a bond that yields 5 percent, but yields on similar bonds rise to 6 percent, your 5 percent looks pretty paltry. If you tried to sell your bond, you'd have to cut the price to find a buyer. If someone tells you bonds are down, make sure that you know whether that person is talking about bond yields or bond prices.

>> **Duration:** A bond's duration measures the time it takes, on average, for the bond buyer to get his or her money back. Duration differs from maturity in that it counts the interest payments made before the bond comes due. Duration is very handy because it can help you compare different bonds and determine which ones are more volatile. The larger the duration, the longer it takes for investors to get their money back, which makes them more volatile. Investopedia's Bond Duration calculator (www.investopedia.com/calculator/BondDurCDate.aspx) can tell you a bond's duration if you enter the bond's details, including face value, yield to maturity, interest rate, current maturity, and the schedule for payments.

TABLE 16-2

Maturities Determine What a Fixed-Income Security Is Called

Fixed-Income Security Name	Maturity
Short-term note	5 years or less
Intermediate-term notes/bonds	More than 5 years but less than 12 years
Long-term bonds	12 years or longer

Source: Securities Industry and Financial Markets Association

UNDERSTANDING THE YIELD CURVE

Anytime you read about or investigate bonds, you'll inevitably hear someone mention the yield curve. The *yield curve* is a chart that shows you how yields on short-term fixed-income securities (with maturities of three months or less) compare with long-term bonds (with maturities of 30 years or so). The Project : Invested site (www. projectinvested.com/markets-explained/bond-basics/#topic-what-factors-should-you-consider-when-investing-in-bonds-part-2) describes the yield curve. But I step you through the basics here. Generally, yield curves come in four shapes:

- **Normal:** Most of the time, investors demand higher interest rates on long-term bonds than they do on short-term notes. That's natural. If you let someone borrow money for 30 years, you'll want more interest because there's a greater chance you'll never see your money again. That's why yields (most of the time) will be at their lowest point for the short-term fixed-income securities and gradually move higher.

- **Steep:** Most of the time, investors demand two or more percentage points in extra yield when lending money for 30 years compared with loaning money for a short time. If the interest rate on a three-month note is 4 percent, investors will demand 6 percent or higher on a comparable long-term bond in normal times. But, if the difference between the short-term and long-term rates gets even wider, that creates a steep yield curve. A steep yield curve often indicates that investors expect economic growth to speed up.

- **Inverted:** When investors are willing to lend money for the long term and accept lower interest rates than they'd take for a short-term loan, the yield curve is inverted. Inverted yield curves can indicate that investors are worried the economy is about to slow down for a prolonged period of time. If the economy slows down, interest rates in the future might also fall. That means investors want to lock in current interest rates for the long term before they decline.

- **Flat:** When the interest rates on short-term loans equal long-term rates, you have a flat yield curve. A flat yield curve indicates that investors aren't at all too sure about where the economy is headed.

The U.S. Department of the Treasury uses a visual representation of bond yields to expect the yield curve. The online tool lets you see how the yields on bonds of different maturities compare to each other and how they've changed over time. To see how it looks, go to www.treasury.gov/resource-center/data-chart-center/Pages/index.aspx. You can choose the date you want to analyze and the site will plot the yield curve so you can understand and see what's happening with interest rates.

Finding and Buying Bonds Online

Just as with stocks, there's no single way to buy bonds. You can buy individual bonds using a mainstream online broker, you can buy directly from the borrowers, or you can deal directly with brokers who specialize in bonds. But you can also buy bonds through a mutual fund or exchange-traded fund (ETF). In the following sections, I show you how to buy bonds using these major methods.

Finding individual bonds online

Finding and buying an individual bond is similar to finding and buying an individual stock. It's up to you to find the bonds that have what you're looking for in terms of risk and reward.

Online tools can help you find bonds that fit your needs. You can use various bond *screening tools*, which let you define characteristics of a bond you'd like to find. The bond screener then cross-checks what you're looking for in a bond against its database of available bonds. A few bond screeners that can help you quickly find bonds you're interested in include the following:

>> Financial Industry Regulatory Authority: (finra-markets.morningstar.com/BondCenter/Screener.jsp): Finra's bond searching tool is a powerful way to find bonds that might fit your needs. The Finra bond screener first asks you whether you're interested in buying a corporate, a government, securitized, or

municipal security. (If you're looking for a muni bond, you can also indicate what state you're interested in.) You can narrow your search by other factors, ranging from the bond's price, coupon, yield to maturity, and credit rating. After you enter what you're looking for, click the Find Bonds button to get a list of all the bonds that meet your standards. Click a bond and write down the name of the issuer, coupon, and maturity date. You need this information to buy the bond.

>> **Municipal Securities Rulemaking Board's EMMA:** If you're looking for a muni bond, EMMA will be your best friend. The site is operated by the MSRB, which is the governing body of the muni market. The Browse Issuers tab at the top of the screen lets you click a map of the U.S. and find issuers in specific states. Use the Advanced Search tab to look for muni bonds that meet your requirements, such as interest rate or maturity date. The Market Activity tab is fascinating, too, in a bond market kind of way. You can look up what kinds of muni bonds are being bought and sold.

>> **BondView (**www.bondview.com/bonds-screener**):** The BondView site provides a full-fledged screener that lets you be even more specific about what you're looking for in a municipal bond. You can filter not only on states and rates but also on how the bond proceeds will be used. On the BondView screener site, enter in the appropriate text fields the characteristics of muni bonds that interest you. When you're finished, click the Submit button, and you see the list of muni bonds that make your cut. Write down the name of the issuer, coupon, and maturity date.

>> **Online brokers' sites:** Most of the large online brokers mentioned in Chapter 4 — including Charles Schwab, Fidelity, TD Ameritrade (see Figure 16-2), and E*Trade — all provide bond-screening tools on their sites. Check with your online broker to see whether it has a feature that lets you screen for fixed-income securities.

FIGURE 16-2:
TD Ameritrade's bond-screening tool helps you find bonds that fit your individual needs.

TIP

Bond screeners tell you the all-important yield to maturity of a bond, saving you the hassle of measuring the yield to maturity yourself.

Sealing the deal: Buying individual bonds online

After you've found the perfect individual bond, you need to know how to buy it. You can buy bonds in several ways:

>> **Buying straight from the government:** If you're interested in buying Treasurys, you can cut out the middleman and buy directly from the U.S. Treasury at TreasuryDirect (www.treasurydirect.gov). TreasuryDirect lets you buy

- *Treasury bills, notes, and bonds.*

- *Treasury Inflation-Protected Securities (or TIPs):* TIPs are unique securities that pay you more interest and principal if interest rates rise.

- *Savings bonds:* These bonds, designed for individuals, don't pay very high interest rates and aren't appropriate for investors looking for the best returns. But savings bonds might have some tax advantages, are backed by the government, and pay predictable interest. TreasuryDirect's Tax Advantage Calculator (www.treasurydirect.gov/BC/SBCTax) can help you measure whether you can get a tax benefit from owning savings bonds. The Savings Bond Calculator (www.treasurydirect.gov/indiv/tools/tools_savingsbondcalc.htm) can help you decide whether savings bonds are right for you.

TIP

Buying Treasurys from the government is a good option because there's no fee for most investors. You also don't have to invest much. The minimum investment is just $100 for Treasurys and TIPs and $25 for savings bonds. Not sure how to use TreasuryDirect? TreasuryDirect's Guided Tour (www.treasurydirect.gov/indiv/TDTour/default.htm) steps you through the specific process of buying bonds through the site.

>> **Buying from a mainstream online broker:** Several of the bigger online brokerage firms (including Charles Schwab, E*Trade, Fidelity, and TD Ameritrade) also let you buy and sell bonds. But remember that the stock-trading commissions don't apply because you're buying bonds, and the bond commission can vary wildly depending on the broker and what kind of bond you're buying.

Several online brokerage firms have slashed the fees to buy bonds. At Fidelity, Schwab, and E*Trade, you can buy Treasurys online for no commission and most other types of bonds — including agencies and corporate bonds — for $1 per bond.

WARNING

Some brokers charge *mark-up fees* for bonds, which are added to the price of the bond. For instance, you might buy a bond for $1,000 but later see that you actually paid $1,045, where $1,000 is the price of the bond and $45 is the mark-up. Nothing is illegal about mark-up fees, and they've been a common way for brokers to charge commissions for buying bonds. You just want to find out ahead of time how much the mark-up fee will be and confirm that you weren't overcharged by reviewing the confirmation of your order.

TIP

Some brokers charge commissions when you buy Treasurys. E*Trade, for instance, charges $1. You should think long and hard before paying any commissions or fees to buy Treasurys because you can buy them for free and online from TreasuryDirect.

>> **Buying with the help of a bond broker:** Some brokers specialize in just bond trading. Zions Direct and JW Korth (`https://jkworth.com/`) are two examples. FMSbonds.com (`www.fmsbonds.com`) specializes in munis.

>> **Buying through a bond mutual fund:** Buying individual bonds can be somewhat complex. You need to understand yields, prices, duration, and other cryptic measures of value. And that doesn't even scratch some advanced bond techniques, such as laddering.

TECHNICAL STUFF

Laddering is a technique used to lower your risk when investing in bonds. When you ladder, you buy bonds that expire at different times, say at one year, two years, and ten years. That way, if you buy bonds and interest rates rise, when your one-year bonds mature, you can reinvest the proceeds at the higher interest rate. Fidelity (`www.fidelity.com/viewpoints/investing-ideas/bond-ladder-strategy`) provides a helpful description of what laddering is and how it can help you.

You can ladder and diversify your own bond portfolio. But for many investors, it's easier to just buy a bond mutual fund that does it for you. With a bond mutual fund, the laddering and diversification is taken care of for you. Just as with stock mutual funds, you can buy actively managed bond funds run by portfolio managers who try to beat the market or passive index bond funds.

You can find bond funds with the mutual fund–screening tools discussed in Chapter 10, but a good bet here would be the Vanguard Total Bond Market index. The index can be bought as a mutual fund that owns a smattering of government, corporate, agency, and other bonds and charges a reasonable 0.15 percent annual expense ratio. If you're looking for an easy way to add bonds to your portfolio, this might be a good choice.

WARNING

Think twice before buying an actively managed mutual fund invested in long-term government bonds. You might pay an annual fee for the mutual fund, sometimes 1 percent a year. That's probably not a good idea considering you can buy Treasurys for free from TreasuryDirect.

>> **Bond exchange-traded funds (ETFs):** Another option for buying bonds is through exchange-traded funds. ETFs, explained in depth in Chapter 11, are baskets of investments that trade like stocks. A bond ETF is ideal for investors who primarily buy stocks but want to easily add bonds to their portfolio and keep fees down. These ETFs track bond indexes, such as the Barclays Aggregate Bond index, which tracks a broad basket of bonds. Buying a bond ETF is the bond version of investing in a stock index like the Standard & Poor's 500.

It's easy to get started. Just pick the bond ETF you want and buy it through your online broker just as you'd buy a stock. You can read how to buy and sell stocks in Chapter 5. Note as well that you can find bond ETFs using the ETF-screening tools discussed in Chapter 11. Three ETFs you may want to check out are iShares Barclays Aggregate Bond (AGG), SPDR Barclays Capital Aggregate Bond (LAG), and Vanguard Total Bond Market (BND). All three are diversified and have low fees.

Considering Bond Alternatives

The relative safety of bonds as well as their lower volatility make them well suited for many investors' portfolios. But don't make the mistake of thinking bonds are without risks. The Project : Invested site (www.projectinvested.com/markets-explained/what-you-should-know) describes the risks of bonds in detail. But these are the risks you should be most aware of:

>> **Default risk:** Unless you're buying Treasurys, you're taking a chance that the borrower won't pay you back.

>> **Market risk:** If bonds go out of favor because investors are seeking higher returns, the price of your bonds might decline.

>> **Liquidity risk:** From time to time, investors get nervous about the economy or about bonds, and they simply refuse to buy bonds. This is generally more of a problem with unusual or rare bonds, and it isn't a worry with Treasurys or investment-grade bonds.

>> **Interest rate risk:** The threat of higher interest rates is one of the biggest risks you face when you buy a bond. If rates rise, the interest rate you locked in suddenly isn't so lucrative, which decreases the value of your bond.

Some investors have an aversion to bonds for these reasons and others. These investors don't like the fact that bond values can fall, because bonds are supposed to be safer investments. If you're a bond hater, keep reading. The rest of this section explores a few bond alternatives.

Money market funds and certificates of deposit

If you're looking for safe investments but want to get more interest than you're getting in a bank savings account, you might consider money market funds or certificates of deposit:

>> **Money market funds** are a place to park money you need in case of emergency. They invest in very safe fixed-income securities, such as highly rated investments that come due in 90 days or less. Money markets generally invest in short-term Treasurys and commercial paper. *Commercial paper* obligations are loans generally given to creditworthy companies to fund short-term needs, such as buying goods to be sold in a few months. Money markets, however, aren't insured by the Federal Deposit Insurance Corporation (FDIC). Money markets are relatively safe, but not bulletproof. During the financial crisis that erupted in 2007 and 2008, one money market fund, the Reserve Primary Fund, "broke the buck" and returned just 99 cents of every investor's dollar. (You can find out what is, and isn't, insured by the FDIC at www.fdic.gov/consumers/consumer/information/fdiciorn.html.)

TIP

Bankrate.com (www.bankrate.com) is a useful site to find the best money market fund for you. The site's CD & Investments tab has a great money market account screener that you can use to pick a money market account that best suits your needs.

>> **Certificates of deposit (CDs):** If you want an even safer investment than a money market — and are willing to take a lower return — you might want to consider a certificate of deposit. CDs are typically issued by banks, and their interest rates can vary quite a bit. CDs are also usually insured by the FDIC.

WARNING

If you buy a CD, your money is locked up, and you'll usually get hit with a penalty if you need the money earlier than its maturity. If you need access to your money, a money market might be a better choice.

If you're looking for the highest CD rates, these sites might help:

● *Bankrate.com* (www.bankrate.com): Bankrate.com can help you track down a money market fund, and it can also help you pinpoint the highest-yielding CDs. Just click the CDs & Investments tab to bring up a page with various CD tables, CD calculators, and CD search tools.

- *MoneyRates.com* (`www.money-rates.com`): This site lists national averages for CDs, money markets, and Treasurys.

You might be able to buy some money market funds through your online broker, but sometimes you need to contact the money market provider directly through its website. With CDs, you need to sign up over the bank's website.

Wall Street's lost child: Preferred stock

You find advantages and disadvantages to bonds and stocks, which is probably why there's room for both in most portfolios. But there's a unique security that's kind of like the Dr. Jekyll and Mr. Hyde of Wall Street: preferred stock.

Preferred stocks, commonly called *preferreds*, try to give investors the best of both worlds. *Preferred stock* is a special type of stock that's sold by companies and acts more like a bond. Companies pay preferred stockholders a fixed dividend from earnings. Unlike with bonds, though, the company isn't obligated to pay the dividend if it doesn't have adequate earnings. If a company hits a tough patch, it can delay paying the preferred dividend until it regains its footing, after which it must pay the dividends it missed.

Preferreds have some advantages over bonds, though. Many preferreds give investors the option to convert their preferred stock into common stock. You might have the right to own a part of the company and enjoy the upside, rather than just collect a fixed interest payment. You can also buy preferred stocks through most online brokers.

Keep in mind, though, that many preferred stocks are *callable*, meaning that a company can retire the shares by paying investors' money back, at any time. If that happens, you'll no longer receive the interest payments.

You can find out more about preferred stock at these websites:

- **Winans International** (`http://winansinvestments.com/WinansIndexes.html`): Winans International maintains an index that tracks the value of preferred stock, called the Winans International Preferred Stock Index, or WIPSI. Click the WIPSI tab and scroll down the page, and you can see a plot of the index at this website.

- **iShares** (`www.ishares.com/us/products/239826/ishares-us-preferred-stock-etf`): iShares offers an EFT that tracks preferred stock. iShares' S&P U.S. Preferred Stock Index Fund (symbol PFF) lets you invest in a basket of preferred stocks. Check out Chapter 11 for more details on ETFs.

» **QuantumOnline** (www.quantumonline.com)**:** This site lets you search for preferred stock that might suit your needs. Just choose the All Preferred Stocks option from the Income Tables menu at the top of the page, and you'll call up a new page with a list of all preferred stocks, their trading symbols, and interest rates. If you find one you're interested in, write down the trading symbol and buy it through your online broker. The site is free, but you must register to use it.

» **CD3** (www.preferredstockinvesting.com/index.htm)**:** This site provides news and quotes on preferred stocks, but it's not free. Subscriptions range from $25 for access to some features for a month to $225 a year.

The Part of Tens

Chapter **17**

Ten Top Mistakes Made by Online Investors

When people tell me they're afraid to start investing online, most of the time it's the fear of making a mistake that's holding them back. With its jargon, formulas, charts, and Wall Street slang, investing online can seem scary and intimidating. For some investors, the thought of managing their money by themselves is overwhelming. The fear of making a mistake and losing hard-earned money is too much to bear.

Calming these fears is what this chapter is all about. After answering thousands of emails sent to me by readers of my various columns over the years, I've heard it all. Most of the mistakes investors make can be neatly placed into ten categories, each of which I explain in this chapter. By reading about the common mistakes other online investors make, you'll probably think twice before committing them yourself. I discuss the ten most common mistakes, explain why they're made, and show you how to avoid them.

Buying and Selling Too Frequently

One of the greatest things about online investing is that it gives investors the power to buy and sell stocks whenever they want. Unfortunately, though, some investors turn this 24/7 access to their portfolios and stock trading into a liability.

Don't get me wrong; it's great that investors can check their portfolios whenever they want instead of calling a broker or waiting for a printed brokerage statement to arrive in the mail. It's just that constant access turns some investors into

>> **Obsessive portfolio checkers:** These investors are constantly logging on to their online brokerage accounts and checking the value of their portfolios. And I mean constantly — often several times a day. This behavior is a problem because it makes investors get overly concerned about the short-term swings in their stocks.

If the market falls 1 percent one day, these investors measure how much money they lost and start thinking about all the things they could have bought if they'd just sold the day before. Clearly, no one can have the foresight to sell ahead of a 1 percent downdraft, much less a 10 percent correction. But these obsessive investors start to take every $1 move in their portfolio personally.

TIP

Checking your portfolio's value online is fine, unless it starts to affect your judgment. If you find you're telling yourself you should have sold or bought because the market is up or down in a given day, you might be missing the point of investing.

>> **Trigger-fingered investors:** These investors are so antsy that they can't help but trade. They buy and sell stocks in a flash, well, just because they can. Trigger-fingered investors figure commissions are so cheap that there's no harm in picking up shares of a stock, trying it out, and then dumping it if it doesn't work out. Trigger-fingered investors also seem to get a rush out of trading online, much like someone might get when pulling on the arm of a slot machine.

The trouble, though, is that these investors are hurting themselves more than helping. Not only are they paying more in taxes than they should (you can find out more about how taxes can reduce your returns later in this chapter and also in Chapter 3), but they're also setting themselves up for losses as they dump stocks they can't remember why they bought in the first place. Without an asset allocation plan in place, these investors are just haphazardly buying stocks and have no idea what their plan is. You can find out how to determine the perfect asset allocation for you in Chapter 9.

Letting Losers Run and Cutting Winners Short

Human nature, in some respects, is your worst enemy when investing online. Humans react in particular ways when faced with certain circumstances, but those reactions can work against you in investing. Two of those elements of human nature are defending bad decisions too long and cashing in on good decisions too early.

If you've ever been to Las Vegas, you've seen this before. Just walk over to one of the ATMs scattered on the casino floor, and you're sure to bump into people who lost all the cash they brought, so they're pulling out another $500. These people figure they'll win it all back if they keep trying. The same thing, sadly, happens with some investors. Investors who buy an individual stock that collapses often hang onto it, figuring that it will come back because it's a good company.

When you're buying individual stocks, it's critical that you cut your losses. Pick a percentage you're willing to risk and stick with it. You can use stop market orders or protective puts, both described in Chapter 5.

Other investors make the opposite mistake by cashing in winning stocks too soon. Say your asset allocation tells you to put 20 percent of your stocks in emerging markets, so you buy an emerging markets index mutual fund. If emerging markets soar in the following few weeks, but your emerging market index fund still accounts for 20 percent or less of your portfolio, you should resist the temptation to sell it all to lock in your gains. Instead, you should stick with your asset allocation. To understand how asset allocations can boost your returns and cut your risk, read Chapter 9.

TIP

The rule of cutting losses short applies to individual stocks. If you don't think you'll have the courage to sell individual stocks when they sink, you should instead invest in mutual funds or exchange-traded funds (ETFs) that own a broad basket of stocks, such as the Standard & Poor's 500. These investments are already diversified and less risky than individual stocks, so you don't have to worry so much about a complete wipeout due to a company-specific problem.

Focusing on the Per-Share Price of the Stock

The fact that one stock is $2 a share and another is $500 a share tells you absolutely nothing about either stock. The $2-a-share stock might actually be more expensive than the $500-a-share stock because it either doesn't grow as rapidly, doesn't earn as much relative to its stock price, or is riskier.

A stock's per-share price is meaningful only if you compare it with something else. Typically, investors multiply the stock price by the stock's number of shares outstanding to get the company's *market value* or market capitalization. A stock's market value tells you whether a stock is small, medium, or large, and gives you a good idea of its valuation. Chapter 9 explains why the size of a stock's market value is so important.

Don't be fooled into thinking it's better to own 1,000 shares of a $2 stock than owning 100 shares of a $20 stock. What really matters is the company's valuation and market value. Think of it this way: What's better — buying one reliable car for $8,000 or ten unreliable and broken-down $800 cars?

Failing to Track Risk and Return

For some reason, prudence often vanishes when it comes to online investing. Many online investors, perhaps because it takes some effort and practice, don't take the time to see how much risk they're taking on to get the reward they're expecting from stocks they buy.

The biggest danger of investing without knowing your risk and return is that you gamble not knowing whether you're doing more harm than good to your portfolio. You might be spending a great deal of time and effort buying individual stocks, thinking the effort is worthwhile, but it might turn out you'd be better off buying and holding index mutual funds. Instead of burning hours looking at stock charts, you might be better off spending the time with your family, on hobbies, or at work.

Chapter 8 shows you the techniques of measuring your portfolio. You can find out how to calculate the returns and risk yourself or check out websites that can do it for you.

Taking Advice from the Wrong People

It's almost hard not to get stock tips. Turn on the TV. Talk to people sitting next to you on an airplane. Chat with other browsers in the financial section of the bookstore (unless they're reading *Online Investing For Dummies*, of course). Connect with other investors online. You'll constantly encounter people who are convinced that such-and-such a stock is going to take off and that you need to buy in now. Some of my readers have told me they've bought shares of retailers because employees told them to.

Here's my advice: Unless Warren Buffett is the guy sitting next to you on the airplane, you're better off politely nodding and wiping your memory clean of all the investing advice you get. Stick with your asset allocation plan.

You should also be cautious of advice you're getting from a financial advisor that you hire. The two things you should do when evaluating your advisors are

>> **Use online broker screening tools.** You want to meticulously check to make sure that the person giving you advice has the right licenses. Chapter 4 contains some online ways to check out your broker. You want to make sure that you use the Financial Industry Regulatory Authority's BrokerCheck (`www. finra.org/Investors/ToolsCalculators/BrokerCheck/index.htm`). Just enter the name of the broker you're checking on into the search box and follow the directions. I give you additional tips on how to avoid scams in Chapter 18.

>> **Track the advisor's performance.** You might not be making the calls in your portfolio, but you still want to make sure that your advisor is getting you adequate returns for the risk you're taking. That also goes for any stock-picking newsletters or websites that promise to make you fabulously rich. Use the tools and techniques in Chapter 8 to make sure that you're getting what you're paying for.

Trying to Make Too Much Money Too Quickly

The reason you invest is to make money. That's the American way. But as an investor, you need to appreciate that wealth is built over time as companies you've invested in expand their revenue and earnings. Generally speaking, stocks have returned about 10 percent a year. You may be able to boost that 10 percent a bit with smart asset allocation and exposure to riskier types of stocks like emerging markets and small companies.

Some investors, though, just aren't satisfied with that. They chase after brand-new IPOs, pile into stocks that have been the market's leaders, and load up on penny stocks. These investors are typically the ones who get sucked into get-rich-quick emails, stock conferences, and other dubious stock promotion schemes that make only their promoters rich.

Sometimes things work out okay for these speculators, and they might buy shares of the right stock at the right time. But more often than not, these speculators suffer as the stocks whip around more than they expected. The volatility proves too much to bear, and the speculators buy and sell stocks at the wrong times. Before they know it, speculators are down 50 percent or more and then write to me asking what to do.

I suppose that if you limit your outlay in speculative investments to a small amount, there's no harm. But for the bulk of your portfolio, you'll find much better success over the long term if you read Chapters 8 and 9 and find out how to track your risk and return.

Letting Emotions Take Over

It's happened to you before: You've fallen in love. No, I'm not talking about your spouse or significant other. I'm talking about your favorite stock. Everyone has had one. The stock you fall in love with is the one that you happened to buy at just the right time and have never lost money on. It might be the one that soars and always shows up on the Top Performers lists printed by magazines and websites. It's easy to be proud of a stock just like parents who see their kid's name in the paper for being on the honor roll.

The opposite happens, too. Say your asset allocation calls for you to own large-company stocks, you invest in them, and they do nothing. There you are; you own shares of big companies and watch your portfolio go sideways while your friends brag about the tiny upstarts and penny stocks they make a fortune on.

Periods of self-doubt and second-guessing account for many investors' worst decisions. These investors might be so blinded by their enduring affection for a stock that they proudly ride it down lower and lower. It's funny, but the love for the stock wears pretty thin by the time the stock is down 50 percent or more. What's the answer to this? Unless you're a robot or computer, you're stuck with your emotions. But you can stop these emotions from meddling with your portfolio by sticking with your asset allocation plan. Yes, I know this asset allocation stuff is getting repetitive, but trust me: It will protect you from yourself.

Emotions can burn you badly with investments that just keep going down. It's easy to get so fed up with certain stocks you can't bear to keep buying more. You curse at your asset allocation for ruining your portfolio. You might get so disgusted with stocks you either inquire about CDs from your local bank or start scanning the "new high" lists for stocks you think will be your ticket to riches.

If you let your greed for huge returns and fear of losses run your investment decisions, you can practically guarantee you'll buy and sell at the wrong time.

If you find that you're an emotional investor and take the market's movements too close to heart, you're probably a good candidate to invest in mutual funds and ETFs. You can just buy these investments and let them ride, removing the temptation to tinker with your portfolio and almost guaranteeing you better results.

Looking to Blame Someone Else for Your Losses

No one likes to lose money on stocks. And everyone loses money on stocks from time to time. It's how you react to the losses that makes the difference. Some investors go on a witch-hunt and start trying to track down anyone who might have mentioned a stock as a good buy, ranging from publications and websites to friends or the company's executives. These investors are generally the first in line to join securities class-action lawsuits and try to sue the company or executives.

Certainly cases of fraud exist, in the mold of Enron and Worldcom. These cases are regrettable because even investors who attempted to do their homework by studying the company's financials were misled. But if you just lose money because you bought a stock at the wrong time or overestimated the company's profit potential, you can only look to yourself. It's best to analyze what you did right, what you did wrong, and learn from it as opposed to playing an unproductive blame game.

Sometimes investors truly are wronged by companies' managements. In those cases, securities class-action lawsuits attempt to extract money for the shareholders. You can find out whether shareholders are suing a company by using Stanford Law School's Securities Class Action Clearinghouse (securities. stanford.edu). If there's a suit, you generally must fill out a claim form. You can obtain the claim form from the law firm assigned to handle the case by the court. You can get the name and contact information of the law firm in charge using the Stanford Law School's Securities Class Action Clearinghouse.

Ignoring Tax Considerations

Come tax time, each April, it's amazing the lengths that taxpayers go to cut their tax bill by just a few bucks. Some go as far as to get married or have a child to pay less tax to Uncle Sam. But many of these same investors ignore or aren't aware of ways of investing that can save them thousands on taxes.

Uncle Sam offers extremely generous tax breaks for investors, if you just know how to take advantage of them. Tax breaks investors should never pass up on include

>> **Lower tax rates for long-term capital gains:** If you can wait more than a year before selling winning stocks, you'll be much further ahead than investors who trade with no regard to taxes. By holding onto stocks for longer than a year, you usually qualify for long-term capital gains taxes, which in many cases are half what you pay if you sell stocks in a year or less.

>> **Major tax breaks on education savings:** If you're trying to save for your child's college, you can let Uncle Sam help out. Special education savings accounts, such as the 529 plan, let you largely shield your money from taxes as long as it's used to pay for school.

Say you need to save $50,000 to pay for your kid's college education. If you ignore the tax breaks available to you through educational savings plans like 529s, you might actually need to save $58,824. You'll need the extra $8,824 to pay the 15 percent long-term capital gains tax that might apply.

>> **Major tax breaks on retirement savings:** Always take advantage of any retirement savings tax breaks you can get. Researching what's available to you should be the first thing you do when you start to invest. If your company matches contributions to a 401(k) or other profit-sharing plan, take advantage of it as soon as you can. If you have no such plan at your job, don't assume that nothing is available to you. Many taxpayers are entitled to invest in a Roth IRA, which offers tremendous tax benefits, as I describe in Chapter 3.

Dwelling on Mistakes Too Long

It might sound funny to tell you to not think about investing mistakes in a chapter dedicated to mistakes, but it's important to not let a mistake in the past paralyze you. So, you bought a stock and rode it down too long before selling it. Don't linger on the mistake. Just don't do it again, and over time, you'll obtain the success in investing you're shooting for.

Chapter **18**

Ten Ways to Protect Your Investments and Identity Online

P romising a big return to investors is kind of like waving red meat in front of a hungry tiger. Even educated investors can't help but salivate when offered what seems to be a plausible chance at winning big-time returns. Investors' innate craving for that big score makes them easy targets for less-than-honest financial snake oil salesmen.

It's always been amazing to me how people are so careful about their money in everyday life but let their guard down when it comes to investing. The same people who clip coupons and shop at discount stores to save a few bucks will readily hand over their life's savings to a stranger with dubious qualifications selling questionable investments.

It's up to you to do your homework when checking into any investments. Online tools make it easier than ever to sniff out unscrupulous people hawking investment products. Unfortunately, though, the Internet is also a boon for the bad guys. Email lets fraudsters reach millions of users with the click of a button.

Fraudsters can also glean basic information about you online, perhaps from your *blog* or Facebook page, and craft a pitch that seems more realistic and personable. Keeping these things in mind, this chapter points out some of the main types of investments frauds and shows you how to dodge them.

Beware of Pyramid Schemes

When it comes to investment frauds, *pyramid schemes* are among the greatest hits. Organizers behind pyramid schemes try to convince investors to contribute money and tempt them with promises of a giant payout. That sounds like playing the lottery, I know. But what makes pyramid schemes so insidious is that they're based on a sham that eventually collapses.

Generally, pyramid schemes work like this: Six fraudsters send out emails to as many people as they can, each hoping to get six additional "investors." These initial promoters convince investors to sign up by telling them that if they contribute money, they'll get a 100 percent or greater return in just 90 days. If the six initial promoters are successful in lining up other participants, they pocket the money from the new investors. But that's just the tip of the pyramid, so to speak. The 36 just-recruited investors are then instructed to get six more investors each, which brings the total number of investors in the scheme to 216. The scheme then continues, and each time more investors are brought in, the previous investors get their payout.

There's just one big problem: The pyramid collapses under its own weight. After 13 rounds of this pyramid scheme, for instance, more than 13 billion people are required to keep it going. That's impossible because it exceeds the world's population. So unless you think you can find six suckers on Mars or Jupiter to buy your stake of a pyramid scheme, you could end up losing your investment. The Securities and Exchange Commission provides helpful information on pyramid schemes at www.sec.gov/answers/pyramid.htm.

REMEMBER

Pyramid schemes have a close relative: *multilevel marketing plans.* In a multilevel marketing plan, a company emails you with an offer to make you a distributor of its products — usually pills or medical devices — that promise miraculous benefits. These plans not only promise to pay commissions if you're able to sell the products, but also pay you if you find other distributors. The problem is that these are often based on pyramid schemes. You should also always run a company through the Better Business Bureau's website (www.bbb.org) to make sure that it's legitimate.

REMEMBER

Just because a company is in the BBB database and doesn't have any complaints, that doesn't mean it's safe. The company could be new and looking for fresh victims. The BBB site, though, is a good place to start. It's a good idea to also run the owners' names through the SEC's website (www.sec.gov) to see whether there have been any prior run-ins with regulators.

Steer Clear of Ponzi Schemes

Ponzi schemes are some of the oldest frauds in the book. But they've also enjoyed somewhat of a renaissance in the wake of the financial crisis that erupted in 2007 and 2008. The Bernard Madoff scheme, which defrauded investors of more than $60 billion, was discovered in late 2008 and is considered the biggest Ponzi scheme ever. The scheme was so complicated some people involved in running it were still facing sentencing years later. Regulators discovered another massive Ponzi scheme in 2009 headed by Texan Allen Stanford, accused of operating a more than $7 billion fraud.

Ponzi schemes are a type of pyramid scheme with one key difference: All the "investors'" money goes to one person — the organizer of the fraud.

Ponzi schemes are pretty simple. The organizer sends out emails or pitches investors in other ways offering fabulous returns, often in a short period of time. In Madoff's case, it wasn't so much a get-rich-quick pitch, but rather an unbelievably steady return of 10 percent a year. If you remember, while stocks have returned 10 percent a year over time, those returns are not guaranteed and come with a great deal of risk and volatility. After the initial investors eagerly sign up, the Ponzi promoter takes a cut and then seeks a second round of investors. When the money comes in from the second round of investors, the Ponzi operator takes another cut but also returns a slice of the money to the first round of investors. Clearly, the first investors are ecstatic and eager to tell others about their great investment. Those testimonials play right into the Ponzi operator's hand, who keeps repeating the process until it falls apart.

Although Ponzi schemes are classic scams, investors seem to keep falling for them. Just in 2017 and 2018, 100 Ponzi schemes were uncovered, according to Ponzi tracking site www.ponzitracker.com. More than $1.6 billion was potentially lost from these schemes in 2018. It's a shame investors keep getting sucked in by these frauds. To inform yourself of how common Ponzi schemes are, you owe it to yourself to read the SEC's summary of recent enforcement actions against them here: www.sec.gov/spotlight/enf-actions-ponzi.shtml. And if you want to learn of some of the signs investors should look for to avoid Ponzi schemes, the SEC has a primer here: www.sec.gov/answers/ponzi.htm.

Avoid Tout Sheets and Know Whom You're Taking Advice From

You find no shortage of investment and stock-picking newsletters that claim to have the inside track on the stocks you need to buy now. But some of these newsletters, known in the trade as *tout sheets*, have nefarious intentions. Tout sheets are investment newsletters or websites distributed for the sole purpose of hyping stocks with exaggerated or false information to stir up investors' interest. Tout sheets have proliferated due to the Internet, which makes distributing and promoting such things a cinch. (You can read more about investment newsletters in general in Chapter 15.)

Above all, you need to be perfectly sure that an online newsletter, blog, or website is above board. Whenever considering subscribing to a newsletter or following its suggestions, you want to be 100 percent clear on whether the newsletter writer is paid by the companies to be a *tout*. Touts are hired by companies or shady brokerage firms to stoke interest in stocks by putting out glowing reports on the company based on exaggeration or lies. If the tout is successful in attracting investors and driving up the stock price, the company's executives and brokerage firm can then sell and pocket the quick profit.

The SEC is somewhat restricted in its capability to crack down on newsletters. The First Amendment allows anyone to make statements, including about stocks. The SEC can get involved, though, when the newsletter writers are paid for issuing misleading statements about a stock for personal gain.

The SEC (www.sec.gov/investor/pubs/cyberfraud/newsletter.htm) warns investors to be especially skeptical of online newsletters that vaguely say how they're paid. A statement like "From time to time, XYZ Newsletter may receive compensation from companies we write about" is a huge red flag, says the SEC. You should also avoid newsletters that say in tiny or hidden places in the newsletter that they're paid to promote stocks.

Check up on newsletters, or any other stock promoter, for that matter, by searching the following sites:

>> **The SEC's Division of Enforcement page** (www.sec.gov/divisions/enforce. shtml) is a great site for all things fraudulent. You can click the Enforcement Actions link to see whether the newsletter you're looking at has been accused of wrongdoing by the SEC.

>> **The SEC's Investment Adviser Public Disclosure page** (www.adviserinfo. sec.gov/IAPD/Content/IapdMain/iapd_SiteMap.aspx) is an excellent way to check up on "investment advisers." Many, but not all, professionals

who dispense advice to investors are required to file Form ADV with the SEC. The Form ADV contains information about the adviser or advisory firm, including any disciplinary actions. To access the site, just click the Investment Adviser Search link on the left side and follow the directions.

>> **The North American Securities Administrators Association** (www.nasaa. org/about-us/contact-us/contact-your-regulator) provides helpful information about securities crackdowns in various states. Just click your state in the list, and the site directs you to the appropriate state regulators that punish securities fraudsters.

>> **Certified Financial Planner Board of Standards** (www.letsmakeaplan. org/choose-a-cfp-professional/verify-a-cfp-professional) lets you quickly see whether someone who claims to be a Certified Financial Planner, or CFP, really is. Just enter the person's last name, choose the state, and click the Submit button.

Don't Fall for Investment Spam Emails

Open your email box, and you're likely to find all sorts of offers. You'll see pitches from alleged Nigerian millionaires who need your help, ways to get Microsoft to write you a giant check, and hot tips on stocks about to take off.

Generally these *spam* emails, or unsolicited promotional email messages, are all similar. The emails masquerade as legitimate reports from stock research firms or investors who are in the know and are simply passing along their tips out of generosity. The messages talk about some major development that will move the stock by a huge amount in a short period of time. And the emails generally pitch stocks with very low share prices that trade on lesser regulated markets, like the Pink Sheets.

If you get such spam, don't even read it. Trash that rotten spam immediately. They're almost always *pump-and-dump* schemes. They work like this: The fraudsters first pick a few lightly traded stocks and buy them up. After the promotional email goes out, the fraudsters wait for gullible investors to buy shares and drive the stock price up. That's the *pump* part of pump and dump. Next, these investors sell their shares. That's the *dump*.

Sadly, many investors fall for these schemes. A study from Rainer Bohme (Dresden University of Technology) and Thorsten Holz (University of Mannheim) found stock prices do react to these emails, indicating that investors are reading them and buying the stocks. (You can check out their research at https://papers. ssrn.com/sol3/papers.cfm?abstract_id=897431.)

TIP

Don't fall for the emails from supposed Nigerian nationals hoping to transfer cash to the United States, either. They're scams called *advance fee frauds*, or *4-1-9 frauds* after that section of the Nigerian penal code. Don't participate in these. The U.S. Secret Service (www.secretservice.gov/about/faqs) provides information on these scams in the Protecting Yourself section.

Understand Loopholes Scammers Can Use

Before you invest your money in anything, your first stop should be the SEC's website at www.sec.gov. You should always find out whether any regulatory filings exist on the investment or person selling the investments.

If you're looking to buy a stock, for instance, you can download the company's regulatory filings, as I explain in Chapter 2. Companies with more than 500 investors and $10 million in assets must file statements with the SEC. Companies listed on major exchanges, such as the New York Stock Exchange and NASDAQ, must also file statements. If it's a broker or an investment newsletter you're interested in checking up on, you can follow the instructions in the section that tells you how to research tout sheets.

If you're not able to turn up any filings, your defenses should go up. Scamsters know that loopholes exist in SEC rules — originally designed to help small companies avoid bureaucratic red tape — that allow them to avoid filing potentially troublesome documents. You can read about these loopholes on the SEC's website (www.sec.gov/info/smallbus/qasbsec.htm) in the section entitled "Can my company legally offer and sell securities without registering with the SEC?"

But to save you the trouble, following are summaries of the primary loopholes that may allow certain firms to avoid filing documents with the SEC:

>> **Intrastate offerings** occur when a local business sells investments to residents of the state it primarily does business in. This is called the *intrastate offering exemption.*

>> **Private offerings** take place when companies only sell investments to investors who have a deep understanding of business and also provide financial information to these investors.

>> **Regulation A** is an SEC exemption that kicks in when firms raise less than $5 million in a 12-month period. Regulation A allows companies to file paper statements called *offering circulars* with the SEC instead of making their information readily available online. Offering circulars contain limited

information and can be hard to get because they're often filed only on paper in Washington, D.C.

>> **Regulation D** is a more common SEC exemption that applies to firms that meet a variety of requirements, including raising less than $1 million in a 12-month period or selling investments only to "accredited investors" who are sophisticated. These firms need to file only a *Form D* with the SEC. A Form D offers just bare-bones information and provides few details other than the names of the company's owners. You can read more about Regulation D at www.sec.gov/answers/regd.htm.

If you can't find a company on the SEC's website, call or email the SEC (www.sec.gov/contact.shtml) to see whether paper forms are available. You should also contact your state's regulator, which you can find from the North American Securities Administrators Association (www.nasaa.org).

TIP

Thousands of legitimate companies have shares trading on the major U.S. exchanges. If you want to invest in an individual stock, choose from one of these listed stocks.

Familiarize Yourself with the Fingerprints of a Scam

There are only so many ways to rob a bank. Face it; most of the scams that fraudsters use online and off generally fall into just a few categories, most of which are variants of pyramid or Ponzi schemes. Sure, you find twists, such as *affinity fraud* (www.sec.gov/investor/pubs/affinity.htm), where the scammers infiltrate a group of investors of a similar age, race, or hobby; gain the trust of the group; and then use the group members to promote the scheme to each other.

Still, a few common traits should set off alarm bells in your head:

>> **Promises of guaranteed returns that seem abnormally large:** By reading Chapter 1, you know that stocks have returned roughly 10 percent average annual returns. If someone tells you he can get you a return of 10 percent or more a year, you know the investment is riskier than stocks. So if the promoter says the returns are guaranteed or risk-free, you know something isn't right.

>> **Pressure to act right now:** Perpetrators of frauds know they have to get your checkbook open now, or you might get cold feet and start thinking about the risks. If you're told you have to invest now or you'll miss out, you're better missing out on the "opportunity."

>> **No documentation on paper:** Bad guys hate paper trails and try their best to avoid documenting anything. If you can't print out the information about an investment, you shouldn't invest in it. Proper investment proposals should be registered with regulators and come with a prospectus, an annual report, and other financial statements.

The SEC provides a list of other telltale signs of online frauds that are worthwhile checking out at www.sec.gov/investor/pubs/cyberfraud/signs.htm.

Learn to Be an Online Sleuth

Scammers often reinvent themselves and try different scams until they get caught. If you're being pitched an investment or seminar, try to find out whether the person is working under an alias or has sold investments before. Get as much information as you can about the person, and use the web search techniques described in Chapter 2 to see whether you can turn up more information.

It's also important to find out whether a regulator or private party has gone after a company or broker to recover funds. You have three main places to check:

>> **The SEC's Investors Claims Funds** (www.sec.gov/divisions/enforce/claims.htm) is a list of all the companies that have been targeted by enforcement actions that resulted in funds being given back to investors.

>> **The Securities Investor Protection Corporation** (www.sipc.org/cases-and-claims/open-cases) maintains a list of brokers that have gone out of business and are being liquidated. You also find instructions on how to fill out a claim form to make sure that you get your money back.

>> **The Stanford Law School Securities Class Action Clearinghouse** (securities.stanford.edu) provides a free database of companies that are being sued by investors for securities fraud.

Know How to Complain If You Suspect a Fraud

It might be embarrassing if you've been taken in by a fraud. But if you feel that you've been had, it's critical that you let regulators know right away. The sooner you can tip off the authorities, the greater the chance the fraudster can be nailed and the better the chance of recovering money.

The SEC's Center for Complaints and Enforcement Tips (`www.sec.gov/complaint.shtml`) allows you to fill out electronic forms to alert regulators to a possible fraud. Give as much detail about the alleged fraud as you can to help investigators who might decide to take your case.

Make Sure That Your Computer Is Locked Down

You should always be concerned with computer security. Make sure that you have the proper software and other safeguards installed to protect your computer from viruses and hackers. You have many options, including some offered by the online brokers themselves. When you're online using a public wireless network service, such as those in Starbucks coffeehouses, you should be especially careful. You can read more about ways to lock down your computer in Chapter 2.

But online criminals also use other low-tech methods to bilk investors. The most common trick used is phishing, which is pronounced "fishing." In *phishing scams*, the fraudster sends out millions of emails purporting to be from a bank (say Citibank), a store (such as Best Buy), a government agency (say the Internal Revenue Service), or an online service (such as PayPal or eBay). These emails are carefully crafted to appear official and generally ask the recipients to click a link to confirm or update personal information.

Here are a couple ways to protect yourself from these scams:

>> **Log on routinely:** Log on to your bank, online broker, PayPal, and other important accounts directly, and routinely check the Messages section. Generally, when these companies want to reach you, they leave a message for you on the site.

>> **Never click links in emails:** If you get an email claiming to be from your online brokerage, assume that it's a fraud. Don't click the link in the email that claims to direct you to the website. Instead, manually enter the site's address into your browser or click the Favorite for the site that you set up.

TECHNICAL STUFF

>> **Hover your cursor over the link:** If you want to know whether the email is phishing for information, put your cursor over the link in the email. Do *not* click the link, but look for a pop-up window or information near the status bar. You see the address the link wants to take you to. If it's not the complete address of the site it purports to be, you know instantly it's a fraud.

WARNING

THE CASE(S) OF BARRY MINKOW

When it comes to money, you need to be on guard at all times. Scammers often use the trust they've built up to get them in a position to abuse, cheat, and steal. Consider the case of Barry Minkow, who not just once, but twice, abused his reputation to allegedly generate ill-gotten gains. Minkow first became known as a fraudster for being the mastermind behind the Zzzz Best "carpet-cleaning" business that bilked investors out of millions in the 1980s. After being released from prison in 1995, Minkow become a Christian minister. He also, ironically, started a business called the Fraud Discovery Institute, where he would serve up warnings of potential corporate frauds. However, on March 30, 2011, Minkow pleaded guilty to charges in connection with insider trading. Minkow allegedly trumped up claims of accounting problems at homebuilder Lennar, only to profit by betting against the stock. Minkow in 2011 was sentenced to five years in prison. But then in 2014, he was sentenced to another five years of jail time connected with his swindling of members of his church. All told, Minkow is ordered to pay hundreds of millions of dollars in restitution. You can read the complaint filed against Minkow in connection with Fraud Discovery Institute here: www.justice.gov/usao/fls/PressReleases/Attachments/110324-01.Information.pdf.

Be Aware of Online Sources for More Information

Scams are constantly evolving. It's up to you to be constantly vigilant and be aware that the Internet is a perfect environment for people trying to fool you and take your money. That doesn't mean you should unplug your computer and give up on online investing. It's just that it's up to you to be aware of the potential risks.

Internet sources can help online investors understand how to protect themselves, including

>> **The SEC's website** (www.sec.gov/investor/pubs/cyberfraud.htm) explains many of the common online investing frauds and gives detailed examples. If you're new to online investing, this site is worthwhile and can make you more street-smart and aware of the dangers.

>> **Investor Protection Trust** (www.investorprotection.org) provides links to a variety of investor education materials. You can view a number of videos that show you how to recognize and avoid common investment scams.

Chapter **19**

Online Investors' Ten Most Common Questions

f you're new to online investing, your mind might be overflowing with questions before you ever click the Buy or Sell button on your online brokerage's website. And even if you're an experienced investor, you might question whether you're doing everything you can to maximize your success and profit.

I hope that by the time you finish reading this chapter, those pesky questions lingering in the back of your head will be answered. I have a pretty good idea of the questions online investors have because thousands of readers have emailed me over the years to ask everything they want to know about investing. I've noticed some of the same questions keep popping up. The most common question from investors by far is "How much money do I need, and how do I get started investing online?" You can find the answer to that number one question in Chapter 1. This chapter tackles many of the other burning questions you might have.

How Do I Find Out Which Companies Are Going to Split Their Stock?

It's almost like clockwork. Shortly after beginning investors get started investing online, they start wondering about stock splits. Stock splits are appealing to investors interested in buying a stock because they bring the per-share price down. And beginning investors who own shares already like splits because they get more shares overnight.

You can read about stock splits and why companies do them in Chapter 6. The short version is that many companies perform stock splits when their per-share stock price gets high enough to presumably scare off individual investors. Some companies might start thinking about splits when their stock gets to $75 a share or higher. When that happens, the company cuts its stock price but then increases its number of shares outstanding.

REMEMBER

Savvy investors understand that a stock's per-share price, by itself, is meaningless. What matters is a company's valuation, which you can find out by using the tools and techniques explained in Chapter 12.

Still, I get the question often enough that I'm happy to answer it. NASDAQ.com (www.nasdaq.com) is a convenient source for a calendar of upcoming stock splits. To get the information, after going to the NASDAQ site, hover your mouse cursor over the Markets tab and then click the Upcoming Splits link. You see a list of all the companies expected to do a stock split (or reverse split), the ratio of the split (such as two-for-one), and the date it's set to happen. You can find this list directly here: www.nasdaq.com/markets/upcoming-splits.aspx.

Can I Use Options to Boost My Returns?

Options, which are contracts that give owners the right to buy or sell stocks by a certain time in the future, can be used aggressively or conservatively. Options can be used by speculators to place giant bets on stocks with little up-front money, as I describe in Chapter 5. However, if used properly, options can add some extra return to your portfolio without necessarily increasing your risk too much.

Selling covered calls is a great example of how you can boost your returns without significantly increasing your risk. When you sell a call for a stock that you already own, it's a *covered call*. When you sell a covered call, you collect a fee, or *premium*, from the buyer of the call. The person who buys your call has the right to force you to sell the stock to him or her at a set price, called the exercise price, before a set date in the future. If the stock never goes above the exercise price, though, you keep the stock and the premium. It's like money for nothing. Covered calls can be lucrative if the stock you own doesn't move much.

WARNING

Selling a call without owning the stock is risky. If the stock rises, you're required to buy it and sell it to the person who bought your call. If the stock soars, you keep losing money.

Can I Still Lose Money If I Invest in Bonds?

Investors who are nervous about market swings are often told to load up on bonds and lighten up on stocks. There's logic to that because bonds and Treasurys, in particular, tend to swing less severely in value than stocks. You can see how the risks of different types of bonds compare with stocks in Chapter 15.

But don't think you can't lose money on bonds, because you still can. Bonds have three main types of risk:

>> **Default risk:** When you buy bonds issued by companies, cities, or borrowers other than the U.S. Treasury, you're accepting the chance that the borrower won't pay you back.

>> **Inflation risk:** You own a bond from a well-known company that pays 6 percent interest, inflation is just 3 percent, and Treasurys are paying 5 percent. You're pretty happy. But what if inflation ticks up, and the yield on Treasurys rises to 8 percent? Suddenly your 6 percent isn't looking so hot. The price of your bond will fall to make up for the fact that the 6 percent interest rate isn't competitive.

>> **Reinvestment risk:** You buy an 8 percent bond, the company pays the interest on time, and everything is going great. But then, the bond matures. The company returns your principal, and you have a pile of cash again. Now what? You must reinvest that cash in another way, perhaps by buying a bond that has a lower interest rate.

TIP

Because bonds have risk, they might not be appropriate places to park cash you might need in case of emergency. Money market funds, described in Chapter 15, can be much safer. You might also consider high-yield savings accounts that can give you ready access to your cash and pay decent rates of return. Bankrate.com (www.bankrate.com/brm/rate/mmmf_highratehome.asp?params=US,416&product=33) offers a great way to find high-yield savings accounts to park cash in.

REMEMBER

It doesn't pay to be overly conservative either and put all your cash in money market funds. Returns on stocks and bonds, over time, will likely far outstrip the interest you'll collect on money markets or high-yield savings accounts. If you play it too safe, you might find that your portfolio isn't growing fast enough to meet your financial goals.

What's the Easiest Way to Invest in Commodities?

Investing in commodities can be another way to diversify your portfolio. Investors who may fear inflation in the wake of economic stimulus packages put in place by the U.S. government, say, may see commodities as a way to protect themselves if prices skyrocket in the future. Whether commodities add value is a topic of debate. Supporters say commodities tend to move differently than stocks, which can help lower your portfolio's risk. You can read more about this in the freely available academic research paper "Facts and Fantasies about Commodity Futures," by Yale University's K. Geert Rouwenhorst and University of Pennsylvania's Gary Gorton (https://papers.ssrn.com/sol3/papers.cfm?abstract_id=560042). Another look at the topic is available in a paper published in the Journal of Asset Management titled "Investing in commodities: Popular beliefs and misconceptions," available here: https://link.springer.com/article/10.1057%2Fjam.2011.35.

WARNING

Investing directly in commodities, such as livestock, grains, metals, and energy, can be messy. You need to understand the futures market, which is where these investments trade, and set up a separate brokerage account just to buy and sell commodities.

You can find much easier ways to invest in commodities. You can find exchange-traded funds (ETFs) that let you invest in commodities like gold, steel, and energy. You can just buy these ETFs much like you'd buy a stock. You can read more about mutual funds in Chapter 10 and ETFs in Chapter 11.

How Long Will It Take for Me to Double My Money?

Something is satisfying about hitting a double. When you hit a blackjack in Vegas, for instance, you double your wager. And who doesn't like a good double-header or double feature? Even the percentage gain on an investment that doubles is a nice even 100 percent.

A popular shortcut is used by many money pros to measure the time it will take to double an investment: It's called the Rule of 72. You simply divide the number 72 by the rate of return of your investment. MoneyChimp (www.moneychimp.com/features/rule72.htm) provides more details on this rule and can do the math for you.

Say you own a basket of stocks that you expect to increase in value by 10 percent a year. Using the Rule of 72, you'll double your investment in 7.2 years (72 divided by 10).

Do I Have a Say in How a Company I'm Invested in Operates?

As a shareholder, you're one of the owners of a company. And yes, that entitles you to a say in the important elements of a company's affairs. Generally speaking, the pecking order goes like this: The company's board of directors hires professional managers to run the company on a day-to-day basis. These hired hands — the CEO, chief financial officer, and other key management — answer to the board of directors. The board of directors, in turn, answers to the shareholders.

Major issues, such as whether a company accepts an offer to be acquired, must be approved by shareholders. Shareholders also have the right to vote for the members of the board. All the items you can vote on are printed on a company's proxy statement. Proxy statements will be mailed to you by your online broker or sent to you electronically. You can also vote online because most companies use Internet-based voting systems such as ProxyVote (https://east.proxyvote.com/pv/web.do). All you need to vote is the Control Number of the proxy, which will be provided to you by your online broker.

TIP

Unless you're willing to spend a great deal of time researching all the matters on the proxy, you might not be sure how to vote. It's important, though, to vote because it's your only say in the company's matters. Professional investors get a big hand when it comes to evaluating all the items up for a vote in the proxy. A company called Institutional Shareholder Services (www.issgovernance.com) provides research and data to mutual funds, pension funds, and other large owners of stock. But those reports aren't available to individual investors. That means you need to take the time to read the proxy statement and understand what investors are being asked to vote on. It's not as hard as it sounds. You just need a copy of the proxy statement. Brokers may mail these documents to you, or more likely, email a link for you to view them online. Proxy statements can also be downloaded from the Securities and Exchange Commission's website. Review Chapter 2 for help on how to get a proxy statement from the SEC.

After you have the proxy statement in front of you, check the section of the report usually called Management Proposals. These are the items the company's management must get shareholders to vote for or against. The proxy statement spells out each proposal and provides some background to help you make a decision. You can also consult with other investors, using social media tools described in Chapter 7.

How Can Deep-Discount Online Brokers Make Money Charging $5 or Less for Trades?

Don't feel too bad for the online brokers. Although commissions have fallen through the floor and are free in some cases, as described in Chapter 4, brokers are doing fine. Keep in mind that the costs to execute trades have also fallen. It generally costs online brokers between $2.00 and $6.50 to execute a trade. Larger brokers usually pay closer to $2.00, meaning that a vast majority of online brokers are able to make money from the commissions they charge.

Online brokers also make money on additional services. Some brokers charge interest to investors who borrow money to buy stocks or other investments. Other brokers make money charging higher fees for more exotic investments, such as options, foreign stocks, and currencies. It's also fairly common for online brokers to sell some of their customers' orders to other investment firms that execute the trades. Some larger brokerage firms also make money selling investing advice. Brokers with free trades generally rely on these additional services to pay for the $2.00 or so they're losing on regular trades.

How Are Hedge Funds, Private-Equity Funds, and Venture Capital Funds Different?

Ever hear the term *alternative investment*? It's a blanket term used to describe most investments other than just plain old stocks, bonds, and mutual funds. Stamp, art, and car collecting, when done with the intent of making money, are technically alternative investments. But typically, when you hear the term alternative investment, what's being referred to are hedge funds, private-equity funds, and venture-capital funds. Here's a rundown of what they are:

>> **Hedge funds:** These are pools of money collected by largely unregulated investment managers who aim to get returns that beat the stock market. Unlike mutual fund managers who generally invest in stocks and bonds, hedge fund managers are free to invest in just about any asset they choose. This freedom to invest with little regulatory oversight is supposed to let hedge funds make money even when stocks are falling.

Due to their structures, though, hedge funds aren't held to the same regulatory scrutiny that other investments are. Rules require hedge funds to be offered only to "accredited investors" who have an annual income of $200,000 or more, or $1 million in net worth. Hedge funds also charge hefty fees, making them largely unattractive to individual investors.

>> **Private-equity funds:** Leveraged-buyout firms use money from large investors like pension plans to buy public and private companies. These firms, also called private-equity firms, generally borrow money so that they can afford to buy big companies. Investment funds run by private-equity firms usually have a different strategy than hedge funds do. Private-equity firms generally try to run the companies they bought for a short time, fix them, and sell them for a profit. Private-equity firms generally have a stable of experienced businesspeople they can call in to run companies.

>> **Venture capital:** If you've ever wondered how young companies can afford to launch new high-tech products, it's probably thanks to venture capital firms. These firms make relatively small investments in scores of highly risky and immature companies. Most of the investments go up in smoke as the fledgling companies fail to get off the ground. But when venture capital firms hit a Facebook or Twitter, they can make big bucks. Chapter 6 gives more details about venture capital.

If a Company Is Buying Back Its Stock, Does That Mean the Stock Is Cheap?

Some investors think it's the ultimate buy recommendation when a company says it's planning to buy back its own stock. Stocks often rise after a company tells Wall Street it's launching a stock-buyback program. After all, who better to know whether the stock is undervalued than the company itself?

But investors should be skeptical of buybacks. For one thing, just because a company says it will buy back stock doesn't mean it will. Academic studies show about a third of companies that say they will buy back stock never do.

WARNING

Companies have had lousy timing when it comes to buying their own stock. Stock buybacks were soaring in the quarter that ended in March 2000 and in late 2007, just as the stock market was topping and about to suffer a nasty bear market. Similarly, in the fourth quarter of 2002 and in early 2009, when the stock market was hitting rock bottom, companies were shying away from buybacks.

If I Own a House, Do I Need to Hold Real-Estate Investment Trusts in My Stock Portfolio, Too?

It's easy to confuse *real-estate investment trusts,* or REITs, with housing. But your home and an investment in REITs are different. First, REITs largely invest in commercial real estate, such as office buildings, shopping centers, hospitals, and malls — not single-family homes.

Another thing to remember is that your home, although it can appreciate in value over time, isn't an investment per se. It's your shelter. You own your home as a place to live, and if you make money on it, that's a secondary perk. REITs, on the other hand, are purely designed to be investments. Cohen & Steers (www.cohenandsteers. com), an investment research firm dedicated to real estate, provides comprehensive details about REIT investing.

REMEMBER

Most importantly, REITs tend to be a great way to diversify a portfolio. REITs are attractive because they have relatively low correlations with stocks. If stocks are down, for instance, REITs might not be down as much or might be rising. And when REITs are down, your stocks might be up. By owning REITs and stocks together, you can smooth out your portfolio's ups and downs, which cuts your risk and boosts returns. (See Chapter 9 for more info on asset allocation.)

Index

A

AAII (American Association of Individual Investors), 59

ABR (average broker recommendation) number, 161, 331

account maintenance fees (529 plans), 89

accounts. *See also* brokerage accounts; education savings accounts; retirement accounts

cash account, 132

margin account, 132

ownership of, 80

sweep account, 113

accredited investor, 153

ACH (Automated Clearing House), 113

Acorns, 109

activation price, 128

active investing, 34

actively managed mutual funds, 238, 240

advance fee frauds (4-1-9 frauds), 378

affinity frauds, 379

AFL-CIO, 165, 294

after the close, 135–136

after-hours trading, 135

after-hours volume, 136

aggregate data, 193

aggregator, 54

AIP (automatic investment plan), 251

Ally Invest, 96–97, 141

alpha (mutual funds), 254

alternative investment, 388–389

American Association of Individual Investors (AAII), 59

American Century, 252

American Institute of Certified Public Accountants, 81

analyst reports, 330–337

analyst revisions, 161–162

analysts, analyzing of, 329–343

Analyze Now!, 86, 214

Annual Report Service (The Public Register), 280

annual report to shareholders, 280

annualized number, 209–210

AnnualReports, 280

antispyware software, 57

antivirus software, 57

Apple, 53

appreciate, defined, 64

apps, 38, 111, 145–146, 192

Argus, 330

The Arithmetic of Active Management, 32

ask (stock quote), 40

ask price (ETF), 271

asset allocation, 30, 201, 220–227, 227–235

Asset ClassDashboard (Russell), 211

asset classes, 219, 222, 227

AssetBuilder, 230–231

assets, 282

The Associated Press, 158, 159

audio software, for finding podcasts, 53

audit, 292

Automated Clearing House (ACH), 113

automatic investment plan (AIP), 251

automatic withdrawals, 21

average broker recommendation (ABR) number, 161, 331

average daily share volume, 132

average price target, 331

average return, calculation of, 206–209

Average Return Calculator, 208

B

back-end loads, 248

balance sheet, 279, 282–283

balanced funds, 244

Bank of America, 98, 99, 102, 103, 104

C

G

H

I

O

Oakmark, 252
offering circulars, 378
One-Click Scorecard (Quicken), 323–324, 325
OneSource Select program (Schwab), 116
online articles, 3
online blogs, 51–52
online broker screening tools, 369
online brokers/brokerages
 for analysts' research reports, 330
 checking if your money is safe with, 110–111
 deep discounters, 95–97, 388
 factors to consider in selection of, 92–94
 finding out what reviewers think, 108–109
 finding the best broker for you, 92–94
 full-service traditional brokers, 93, 104–106
 gotchas to watch out for, 94
 self-service brokers, 93
 Twitter feeds from, 190–191
 types of, 94–106
 websites of for tracking investments, 75–76
online capital gains calculators and sites, 76
online investing
 benefits of, 8–9
 danger of doing nothing, 11
 getting started, 9–12
 lingo, 22–23
 measuring how much you can afford to invest, 12–20
 social networking meets, 196–198
online performance-measurement tools, 212
online screening sites, 317–319
online simulations, 60–61
online sites dedicated to optimizing tax strategy, 76
online tutorials, 59–60
open-end investment companies, 241
OpenOffice, 209
operating margin, 321
operating profit, 281

options
 basic strategies for, 137–139
 defined, 136–137
 discovering more about, 142–143
 getting prices of online, 140–141
 how to buy online, 141–142
 as offered by ETFs, 259
 types of, 137
 use of to boost returns, 384–385
options chains, 140
Options Clearing Corporation, 141
Options Industry Council, 143
options quotes, 140
The Options Guide, 138, 143
Oracle, valuation of, 304
OTC Bulletin Board, 41, 184, 185, 186, 348
OTC Markets, 73, 186
OTC Pink, 184
out of the money (call option), 140
Outlook.com, 342

P

paper stock certificates, 120, 122–123, 124–125
passive investing/passive investor, 51
Patient Protection and Affordable Care Act, 79
P/E ratio (price-to-earnings ratio), 264–265, 298, 300, 301, 302
PEG ratio (price-earnings-to-growth ratio), 298, 302
penny stocks, 41, 185–187
The Penny Hoarder, 13
performance, measurement of, 199–217
performance-analytics websites, 216–217
performance-tracking websites, 213
Personal Capital, 16, 18, 216, 230, 267
personal finance app, 17–18
personal finance information sites, 17–18
personal finance software, 13–15, 75–76, 229
personal finance websites, 15–17
Personal Fund, 249

About the Author

Matt Krantz is a nationally known financial journalist who specializes in investing topics as personal finance and management editor for *Investor's Business Daily*. In addition to writing for IBD, his work has appeared in *USA TODAY* and *Money* magazine. He's covered financial markets and Wall Street for decades, concentrating on developments affecting individual investors and their portfolios. His stories routinely signal trends that investors can profit from and sound warnings about potential scams and issues investors should be aware of. Krantz has written or co-written several books in addition to this one, including *Fundamental Analysis For Dummies* and *Investment Banking For Dummies*.

Readers often tell Matt he's the only one who has been able to finally solve investing questions they've sought answers to for years.

Matt has been investing since the 1980s and has studied dozens of investment techniques while forming his own. And as a financial journalist, Matt has interviewed some of the most famous and infamous investment minds in modern history.

He has also spoken to investing groups, including at the national convention of National Association of Investors Corporation, and has appeared on various financial TV programs.

Matt is based in Los Angeles. When he's not writing, he's spending time with his wife and young daughter, running, playing tennis, mountain biking, or playing Xbox games.

Dedication

This book is dedicated to my wife, Nancy, and daughter, Leilani, who are always available to help me think of a better word or a new way of thinking.

Author's Acknowledgments

Wiley personnel have been tremendous to work with on this project, including senior acquisitions editor Katie Mohr, project editor and copy editor Susan Pink, who found ways to make this edition of the book even more useful to readers with great edits and suggestions. Guy Hart-Davis, technical editor, made sure that the book was free of "dead links" by checking every URL and link. A big thanks to Matt Wagner, my literary agent, for thinking of me for the project and first presenting it to me. Fane Lozman provided input by sharing his options expertise.

Thanks to my mom and dad for instilling, at a very young age, a curiosity in investing, writing, and computers (and for buying me my first computer well before having a PC was common). And thanks to my grandparents for teaching me the power of saving and investing.

And thanks to the readers of this book and the previous editions for telling me how much you like it.

Publisher's Acknowledgments

Executive Editor: Katie Mohr

Project Editor: Susan Pink

Copy Editor: Susan Pink

Technical Editor: Guy Hart-Davis

Production Editor: Magesh Elangovan

Proofreader: S. Hobbs

Cover Photo: © Who is Danny/Shutterstock

Take dummies with you everywhere you go!

Whether you are excited about e-books, want more from the web, must have your mobile apps, or are swept up in social media, dummies makes everything easier.

Find us online!

dummies.com

dummies
A Wiley Brand

Leverage the power

Dummies is the global leader in the reference category and one of the most trusted and highly regarded brands in the world. No longer just focused on books, customers now have access to the dummies content they need in the format they want. Together we'll craft a solution that engages your customers, stands out from the competition, and helps you meet your goals.

Advertising & Sponsorships

Connect with an engaged audience on a powerful multimedia site, and position your message alongside expert how-to content. Dummies.com is a one-stop shop for free, online information and know-how curated by a team of experts.

- Targeted ads
- Video
- Email Marketing
- Microsites
- Sweepstakes sponsorship

20 MILLION PAGE VIEWS EVERY SINGLE MONTH

15 MILLION UNIQUE VISITORS PER MONTH

43% OF ALL VISITORS ACCESS THE SITE VIA THEIR MOBILE DEVICES

700,000 NEWSLETTER SUBSCRIPTIONS TO THE INBOXES OF *300,000* UNIQUE INDIVIDUALS EVERY WEEK

# of dummies

PERSONAL ENRICHMENT

Staying Sharp
9781119187790
USA $26.00
CAN $31.99
UK £19.99

Facebook
9781119179030
USA $21.99
CAN $25.99
UK £16.99

Guitar
9781119293354
USA $24.99
CAN $29.99
UK £17.99

Investing
9781119293347
USA $22.99
CAN $27.99
UK £16.99

Beekeeping
9781119310068
USA $22.99
CAN $27.99
UK £16.99

Digital Photography
9781119235606
USA $24.99
CAN $29.99
UK £17.99

Meditation
9781119251163
USA $24.99
CAN $29.99
UK £17.99

Pregnancy
9781119235491
USA $26.99
CAN $31.99
UK £19.99

Samsung Galaxy S7
9781119279952
USA $24.99
CAN $29.99
UK £17.99

iPhone
9781119283133
USA $24.99
CAN $29.99
UK £17.99

Crocheting
9781119287117
USA $24.99
CAN $29.99
UK £16.99

Nutrition
9781119130246
USA $22.99
CAN $27.99
UK £16.99

PROFESSIONAL DEVELOPMENT

Windows 10
9781119311041
USA $24.99
CAN $29.99
UK £17.99

AutoCAD
9781119255796
USA $39.99
CAN $47.99
UK £27.99

Excel 2016
9781119293439
USA $26.99
CAN $31.99
UK £19.99

QuickBooks 2017
9781119281467
USA $26.99
CAN $31.99
UK £19.99

macOS Sierra
9781119280651
USA $29.99
CAN $35.99
UK £21.99

LinkedIn
9781119251132
USA $24.99
CAN $29.99
UK £17.99

Windows 10
9781119310563
USA $34.00
CAN $41.99
UK £24.99

SharePoint 2016
9781119181705
USA $29.99
CAN $35.99
UK £21.99

Fundamental Analysis
9781119263593
USA $26.99
CAN $31.99
UK £19.99

Networking
9781119257769
USA $29.99
CAN $35.99
UK £21.99

Office 2016
9781119293477
USA $26.99
CAN $31.99
UK £19.99

Office 365
9781119265313
USA $24.99
CAN $29.99
UK £17.99

Salesforce.com
9781119239314
USA $29.99
CAN $35.99
UK £21.99

Coding
9781119293323
USA $29.99
CAN $35.99
UK £21.99

CPSIA information can be obtained
at www.ICGtesting.com
Printed in the USA
LVHW050621130421
684313LV00002B/16

9 781119 601487